FORTHCOMING TITLES

Unified Gridlock, David Brady and Craig Volden

Broken Contract? Changing Relationships Between Citizens and Their Government in the United States, edited by Stephen C. Craig

Congress and the Administrative State, Second Edition, Lawrence C. Dodd and Richard L. Schott

Governing Partners and State-Local Relations in the United States, Russell L. Hanson

Young Versus Old: Generational Gaps in Political Participation and Policy Preferences, Susan MacManus and Suzanne L. Parker

Cold War Politics, John Kenneth White

The New American Politics

REFLECTIONS ON POLITICAL CHANGE AND THE CLINTON ADMINISTRATION

EDITED BY

Bryan D. Jones

Texas A&M University

Westview Press

BOULDER · SAN FRANCISCO · OXFORD

Transforming American Politics

Copyright © 1995 by Westview Press, Inc.

Published in 1995 in the United States of America by Westview Press, Inc., 5500 Central Avenue, Boulder, Colorado 80301-2877, and in the United Kingdom by Westview Press, 12 Hid's Copse Road, Cumnor Hill, Oxford OX2 9JJ

Library of Congress Cataloging-in-Publication Data
The New American politics : reflections on political change
and the Clinton Administration / edited by Bryan D. Jones.
    p.   cm.—(Transforming American politics)
  Includes bibliographical references and index.
  ISBN 0-8133-1972-2.—ISBN 0-8133-1973-0 (pbk.)
  1. United States—Politics and government—1989–1993.   2. United
States—Politics and government—1993–   3. Presidents—United
States—Elections—1992.   I. Jones, Bryan D.   II. Series.
JK271.N43   1995
320.973'09'049—dc20

94-45163
CIP

Printed and bound in the United States of America

The paper used in this publication meets the requirements
of the American National Standard for Permanence of Paper
for Printed Library Materials Z39.48-1984.

10   9   8   7   6   5   4   3   2   1

Contents

1

Continuity and Change in American Politics

BRYAN D. JONES

This book is about the nature of change in the American political system. President Bill Clinton has often stated his belief that his election was about change, or rather the public's desire for change. But many journalists and academic commentators stress stability: The American system, they say, is particularly designed to thwart major and meaningful change. Moreover, the nature of political, social, and economic change itself has been the source of academic controversy. Emblazoned across the title page of *Principles of Economics,* by the great late-nineteenth-century economist Alfred Marshall, is the Latin phrase *Natura non facit saltum:* Nature does not make leaps. Encapsulating the belief that nature is well-behaved, this aphorism can be traced at least to the biologist Carolus Linnaeus in 1750; but Marshall may have been the first social scientist to popularize it.

In political science, *Natura non facit saltum* comes in various guises. Indeed, many analysts of American government seem compelled to claim that government not only doesn't make leaps, it doesn't make moves. In 1989 *Time* carried a cover story entitled "Is the Government Dead?" It seems that so many politicians were beholden to interest groups, so much money was pouring into image-making in elections, and the institutions of government were enmeshed in so much divided control and deadlock that bold leadership at the national level was impossible. From James Madison's schemes to try to make government less oppressive by making it less active, to James McGregor Burns's classic *Deadlock of Democracy* in the early 1960s, to *Time's* dead-government claim and Brookings scholars John Chubb and Paul Peterson's book *Can the Government Govern?* (1989), to the present-day claim that government cannot act because the deficit has gotten too big, it has been fashionable to point to the inherent inaction and conservatism of national government in the United States. The most recent entries in the "government can't govern" refrain point to interest groups as the problem—journalist Jonathan Rauch calls it "demosclerosis" (Rauch, 1994).

The pessimism regarding the capacity of U.S. government to make major changes carries over into the more abstract analyses of political scientists. The belief in the impossibility of large change can be seen in group theory, where actions always beget reactions and existing interest groups, when threatened, will mobilize to block major disruptions; and in the incremental decisionmaking models, where public decisionmakers are supposed to take only minimal steps so as not to ruin what works pretty well. Empiricists also get into the act, claiming that everything in politics is incremental anyway. James Stimson claims that "if we observe almost any phenomenon at regular intervals over time, we will see change produced by the cumulation of small and irregular increments. If we do this for a while . . . the idea of change occurring as discontinuous jumps becomes increasingly an idea of oddball irregularities" (1991: 6).

For a long time, I have been unhappy with the idea that the American system—owing to deliberate institutional design or to a conservative political culture, or because norms of openness are exploited by an interest group system with an upper-class bias—cannot manage meaningful change. In this book I have asked several political scientists—some very distinguished, some younger and bringing fresh approaches to the analysis of politics—to comment on the nature of political change, upon examining it through the lenses of the early Clinton years. All were requested to think about the nature of political change: Is government deadlocked and unable to act boldly? Is political change in the United States invariably incremental? Is divided government inevitably gridlocked?

ASSESSING POLITICAL CHANGE

The chapters that follow are diverse, covering topics ranging from elections and the role of minorities to foreign policy, interest groups, and the Supreme Court. The authors sometimes emphasize continuity, and sometimes change, but I will focus on change here. At the risk of oversimplification, I suggest that three broad themes relating to political change may be found in the chapters of this book. First, major episodic political change is not only possible in the United States, it happens with considerable frequency. Sometimes such change is a result of the deliberate actions of major political actors or of major unforeseen events, as Lawrence Baum (in Chapter 9) notes can happen when new appointments join the Supreme Court. At other times major change results from seemingly minor alterations of political structures or cultural norms or from the cumulation of forces over an extended period of time. For example, Barbara Norrander points out (in Chapter 5) that the seemingly large jump in the success of women in capturing high elective and appointive office is best viewed as a cumulation of past changes. And Morris Fiorina suggests (in Chapter 8) that seemingly minor changes in the organization of legislatures can shift the party balance, thereby altering policy outputs.

Second, the nature and direction of that change is, to a considerable extent, unpredictable. When change occurs, it is not always what many of us would define as "progress." In Chapter 4 Rodney Hero notes a "populist backlash" toward minorities among whites. This illustrates a general point about American politics. Leaders may be able to highlight an issue, but they are often unable to control the subsequent course of events. For example, President Clinton was able to raise the issue of health care to the agenda, but he was much less able to control the course of policy "solutions" to the issue he raised. And William Thompson shows in Chapter 11 that the success of President Bush in the Gulf War probably would not have translated into electoral success even without the recession that was just abating as the 1992 election took place. In general, foreign policy successes are very difficult to translate into electoral popularity, although such failures must certainly be avoided. Recall that the invasion of Haiti by U.S. forces in 1994 yielded little in the way of improvement in President Clinton's popularity, which was very low as the nation moved toward midterm elections. Finally, many journalists and political analysts predicted substantial political change as the 1994 elections approached, but even the most optimistic Republican politicians failed to anticipate the sea change that occurred.

Third, the longer the time frame within which one assesses political change, the more likely it is that abrupt and discontinuous changes in politics will be noted. At first blush, this generalization may seem obvious: Longer periods of time allow for greater changes. Yet longer time frames may also make immediate shifts less impressive by putting them in context. In this case, major changes might not be detected when they happen, especially when they give rise to vast unintended consequences as government struggles to cope with the changes. As William Mayer notes in Chapter 2, one cannot really judge the impact of an election until one observes the policy activities that follow the election. That can take years. Similarly, as Frank Baumgartner and Jeffrey Talbert show in Chapter 6, one cannot really appreciate the role of interest groups in the policy process without putting the entire interest group system in historical context.

The authors of these chapters generally agree that both political changes and important changes in public policy can and do occur in modern-day America. But assessing the extent of change represented by Clinton's election and his first two years as president is a different matter. Several of the authors stress incrementalism and continuity; others point to factors that suggest broad shifts in the political system. Overall, however, the book focuses on three fundamental aspects of political change: politics, governmental institutions, and public policy. Part I considers the politics of continuity and change: elections, parties, and groups. In Chapter 2, the first of five chapters in this part, William Mayer offers a careful analysis of electoral coalitions in modern times. His key point is that a major electoral realignment *did* occur in the 1964–1972 period, and that the 1968 election was probably a critical one. Thus, claims Mayer, the American system in modern times, characterized as it has been by weak parties and numerous independents, is nevertheless capable of dramatic changes in electoral direction. With respect to the 1992 election, however, Mayer is "extraordinarily skeptical" about assertions that major new policy directions were set, even though a remarkable 19 percent of the electorate voted for independent candidate Ross Perot. And, indeed, 1994 has turned out to be the watershed. In Chapter 3, Shanto Iyengar and Sharmaine Vidanage, in their analysis of campaigning and the media, note that the 1992 campaign was different in many ways. For instance, it involved a great effort by the media to be more responsible than in the past, and it was characterized by extensive attempts on the part of candidates to avoid being completely reliant on the media in getting their messages out. Hence they heavily used electronic town halls, talk shows, and local news stories rather than national outlets. By this means, candidates avoided the responsibility that the national media had hoped to impose, reinstituting symbolic appeal and "sound-bites."

In Chapter 4, Rodney Hero observes both continuity and change. Examining the role of minorities in the 1992 election and the early Clinton years, he sees the Democratic Party moving to diversify symbolically (given two Latino and two black Cabinet members), yet split over the "populist" hostility toward minorities that seems to characterize a substantial part of the Democratic electoral coalition. This split seems to have been activated in the 1994 elections, especially in the South, as whites moved decisively toward the Republicans. Conversely, in Chapter 5 Barbara Norrander sees in 1992 the result of a sea change in women's accomplishments, especially in the area of high elective and appointive office. In particular, she points to Hillary Rodham Clinton as a very different kind of First Lady, one who remains a policy leader in spite of questions concerning her activities as a lawyer in Arkansas when Bill Clinton was governor there. The downside of her approach was evident in the criticism she received for the failed health care initiative that she led. Then, in Chapter 6, Frank Baumgartner and Jeffery Talbert note the vast changes that have characterized the interest group system over the past thirty years. They conclude that the changes in this system offer the president and Congress a great opportunity to shift the direction of policy. More generally, they argue that interest groups do not just act to block popular demands for change but also are a major catalyst for policy shifts themselves.

Part II of this book focuses on continuity and change in governing institutions. In Chapter 7, David Mayhew provides an update of *Divided We Govern* (1991), his important study of the role of divided government in the policy process. Again he stresses that divided government does not "gridlock" the policy process, because activist moods are able to wash out party gridlock. Even in the absence of an activist mood, such as existed in the late 1960s and early 1970s, major legislation can be accomplished, because so many influential actors recognize that it *must* be accomplished. Such recognition can be more important that the partisan coalitions that are assembled for policy action. For example, the coalitional structure of deficit reduction changed between the 1990 budget agreement involving the Democratic-led Congress and President Bush (a bipartisan coalition) and the 1993 Clinton-engineered deficit-reduction budget bill (a Democratic-only coalition). Here, the issue was constant even though its coalitional basis shifted. Mayhew also notes that health care is just the kind of issue that is poised for great legislative change, with most major actors agreeing that something needs to be done; but he warns that such great initiatives could go the way of President Carter's energy plan. The energetic Republican Congress convening in 1995, opposing a Democratic president vitally concerned with accomplishments, could set the stage for a Mayhew-type divided government activism.

Morris Fiorina, in Chapter 8, notes that subtle changes in institutions can produce dramatic change later on. His analysis of divided government in the states points to increased professionalism in state legislatures as a major reason for which fewer Republicans serve there. Republicans did much better in state legislative races in 1994, gaining over 450 seats nationally, according to some early estimates, and they gained eight governorships. This gain has not changed the picture of divided government in the states. In particular, almost all of the most populous states now have some form of divided government. Moreover, term limits and other citizen initiatives could have the effect of "deprofessionalizing" state legislatures, aiding Republican candidates in the long run. Divided government at the subnational level clearly has important policy consequences, because so much of domestic policy is set and implemented by the states. Republicans in Congress want to shift more policy responsibility to the states, so the big-state divided government issue will play a large part in national politics in the years to come.

In Chapter 9, Lawrence Baum's analysis of change in the Supreme Court points to selection as the major factor in departures from incrementalism in judicial policy, such that selection decisions introduce "an unusually large element of chance in the pace of policy change." Baum argues that chance operates in two ways: in terms of the number of justices a president gets to appoint and the direction the new justices take. Clinton had recently announced his second appointment to the Court, centrist jurist Stephen Breyer, to fill the vacancy left by the retiring Justice Blackmun. Given the earlier appointment of Ruth Bader Ginsburg, Clinton's list suggests a "center left" strategy in appointments; but as Blackmun's retirement demonstrated, presidents are not infrequently surprised by the direction taken by their newly independent appointees. Baum also concludes that, although the Court is often in the grip of incrementalism, it is actually more likely to strike out in new policy directions than is Congress. Next, Bert Rockman examines the federal executive branch in Chapter 10. Even though the executive bureaucracy is designed to provide "ballast" to shifts in party control of government, he argues, "presidents with a mind to do so and available opportunities can impose change on the executive."

The chapters that constitute Part III examine change in the policy process. In Chapter 11, William Thompson focuses on the effects that policy has on politics—in this case, the effects of foreign policy on the 1992 electoral outcome. According to Thompson, the majority view that economic conditions were the factor in explaining George Bush's defeat may have validity, but the rush to that judgment leaves much unexplained. In particular, why did economics so overwhelm the foreign policy accomplishments of President Bush? By way of an answer, Thompson points out that "rally 'round the flag" effects, which boosted Bush's popularity, are historically short-lived; that American voters have traditionally punished parties that engage in wars, even winning ones; and that the end of the Cold War did not bring the electoral "peace dividend" that can benefit presidents. Rather than aiding Bush, the end of the Cold War probably helped Clinton, whom the American public viewed negatively on this issue. With the demise of Cold War tensions, the nation could focus almost exclusively on domestic issues, on which Clinton had a decided edge with the American public.

In Chapter 12, Billy Hall and I pose the question as to why presidents choose to pursue the policies that they do. In the first year of the Clinton administration, three major domestic initiatives emerged: deficit reduction, health care, and the "investment and jobs" program. Of these, neither health care nor the deficit was of particular importance to the mass public, although jobs were. Yet Clinton chose to pursue the first two initiatives, pushing half-heartedly on the jobs program and dropping it after it was defeated in Congress. We conclude that much policy change comes from the choices made by the president, who tries to activate latent preferences in the public for the policies that he has chosen to pursue.

Because no volume on public policy would be complete without a consideration of federalism, Dennis Judd's analysis of urban policies in a federal system is included here as Chapter 13. This issue is critically important for understanding policy change in America. Federalism has been viewed through two lenses by political scientists. Many authors have seen a system that hamstrings and deadlocks, allowing and even encouraging the frustration of national majorities bent on change. Other authors, myself among them, have viewed federalism as a contributor to rapid policy change. From this latter perspective, states and localities are seen as "laboratories of democracy," trying out policies on a local scale where consensus is easier to reach. Judd details the difficulty of maintaining a single voice for urban issues in Washington, partly because they are not central to the implementation of national policies, as they are in Europe. Consequently, they may be abandoned nationally when convenient. Yet inner cities are not powerless—especially in their metropolitan regions, where their interests are shared with suburbs. So even in an era of national neglect, considerable policy change can be forged.

In Chapter 14, James Lester and W. Douglas Costain show just how much change has occurred in environmental politics during the last century, detailing the shifts in issues over time that fall under the rubric of "environmental policy." Although they categorize the Clinton administration's environmental policy within the broad trends of decentralized, participatory policymaking, they also see important new issues that are being raised by the administration. Two of the most important are the internationalization of environmentalism and the construction of a new issue from old truths: environmental racism. The emergence of this latter issue, in light of the undeniable fact that minorities are more likely to live near polluting facilities, dramatically illustrates the changing debate over political issues in American politics.

Finally, in Chapter 15, Larry Dodd details the elements of what he calls a changing mindset that underpins the conduct of American politics. This changing mindset, he believes, is fundamentally and irrevocably altering the political and governmental landscape. Although the outlines are not yet clear, the mindset in its newest form seems to involve four elements: a reduced expectation for presidential action; a shift to an incentive-driven unbureaucratic governmental ideal; a replacement of the interest-satisfaction, careerist representative model of representation with constitutional limits on the service of representatives; and an increase in the intrusion of average, opinionated citizens into the democratic dialogue.

If Dodd is correct, then one must ask, Who will benefit from the new configuration of political forces? First, we must note that these new mass attitudes may, ironically, reinforce the interest-driven liberal state as all political actors, from presidents to political parties, are diminished and groups remain free to engage in mass-based propaganda campaigns that mobilize the new opinionated talk-show political activists. Second, it would seem that the Republican Party is most poised to benefit from this new mindset, as it has traditionally been the party of limited government. At the same time, the Republicans have also dropped their old mantle of fiscal responsibility and balanced budgets, instead demanding specific tax cuts while promising generalized, unspecified spending cuts. On the one hand, this circumstance would seem to offer Democrats, with their newfound free-trade and reinventing-government themes, an opportunity to claim the mantle of fiscal responsibility. On the other hand, the opportunity may be exploited by Ross Perot. Former American Political Science Association president Theodore Lowi has argued that America is ripe for the emergence of a third party, but third parties have been notoriously unsuccessful in the United States.

THE 1994 ELECTIONS
AND THE NEW AMERICAN POLITICS

The 1994 elections proved decisively that the Republicans could exploit the political openings offered by the new American mindset. The sweep of the Democrats was as deep as it was wide: When the dust had settled, the Republicans had captured control of both houses of Congress by adding 52 House and 9 Senate seats (8 by election and 1 when Senator Richard Shelby of Alabama switched parties), but they had also captured 9 gubernatorial seats and a number of state legislative chambers. One early report indicated that Republicans captured nearly 500 previously Democratic state legislative seats while losing only 11 ("Now the Schools," 1994). How the GOP captured the American political momentum was as impressive as what it captured: In the House of Representatives, Republicans captured 21 of 25 open seats and defeated 35 Democratic incumbents while suffering not a single defeat of one of their own incumbents! At the state level, and particularly in the South, Democrats suffered disastrous defeats as well. Republicans gained a majority in the Florida Senate and North Carolina House of Representatives and came up only 2 seats short of control in the South Carolina House. Southern straight-ticket Republican voting ousted all Democratic state district judges in the Harris County, Texas (Houston), at-large district, not only sweeping out of office a number of black and Hispanic judges but also elevating several less-than-qualified candidates recruited in what was thought to be a losing effort.

A Partisan Realignment?

Was 1994 the culmination of a partisan realignment that began in 1968? In the next chapter, Mayer makes the case that a presidential realignment occurred in the 1964–1972 period. It is certainly plausible that 1994 completed the realignment as white Southerners, long accustomed to ticket-splitting, shifted their local allegiances to the Republicans. There are other indications that the long-awaited realignment occurred in 1994, yet there are also suggestions that the period of instable dealignment continued, in which few citizens had strong allegiances to either party and many claimed independence from both. Let us briefly survey the evidence.

Political scientists look for several facets in determining whether a bona fide realignment has occurred in an election (or a series of elections). Many one-sided elections occur even when no realignment is in progress. In 1984, President Reagan captured all states except Massachusetts, Minnesota, and the District of Columbia. In congressional midterm elections, the Democrats lost 55 seats in 1946, only to gain 72 in 1948. The key facets of a partisan realignment include the breadth and depth of the election move; the extent to which the election results can be tied to broader social, economic, and political trends; and whether identifiable groups in the electorate seem to have shifted allegiances in line with the broader social trends.

Element 1: The breadth and depth of the Republican sweep is undeniable, as noted earlier.

Element 2: The 1994 election occurred on top of major social and political trends that have been going on for some time. These trends include (1) the growth of Republican power in the South as a consequence of the union of class-based Republican voting and resentment against black empowerment; (2) the politicization of the "social issues" in elections since 1972; and (3) the marginalization of white male industrial workers since 1970 and the emergence of women as an economic and political force.

In the South the move toward Republicanism in 1994 was glaringly apparent, but that movement had been going on at least since the enactment of the Voting Rights Act in 1965, and probably long before. Even in the 1950s, well-to-do Southern urbanites had been moving toward the Republican party; after the Voting

Rights Act, class-based Republicanism became appealing to working-class white Southerners resentful about the progress of blacks. State and local offices have drifted toward Republicanism in the South at least since 1972. In Texas, for example, according to the Texas Republican Party, Republicans held only 53 local offices in 1974. By 1980, they held 166; by 1986, 504; and by 1992, 814. They gained only 76 in 1994, along with 1 state Senate seat and 2 House seats—but this gain moved them to a total of more than a third of each body (Ratcliffe, 1994: 16A). This development looks more like incremental growth in Republican strength than a radical break with the past—but it is all the more powerful because of the force of the underlying trends set in motion as early as 1972.

Resentment against black empowerment was but one of several elements that mobilized what was termed "the silent majority": middle- and working-class Americans resentful about countercultural lifestyles; perceived military weakness abroad; and the decline of living standards, in particular for industrial workers and their dependents. Political scientists have shown that, beginning in 1968, a new dimension of conflict began to structure American politics, one that acted to undermine the Democratic "New Deal" coalition constructed in the realignment of 1928–1932 (see Jones, 1994). That coalition was centered on economics and the politics of class conflict. In contrast, the new issues included concern about the declining moral values of America and often focused on abortion, women's rights, crime, homosexuality, and media depictions of sex and violence. The politicization of such social issues activated the Christian right, a major new force in American politics. In 1994, resentment toward immigrants, especially in California, joined distrust of minority progress and women's changing roles as part of the complex jumble of issues that political scientists have termed, somewhat imprecisely, *the* social issue. Regardless of the confusing tumult associated with this new-issue cluster, two things are clear. First, the cluster is real and has joined class issues (and maybe eclipsed them) as critical to political conflict in America. Second, nativist, antiforeign, Christian movements are recurrent in American politics, and the social issues are nothing less than the current reincarnation of this element in American political life. As such, they are both important and somewhat dangerous.

The third trend in American political life that points to a Republican realignment is the marginalization of the white male industrial worker. Although in the 1980s and early 1990s the United States experienced an economic boom of great proportions, the distribution of the benefits of that boom have been concentrated. Labor Secretary Robert Reich recently noted that working men who lack college degrees, a group that includes nearly three-quarters of working men, have "suffered a 12% decline in average real incomes since 1979" (Farney, 1994: A4). This working man, a traditionally Democratic voter, saw his economic prosperity decline at the same time that he saw the emergence of women in the workforce and apparently unfair advantages going to minorities. Labor Secretary Reich went on to state, "We are on the way to becoming a two-tiered [middle class]

composed of a few winners and a larger group left behind, whose anger and disillusionment are easily manipulated. Today the targets of rage are immigrants, welfare mothers, government officials, and an ill-defined 'counter culture'" (Quoted
in Farney, 1994: A4).

A major reason for the marginalization of the white male worker is the increasing internationalization of the American economy. As international competition forced companies to cut payrolls and lower wages and benefits, the previously enviable lifestyle of the American industrial worker took a nosedive.
Perhaps more important than declines in real income was the increasing insecurity of job tenure as companies slashed payrolls mercilessly. Even though some
evidence has indicated that mindless downsizing actually hurt profitability, companies were handsomely rewarded by investors for doing so. Organized labor
fought a losing battle with its traditional corporate enemies on the one hand and
its traditional friend, the national Democratic party, on the other. President Clinton strongly backed the North American Free Trade Agreement (NAFTA) and the
ratification of the Uruguay Round of amendments to the General Agreement on
Tariffs and Trade (GATT), both of which passed Congress with some Democratic
skepticism and considerable Republican support. As protectionism for industry
declined, the high wages for American factory workers became more of a liability
for American companies, and free trade became an issue dividing the Democratic party.

Element 3: Exit polls from the 1994 elections show movement among groups
that are heading in the direction one would expect, given the trends discussed
above. One notes, first, that all groups moved toward the Republicans, but this
movement is not particularly important in gauging a realignment. For example,
according to Voter News Service Exit Polls, Hispanics voted 28 percent for Republican congressional candidates in 1992 but 39 percent for Republican candidates in 1994. Those making less than $15,000 a year voted 31 percent for Republi-
cans in 1992 but 39 percent for them in 1994. In 1994, as in every election since the
advent of modern polling techniques, upper-income voters supported the Republicans more solidly than lower-income voters (Schneider, 1994). The emergence of the new social issues did not erase class-based election distinctions, but
it did weaken them.

However, 1994 highlighted new social fissures: region and the gender gap. The
South, long a bastion of Republican strength in presidential elections, became a
regional source of Republican congressional strength in 1994. Gender differences
were also magnified in 1994. In 1992, women and men barely differed in their
voting for congressional candidates: Men voted 48 percent Republican; women,
45 percent. In 1994, women moved gently toward the Republicans, with 47 percent supporting the Republicans, but men voted 57 percent for GOP candidates.
(Schneider, 1994: 2631). The New York Times exit polls showed a similar split:
Men voted 54 percent for the Republicans; women, 46 percent. White men, however, voted 62 percent for Republicans; white women, 55 percent. ("Portrait of the
Electorate," 1994: A15). Whites generally moved toward the Republicans, but

white men virtually raced in that direction. It is worth noting that Ross Perot's independent candidacy for president in 1992 drew disproportionately from male voters; third-party and independent candidates sometimes act as "halfway houses" for voters who are disaffected from their current party but are not quite ready to shift to the other party. Although the gender difference does not reach the proportions of class differences or ethnic differences (blacks voted 88 percent for the Democrats), it is significant because it would be confirmation of a partisan move on the part of a clearly disaffected segment of the citizenry. In some cases, the gender difference reached very large proportions: In California, 57 percent of men voted for Republican Senatorial candidate Michael Huffington, while 57 percent of women voted for Democrat Dianne Feinstein. In Texas, 67 percent of white males voted for Republican George Bush for governor, while Ann Richards garnered a bare majority of white women (Wallace, 1994). Note that this gap was activated when women ran as Democrats against male Republicans.

A Continuing Dealignment?

There also exists evidence of a continuing dealignment in the returns of 1994, or a realignment that does not damage the Democratic party quite as much as the election seems to indicate. First, although the Republicans did extremely well in capturing offices, they did not do so well in capturing the actual votes of the American electorate. In 1990, Democrats captured 52 percent of the votes for the House of Representatives to the Republicans' 48 percent. In 1992, Democrats boosted their percentage to 54 percent to the Republicans' 46 percent even though the Democrats lost ten seats. In 1994, the parties split evenly: 50 percent for each. (Portrait, 1994). A slight shift of votes in the proper districts yielded a landslide for the Republicans.

Second, the existence of at least two primary issue dimensions in American politics, one centering on economics and one on the "social issues," means that conflict is far less stable than during the period of American life in which one dimension was dominant (from 1932 to 1968). The electoral fortunes of the parties depend on (1) how salient each dimension is in any given election and (2) how the parties define themselves on the two dimensions. It might seem sensible to assume that the Republicans have captured the social issue dimension whereas the Democrats hold sway on the economic dimension, their traditional strength, but this assumption is not necessarily the case. First, the Democrats, especially the more conservative "New Democrats," have refused to yield the social issues and continue to support crime bills and welfare reform. This refusal has had the immediate effect of depoliticizing, at least for the present, the crime issue: Of citizens citing the crime issue as their most important concern (and this was 25 percent of the electorate), 51 percent voted for Republican candidates (Schneider, 1994: 2632). Similarly, Republicans have laid claim to be the party of economic prosperity, touting tax cuts to stimulate economic growth (although of those concerned about the economy, only 43 percent voted for the Republicans).

Finally, there exists a great deal of disillusionment about government among

Americans, and it is not clear that Republicans will be able to capitalize on that disillusionment. One of the major elements of their "Contract with America" is a capital gains cut, something that clearly does not benefit the disaffected male voter who moved so dramatically toward the party. Such an obvious Republican move to reward wealthy supporters gives Democrats the opportunity to reassert the economic issue. Similarly, the harsh antiwelfare measures directed toward the poor that Republicans have proposed could exacerbate the gender gap by causing many women to move toward the Democrats.

REPUBLICANS AS THE GOVERNING PARTY

As William Mayer notes in Chapter 2, realignments are not made in elections: They are made through the actions of the winning party after the election. Republicans sense this fact and, particularly under Speaker of the House Newt Gingrich, have moved aggressively with an agenda of their own, not waiting for President Clinton to act. Their Contract with America, announced with great fanfare before the election, promised early votes on a series of measures ranging from term limits to tax cuts to welfare reform to increased military spending. Moreover, in a Wall Street Journal–NBC News poll just after the election, 55 percent of voters polled said they wanted Congress to take the lead now, as opposed to only 30 percent who wanted to see President Clinton lead (Seib, 1994). Let us turn briefly to the ambitions and prospects of the Republican congressional majority.

The task of the Republicans as governing party seems fourfold. The first task is institutional reform. Citizens demanded, through their distaste for politicians in general and congressmen in particular, reform of Congress. Republicans are aggressively pursuing a reform strategy as they anticipate taking control of Congress, particularly in the House. One advantage the Republicans have in the House is that they are so junior: Of the 230 Republican representatives, 122 were elected in 1992 or 1994. This "new-breed" Republican is less willing to compromise concerning the accepted practices of the legislature and apparently more willing to allow House Speaker Gingrich to centralize matters. The Republican caucus is cutting committees, cutting committee staffs, and vowing to open up the legislative process. Yet Republicans in the last term of Congress blocked lobbying reform, and Gingrich is already having to contend with more-established members who do not want to let their opportunity for influence disappear in a more centralized house.

Second, the party must serve the constituency that elected it. The antitax, antiregulation, anti–big government refrain has always been popular with the upper-income base of the party. What is new is that a majority of Americans have, at least temporarily and maybe permanently, signed on. But much of the money financing Republican campaigns comes from large donors, particularly companies and groups wanting governmental action. Big business gave large amounts of money to the Democrats while they governed, even though most corporate executives were themselves Republicans. Now money can go to the powerful *and* to the ideologically sympathetic. Serving the constituency providing the money will doubtless conflict with the desire for institutional reform, particularly reform directed at the role of money in the governing process.

Third, the Republicans ought to move to reintegrate the disaffected white voter into the political system without resorting to attacks on minorities, immigrants, and other traditionally disadvantaged groups. The big move to the Republicans came from resentful groups who can be mobilized in either a positive or a negative manner. For example, one can envision a move directed at the media concerning the depiction of violence and sex on television and in the movies, a move that would conflict with free-market rhetoric but that would be solidly grounded in social science findings about the role of exposure to television in the propensity to violence. On the other hand, one can envision a covert or direct attack on immigrants, gays, and other groups already singled out as target groups for hate campaigns by disaffected whites.

Fourth, the party will need to establish a governing philosophy that goes beyond attacks on the governing Democrats. Elements of that philosophy are in place: limited government, institutional reform, and tolerance without preferential treatment. Where the Democrats, in the later stages of the New Deal coalition, seemed to seek subsidies for all constituencies, the Republicans could demand uniformity in fair treatment for all. But this would mean eschewing special treatment in the tax codes, including lowering the capital gains tax. Whereas the Democrats stood for professional politicians and an experienced "governing class," the Republicans could really enact term limits and lobbying reform, but such action would conflict with the desire to exercise the power they have won. Whereas the Democrats stood for special consideration for the disadvantaged, the Republicans could demand equal treatment before the law. But this tactic already seems unduly cruel to the truly disadvantaged or needy.

It will not be any easier for the Republicans to maintain a consistent but flexible governing philosophy than it was for the Democrats. And every seeming advantage carries with it significant potential disadvantages.

In the end, whether the Republicans forge a long-run governing majority depends both on what they do and on what the Democrats do. Republican House members revere Gingrich for good reason: He and a limited number of Representatives saw the fallacy of playing the governing Democrats' game by offering electoral alternatives but scrambling for constituency benefits between elections. Rather, these Republicans melded strong criticism of the Democrats with clear programs of their own, including in particular the painful spending cuts that President Reagan was never able to engineer. Only early in the Clinton administration did it become clear that the distributional benefits approach that had cemented the Democratic majority was as vulnerable as it turned out to be. As representatives rushed to make cuts beyond what President Clinton had proposed in his budget bill and voted by a nonpartisan majority to end funding for the superconducting supercollider, the real importance of the limited government appeal became obvious to all who would listen.

President Reagan used a "supply-side" argument, in which tax cuts would stimulate economic growth so strong that government revenues would actually grow. This argument justified his program of cutting taxes, increasing defense spending, and protecting entitlements. It also resulted in the infamous deficit problem. Now Republicans have promised to offer a program of tax and spending cuts, and President Clinton has joined them with his own tax cut proposal. What remains to be seen is whether Republicans will offer serious spending cuts, even the unpopular cuts in entitlements such as Medicare and Social Security, to balance the proposed tax cuts. Given that the defense budget has been cut considerably since the mid-1980s, and that both parties seem committed to modest growth in that portion of the budget, such entitlements are the only areas ripe for serious savings. If the Republicans do make these cuts, they will doubtless antagonize powerful constituencies. If they do not, they will run the risk of being tagged as the "party of fiscal irresponsibility" by the Democrats and will suffer rising interest rates and an economic downturn by 1996, just at the time when they would like to tout their new policies as the wave of the future.

Democrats, on the other hand, have a different task. It is clear that Democrats ought to try to depoliticize certain issues—such as crime and welfare reform. And they are likely to continue to agree with Republicans on free trade. But if they become the "me too" party on tax cuts, limited government, and every other issue in sight, they surely will be relegated to the status of semipermanent minority. So what issues should they highlight for maximum political advantage? Economic insecurities continue to plague Americans even in this period of economic recovery. In the Wall Street Journal–NBC News postelection poll, 70 percent of respondents cited lack of affordability in health care as an economic problem, and 68 percent worried about unreliable retirement benefits. On the other hand, only 51 percent cited unemployment, although 77 percent indicated that available jobs are too low paying ("Washington Wire," 1994). So the Democrats should probably highlight the class-based economic issues that have always served them well—for example, they should fight capital gains tax cuts and continue to promote public works, investment spending, educational grants and loans, job training, and early intervention programs for children. President Clinton is likely to recommend raising the minimum wage—something that 75 percent of Americans support ("Washington Wire," 1994). Republicans, I suspect, will both be serious about spending cuts and will want to avoid Social Security as a target and therefore will be drawn to cut the limited parts of the federal budget that go to investment spending. A second major area of advantage for Democrats will come in the area of regulation. Republicans have a distinctly probusiness approach to regulation, and this approach may not play well in the areas of health and safety regulation. Finally, the nature of governmental downsizing offers some advantages for the Democrats. For example, Clinton's welfare proposal, stressing job training and public-sector jobs, is favored over the Republican alternative put forth in the Contract with America by 62 percent to 27 percent ("Washington Wire," 1994).

WAS THE 1994 ELECTION A MANDATE?

Elections are almost never mandates. The 1994 midterm elections were almost certainly not a mandate for a vast shift toward a more conservative America. Voters were troubled by many things, and most of the things they were troubled by were epitomized by President Clinton and the Democrats. However, fully 50 percent voted Democratic—only 2 percent less than in 1990 and 4 percent less than in 1992—and a variety of issues motivated those who voted Republican. Even though the Republicans have assumed that their victory had something to do with tax cuts and spending limits, polling data do not fully support this interpretation. Table 1.1 shows the major reasons for voting given by Americans on election day as well as the proportions voting Republican (Schneider, 1994: 2632).

Note that the largest majorities for the Republicans come from people citing taxes, Clinton's performance, and "time for a change" but that the number of people citing these items are considerably lower than those citing health care and the economy, where the Republicans are not favored, and crime, where they split evenly with the Democrats. Note particularly how few Americans cite taxes as an issue that mattered in voting. In the Wall Street Journal–NBC News postelection poll, citizens ranked reducing the deficit as more important than reducing taxes by 58 percent to 35 percent ("Washington Wire," 1994). In that poll, citizens were asked to explain election results. Over half, 53 percent, said "change in Washington," and 19 percent said "voting against Clinton." Only 12 percent said "a more conservative Congress" (Seib, 1994).

The Republican victory, in terms of issues, seems to be a function of general disgust with the Democrats in general and President Clinton in particular.

TABLE 1.1
Reasons for Voting and Numbers Voting Republican in 1994 Elections

Problem	Percentage Citing Issue (Multiple mentions possible)	Percentage Citing the Issue Who Voted Republican
Health care	30	35
Crime	25	51
Economy, jobs	22	43
Taxes	18	72
Budget deficit	17	58
Clinton's performance	17	72
Time for a change	15	70
Candidate's experience	12	39
Foreign policy	5	47

Moving to dismantle the welfare state "brick by brick," as Republican majority leader Dick Armey has indicated his majority would do, might well play into Democratic hands. My guess is that Americans voted for moderation and political reform in 1994 and sensed that the Democrats were too left and too long in power. If the Republicans are too right and too cozy with the lobby, they may well suffer the same fate.

CONCLUSIONS: CHANGE OR CONTINUITY?

In short, the aim of this collection is to examine one of the great issues of politics: the very nature of democratic change. Is it fundamentally incremental, such that nonincremental shifts are to be classified as mere "oddball irregularities"? Is it fundamentally crisis-driven, with crisis compounded upon crisis the way some scholars of presidential decisionmaking describe the process? Or is it characterized by periods of stability interspersed with crises? As if to underscore the importance of this topic, President-elect Bill Clinton, after running a campaign stressing change, emphasized stability in his first statement to the press.

It will become clear that the authors in this book do not completely concur on the nature of change. Some stress change in American politics, whereas others point to continuity and limits. And many of the authors disagree over the pace and direction of change represented by the 1992 election and the first eighteen months of the Clinton administration. This variability is only partly a consequence of the differing subject matter of the chapters.

Even given the obvious political upheaval in 1994, one could debate the extent of change for the Washington establishment. Will interest groups and lobbyists reestablish their traditional relationships with those in power? Will business be even more protected under the Republicans than under the Democrats? Will bureaucrats prove too resilient? Will policy subsystems and "iron triangles" composed of congressional committees, executive agencies, and interest groups be able to resist the demands for change from the Republican majority? Will gridlock, a seeming implication of the constitutional arrangement of divided government, simply reestablish itself?

These forces are powerful. Yet the Republican victory last fall shows just how vigorous American democracy is. Some kind of inevitable "demosclerosis" may set in with Republican governance as lobbyists seek out the new governing power centers, or a kind of obverse gridlock, with a Democratic president and a Republican Congress, may occur. I doubt it. But even if these things happen, we should not forget about the states and localities as sources of major policy changes.

There is simply no doubt that American political institutions make major policy change difficult, but there seems to me to be little reason to assume that these institutions make major alterations in policy impossible. The case for the emergence of a new American politics is made much stronger by the Republican victory in 1994.

PART I

The Politics of Policy Change

2

Changes in Elections and the Party System: 1992 in Historical Perspective

WILLIAM G. MAYER

For those interested in the general phenomenon of political change, the American system of elections and political parties presents a remarkable, almost unique venue of inquiry.[1] Within a constitutional order whose basic parameters have changed relatively little since 1789, we now have regular measures of American voting behavior extending back 150 or even 200 years. For the first forty years or so of this period, election returns were a confusing jumble of personal followings, local cliques, and short-lived factions that defied easy analysis or interpretation; but by the 1840s, a system of organized and competitive political parties had arisen to help structure the contest for public office (see especially Formisano, 1983). Voting and elections also have a very clearly defined universe (in the United States, at least, it isn't really difficult to figure out what constitutes an election and what does not) and come in units that are inherently and meaningfully quantifiable. If we wished to draw a political portrait of New York State in the 1840s, we might have some difficulty in describing how the average person thought about politics; how many interest groups there were, whom they represented, and how active they were; the precise mix of governmental policies and who benefited and lost from them; or the norms and rules that governed its major institutions. But as to how New York voted, we can make a number of quite precise statements.

Changes in partisan electoral outcomes can be classified in several different ways. In this chapter, I divide such changes along two dimensions. First, I distinguish between changes that are long term and enduring versus those that are temporary and short-lived. Then, within the category of enduring changes, I make the further distinction between changes that occur quite rapidly and abruptly and those that are more gradual and take place over an extended period of time. Obviously, each of these distinctions should be thought of as a continuum rather than as a dichotomy, and many elections may display a complicated mixture of changes of varying speed and duration. Yet there seems little doubt that these distinctions do represent important characteristics of change, and that meaningful comparisons can be made along both dimensions. The purpose of this chapter, then, is to explore these three kinds of change—abrupt long-lasting changes, gradual long-lasting changes, and short-term changes—both as general phenomena and with specific reference to the events of 1992.

THE CONCEPT OF A PARTISAN REALIGNMENT

Of the two dimensions of electoral change just described, it is clearly the distinction between long- and short-term changes that has exercised the greatest fascination for scholars, practioners, and journalists alike. When an election such as that in 1992 takes place, it is not especially difficult to see that some substantial changes really did occur. Bill Clinton's victory put an end to twelve years of Republican presidents, while George Bush's 37 percent share of the popular vote represented one of the weakest showings for a Republican candidate in the last fifty years and a decline of more than 20 percentage points from Ronald Reagan's totals of just eight years earlier. Still, we would like to know, are these developments a short-term reaction to the particular failings of one man, or part of a long-term decline in Republican fortunes? Will the next Republican candidate (who will presumably not be George Bush) get 160 electoral votes or 360? And what about Ross Perot, who signaled his willingness to run for the presidency in February, led the polls in June, dropped out of the race in July—and then went on to post the second-best showing for a third-party candidate since the Republicans replaced the Whigs in the 1850s? Was this a unique, one-shot phenomenon—or a sign of a more serious and enduring rupture in the American two-party system?

Questions such as these have animated one of the most influential bodies of theory and evidence in American political science: the theory of critical elections and party realignments. In an immediate sense, most of this scholarly outpouring can be traced to a single article written by V. O. Key, Jr., in 1955. Yet the basic insight behind Key's article is not an especially complicated one, and there are clear intimations of it in a number of other books and articles written in the decade and a half before Key's seminal work (e.g., Bean, 1940: ch. 7; Merriam and Gosnell, 1949: ch. 3; and Lubell, 1952: especially chs. 10 and 11).

Key began his article by observing that while elections are a defining characteristic of a democratic order, they vary widely in "their nature, their meaning, and their consequences."

> Even the most fleeting inspection of American elections suggests the existence of a category of elections in which voters are, at least from impressionistic evidence, unusually deeply concerned, in which the extent of electoral involvement is relatively quite high, and in which the decisive results of the voting reveal a sharp alter-

ation of the pre-existing cleavage within the electorate. Moreover, and perhaps this is the truly differentiating characteristic of this sort of election, the realignment made manifest in the voting in such elections seems to persist for several succeeding elections (1955: 3–4).

As we shall see, a number of intricate methods have been devised to isolate these "critical" or realigning elections from their less consequential fellows. But as Key implies, if the changes really are so significant and enduring, one should not have to resort to heavy-duty statistics in order to distinguish them. All one really needs is to look at the kinds of gross patterns shown in Table 2.1. For relatively long periods of time, it seems clear, there exists a fairly stable balance of power between the two parties. And then, often quite suddenly, a decisive election or series of elections occurs that substantially rewrites the pattern of electoral outcomes. Between 1896 and 1928, for example, the Republicans almost always won both the White House and majorities in both houses of Congress. Over the

TABLE 2.1
Partisan Strength During
Various Periods in American History

Period	Number of Presidential Elections Won by Each Party	Number of Times Each Party Won a Majority of Seats in the House of Representatives
1788–1822	6 Democratic-Republican 2 Federalist	13 Democratic-Republican 4 Federalist 1 Other
1824–1858	6 Democratic 2 Whig 1 Other	12 Democratic 2 Whig 2 Republican 2 Other
1860–1894[a]		
1860–1874	4 Republican 0 Democratic	7 Republican 1 Democratic
1876–1892	3 Republican 2 Democratic	2 Republican 7 Democratic
1894–1928	7 Republican 2 Democratic	14 Republican 4 Democratic
1930–1964	7 Democratic 2 Republican	16 Democratic 2 Republican
1966–1992	5 Republican 2 Democratic	13 Democratic 0 Republican

[a]This period is split in two on the grounds that the most Democratic section of the country, the South, did not participate in most of the elections held between 1860 and 1874.

SOURCE: Compiled by the author on the basis of results reported in Congressional Quarterly's *Guide to U.S. Elections,* 2nd ed. (1985).

next four years, however, the Republicans quickly lost their hold over the presidency and Congress, inaugurating an era of Democratic dominance that lasted until at least 1964.

At its most basic level, then, a critical election is one that inaugurates a "sharp and durable" change in American electoral outcomes. But exactly what kinds of "change" did Key have in mind? On this score, Key was somewhat ambiguous. In the early parts of his 1955 article, he was concerned mainly with *changes in the coalitional structure of politics:* changes in the kinds of groups that could be counted on to support one party rather than the other on a regular, reliable basis. The 1928 election thus emerged as a critical one, in Key's view, because it first established the Democratic Party as the party of "low-income, Catholic, urban voters of recent immigrant stock." Prior to that time, there had been no discernible difference in voting behavior between low-income Catholic cities and rural Protestant areas.

It was largely this type of change that concerned the first wave of political scientists who attempted to flesh out Key's thesis (e.g., MacRae and Meldrum, 1960; Pomper, 1967). Operationally, they looked for evidence of realignments by examining the geographic pattern of partisan voting over an extended period of time. If a party's basic sources of support seemed to remain fairly constant—as reflected, for example, in a high correlation between the party's vote percentage on a state-by-state level in successive elections—one could speak of a stable party system. Lower correlations, by contrast, signaled a shift in the party coalitions and the onset of a realignment.

But later in the same article, Key shifted ground somewhat. As he noted, "One of the difficulties with an ideal type is that no single actual case fits exactly its specifications. . . . If taxonomic systems are to be of analytical utility, they must almost inevitably group together instances that are unlike at least in peripheral characteristics irrelevant to the purpose of the system. All of which serves to warn that an election is about to be classified as critical even though in some respects the behavior involved differed from that of the 1928 polling" (1955: 11).

The election Key referred to here was that of 1896, and he classified it as critical not because it altered the coalitional structure of the parties but because it had a decisive effect on *the parties' relative balance of strength.* In 1896, Key observed, "the Democratic defeat was so demoralizing and so thorough that the party could make little headway in regrouping its forces until 1916." But the 1896 contest "did not form a new division in which partisan lines became more nearly congruent with lines separating classes, religions, or other such social groups. Instead, the Republicans succeeded in drawing new support, in about the same degree, from all sorts of economic and social classes" (1955: 12). Empirically, trying to find this kind of realignment requires that one examine the sort of evidence presented in Table 2.1, showing sharp, long-term changes in the parties' success at winning various kinds of offices.[2]

Spurred on by Key's basic insight, scholars in political science and history soon began an intensive search for critical elections throughout American history. In short order, they compiled not only a list of plausible candidates—the elections in or around 1828, 1860, 1896, and 1932 were almost always singled out—but also a lengthy inventory of characteristics that seemed to be associated with critical elections. This latter list included the following:

- a high level of voter participation;
- a remarkably periodic character, such that critical elections seemed to occur about every thirty-six years;
- a substantial level of issue polarization, first within and then between the two major parties;
- the existence of extensive third-party activity immediately preceding the realignment;
- a major change or displacement in the *issue agenda* of American politics—meaning changes in the kinds of issues on which the parties took opposing stands and that formed the substance of most election campaigns;
- a major shift in the distribution of party identifications;
- significant turnover in governing elites; and
- significant changes in public policy.

Most of this literature contributed a great deal to our understanding of both American political history and the ongoing operations of contemporary American politics. The problem, however, was that a fascination with the details and nuances of realignment theory soon began to overwhelm the basic concept. Properly speaking, the kinds of characteristics I listed earlier should have been treated as the usual (though not invariable) *empirical accompaniments* of realignment—meaning that when a sharp and durable change in voting occurred, these sorts of things also tended to occur.[3] Instead, in a number of cases, these empirical accompaniments came to be seen as a rather rigid list of defining characteristics.[4]

The most influential example of this tendency came at the end of *The American Voter* (1960), where Angus Campbell and his colleagues attempted to apply their findings about the political centrality of party identification to Key's concept of a critical election. And had they simply hypothesized that critical elections in the past were probably associated with major changes in party identification, their insight would have been unassailable. Instead, the authors actually *defined* a realigning election as one that resulted in "a shift in the distribution of party identification"—an intriguing leap of faith given that they had reliable party identification data on exactly *none* of the past elections that were reputed to be realignments. Problematic or not, the Michigan group's definition soon became perhaps the leading criterion for assessing whether or not a realignment had occurred. Thus, in 1973 James Sundquist could confidently, almost off-handedly, assert that 1972 was not a realigning election because it was not accompanied by any major changes in party identification. As for the kinds of changes in aggregate voting behavior that Key had been so concerned with in his original article, Sundquist apparently felt it was unnecessary to examine them (1973: 5–6).

THE CONTEMPORARY ERA

It is against this background that we now turn to the recent sequence of events that culminated in the election of William Jefferson Clinton to the presidency in November 1992. Two questions, in particular, need to be addressed: (1) What are the major characteristics of the electoral era that existed in the years immediately prior to Clinton's triumph? (2) What reasons, if any, do we have for believing that the election of 1992 ushered in a substantial, long-term change in that era?

As to the first question, one can see a growing consensus beginning to emerge about the basic contours of contemporary American electoral politics. Not surprisingly, the 1960s and the first few years of the 1970s—especially the years from 1964 to 1972—show up as a time of substantial change and upheaval. During that period, a number of the most important features of the New Deal order began to weaken and then to fall apart entirely. Some characteristics of the old system still survived, of course—no political change ever entirely wipes out the past—but enough had changed to suggest that the party system of the 1970s and 1980s was distinctively different from that of the 1940s and 1950s. The most significant features of this new era, most authors agree, are the following:

1. The Republicans, who have won five of the last seven presidential elections, are now the normal majority party in presidential voting. During the New Deal party system, Republicans won the White House only under exceptional circumstances: specifically, when their ticket was led by the most popular American war hero of the twentieth century. Since 1968, the reverse has been true: Now it is the Democrats who must wait for a lucky break. Writing in the wake of the last great Democratic landslide, Philip Converse (1966a) estimated that the Democrats had an expected or "normal" vote of 54 percent in national elections. But such an outcome has definitely not been the norm in recent American politics: Indeed, not one Democratic presidential candidate since 1964 has managed to win 54 percent of the popular vote, total or two-party.

2. The Democrats, however, continue to win the lion's share of elections for the U.S. House of Representatives and (to a lesser extent) the Senate, and to win a clear majority of elections for state and local offices.

3. Party labels and identifications have lost much of the meaning they once held, owing to a pronounced growth in the ranks of independents and ticket-splitters. Perhaps the most important reflection of this development has been the enormous increase in the number of congressional districts that vote for a presidential candidate of one party and a congressional candidate of the other (see Jacobson, 1990).

4. The issue agenda of American politics has been substantially transformed. The New Deal, as I have shown in greater detail elsewhere (Mayer, 1992), was al-

most entirely an economic phenomenon, and Democratic presidential candidates enjoyed their greatest success whenever they could keep the election focused on economic issues. Beginning in the early 1960s, however, American national politics became increasingly preoccupied with a new cluster of social and cultural issues. The most prominent of the new issues was race, but abortion, crime, drugs, gay rights, school prayer, and the ERA were also important parts of the mix. Prior to 1960, these matters were rarely discussed in national politics; and on those occasions when they were, they were a source of division *within* the parties, rather than between them.

At almost the same time, the parties also became associated with distinctive positions on foreign policy issues. International affairs had been an important item on the agenda of American national politics since the late 1930s, of course, but not in a way that involved clear and recurring ideological differences between the parties. Especially in the two decades after World War II, both parties professed to be vigorously and determinedly anticommunist; and although each party was happy to take advantage of the mistakes and failures of the other, the criticism generally had much more to do with performance and results than with basic goals or policies. Not until the late 1960s, when Lyndon Johnson had left the White House and Vietnam had become "Nixon's war," did liberal Democrats become closely identified with a foreign policy that, when compared to that of the Republicans, was less sympathetic to defense spending and military intervention and more supportive of arms control and negotiation with the Soviet Union.

5. The voting coalitions of the two parties, especially at the presidential level, have also undergone significant changes. The Republicans have made substantial gains among groups that are culturally traditional (white southerners, the white working class, the devoutly religious) while losing ground among groups supportive of culturally liberal policies (blacks, the highly educated, white-collar women).

A number of very good attempts have been made to trace this partisan reshuffling within the survey data on voting and party identification (see especially Petrocik, 1981, 1987). As a way of preserving some continuity with previous realignment studies, however, I will be using a somewhat more traditional method to make the point. Much of the early realignment literature, as I have indicated, looked for evidence of political change by examining the geographic patterning of the vote. When two or more elections showed a high correlation in the state-by-state results, it was seen as evidence of substantial continuity in the party coalitions. Low or negative correlations, by contrast, were a sign of major changes in the parties' base of support.

Between 1936 and 1944, these correlations clearly mark off a period of great stability. Where the 1932 election seems to have reflected a more uniform, across-the-board rejection of Hoover's leadership, by 1936 the basic character of New Deal policies was clear, as was the lineup of groups and states that favored and opposed them. Take the Democratic or Republican vote for any two presidential elections between 1936 and 1944, and the state-by-state results will correlate at a level of .89 or higher. Suppose, then, that we compute an average Democratic and average Republican vote for the presidential elections of 1936, 1940, and 1944, as providing a good measure of the parties' base of support during the high-water mark of the New Deal party system.[5] By examining how these average votes correlate with subsequent elections, we have a good way of following the degree of continuity and change in the party coalitions.

As the figures in Table 2.2 make clear, the first major departure from the New Deal system came in 1948, when the States' Rights candidacy of Strom Thurmond made major inroads into the Democratic Party's southern base. But as the Republican correlations make clear, 1948 had no observable effect on the shape of the Republican presidential coalition, which still bore a very strong resemblance to the pattern of the New Deal years. In any event, most of the States' Rights vote soon returned to the Democratic fold: The Stevenson vote in 1952 and 1956 continued to show a high (though clearly reduced) correlation with the results of 1936–1944. That correlation plunged even lower in 1960, however, and turned strongly negative in 1964, 1968, and 1972. Of the last seven Democratic presidential candidates, only Jimmy Carter managed to assemble a coalition that even remotely resembled the one that had elected Franklin Roosevelt. The old Republican coalition took a little longer to leave the stage: As late as 1968, Nixon's vote still correlated fairly strongly with that of Landon, Wilkie, and Dewey. But by 1972, the geographic pattern of the Republican vote also looked nothing like its New Deal–era predecessor.

So the New Deal system has dissolved. Has a new one arisen to take its place?

TABLE 2.2
Correlation of Democratic and Republican
Presidential Vote with 1936–1944 Party Averages

Correlation with Average Democratic Presidential Vote, 1936–1944		*Correlation with Average Republican Presidential Vote, 1936–1944*	
Truman 1948	−.37	Dewey 1948	.96
Truman + Thurmond 1948	.95		
Stevenson 1952	.76	Eisenhower 1952	.74
Stevenson 1956	.67	Eisenhower 1956	.84
Kennedy 1960	.24	Nixon 1960	.65
Johnson 1964	−.68	Goldwater 1964	−.69
Humphrey 1968	−.62	Nixon 1968	.72
McGovern 1972	−.47	Nixon 1972	−.40
Carter 1976	.45	Ford 1976	.46
Carter 1980	.43	Reagan 1980	.13
Mondale 1984	−.11	Reagan 1984	−.10
Dukakis 1988	−.38	Bush 1988	−.36
Clinton 1992	.09	Bush 1992	−.52

SOURCE: Data compiled by the author.

The correlation matrices shown in Table 2.3 suggest that the answer is yes. Particularly over the last four elections (1980–1992), there *is* a pronounced regularity to the Democratic and Republican vote. The correlation coefficients are not quite as high as those in previous party systems,[6] perhaps reflecting the greater volatility of the vote in a less partisan, candidate-centered era. Nevertheless, one *can* use the party votes in 1980–1992 as a way of predicting the general shape of the presidential vote in 1996, whereas the New Deal results are clearly no help at all in this respect.

With the possible exception of the Republican presidential dominance, which a few brave souls continue to dismiss as a product of luck or macroeconomics, the existence of all these changes is not really in doubt. Neither is their timing: Though one can find omens of some of these developments in the 1940s and 1950s, the decisive, durable break with the past can generally be localized to the years between 1964 and 1972. But political scientists do disagree about how to interpret this sequence of events: Is it a realignment or isn't it? From the vast profusion of writings on this topic, three basic positions have emerged.

In one corner are authors like Jerome Clubb, William Flanigan, and Nancy Zingale (1990), who have described these developments as simply the "decay phase" of the New Deal party system.[7] The issues, symbols, and loyalties of the old order have clearly deteriorated, in their view, but nothing has yet arisen to take their place, because a "triggering event" of sufficient magnitude has not occurred. There are several problems with this argument. In the first place, I think it considerably understates the immensity of recent changes in American elections. The New Deal order has not just decayed; it has passed from the scene, altered beyond recognition. To take just one example: Clubb, Flanigan, and Zingale

TABLE 2.3
Correlation of Democratic and
Republican Presidential Vote, 1976–1980

	Democratic Vote			
	Carter 1980	Mondale 1984	Dukakis 1988	Clinton 1992
Carter 1976	.92	.76	.61	.82
Carter 1980		.80	.63	.83
Mondale 1984			.93	.92
Dukakis 1988				.83
	Republican Vote			
	Reagan 1980	Reagan 1984	Bush 1988	Bush 1992
Ford 1976	.83	.78	.62	.46
Reagan 1980		.90	.78	.67
Reagan 1984			.94	.77
Bush 1988				.84

SOURCE: Data compiled by the author.

describe the Republican victories in recent presidential contests as "deviating elections." This label may have made sense in 1968—but by the late 1980s, it seemed a strange way, indeed, to characterize a result that had occurred in five of the last six elections. Even more telling is evidence suggesting that the elections of the last decade and a half have acquired certain stable characteristics of their own. Not only is the New Deal system gone, but *something* clearly has arisen to take its place. One must also wonder about the authors' contention that realignment has been forestalled for lack of a sufficiently serious triggering event. If the remarkable combination of racial change, the Vietnam War, exploding crime rates, urban riots, and cultural ferment that took place in the 1960s do not qualify as a crisis of sufficient magnitude, is anything ever likely to meet this standard?

It is this last question that forms the starting point for a second school of thought, whose proponents agree that the New Deal party system has ended but deny that the changes of the recent past can be called a realignment. As both Everett Ladd (1991) and Byron Shafer (1991) have argued in a recent book on the realignment controversy, whatever happened in the 1960s differs in too many significant ways from what occurred during previous realigning periods. Indeed, they conclude that America has probably seen its last realignment, for the entire concept is now outdated—quite descriptive, perhaps, of electoral politics during the more partisan eras of the past, but no longer applicable to a time when party labels have lost much of their intensity and meaning. Yet no sooner do both authors reach this conclusion than they introduce a new term—*party system* in Ladd's case, *electoral era* in Shafer's—that seems to be little more than the old realignment idea, wrapped in new clothing and stripped of some of the more elaborate encrustations that had grown up around Key's original theory.[8] Like the character of Jason in that endless succession of "Friday the 13th" horror movies, realignment is no sooner killed off than it somehow springs back to life.

A third school of thought, with which I associate myself, offers a simpler solution: Retain the realignment terminology, but distinguish more carefully between the core concept and all of its numerous manifestations and accompaniments.[9] That core concept, to repeat, is that realignments set in motion major, long-term changes in the electoral order—in particular, changes in the balance of power between the parties and in the types of groups and voters who support them. As for all the rest, it tells us much that is useful and valid about why realignments occur and what happens when they do, but we should not be shocked or disillusioned (as Key himself had pointed out) if one or more of these characteristics is absent in any particular instance of realignment. Party identifications may have changed substantially during the realignment of the 1930s, but there was no reason to think that this had to be the case in the next realignment.

By this criterion, a realignment clearly did occur between 1964 and 1972, with 1968 probably having the best title to "critical election" status. Those who adhere to this view, however, are forced to make one important concession to scholars like Ladd and Shafer: that the realignment of the 1960s was, in a number of respects, different from that of 1932 (though, by the same token, the 1932 realignment was in some ways different from that of 1896, which in turn was not the same as that which took place in 1860). In particular, the 1960s realignment went nowhere near as deep as its predecessors had gone. It redefined the nation's issue agenda, the party coalitions, and the dynamics of presidential voting, but it did not turn the Republicans into the majority party or give them unified control of national government and most state governments. The reasons why recent electoral changes were so stunted have been amply explored elsewhere (Burnham, 1970; Chubb and Peterson, 1985; Brady, 1988; Silbey, 1991). Particular weight must be given to the long-term decline in partisanship and to the many changes in Congress, state legislatures, and governmental bureaucracies that have helped to insulate them from the more volatile forces that affect presidential voting. However explained, it remains the case that the realignment of the 1960s transformed some aspects of the American party system more comprehensively than did any previous realignment—and yet left other parts of the system largely untouched.

THE LONG-TERM IMPLICATIONS OF 1992

What reason do we have for believing that Bill Clinton has rewritten the rules of American electoral politics, ushering in a new and more Democratic era? The answer is: scarcely any. In reaching this conclusion, I do not think that I am breaking any new ground. Though almost every recent presidential election has been anxiously scrutinized for even the slightest evidence of an emerging realignment, such speculations were strikingly absent from the 1992 postmortems. As a way of putting the 1992 vote into clearer long-term perspective, however, it is worth making a brief examination of Clinton's victory in the light of realignment theory.

1. As V. O. Key emphasized in a 1952 article that previewed some of his developing ideas on realignment, critical elections are usually associated with some kind of significant catastrophe. The elections of 1932 and 1896, for example, were preceded by the worst and second worst depressions in our nation's history; the decade of the 1960s, though quite prosperous, was one of the most contentious, violent, and unsettling periods in the twentieth century. Measured against this yardstick, the Bush presidency surely looks a little pale. It was a disappointment no doubt, and many people have suffered during the country's recent economic travails. But it is difficult to describe as a "catastrophe" a time of slow or stagnant growth when inflation was low and the unemployment rate never rose above 7.7 percent. Nor is there any indication that the Iran/Contra affair has left any lasting scars on the Republican Party's image. (Even the far more serious events of Watergate, it is worth noting, were not a significant issue in any election after 1976.) Bush clearly caused many normally Republican voters to desert the GOP ticket, but there is no evidence I know of, nor any obvious reason to suspect, that Bush's failures have done substantial, long-term damage to Republican prospects.

2. Realignments, it has been argued, are usually characterized by "a considerable increase in ideological polarization" between the parties. But this scarcely seems like a very accurate way to characterize the presidential campaign of Bill Clinton. Though there were a few issues on which the Democratic ticket did its best to accentuate its differences with the Reagan-Bush program (abortion, for example), on most topics Clinton did his best to portray himself as a more moderate, "new-style" Democrat, in a way that actually muted his differences with traditional Republican positions. He planned to increase taxes on the rich, to be sure, but he also promised the middle class a tax *cut* and said that most of his deficit-reduction plan was based on cuts in spending. Having learned the lesson of Michael Dukakis, Clinton did everything possible to avoid being labeled "soft on crime"—even returning to Arkansas during the campaign to be present for an execution. "I don't think the old words 'liberal' and 'conservative,' 'left' and 'right' have much descriptive meaning any more," said one Clinton adviser in an interview during the fall campaign (as quoted in O'Sullivan, 1992). This is not the kind of emotional rallying cry that seems likely to provoke a partisan realignment.

3. One of the key characteristics of a realignment is that it leads to the formation of "new and durable electoral groupings" (Key, 1955: 4). Since this result often requires several elections to become apparent, any judgment we render here must be regarded as preliminary. But we can say that there is precious little evidence of it in the 1992 voting. As the data in Table 2.3 make clear, Clinton's state-by-state results in the 1992 general election correlate quite strongly with those of Walter Mondale in 1984 and Michael Dukakis in 1988. As Gerald Pomper (1993: 134) has observed, "The Arkansas governor extended the Democratic coalition; he did not transform the political map."

4. One way in which the 1992 election *did* differ from its predecessors of the last half-century had to do with the nature of the issue agenda. A unique feature of the 1992 campaign—noted in almost every postelection analysis—was the virtual disappearance of foreign policy as a significant concern among the voters. In the network exit polls, only 8 percent of the voters mentioned foreign policy as one of their major voting issues, even though they had the opportunity to check off more than one issue (Pomper, 1993: 146).

In 1992 there seems little doubt that this change was a significant disadvantage to George Bush. In an early September Gallup poll, in which Clinton was seen as better able than Bush to handle almost every other important issue (taxes, education, the economy, the deficit, the environment, and crime and drugs), Bush was still viewed by a wide margin—67 to 24 percent—as superior in handling "foreign affairs." But it is much less clear what this finding foretokens for future presidential elections. In the first place, it is premature to suggest that foreign policy will never again play a major role in presidential elections until we have a much firmer sense of what the "New World Order" will look like. And even if future elections do focus more narrowly on domestic issues, it is still unclear which party will benefit from this development. Most analysts of the 1992 vote have emphasized that the disappearance of foreign policy eliminates one of the Democrats' major weaknesses in presidential contests: the perception that they were too weak to stand up to the Soviet Union and to protect American interests abroad. But this flaw in the Democratic armor, it is worth recalling, was frequently counterbalanced by the claim that Republicans were too trigger-happy, too willing to get the United States involved in foreign military adventures. In a 1980 Harris survey, for example, voters regarded Reagan by a substantial margin as more likely to keep the United States militarily stronger than the Soviet Union. But they also regarded him as the candidate "most likely to get the U.S. into another war." When asked more broadly about which candidate "would best handle foreign policy," Reagan and Carter came out essentially tied.

Ultimately, of course, whether any particular election result is an instance of long- or short-term change does not become truly clear until decades after the votes are cast. This is especially true of partisan realignments since, as several recent studies have emphasized, much of what leads us to classify a particular election as realigning depends on events that occur only *after* the election: in particular, on how well the new incumbents craft a set of policies that deal with the issues and crises that brought them to office (Clubb, Flanigan, and Zingale, 1990; Brady, 1988). Perhaps there really is something to Clinton's claims that he is a genuinely new kind of Democrat, whose policies will resolve the problems and tensions that have afflicted the Democratic Party over the last thirty years. But after reading a substantial amount of the Clinton campaign literature and the books and articles written by policy experts prominently associated with the Clinton campaign, I must confess to being extraordinarily skeptical.

Finally, I wish to reiterate that I have examined such factors as ideological polarization and changes in the issue agenda, not because I see these as the defining characteristics of a realignment but because, in the past, these developments have usually accompanied the onset of a critical election. In the end, however, the real question is whether the events of 1992 will lead to sharp and durable changes in American voting behavior. If the Democrats win the next seven presidential elections in a row and gain new sources of support among previously Republican voting groups, 1992 will have to be classified as a critical election even if it was not accompanied by a full-blown catastrophe or an increase in ideological polarization. In the absence of a crystal ball, however, it is quite reasonable to examine what I have called the empirical accompaniments of realignment as our best evidence for what lies ahead.[10] And almost all of this evidence, as I have indicated, weighs against a realignment interpretation.

THE PEROT PHENOMENON

It is much more difficult, however, to say anything definitive about the future of Ross Perot or of the 19 percent of the electorate who voted for him. To be sure,

almost everything that political scientists have learned over the last fifty years indicates that a two-party system is a stable and enduring feature of American politics and that third-party movements will be short-lived and generally unsuccessful. At the same time, most of that same body of knowledge suggests that Perot
should never have done as well as he did.

Nor is there much in the voter surveys to help us understand the nature of
Perot's appeal. Unlike other recent third-party candidates, the Perot vote was *not*
characterized by any particularly distinctive set of demographic or attitudinal
traits. To the contrary, Perot drew about equally well from both parties (though
he did best, of course, among independents), from all parts of the ideological
spectrum, and from all major demographic groups except blacks and Jews. In
general, the Perot constituency was closer to the Bush voters in their economic
attitudes and closer to the Clinton voters on social and cultural issues—but I
think these findings say more about why some people stuck with Bush and Clinton than about why others turned to a third-party candidate. Perot voters did
stand out for their *concern* about the federal deficit, but they were much less
united in their attitudes about specific policies designed to reduce it. They were
also more likely than average to believe that the economy was bad and that the
country was headed in the wrong direction—but this is no more than one would
expect from any group that votes against an incumbent president (see Pomper,
1993; Ladd, 1993).

The picture of the Perot vote that emerges, in short, is of a large and rather
diffuse protest movement, dissatisfied with politics and politicians as usual, but
not possessed of any clear ideological or programmatic commitments. Though
one can surely say that the Perot candidacy seemed a good fit for the "alienated"
electorate of the 1992, one could probably make the same claim about the mood
of the voters in 1968, 1976, or 1988.

The cause of Perot's impressive showing, then, probably had less to do with
underlying issues and ideologies than with the peculiar dynamics of the 1992
campaign. The general pattern of modern-day third-party candidates is that their
support peaks in the summer or early fall of the election year and then declines
steadily until the day of the actual voting. In 1980, for example, John Anderson
had polled 24 percent of the vote in mid-June, but this figure fell to about 15
percent in September, to 9 percent in October, and then to 6 percent of the final
vote. The same thing was clearly happening to Perot in the early summer, just
before he withdrew. In the fall, however, the opposite pattern occurred. According to the Gallup polls, Perot's vote rose from 7 percent in late September (shortly
before he formally reentered the race), to 10 percent in early October, to 15 percent in late October, finally cresting at 19 percent in the actual voting.

Two factors, in my judgment, explain this surprising turn of events. The first,
of course, was that Perot had considerably more money at his disposal than any
previous third-party candidate. For more typical third-party candidates, such as
John Anderson in 1980, the campaign finance laws enacted in 1974 have worked a

significant hardship on their ability to wage a vigorous general election campaign. Though denied the huge federal subsidies that went automatically to the Republican and Democratic candidates, Anderson still had to abide by the new contribution limits. No individual could give more than $1,000 to his campaign, no political action committee more than $5,000. Perot, however, took ample advantage of a loophole in the law (actually carved out by a 1976 Supreme Court decision) that allows candidates to spend unlimited amounts of their own money on their campaigns. So where Anderson was outspent by Reagan and Carter by a margin of about 2 to 1, Perot actually spent about $23 million *more* than either Bush or Clinton in the fall campaign.

The other remarkable fact about Perot's fall campaign was that neither Bush nor Clinton made any real attempt to attack or challenge him: To the contrary, they both went out of their way to appear respectful and accommodating. Perhaps because Perot's vote did seem so heterogeneous, the Bush and Clinton campaigns seem to have decided that any attempt to deflate his candidacy would only drive his disaffected supporters into the arms of the other candidate. Whatever the reason, Perot was treated throughout the fall campaign in a manner that makes phrases like "kid gloves" and "a free ride" seem distinct understatements.

The best example of this, of course, was Bush and Clinton's willingness to include Perot in the presidential debates. In 1980, it may be recalled, the League of Women Voters, which then sponsored the debates, dealt with John Anderson's candidacy by saying that he would be invited to debate Carter and Reagan only if he was registering at least 15 percent in the national polls. Anderson ultimately did reach this threshold—and Carter still refused to share the stage with him. By contrast, Perot was included in the 1992 debates at a time when his poll support was no more than about 9 percent of the vote.

And once the debates were held, everything Perot said was almost entirely exempt from criticism or rebuttal by either Bush or Clinton. As Al Gore was to show when he debated Perot about the North American Free Trade Agreement (NAFTA) in the fall of 1993, the Texas billionaire clearly did have weaknesses that could have been exposed. He was generally short on facts and a detailed understanding of the issues, and he reacted quite poorly to criticism. But none of this came out in 1992. In the first debate, for example, I counted 23 separate instances in which Clinton criticized either Bush or the Republicans, and 17 times when Bush attacked Clinton and the Democrats. But Perot was criticized only five times by Bush and just twice by Clinton.

Given such a charmed life, Perot's image with the electorate could go nowhere but up. When Gallup asked the participants in a national sample in late September whether they had a favorable or unfavorable opinion of Perot, the results were 20 percent favorable, 66 percent unfavorable. When the same question was asked in late October, the tally read 41 percent favorable, 41 percent unfavorable.

If this account of the Perot phenomenon is correct, however, it clearly suggests that there are limits to Perot's political future. The Perot money will presumably always be there to finance his campaigns; but if he ever does show signs that he has a real chance to win the White House, or that he is drawing votes disproportionately from one party, his immunity from attack will end. And as Gore showed, there is much there to attack.

I am similarly skeptical about the possibility that Perot's followers are cohesive enough to be transformed into an important and lasting pressure group or voting bloc. Even in 1992 Timothy Prinz (1993) has demonstrated that casting a ballot for Perot had no effect at all on how people voted for Congress. After controlling for factors like party identification, Perot voters were neither more nor less likely to vote for incumbent representatives, or for Republicans or Democrats. Realignments, as I have noted earlier, are often foreshadowed by major third-party movements. But the converse is not true: Not all major third-party showings occur just prior to realignments. Those that took place in 1912 and 1980, for example, had at best very small effects on the elections immediately following them. Historically, the third-party movements that have had the greatest impact on American politics are those that were organized around quite specific, issue-based grievances and therefore appealed to distinct and identifiable groups of voters. In such cases, a large third-party vote indicated that some particular issue or problem was being ignored by the major parties, and that a major electoral payoff was available to the party that could best reach out to the disaffected constituency. But the Perot vote, as we have seen, had a much more diffuse character than this. As a revolt against politics as usual, the Perot vote also seems extraordinarily difficult movement for either party to incorporate into its ranks on a lasting basis. By the mere act of taking power, such a party would become precisely what the Perot people were protesting against. Third-party movements organized around the personal appeal of a particular individual tend not to be transferable to other candidates or causes and usually dissolve once their leader withdraws from active combat. Such, I would argue, is likely to be the fate of the Perot "movement."

Yet, even if it does not prefigure a major realignment, the Perot phenomenon does reveal some important features of American electoral politics in the late twentieth century. If nothing else, Perot's 19 percent showing is testimony to the substantial weakening of party allegiances within the electorate and to the large number of people who are dissatisfied, in some way, with politics as usual. Perhaps more significantly, Perot's candidacy is a fascinating case study of the potential uses of modern campaign technology. For the first century and a half of American politics, a wealthy individual who wanted to run for president without party endorsement would have needed to build an organization in order to get his message out to the voters. Perot did, in fact, attract a sizable number of volunteers to his banner, but there is no evidence that these people did anything other than gather signatures to get him on the ballot. Especially during the fall, the Perot campaign was run almost entirely through the media, both for free and, especially, on a paid basis. For television time, unlike an organization of diverse, far-flung, and frequently recalcitrant individuals, is available to anyone with the money to buy it, takes very little time to acquire, and makes no other demands upon the user. Perot enthusiasts will perhaps see this development as a welcome new way of undermining support for the two established parties and introducing new competition into American elections. But most political scientists, I suspect, will see it as a reminder of the healthy discipline that political parties exercise over the behavior of ambitious officer-seekers.

SECULAR REALIGNMENTS

Up until now, I have used the word *realignment* as though it were synonymous with the concept of a *"sharp* and durable" change in electoral behavior. And so it would seem from Key's original article. But four years later, Key took note of another level of complexity in the American party system. "Some elections," he still believed, "may be 'critical' in that they involve far wider movements and more durable shifts than do other elections. Yet the rise and fall of parties may to some degree be the consequence of trends that perhaps persist over decades and elections may mark only steps in a more or less continuous creation of new loyalties and decay of old. . . . A secular shift in party attachment may be regarded as a movement of the members of a population category from party to party that extends over several presidential elections and appears to be independent of the peculiar factors influencing the vote at individual elections" (1959: 198–199). So some realignments were sharp and abrupt, but others were gradual and incremental. Long-term changes come in two varieties.

Of Key's two path-breaking articles on change in the party system, the one on secular realignments has had distinctly less effect on the course of subsequent scholarship. Everyone who works in the field has read it, it is often footnoted, a few even lament the fact of its being slighted—and then everyone moves on to the sexier topic of critical elections. Perhaps political scientists, like journalists, are overly fascinated with sharp changes and "new eras" and are unwilling to devote much effort to the slower and less dramatic trends that may nonetheless be remaking our politics. Yet it must also be said that the concept of secular realignment—both in Key's original article and in the small amount of follow-up work that has been done since then—is much less well defined than the idea of a critical election. The theory of critical elections caught on in part because it directed our attention to a fairly well-defined universe of phenomena. We were looking for elections that marked off a decisive, long-lasting change in the state of American electoral politics. That quest pretty much limited the roster of possible candidates to the fifty-two presidential elections held since the ratification of the Constitution; and it further suggested that we should be able to find evidence of these shifts in either national voting data or in state data that could be taken as indicative of national trends.

A secular realignment, by contrast, could involve almost any sufficiently defined subgroup of the population, in any region (or regions), and over any span of years. Though it was surely possible to locate individual instances of secular change, it was probably impossible to devise a general method for locating or classifying them. Just within Key's original article, there was one example involving industrial towns in New England; a second occurred in a single, apparently German county in rural Ohio; a third was set in a Jewish ward in Boston. The first of these took place primarily between 1900 and 1928, the second over the years 1880 to 1956, and the third from 1928 to 1952. And although each of these changes involved a group that was becoming "more or less homogeneous in its partisan attachments" (Key, 1959: 199), different types of processes seemed to be at work in each case.

I suspect, in short, that there may never be an adequate, general-purpose theory of secular realignment: The range of phenomena drawn together under one label is simply too diverse. Yet one aspect of the secular realignment concept does link up more directly with the issues considered in this chapter. Key's 1955 article, as we have seen, clearly implied that long-term changes in the party system revolved around a single, critical election that set the pattern for decades to come. But many subsequent studies have argued that the changes are actually more gradual than this: that rather than speaking of one realigning election, we would be more accurate to think in terms of a realigning era. Which view best describes the upheavals in the American party system? Just how sharp and abrupt are the changes associated with a partisan realignment?

To answer these questions, let us look at several kinds of data. Table 2.4 presents the presidential and congressional election results from immediately before and after three elections widely regarded as critical: 1896, 1932, and 1968. And here the evidence clearly *is* of a sharp and quite abrupt break with the past. We may take the 1896 results as representative of this pattern (though the 1932 results are an even stronger case in point). In the last two decades of the third-party system, the Democratic and Republican parties were more evenly balanced than in any other sustained period in American history. Democrats won two of the three presidential elections preceding 1896, though in all three cases the division of the popular vote was extremely close. Democrats also won a majority of seats in the House of Representatives in four of five elections between 1884 and 1892, though again the margins were usually small. And then, beginning in 1894, the American political universe was quite suddenly turned upside down. The Republicans won a clear majority of House seats in the 1894 midterm elections, reclaimed the White House in 1896—and then never lost control of either until 1910. The transition between party systems could hardly have been more abrupt.

The evidence regarding the 1968 realignment is less decisive, though the pattern would probably be clearer if Table 2.4 included data for a longer span of elections. To begin with, as I have already indicated, there is no change in the congressional results: The Democrats won a majority of House seats in every election held just before and after 1968. At the presidential level, however, the

TABLE 2.4
Presidential and Congressional Election Results
Before and After Three Realignments

Year	Party That Won the Presidential Election	Margin of Victory in Popular Vote	Party that Won a Majority of House Seats	Majority in Seats
1884	Democratic	0.2	Democratic	43
1886			Democratic	17
1888	Republican	−0.8	Republican	7
1890			Democratic	147
1892	Democratic	3.1	Democratic	91
1894			Republican	139
1896	Republican	4.3	Republican	91
1898			Republican	22
1900	Republican	6.2	Republican	46
1902			Republican	30
1904	Republican	18.8	Republican	114
1920	Republican	26.1	Republican	170
1922			Republican	20
1924	Republican	25.2	Republican	64
1926			Republican	42
1928	Republican	17.4	Republican	100
1930			Democratic	6
1932	Democratic	17.8	Democratic	193
1934			Democratic	216
1936	Democratic	24.2	Democratic	242
1938			Democratic	97
1940	Democratic	9.9	Democratic	106
1956	Republican	15.4	Democratic	33
1958			Democratic	130
1960	Democratic	0.2	Democratic	89
1962			Democratic	81
1964	Democratic	22.6	Democratic	155
1966			Democratic	60
1968	Republican	0.7	Democratic	51
1970			Democratic	74
1972	Republican	23.2	Democratic	47
1974			Democratic	147
1976	Democratic	2.1	Democratic	149

SOURCE: Compiled by the author on the basis of results reported in Congressional Quarterly's *Guide to U.S. Elections,* 2nd ed. (1985).

Democrats triumphed in seven of the nine elections before 1968, with their 1964 candidate amassing the largest popular vote percentage for any Democratic candidate in this century. But the Democrats then lost five of the next six presidential elections, the string being interrupted only by the election that followed the worst political scandal in American history.

What about the party coalitions: Do these change abruptly or incrementally? For previous realignments, this question can be answered only by examining aggregate election returns, usually at the state or county level. For the events in and around 1968, however, mass sample surveys can provide us with a considerably more precise and detailed view of the evolution of party coalitions. Using data from the *American National Election Studies,* I have identified three major groups often seen as central to the political upheavals of the last three decades: blacks, native white southerners, and northern white blue-collar workers. In Tables 2.5, 2.6, and 2.7, respectively, I present three major indicators of each group's partisan inclinations for the presidential election years between 1952 and 1992: their party identification, their presidential vote, and their congressional vote. Depending on which part of these tables one chooses to emphasize, there is support for several different views about the speed and sharpness of electoral change.

In some respects, the new electoral order clearly did come about through an abrupt change rather than a smooth and gradual transition. This is most obviously the case for blacks, who constituted a solidly Democratic group in the 1950s and then, between 1960 and 1964, became an overwhelmingly Democratic constituency. The modest but reliable number of black Republicans bolted that party in 1964 and never returned. Even black party identifications changed quite rapidly, jumping from 50 percent Democratic in 1960 to more than 80 percent Democratic in 1964, and showing little or no change thereafter.

TABLE 2.5
Partisan Inclinations of Blacks, 1952–1992

	1952	1956	1960	1964	1968	1972	1976	1980	1984	1988	1992
Party Identification											
Democrat[a]	62	55	50	82	91	75	85	81	77	80	78
Republican[b]	16	19	20	8	3	11	6	8	10	12	8
Apolitical	17	18	14	4	3	2	1	4	2	3	2
(N)	(171)	(146)	(171)	(156)	(149)	(267)	(291)	(187)	(247)	(267)	(316)
Presidential Vote											
Democrat	80	64	71	100	97	86	94	92	89	90	91
Republican	20	36	29	0	3	13	5	7	9	8	5
Third Party					0			1			2
(N)	(51)	(50)	(75)	(94)	(87)	(139)	(134)	(106)	(131)	(125)	(196)
Congressional Vote											
Democrat	92	83	82	95	87	93	96	95	90	92	88
Republican	8	17	18	5	13	6	3	5	19	8	11
(N)	(36)	(35)	(45)	(63)	(60)	(94)	(108)	(82)	(95)	(99)	(144)

[a]Includes those who say they lean toward the Democratic Party.
[b]Includes those who say they lean toward the Republican Party.
SOURCE: American National Election Studies.

TABLE 2.6
Partisan Inclinations of
Native White Southerners, 1952–1992

	1952	1956	1960	1964	1968	1972	1976	1980	1984	1988	1992
Party Identification											
Democrat[a]	82	75	73	74	62	61	64	60	44	50	40
Republican[b]	10	17	16	15	23	24	21	26	38	39	43
(N)	(260)	(284)	(325)	(199)	(220)	(406)	(337)	(241)	(285)	(264)	(328)
Presidential Vote											
Democrat	50	57	57	59	28	19	49	41	33	38	35
Republican	50	40	41	41	40	80	50	57	66	62	47
Third Party					32			2			17
(N)	(137)	(173)	(222)	(126)	(134)	(196)	(172)	(138)	(155)	(149)	(194)
Congressional Vote											
Democrat	93	87	80	77	71	77	72	60	61	66	49
Republican	5	13	19	23	29	23	28	39	39	34	48
(N)	(95)	(150)	(197)	(115)	(108)	(149)	(149)	(113)	(128)	(128)	(170)

[a]Includes those who say they lean toward the Democratic Party.
[b]Includes those who say they lean toward the Republican Party.
SOURCE: American National Election Studies.

Abrupt, rapid change is also the best description of *presidential voting behavior* among native white southerners and northern white blue-collar workers, though in these cases the key changes occurred later than did the changes in black voting. Both white groups were reliably Democratic presidential voters between 1952 and 1964. But they left the Democratic banner in 1968 and, after flirting briefly with George Wallace, flocked to the Republican standard in 1972. With the exception of the 1976 and 1992 elections, most of them have remained presidential Republicans ever since.

The party identification figures for these two groups tell a somewhat different story, however. Democratic partisanship did decline among both groups between 1964 and 1972 (the falloff is especially noticeable in the number of strong Democrats, which is not reported here). In general, however, both the native white southerners and the northern white working class required a considerable period of time for their more stable and inertial partisan commitments to catch up with the changes in their presidential preferences. Indeed, if we may assume that a group's partisanship should ultimately come into line with its average presidential vote, the process is still not complete.

At one level, this finding should come as no surprise, since party identifications have long been noted for their great stability and resistance to change (see, among others, Campbell et al., 1960; Converse, 1964). Yet, for both groups, the shift away from Democratic partisanship seems to have occurred in several sharp

TABLE 2.7
Partisan Inclinations of Northern White Blue-Collar Workers, 1952–1992

	1952	1956	1960	1964	1968	1972	1976	1980	1984	1988	1992
Party Identification											
Democrat[a]	64	53	54	65	57	51	46	47	46	41	44
Republican[b]	29	36	32	24	31	31	31	31	40	41	40
(N)	(322)	(331)	(338)	(263)	(233)	(365)	(377)	(217)	(286)	(247)	(303)
Presidential Vote											
Democrat	56	48	58	77	43	34	62	42	35	39	40
Republican	43	52	42	23	46	64	35	51	65	59	29
Third Party					11			5			31
(N)	(236)	(256)	(273)	(192)	(150)	(213)	(201)	(114)	(166)	(134)	(199)
Congressional Vote											
Democrat	57	55	57	69	50	54	52	48	47	58	57
Republican	42	45	43	30	50	46	46	51	53	42	42
(N)	(203)	(243)	(231)	(169)	(131)	(188)	(162)	(106)	(150)	(117)	(167)

[a]Includes those who say they lean toward the Democratic Party.
[b]Includes those who say they lean toward the Republican Party.
SOURCE: American National Election Studies.

bursts rather than in the smooth and even increments posited by theories of secular realignment or generational replacement. Among native white southerners, for example, there was a sizable decline in Democratic identifications between 1964 and 1968, accompanied by a somewhat smaller increase in Republican affiliations. These percentages then remained quite stable for the next sixteen years. Not until 1984 is there evidence of a second major surge—this time, toward the Republicans.

As for the congressional voting figures, there is (again, not surprisingly) less change of any kind. There was perhaps a slight increase in Democratic voting among blacks and a slight increase in Republican voting among northern white blue-collar workers. The only significant change in congressional voting occurred among native white southerners—and here the pattern really does correspond to Key's original conception of a secular realignment. Beginning as early as 1956 and continuing through the 1980s, there was a long, slow increase in the percentage of southern whites who cast their ballots for a Republican congressional candidate. As of the late 1980s, however, two-thirds of white southerners were still voting Democratic at the congressional level. For both white groups, there was a sizable gap between their willingness to vote for Republican presidential candidates and their willingness to vote for Republican congressional candidates.

Overall, what these data indicate is that electoral realignment occurs very rapidly at some levels but takes a good deal longer to accomplish at others. The parties' relative balance of strength changes quite abruptly, as does the voting behavior of many particular groups. In previous realignments, such voting changes seem to have occurred in both presidential and congressional elections; but in the most recent upheaval, there is, as I have indicated throughout this chapter, a much greater separation between the two. Party identifications, at least in the contemporary era, have adjusted more slowly. Perhaps this has always been the case. Alternatively, one may wish to read Tables 2.6 and 2.7 as support for Kevin Phillips's (1982) contention that a full-scale realignment was under way in the early 1970s—only to be arrested by the events of Watergate. In either case, it seems highly misleading to call such developments a "secular realignment" in Key's sense of the term: meaning a trend that is "independent of the peculiar factors influencing the vote at individual elections." A more revealing interpretation is to say that these changes were a delayed "aftershock" of the upheaval that occurred in the 1960s.[11]

This is not to deny that *some* secular realignments do take place. We have seen evidence of one such realignment in the data on congressional voting among white southerners. Studies of particular states and regions provide a wealth of other examples (Galderisi et al., 1987; Moakley, 1992). The problem is that, although these secular realignments undoubtedly have important localized effects, no one I know of has been able to demonstrate that they are connected to national changes in party strength. In the case of southern congressional voting, for example, there has been a long-term increase in the number of southern Republican representatives—but it has been counterbalanced by a similar increase in the number of Democratic representatives elected in other parts of the country (Jacobson, 1990). As of 1992, Republicans were no closer to a majority in the House of Representatives than they were in the 1960s. The periods between critical elections—the various "party systems" enumerated in the standard histories of American electoral politics—are, as we have seen, characterized by a fairly stable balance of power between the parties. The implication is that during such times, pro-Republican and pro-Democratic secular changes probably occur in about equal proportions, thus tending to cancel one another. And this, of course, is yet one more reason why political scientists have been reluctant to study such changes.

SHORT-TERM CHANGE

If 1992 did not mark a durable change in American voting habits, then the Republican decline must be attributable to short-term forces: to factors that had a major effect on how people voted in 1992 but are unlikely to have a lasting, persistent impact on the electorate. Perhaps the paradigmatic example of short-term change was the election of 1952. In that year, Republicans won a majority of seats in both houses of Congress and triumphed in the presidential balloting for the first time in twenty-four years. But forty years later, one would be hard-pressed to find any lasting results of this election on the character of the American party system. The Republicans lost their hold on Congress at the first available opportunity (1954) and surrendered the White House as soon as the charismatic figure of Dwight Eisenhower was no longer at the top of their ticket. By 1960 the Democratic dominance of American national government was, to all outward appearances, as solid as it had been in the early 1940s.

Most discussions of short-term electoral change attribute such shifts to three general factors: policy issues, the performance record of the incumbent administration, and the characteristics of the candidates. And though this list is basically accurate, all three factors are often measured and analyzed in ways that actually combine short- and long-term influences.

The attempt to distinguish between long- and short-term components of the vote is especially problematic when we are dealing with policy issues. A stable electoral era, as we have seen, is generally characterized by a recurring issue agenda and a durable clustering of groups that tend to be regular supporters of one party or the other. Under such circumstances, we can expect—and, in fact, do find—that most campaign issues are not events unto themselves but simply individual episodes in a long-running script.[12]

So when John Kennedy attacked Richard Nixon in the 1960 campaign for opposing aid to education, medical insurance for the elderly, and an increase in the minimum wage, it would be misleading to suggest that these were unique, short-term influences applicable only to that election. Though the particulars at stake were slightly different from year to year, disagreements about the spread of the welfare state were a regular feature of elections held during the period of the New Deal party system. Or, to take a more recent example, no other Democratic candidate besides Michael Dukakis will ever have to face the charges that he furloughed a convicted murderer and vetoed a bill that would have required the recitation of the Pledge of Allegiance. But to see these controversies as exclusively short-term forces is a very ahistorical way of looking at the 1988 election. These two issues were only the latest in a series of attempts to portray the Democrats as out of touch with mainstream American cultural values. Much of their success, indeed, probably had less to do with the specific dynamics of that campaign than with the fact that the voters already had a well-established image of the Democratic Party as being soft on crime and suspect on patriotism. By 1988 the Republicans did not need to create such images anew; they merely had to suggest that Dukakis fit the stereotype.

In some circumstances, however, issue effects on the vote do belong in the category of short-term forces. In the first place, there are issues that do not fit into the agenda that defines a particular party system. During the New Deal era, for example, the parties were polarized primarily over economic issues. Racial issues, when they arose (and they did not arise often), cut across the prevailing line of cleavage. It is thus reasonable to regard such issues as a short-term electoral force. An important feature of the post–New Deal electoral order, however, has been an expansion of the issue agenda such that the parties have also become associated with distinctive positions on cultural and foreign policy issues. Thus, the number of potential "cross-cutting" issues has become substantially smaller. Perhaps the only examples of such issues in recent elections are protectionism, policy toward Israel, and the budget deficit.

Another variation on this theme arises when a candidate tries to outflank his opponent by adopting a position usually identified with the other party. In 1976, for example, Jimmy Carter attacked Gerald Ford for making too many concessions to the Soviet Union; in 1985 Ronald Reagan tried to alter his party's economic image by advocating a comprehensive reform of the tax code. In these cases, the issue might be considered a short-term factor in that both men were advocating a position contrary to what one might have expected on the basis of the established party ideologies. In neither case, it might be added, was there much evidence that these gambits yielded a substantial electoral payoff.

Finally, even though issues like crime and the welfare state are regularly discussed in national elections, the particulars present in any one election do matter. For instance, Democrats have often tried to portray Republicans as insufficiently supportive of Social Security—but their task was obviously made easier when the Republican candidate had indicated that he might make Social Security voluntary, as Barry Goldwater did in 1964.

In general, I know of no precise way of separating the long- and short-term components of issue voting. (Normal vote analysis certainly does not accomplish the task.) On the whole, however, I think policy issues are better seen as long-term than as short-term forces in most elections.

A second and more important source of short-term electoral change is retrospective performance evaluations. Again, we must be careful to define the boundaries of this concept. In the leading book on retrospective voting, Morris Fiorina (1981) uses the term to include virtually anything the voters learn from observing how the parties have behaved in the past—including their issue positions. In the more limited sense I have in mind, however, performance evaluations are essentially nonideological. With respect to certain kinds of issues, especially the state of the economy, the evidence strongly indicates that voters are less concerned with the specific policies that each party will pursue (policies that are, in any event, highly technical and never very well defined in the course of the campaign) than with the end product of those policies. Voters want a growing economy with low unemployment and stable prices—and do not especially care how these results are achieved. Hence, in deciding which party is more likely to meet these goals, voters place great emphasis on the parties' past record of performance, especially the performance of the incumbent administration. The same seems to be true of the way that voters reacted to the Korean War in 1952 and to the Vietnam War in 1968: The Democrats lost votes in both cases, not because the voters disapproved of their specific policies or felt that the proposed Republican policies were superior, but because of a more general dissatisfaction with the *results* that the incumbent administrations had produced.

Table 2.8 sets out three commonly used indicators of the incumbent adminis-

TABLE 2.8
Three Indicators of Presidential Performance

Year	Real Growth in GNP in the Year Before the Election[a]	Number of Deaths in a Major War During the Election Year[b]	Approval Rating in the Summer Before the Election[c]
1952	2.30	4,437	30
1956	1.35	0	70
1960	2.22	0	59
1964	5.35	205	74
1968	4.34	16,588	39
1972	5.52	640	58
1976	4.03	0	45
1980	−1.94	0	33
1984	5.63	0	54
1988	3.84	0	51
1992	2.11	0	36
Range	7.57	16,588	44
Average	3.16	1,988	50

[a]Real growth in GNP was measured from the third quarter of the preceding year to the third quarter of the election year.

[b]Figures on war deaths are based on Combat Area Casualties file in the National Archives.

[c]Approval ratings were taken from Gallup Polls conducted during June and July of each election year. When more than one survey included the presidential approval question, the results were averaged.

SOURCE: GNP data are taken from the U.S. Department of Commerce, *National Income and Product Accounts* (multiple years).

tration's performance: the growth in real gross national product (GNP), measured between the third quarter of the preceding year and the third quarter of the election year; the number of Americans who died in a major war during the election year; and the approval rating of the incumbent president as recorded in polls taken during the summer preceding the election. Three points are worth making about these data. First, they really *are* variables; that is, past administrations have varied widely in their success at achieving prosperity, peace, and popularity. Second, successes and failures can be found in both parties. Performance evaluations, in other words, are not simply a reflection of long-term tendencies inherent in the established party issue positions.

Finally, these three indicators go a long way toward defining the predicament of George Bush in 1992. Peace we clearly had. The economic record was more mixed. The economy was growing slowly—but it *was* growing, and at a rate exceeding that achieved by Dwight Eisenhower in his successful reelection bid of 1956. It was in the voters' assessment of his own performance that Bush looked especially like a loser. Estimates indicate that in order to get reelected, an incumbent administration needs a midsummer approval rating of about 50 percent (Brody and Sigelman, 1983). Bush was clearly well below this figure, ranking just beneath Johnson and Ford and just above Truman and Carter, four other administrations that had also been rejected by the voters. Indeed, the only puzzle raised by these data is why the Republicans woke up to their predicament so late in the campaign.

Of course, the Gallup presidential approval question is not only a measure of the incumbent administration's performance. It is also, at least when the incumbent is running for reelection, a reflection of a third source of short-term electoral change: the qualities and characteristics of the candidates. This concept too needs a somewhat clearer focus. In some contexts, issue positions and past performance can also be considered characteristics of the candidates. When most political scientists talk about the influence of candidate evaluations on the vote, however, they are thinking about the candidates' personal qualities: whether the voters see them as competent, moral, intelligent, honest, and so on. Unfortunately, though these aspects of candidate evaluation may be conceptually distinct, they are highly entangled in practice, for one of the principal ways that voters acquire information about the candidates' personal qualities is by observing their issue positions and how they have performed in the past. It is thus, in any particular election, difficult to say what is causing what. Was George McGovern seen as ill-suited for the presidency because various campaign events (especially the Eagleton fiasco) had given the impression of a man who lacked the qualities of steady leadership—or because he advocated a set of policies that the voters regarded as extreme, poorly thought out, and dangerous? Was Ronald Reagan seen as an effective leader because he got his program through Congress and was good on television—or because the economy recovered?

Almost certainly, the sorts of variables commonly used to measure candidate evaluations reflect both sorts of influences; and in Bush's case, the evidence suggests that it was his personal capabilities that were especially in doubt. As many commentators have pointed out (including many affiliated with the Republicans), the most puzzling facet of the Bush presidency was that after pursuing the White House with such energy for most of a decade, Bush had remarkably little apparent interest in doing very much with the office once he got there. With the single, glaring exception of the Gulf War, the Bush record was one of responding to problems only in a belated, reactive fashion, proposing timid and watered-down programs, and then not expending much effort to make sure they got through Congress (see Mayer, 1993). It is only against this background that one can understand how public opinion reacted when the economy began to stagnate shortly after the end of the Gulf War. As political commentator Mark Shields once pointed out, when the economy nose-dived in 1982 Ronald Reagan could plausibly tell voters to "stay the course." But when George Bush presided over an economic downturn that was far less severe, most voters were convinced that he had no course to stay.

The good news for Republicans, then, is that their dramatic slide in the 1992 presidential voting was a reaction to the particular failings of one man, and not a decisive, long-term rejection of the entire party. Though the Religious Right took a severe drubbing for its conduct during the 1992 campaign, I think most of this blame is greatly misplaced. It was Bush and his cohorts who lost the election, not Buchanan and his compatriots. (Indeed, one reason cultural conservatives so dominated the Republican convention was that they at least had a program while Bush had none.)

A BRIEF WORD ON 1994

Most of this chapter was written in the late fall of 1993, when American politics had, at least to all appearances, a vastly different complexion than it was to assume just one year later. Indeed, Bill Clinton seemed, at the time, to be on something of a roll. After a few initial missteps, he had managed to secure congressional approval for his tax and budget package, NAFTA, and gun control legislation, and most commentators were predicting the eventual passage of his recently introduced Health Security Plan. Certainly, nothing on the political horizon of late 1993 indicated that, twelve months later, the Republicans would post stunning gains in both the House and the Senate and secure control of Congress for the first time in forty years.

How can we account for this remarkable turn of events? The analytic categories developed earlier in this chapter suggest three possible interpretations.

In the first place, 1994 may be, like 1992, simply a *reaction to short-term issues and events,* without any significant long-term implications for the American party system. From this perspective, 1994 is basically a replay of 1946, when the Republicans also won control of both houses of Congress and did a little too much premature celebrating, only to see the Democrats surge back into power just two years later.

As a general rule, I would argue, whenever a striking or anomalous election result occurs, our initial assumption should always be that it *is* a product of short-term forces, not a critical turning point; and we should abandon that assumption only when confronted with a good deal of evidence to the contrary. One lesson all election analysts should take away from recent events is how volatile contemporary American politics is and how dangerous it is, therefore, to extrapolate short-term developments into long-term trends. In the last three years alone, the conventional wisdom has confidently assured us: that George Bush was a shoo-in for a second term; that Bill Clinton had too much personal baggage to get elected president; that the post-Democratic convention Bill Clinton was a political genius; that the Republican Party was seriously weakened and hopelessly divided; and that the Clinton presidency was (depending on which month's press coverage one consulted) a huge disappointment, a great success, or a remarkable failure. It is in this spirit that we ought to greet the new predictions of an enduring Republican congressional majority.

In this particular instance, however, there *is* good reason to be skeptical of a purely short-term explanation. Indeed, what is striking about the 1994 results, especially in the House of Representatives, is how difficult it is to account for them on the basis of the usual short-term indicators. The conventional academic models of midterm elections almost all posit that the net change in House seats can be explained by three major factors: the recent growth rate of the economy, the president's popularity, and the current partisan composition of the House. And all of these variables suggest that 1994 should have been a reasonably *good* year for House Democrats. The economy, whatever its long-term problems, was growing at a robust rate; Clinton's approval ratings, press commentary aside, were not that low (in the mid-40-percent range through most of 1994); and the Democratic seat plurality in the House going into the elections was just about at its average level of the past decade. Models that relied on these three factors were routinely predicting that the Democrats would lose about 4–10 House seats in 1994, as compared to the 53 they actually lost. Whatever else one may say about them, the 1994 elections were clearly *not* politics as usual.

A second interpretation of the 1994 vote is that the Republicans achieved their new congressional majorities as the result of a long and gradual series of *secular changes.* Having acknowledged this idea as a logical possibility, however, we can immediately dismiss this explanation as entirely inapplicable to the case of 1994. For the most salient feature of the recent Republican victories was precisely their suddenness, their sharp break with all previous expectations. Prior to 1994, there was simply no evidence that Republican strength in the House or the Senate was growing, slowly or otherwise. Particularly on the House side, the number of Republican seats had reached its recent high point in 1980; after that, the GOP *lost* seats in four of the next six elections.

Perhaps the only aspect of the 1994 vote that can validly be seen as part of a secular trend is the steady erosion of the Democratic congressional party in the South. Much as we might have predicted from the data in Table 2.6, the Republican surge in that region continued: Indeed, for the first time in their history, the Republicans won a majority of southern House and Senate seats. Yet, for all the publicity these results received, they actually made only a small contribution to the total Republican victory. While the Republicans did carry 64 southern House seats to the Democrats' 61, they also won the Midwest 63 to 46 and the West 57 to 42 and lost the Northeast by the comparatively small margin of 45 to 54. Put simply, the Republicans triumphed in 1994 not because they did unusually well in the South but because they ran strongly everywhere.

The third interpretation of 1994, of course, is that it is a *sharp and long-lasting change:* that is to say, a change connected in some way with a fundamental partisan realignment. Actually, one might distinguish two different versions of the realignment explanation. According to Version 1, 1994 was only the congressional "aftershock" of a presidential realignment that had already taken place in 1968 or possibly 1980. The original realignment had thus defined the basic constellation of issues and groups in American electoral politics, but it had taken a while for its effects to be felt in congressional voting. Version 2, on the other hand, would see

1994 as the first sign of a realignment-still-to-come, much as the elections of 1894 and 1930 heralded the upheavals of 1896 and 1932, respectively. In either case, the essential point is that 1994 was not just a short-term aberration but the first in a long string of Republican congressional victories.

For reasons detailed in earlier sections of this chapter, I am inclined to be somewhat sympathetic to at least the first version of the realignment interpretation. One distinctive feature of the 1994 vote is that the Republicans do seem to have been very successful in turning the election into a referendum on national issues rather than a fight over who could do more for each local area. Although President Clinton's popularity was not especially low in 1994, according to the network exit polls those who disapproved of his performance were much more likely to vote for the congressional candidate of the opposition party than had been the case in 1986 or 1990.

Nevertheless, I am reluctant to hop on the emerging Republican bandwagon. The reasons for my skepticism go beyond the natural reluctance of a young academic to make a glaringly inaccurate prediction that could hang over the rest of his career. The more significant point is one I have already made with reference to the events of 1992. As most contemporary versions of realignment theory emphasize, much of what leads us to classify a particular election as realigning actually occurs *after* the election, when the new majority party starts to grapple with the issues and problems that brought it to power. As of the early 1990s, the United States was reasonably prosperous and militarily more secure than it had been at any time in the last fifty years—and yet it was experiencing a severe crisis of confidence, especially in regard to the governing capacity of its major national institutions. The 1994 elections have undoubtedly presented the Republicans with a major opportunity—and if they can succeed in significantly alleviating that crisis, the elections of 1994 may mark a significant turning point in American electoral politics. At the risk of sounding cynical, however, I would add that the problems of the deficit, crime, the family, and the postindustrial economy are difficult and deep-seated ones; that many other elected officials have tried to solve them, without great success; and that, precisely because the Republicans have raised expectations so high, the consequences of failure may also be quite substantial.

CONCLUSIONS

In terms of the 1992 election, the major conclusions of this chapter are easy to summarize and will probably provoke little controversy among those who study American electoral politics. The Democratic presidential victory was an instance of short-term rather than long-term change. It was certainly not a sign of an impending realignment. Clinton won primarily because he had the good fortune to run against a man whom I think history will regard as the most inept and ineffective person to occupy the White House since the creation of the modern presidency under Franklin Roosevelt.

On a more theoretical level, perhaps the most significant position advocated here is that realignment is still a useful and valid concept. This position, of course, is not unanimously held. Indeed, in a very good recent symposium on the topic, it was distinctly the minority view (see Shafer, 1991).

In the end, much of the disagreement about whether a realignment occurred in the 1960s hinges on some thorny and probably unresolvable definitional questions. As I have tried to indicate, once we get past these definitional issues, there is widespread agreement about the ways that American electoral politics has and has not changed over the last three decades. Perhaps we should just leave the matter there, and consign the definitional matters to linguists.

Though occasionally tempted by this way of resolving the controversy, I have ultimately come to feel that there *is* something genuinely important at stake here—something that gets quite close to the subject of this book. At its most essential level, realignment is a theory about the nature of American electoral change. Specifically, it asserts that such change is *discontinuous* and *patterned.* Change in the party system is discontinuous in the sense that it does not occur at a single uniform pace: Some periods witness considerably more change—and more lasting change—than others. But major change does not occur haphazardly and at random. Because of certain enduring features of the American polity, there are regularities and commonalities to these upheavals, though each also has its own distinctive qualities. Is this set of ideas still useful? And does it help us to understand better the events of recent American politics? I believe that the answer to both of these questions is yes. Whatever one chooses to call them, the changes of the 1960s did accord with many of the established features of electoral change in the American past.

NOTES

1. I wish to thank Jay Greene, Bryan Jones, Amy Logan, Thomas Morton, and Gerald Pomper for their assistance in the preparation of this chapter.

2. The best example of this method is Burnham, 1970. See also Sellers, 1965; and Clubb, Flanigan, and Zingale, 1990: ch. 3.

3. I do not mean this statement to endorse an atheoretical approach to studying realignments. The task of theory, of course, is to explain why increased third-party activity, changes in public policy, and so forth have tended to accompany realignments. A number of studies, as I suggest in the text, have made substantial contributions in this regard. See especially Burnham, 1970; Ladd, 1970; Sundquist, 1973; Brady, 1988; and Clubb, Flanigan, and Zingale, 1990.

4. The same observation has been made in McMichael and Trilling, 1980; and in Lawrence and Fleisher, 1987.

5. The 1932 election also shows a substantial, though slightly smaller, correlation with the 1936–1944 results. I exclude it from the averages computed for Table 2.2 because numerous studies of elections during the early New Deal period have concluded that the basic shape of the new Democratic coalition did not become clear until *after* 1932. (See, in

particular, Lubell, 1952; MacRae and Meldrum, 1960; and Shively, 1971). In any case, adding in the 1932 results produces only the most trivial changes in the correlations and alters none of the conclusions drawn from these data.

6. Compare Table 2.3 in this chapter with Tables 1, 2, and 3 in Pomper, 1967. Note, however, that the stability of the coefficients in Table 2.3 is not markedly different from the stability of the partisan vote in the 1828–1864 period, as indicated in Table 4 in Pomper, 1967.

7. Another author who may fit this category is James Sundquist. In 1983, Sundquist described recent changes in American electoral politics as a "revitalization of the New Deal party system" (1983: 444–449). Two years later, however, he seemed more sympathetic to a realignment interpretation (see Cavanagh and Sundquist, 1985).

8. Strictly speaking, both of these terms refer to the periods of stability during which electoral outcomes and partisan coalitions do *not* undergo significant change. But since Ladd and Shafer both make clear that the current electoral era is quite different from the one of fifty years earlier, they obviously believe that changes in the party system do occur. And if such changes occur, then somehow we need a body of theory and evidence to explain how and why electoral eras change—which is exactly what I take realignment to be.

9. A particularly good statement of this position is found in Burnham, 1991. Other scholars who have argued that a realignment took place over the last several decades (though they differ about some of its features) include Petrocik, 1981, 1987; MacDonald and Rabinowitz, 1987; Stanley, 1988; Chubb and Peterson, 1985; and Pomper, 1989.

10. On this score, it is worth pointing out that a number of prescient people were able to anticipate that the upheavals of the late 1960s would bring an end to the New Deal party system, even while those changes were still in an early stage of development. Three good examples are Phillips, 1969; Ladd, 1970; and Burnham, 1970. All of these books contain predictions that turned out to be wrong, but in numerous respects their diagnoses were right on the money.

11. The "aftershock" terminology is borrowed from Sundquist, 1973, 1983.

12. Note that the continuity in issue positions is due not only to the kinds of voters who identify with each party but also to the kinds of interest groups, activists, and public officials who affiliate with the parties.

3

Campaigning Through the Media: Was 1992 Really Different?

SHANTO IYENGAR
SHARMAINE VIDANAGE

Reporters, scholars, and general observers of the political scene unanimously regarded the 1992 election campaign as distinctive. The "standard operating procedures" followed by political campaigns became irrelevant as the candidates discovered new forms of campaign communication. Local news, talk-show, and call-in programs replaced network news and the Washington–New York press corps as the "flagship" outlets for campaign messages. The candidates relied less on attack advertising. Voters seemed more responsive to information about the candidates' political capabilities and policy positions and less interested in matters of personality and character. Reporters abandoned their passive role as recorders of campaign events in favor of a more "adversarial" stance, and campaign messages became legitimate targets for journalistic interpretation and criticism.

Yet despite these manifest changes in the behavior of the key participants, the argument of this chapter is that the underlying relationship between candidates and reporters, and hence the essential dynamic of the campaign, changed little in 1992. Candidates Bush, Clinton, and Perot, like other candidates before them, attempted (in different ways and with varying degrees of success) to maximize their control over news coverage. Reporters, in turn, attempted to maximize their autonomy and objectivity. In short, the 1992 campaign can appropriately be described by the adage *Plus ça change, plus c'est la même chose.*

We begin by summarizing the vast literature on "media effects." Next, we describe three key elements of campaign strategy in 1992—the candidates' attempts to influence the flow of news, reporters' efforts to monitor the candidates, and the effects of campaign advertising. Then, by way of conclusion, we assess the implications of the 1992 election for the quality of discourse in American political campaigns.

HOW MEDIA CAMPAIGNS AFFECT
PUBLIC OPINION

Today, the mass media—especially television news—provide much of the "intelligence" on which voters' choices rest. The ability to influence the flow of news can prove critical to electoral success. Candidates who succeed in shaping the content of television news also succeed in influencing how Americans think about politics.

A considerable body of research has been accumulated concerning the effects of the mass media on American public opinion. This research has identified at least three different ways in which campaign communication affects public opinion: by informing people about the candidates and issues ("learning"), by defining the major political issues ("agenda-setting"), and, finally, by shaping the public's political preferences and choices ("persuasion").

Learning

Candidates enter campaigns with widely disparate visibility. At one extreme are universally recognized candidates (generally incumbents). At the other extreme are candidates about whom the typical voter knows nothing. In the case of the former, campaigns cannot reasonably be expected to make them more well known. But candidates with limited public visibility have two possible trajectories. Most of the time these candidates remain unknown, are labeled hopeless causes by the media, and quickly withdraw from the race. (Senators Harkin and Kerrey represented this category in 1992.) In other cases, however, initially unknown candidates (such as ex-Senator Tsongas) attract significant media attention, usually by doing better than expected in the early primary contests, and catapult into national prominence.

Visibility has benefits that extend beyond mere familiarity. Candidates who bask in the glow of the news are also better able to raise money and attract endorsements (Mutz, 1991). In politics, familiarity breeds support. Although voters' desire for "change" may occasionally lead them to prefer candidates about whom they know little, a familiar name is typically an electoral asset.

Sheer visibility, however, can carry candidates only so far. Name recognition must be enriched with information about what the candidates stand for, the policies and interests they promote, and their personal qualities. This information is crucial to the formation of voters' impressions of the candidates. Frequently, candidates who surge to prominence based on impressive showings in early primaries fade rapidly as voters learn more about them. For instance, once Democratic voters learned (primarily from the Clinton campaign) about Senator Tsongas' anti-union and probusiness stance, his candidacy was doomed. In other cases, the learning process strengthens candidates, allowing them to override early impressions and to redefine their candidacies (as was the case with Bill Clinton in 1992).

Of course, voters do not absorb information like sponges. Instead, their attention is selective (see Iyengar, 1990), and they often resort to various learning shortcuts such as utilizing information that happens to be momentarily prominent. As a result, some campaign themes disseminate rapidly, whereas others remain unknown.

In the area of candidates' specific policy positions, most Americans are poorly informed, and their ignorance is diminished little by campaigns. For instance, public awareness as to where Bush and Dukakis stood on the issues most emphasized by the candidates dropped by 10 percent over the course of the 1988 campaign. Yet voters are able to differentiate fairly accurately between Democrats and Republicans on "traditional" issues such as poverty, taxes, and defense. They also tend to be well informed about the groups and interests that stand to gain from Democratic or Republican policies (e.g., blue-collar workers and senior citizens in the case of Democrats, business executives in the case of Republicans). Overall, therefore, although campaigns may not impart detailed information, voters do learn about the "basic policy directions" of the competing campaigns (Popkin, 1991: 41).

Over the course of a campaign, voters also develop differentiated—though not necessarily accurate—images of the candidates' personal traits, ideology, group connections, and electoral prospects. The traits of competence and integrity are particularly important components of a candidate's image. To be seen as intelligent, decisive, honest, and sincere is a prerequisite for electoral success. Recall that President Carter was widely perceived as an indecisive leader in 1980, and that Bill Clinton's quest for the Democratic nomination in 1992 was nearly derailed by doubts about his honesty. In sum, the campaign serves to "fill in" voters' impressions of the candidates.

Agenda-Setting

There is considerable evidence that the public's social or political priorities and concerns—its beliefs about what constitutes a significant issue or event—are determined by the amount of news coverage accorded various issues and events.[1] (See Rogers and Dearing, 1988.) The most compelling evidence of agenda-setting stems from carefully designed and realistic experiments that manipulated the level of television coverage accorded particular issues. These experiments revealed that the insertion of only a modest degree of coverage into network newscasts induced significant shifts in viewers' beliefs about the importance of a particular issue.[2]

Political campaigns constantly strive to focus media (and voters') attention on issues that provide them with a relative advantage. Whereas incumbents strive to highlight policies that reflect favorably on their performance, challengers tend to harp on policies that have failed. In 1992, for instance, the Clinton campaign continually attempted to spotlight the failing U.S. economy whereas the Bush campaign attempted to revive memories of the war in the Persian Gulf.

Voters' priorities also shift in response to candidates' advertising themes. This effect is most striking when both campaigns devote a considerable portion of their advertising to the same issue. In the 1991 Pennsylvania Senate race, for example, Democrat Harris Wofford made national health insurance the cornerstone of his campaign. When Wofford's support surged, his Republican opponent, Richard Thornburgh, decided to confront the issue by attacking Wofford's proposals and the entire concept of government-sponsored health care. As a result, health insurance became the central issue of the campaign.[3] It was also the issue that determined the outcome of the election. Although Wofford trailed by 47 percentage points in June, he actually won by 10 percent in November.

Naturally, candidates' efforts to influence the public agenda are limited by "real-world cues"—that is, by the course of national and international events. In 1992 the collapse of communism in Europe and the severe recession at home relegated foreign policy issues to a position of near irrelevance and elevated domestic problems to the level of pressing crises. Given President Bush's accomplishments in the foreign policy domain and his apparent failure to stem the recession, the state of the public agenda was a significant boon to the Clinton campaign.

Candidates' efforts to shape the campaign agenda are also limited by public stereotypes concerning their policy capabilities (see Petrocik, 1993). Republicans, for example, are generally considered more capable of maintaining national security and law and order, whereas Democrats are seen as having the edge on most economic issues and at protecting the rights of the underprivileged. Candidates therefore seek to capitalize on the issues they "own" (based on their partisanship). Republicans are better off highlighting foreign policy and defense-related issues; Democrats gain by campaigning on unemployment and civil rights. There is considerable evidence that candidates shape voters' perceptions most effectively when their campaigns resonate with these partisan stereotypes. For example, Democratic candidates were found to elicit more favorable responses than Republicans by advertising on unemployment, whereas Republicans were more persuasive than Democrats when the subject of the advertisement was crime (see Ansolabehere and Iyengar, 1993a).

Persuasion

Voters often alter their political beliefs and preferences in response to a particular stream of messages. Indeed, persuasion can be the end product of learning and agenda-setting. Consider the dramatic drop in President Bush's popularity between 1991 and 1992. In 1991 the news was dominated by events in the Persian Gulf, and this issue became paramount in the minds of Americans. Because the outcome was so favorable, President Bush, as commander in chief, was credited with the responsibility for the lopsided victory. Yet only one year later, when the flagging economy replaced the war in the Gulf as the dominant news story, President Bush appeared in a much different light. Because of the state of the economy, and the president's dismal record on matters of economic policy, Bush's approval ratings dropped precipitously from 83 percent in February 1991 to 46 percent in February 1992.

Clearly, changes in the public agenda contributed to the free-fall in President Bush's popularity. This process is known as "priming." An extension of agenda-setting, priming refers to the power of the media to isolate particular issues, events, or themes in the news as criteria for evaluating politicians. In the context of campaigns, the issues that receive heavy news coverage or campaign advertising are likely to be the issues that determine voters' evaluations of the candidates.

The candidates can also engage in direct persuasion without having to rely on intervening effects such as agenda-setting or priming. Here the central notion is that of diffusion: "Who says what to whom?" The major determinants of persuasion, accordingly, are *source, message,* and *audience* characteristics (see McGuire, 1985; Zaller, 1993).

A source can be evaluated as more or less credible or trustworthy. One advantage of attracting news coverage is that news reports are considered relatively credible. Campaign advertisements, by contrast, tend to be dismissed as misleading and distorted, thus eroding their potential impact. The credibility of particular candidates, however, depends upon the issue on which they advertise. For instance, Republicans tend to be perceived as more credible than Democrats on the issue of crime, whereas female candidates are likely to prove more credible than males on the issue of sexual harassment.

The properties of messages themselves have also been found to affect the likelihood of persuasion. In political campaigns, an important factor is the tone or valence of the message. Campaign strategists have found that negative messages tend to be more persuasive than positive messages; indeed, as discussed in the next section, candidates have increasingly turned to negative or attack advertising. The relationship between message characteristics and the amount of attitude change, however, is complicated by source and audience factors. For example, attack advertisements might be effective when used by a man but counterproductive when aired by a woman.[4] (For evidence of such gender differences, see Ansolabehere and Iyengar, 1993a.)

Finally, candidates' ability to persuade depends upon the composition of their audience. According to William McGuire's famous "two-factor" theory of persuasion, people must first receive some message (exposure) and then agree with it (acceptance) if they are to be persuaded (McGuire, 1968). A particularly interesting finding in relation to this theory is that the people who are most likely to tune in to campaigns are also the people least likely to adopt messages that clash with their prior preferences. Educated individuals, for example, are more likely to become exposed to information about current events. However, as they are also more likely to call upon alternative sources and a greater mass of stored information to question a particular item of new information, they are better able to "counterargue" and hence less likely to accept new information. Because exposure and acceptance work in opposite directions in determining the likelihood of persuasion, McGuire's two-factor model predicts an inverted U-shaped relationship between characteristics of the audience (such as level of education) and the extent of attitude change. Accordingly, voters with the highest and lowest levels of political attentiveness are least likely to be persuaded by campaign communication (Converse, 1966; Zaller, 1993).

In short, candidates can use the mass media to spread information (or misinformation) about their candidacies, to shape the public's political concerns, and to change voters' preferences. Given this wide range of political effects, it is no surprise that the mass media have become the principal battleground of campaigns.

MEDIA STRATEGIES IN 1992

Successful candidates and campaigns are those best able to exploit the media environment in which they operate. Whereas campaigns seek to "spoon-feed" the press, journalists, of course, seek to remain independent. Recognition of the built-in tension between candidates and the press is fundamental to an understanding of campaign strategy. Accordingly, this section describes candidates' and reporters' efforts to influence each other in 1992.

New Media, New Forms of News

Campaign managers understand that the effectiveness of communication depends on reaching a large audience and exercising strong control over the message. In the past, presidential candidates assiduously courted network news coverage. The high ratings enjoyed by network newscasts and the generally benign approach to reporting in which the candidates' sound-bites were relayed without critical commentary provided candidates with a powerful incentive to appear with Messrs. Brokaw, Jennings, or Rather.

These circumstances changed in 1992. First, reporters adopted a more aggressive posture. In the aftermath of the 1988 election, there was widespread agreement that the press had aided and abetted the candidates (especially the Bush campaign) by merely echoing their campaign claims (Rosen and Taylor, 1992; Dionne, 1991; Kamber, 1990). A chorus of analysts urged reporters to reassert their independence by subjecting campaigns to close public scrutiny. David Broder (1990), Ken Bode (1992), and others began to argue that staged events, prepared sound-bites, and campaign advertisements should no longer be guaranteed news coverage, and that when these events were covered, they should be subjected to analysis and criticism. The hope was that by monitoring campaign rhetoric systematically, and by exposing candidates who distorted or blurred the record, the media could deter candidates from making irresponsible claims.

How did this newfound adversary relationship affect campaign strategy in 1992? In the first place, the drive toward more critical reporting meant that a campaign's efforts at "spin" were subjected to immediate analysis and commentary, often leaving candidates in a defensive position. Simultaneously, the candidates discovered that there were vast audiences to be captured elsewhere, and that these alternative sources were more pliable and cooperative. As a result, the candidates avoided network news shows and concentrated instead on obtaining exposure in local news, talk shows, and other "soft" programs. Figure 3.1 compares the frequency with which Bush, Clinton, and Perot appeared in "alternative media" (defined as "Good Morning America," "This Morning," "Today," "Larry King Live," and "Donahue") and on "Nightline." On average, the number of appearances in alternative media more than doubled those in "Nightline."

"Nightline" and other mainstream media news programs, having been snubbed by the candidates, turned their attention to candidates' paid advertisements. A new genre of campaign journalism, now known as the "truth-box," or "ad-watch," was spawned.[5] This genre, which features reports *about* campaign advertisements, was used extensively during the 1992 campaign. The *Los Angeles Times,* for instance, published more than twenty ad-watch stories focusing on the two races for U.S. Senate in California.[6] Ad-watches also appeared regularly on the networks' newscasts. In fact, the producers of CNN's "Inside Politics" program assigned a senior correspondent, Brooks Jackson, full time to the task of inspecting and analyzing the advertisements aired by the presidential candidates.

What constituted the typical ad-watch message of 1992? To answer this question, we examined all ad-watch reports printed in the *Los Angeles Times* and *New York Times,* and coded the level and nature of criticism directed at the candidate or advertisement, the sources used to document the criticism, and, finally, the relative mix between description and analysis. We found that the typical ad-

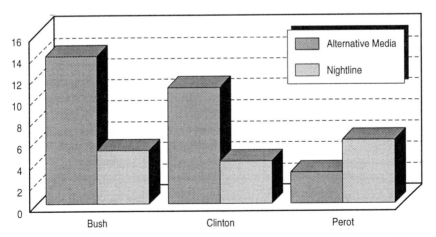

FIGURE 3.1   Appearances on Nightline and Alternative Media. SOURCE: *Vanderbilt Abstracts* (multiple years).

watch report was not particularly adversarial; if anything, its tone tended to be neutral or balanced. Using a five-point tone index that ranged from 1 (clearly negative) to 5 (clearly positive), we determined the average score to be 2.65. The typical ad-watch thus provided relatively muted criticism. In addition to equivocating over the accuracy of the targeted advertisement, it relied extensively on partisan sources to rebut or question the advertisement in question: More than 50 percent of all rebuttal information could be attributed to the opposition campaign or party. Finally, the typical ad-watch provided extensive repetition of the targeted campaign advertisement. In terms of total space, statements describing the visuals and echoing the audio portion of the ad accounted for more than 50 percent of the column inches used. In short, the typical ad-watch report devoted at least half its content to a descriptive summary of the advertisement.

Given its less than adversarial tone, its reliance on partisan sources, and its frequent repetition of the advertisement, the ad-watch may not "work" as intended. Our content analysis shows that ad-watch reports not only send mixed signals regarding the accuracy of the advertisement but also recirculate (at no cost) the candidate's message. Free exposure and repetition are obvious benefits to the sponsor of the target advertisement. In addition, by presenting information in the guise of "news," the ad-watch may enhance the believability of the campaign's message. This sort of "journalism" is especially welcomed by political consultants. As Roger Ailes has pointed out, "You get a 30 or 40 percent bump out of getting it [an advertisement] on the news. You get more viewers, you get more credibility, you get it in your framework."[7] Given these characteristics, exposure to ad-watches, instead of making voters less vulnerable to campaign advertising, may actually play into the hands of image makers and consultants by boosting the stock of the candidate whose advertisements are targeted.

We explored this ominous possibility by designing an experiment to assess the impact of televised ad-watch reports on viewers' political preferences. Our study called for two groups—one consisting of voters who watched either a Bush or Clinton campaign advertisement, and the other consisting of voters who watched a CNN ad-watch report on the Bush or Clinton advertisement. The advertisements and ad-watch reports were inserted into a local newscast that was identical in all other respects. The effects of each advertisement and of the ad-watch story that scrutinized the advertisement could thus be assessed.[8]

After watching the newscast, participants answered a variety of questions concerning their attitudes toward the presidential candidates. Limiting our focus to their voting intention, we asked: Did participants intend to vote for Clinton, Bush, or Perot, or did they remain undecided? We then examined the effects of exposure to the campaign advertisements and ad-watch reports on responses to this question. In order to adjust for the effects of predispositions and thus to isolate the independent effects of the campaign advertisements and ad-watch reports, we regressed the voting-intention question against exposure to each advertisement and ad-watch in addition to a set of control variables that reflected participants' partisan leanings, prior voting histories, and personal backgrounds.[9]

The conventional wisdom led us to expect that participants who watched a Bush or Clinton advertisement would be more favorably disposed toward the sponsoring candidate, whereas participants who watched the ad-watch report would be less favorably disposed toward the candidate whose message was scrutinized. Neither expectation was met.

The analysis was carried out for two groups of participants—both actual and likely voters. The latter group was defined as registered voters who indicated that they would vote. The results of our multiple regression analyses indicated that, for actual voters, neither the advertisements nor the ad-watches significantly influenced political preference after the effects of prior predispositions had been adjusted for. Among likely voters, however, exposure to the ad-watches independently boosted support for the candidate sponsoring the advertisement by 11 percentage points. This effect was statistically significant ($p < .07$). By contrast, the effect of the advertisement was to increase the sponsoring candidate's support by just 4 percentage points, a shift that was not distinguishable from zero.

The results of this study thus suggest that ad-watch reports do not necessarily achieve their basic objectives. In fact, they tend to increase support for the candidate whose advertising has been scrutinized. This effect is especially strong among likely voters, the group that is pivotal to electoral outcomes. The ad-watches not only promoted the interests of the candidates but also proved more persuasive than the campaign advertisements themselves.

From the political consultant's perspective, our results are good news. Not only does televised advertising buy support for the candidate, but media coverage of the advertisements gives candidates a further boost. We do not mean to suggest that journalists should give up on the ad-watch format or that ad-watches are doomed to fail. Advertising is, after all, the dominant mode of campaign communication. Not to report on political advertising is tantamount to ignoring the campaign's message. In addition, ad-watches may provide an indirect monitoring effect by providing ammunition for opposing candidates. The Clinton campaign, for instance, was quick to cite in its own negative advertising the *Washington Post*'s labeling of a Bush advertisement as "misleading." Our results suggest, however, that ad-watch reports will be more likely to achieve their stated "monitoring" effect if they provide less free repetition of the advertisement and are less reliant on obviously partisan sources of analysis.

Advertising Strategy

The spiraling costs of elections over the past two decades can be traced to the enormous expenditures for broadcast advertising. Unlike news coverage, paid advertising permits a candidate to communicate with voters in the absence of screens or filters. Not only have candidates turned increasingly to "paid" messages, but the tone and content of political advertising have undergone significant shifts. First, campaign advertisements have turned increasingly negative and hostile. Candidates, more often than not, sharply criticize or question their opponents' credentials and leadership capability, rather than promoting their own candidacies (see Jamieson, 1992; Hagstrom and Guskind, 1988, 1992). The spurt in negative advertising has been attributed to several factors. These include the presumed "negativity bias" in human information processing, the alleged persuasive advantage enjoyed by information that confirms rather than contradicts existing beliefs,[10] and, most important, the greater ability of negative advertising to attract news coverage and comment.

The second trend in campaign advertising has been a sharper focus on "character"—that is, on matters of lifestyle, personal values, and family background (see Sabato, 1991). With the general decline of partisanship and the news media's insatiable appetite for personality-related stories, character judgments have become especially prominent components of voting decisions. Not surprisingly, candidates seek to project images of dependability, patriotism, and morality in their advertisements.

The 1988 campaign epitomized these dual trends. The Bush message was essentially negative, portraying Dukakis as a failed governor (recall the famous "Boston Harbor" and "Revolving Door" spots) who subscribed to ultraliberal and unpatriotic values (here, Bush relied on the pledge of allegiance and on certain defense-spending issues). The combination of sharp personal attacks and Dukakis's failure to respond is thought to have turned the tide of public opinion toward Bush (e.g., Germond and Witcover, 1989).

Negative advertisements were certainly not in short supply during the 1992 campaign. The Bush reelection strategy relied heavily on attack messages; Clinton's team utilized a roughly equal mix of positive and negative appeals. Seventy-five percent of the Bush spots represented attacks directed at Clinton, whereas 54 percent of all the Clinton spots were positive. Meanwhile, Perot's "infomercials" generally maintained a positive tone. Overall, the 1992 campaign thus appears to have been as negative in tone as the 1988 campaign, during which the ratio of positive to negative advertisements was equal (Jamieson, 1992: 270).

It is in the area of advertising content (as opposed to tone) that we truly see the distinctiveness of the 1992 campaign. Campaign advertisements tended to be relatively "substantive" or issue oriented. No doubt the Bush campaign did attempt to revive suspicions about Clinton's trustworthiness, but by and large, the advertising agenda was dominated by questions about the economy, health care, and the candidates' ability to govern. The Clinton advertisements hammered away at the gloomy economic statistics and Bush's alleged ineffectiveness on domestic issues, while the Bush camp contrasted Clinton's "tax and spend" record in Arkansas with Bush's fiscal conservatism and highlighted Bush's many successes in foreign and military affairs.

Of course, the fact that Clinton aired a higher proportion of positive and issue-oriented advertisements does not, by itself, reveal the distinctiveness of the 1992 campaign. The real question concerns voter response: Were voters more or less persuaded by negative messages and appeals to character? One of our 1992 experiments addressed this question. During the final two weeks of the campaign, 175 residents of the Los Angeles area watched a videotape of a local newscast that included either a positive or negative campaign advertisement aired by either Bush or Clinton.[11] Depending on the experimental condition, the advertisement focused on either performance or character. Our study thus consisted of eight conditions corresponding to the combination of source (Bush or Clinton), tone (positive or negative), and content (performance or character) factors.[12]

The participants, who represented a cross-section of southern California residents, were recruited by a combination of methods including the use of flyers in shopping malls, announcements in employee newsletters, and phone calls to names from voter registration lists. Potential subjects were informed that the study concerned "selective perception" of local news and that they would be paid $15 for their participation.

The study was administered at two different locations—West Los Angeles and an affluent Orange County suburb known as Costa Mesa. In both locales, we rented three-room office suites, each consisting of two viewing rooms and one central administrative area. The viewing rooms were furnished casually (with couches, easy chairs, coffee tables, and potted plants) so as to resemble typical living rooms. Most participants watched the news with a friend or work associate. Random assignment of participants to experimental conditions was used throughout.

Three dependent measures were collected during the posttest. First, participants indicated how they would vote in the presidential election. Responses were collapsed into a trichotomy consisting of Bush (-1), Perot/undecided/not voting (0), and Clinton ($+1$) categories. Second, participants rated the candidates' ability to deal with unemployment and rising health care costs. These ratings were summed to form a "performance index" that ranged from -2 (indicating more positive ratings of Bush) to $+2$ (indicating more positive ratings of Clinton). Finally, participants rated the degree to which the terms *dishonest* and *experienced* described Bush and Clinton. These ratings were summed to form a "character index," at which point we determined a net score by subtracting Bush's index score from Clinton's. The net scores ranged from -2 (indicating that Bush's score was higher than Clinton's) to $+2$ (indicating that Clinton's score was higher than Bush's).

Next, we estimated the effects of the three experimental factors—source, tone, and content—using analysis of variance (ANOVA). The source factor was a measure of the overall persuasive effect of watching an advertisement from one (but not the other) candidate. The effects of the tone factor corresponded to the difference in responses between participants exposed to the positive and negative advertisements. And, finally, the effects of the content factor reflected differences in viewer response to the performance- and character-oriented advertisements.

In addition to the three main effects just described, we examined the interaction effects. That is, we examined whether the effects of source, tone, or content, were interdependent. The source × character interaction, for example, gauged the extent to which the effects of the performance versus character distinction differed between candidates.

The results of the three 2 × 2 × 2 ANOVAS are presented in Figure 3.2. The panels on the left show the effects of the Clinton ads, and those on the right indi-

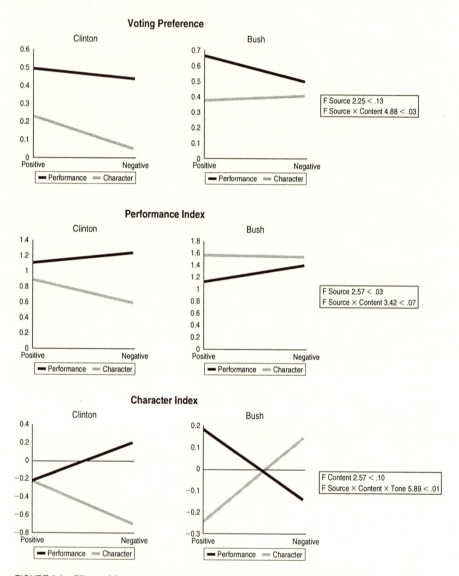

Voting Preference

F Source 2.25 < .13
F Source × Content 4.88 < .03

Performance Index

F Source 2.57 < .03
F Source × Content 3.42 < .07

Character Index

F Content 2.57 < .10
F Source × Content × Tone 5.89 < .01

FIGURE 3.2   Effects of Campaign Ads on Voter Preference (positive ratings indicate Clinton support; negative ratings indicate Bush support). SOURCE: Experimental data collected by Stephen Ansolabehere and Shanto Iyengar.

cate the effects of the Bush ads. In each panel, the mean value of the dependent measures is plotted by advertising content and tone.

The voting-intention question revealed that Clinton enjoyed a massive lead (of 40 percentage points) among our participants. Meanwhile, statewide polls had Clinton leading by an average margin of 25 percentage points (see American Enterprise Institute, 1993), suggesting that, for all practical purposes, the Bush candidacy was doomed in California. We thus concluded that the effects of exposure to a single campaign advertisement on voting preference were minimal; if anything, exposure to an advertisement from either Bush or Clinton tended to reduce the sponsoring candidate's support. Among participants who watched a Bush advertisement, for example, Bush trailed by nearly 50 points; among participants in the Clinton conditions, Bush trailed by 32 points.

Our study also indicated that the tone of the advertisement had no visible impact on voting intention. However, the trend in the means (see Figure 3.2) suggested that Bush gained slightly from the use of negative rather than positive messages (Clinton's lead in the polls was reduced by 7 points among participants who watched his negative advertisements).

It was the content manipulation that proved most relevant to voting preference in 1992. According to our results, both candidates were better off when they addressed the economy, a difference that was especially prominent for Clinton's advertising. Whereas Bush cut Clinton's lead by 19 points when he advertised on the economy instead of character, Clinton's lead fell by 30 points when he addressed character instead of the economy. This sharp divergence between the candidates produced a significant source $\times$ content interaction effect.

Our performance index yielded virtually identical results. President Bush's image as an ineffective problem solver was actually *magnified* when he advertised, yielding a significant main effect for source. As in the case of voting intention, it was advertising content and not tone that affected the candidates' standing. Bush and Clinton both gained by discussing the economy, and the performance-character difference was magnified considerably in the case of Clinton. Clinton's edge in the performance ratings fell by 30 percent when he shifted the focus of his advertising from performance to character.

Finally, the character ratings exhibited a somewhat altered pattern. For the first time, Bush enjoyed an advantage over his opponent, especially among participants who watched a Clinton advertisement. This difference in the character ratings, however, proved insufficient to attain statistical significance. Once again, the candidates elicited uniform responses from their use of negative or positive advertisements, and it was advertising content that proved most influential. Clinton's attack advertisement on character elicited the strongest movement in viewers' ratings, and this movement favored Bush, the target of the attack. Clinton's rating in the character index hit bottom (at $-.70$) in this condition. By contrast, when Clinton attacked Bush in terms of economic performance, his character rating was more favorable than Bush's. The magnitude of this difference produced a significant content main effect ($p < .10$) and a significant source $\times$ content $\times$ tone interaction ($p < .01$). The latter represented the distinctiveness of the Clinton character-attack condition.

Overall, our experimental results suggest that James Carville's diagnosis of public opinion was on the mark: Voters' concerns over the economy and the candidates' abilities to address economic problems did indeed dominate their concerns over the candidates' honesty and trustworthiness.[13] For George Bush, the potential benefits of advertising on either performance or character were negligible; two weeks before the election, his candidacy had been thoroughly repudiated by California voters. Bill Clinton's appeal, however, was significantly strengthened when he focused voters' attention on his ability (and his opponent's inability) to reverse the country's economic decline. Conversely, Clinton's appeal was significantly weakened when voters were asked to judge the candidates on the basis of their honesty and experience.[14]

In summary, our study suggests two respects in which the 1992 advertising campaign was distinctive. First, we could find no evidence to suggest that either candidate registered greater returns by attacking rather than promoting. Second, we found that performance-oriented messages were much more likely to resonate with the audience than were messages bearing on character.

CONCLUSIONS

The 1992 campaign was reputed to be different. In many ways it was. Having learned its lesson in 1988, the press corps was determined to gain the upper hand over the machinations of campaign consultants and spin doctors. News coverage of the candidates became highly interpretative, and campaign messages were subjected to critical analysis. Changes in the behavior of the press, however, were counteracted by changes in campaign strategies. Talk shows, local news programs, and "electronic town halls" became the dominant sources of news about the campaign. By bypassing the mainstream media, the candidates strengthened their abilities to control the agenda and engage in effective impression management. Indeed, the new forums were unlikely to subject the candidates to what Ross Perot (the darling of the new media) dismissed as "gotcha" journalism—sustained cross-examination and scrutiny of policy proposals, campaign claims, or previous records. And when the old media resorted to critical inspections of the candidates' advertisements, they too played into candidates' hands. In short, the emergence of new forms of campaign communication empowered the candidates instead of the voters.

If continuation of the candidates' strategic advantage vis-à-vis the media was the only consequence of these new forms of campaigning, perhaps there would be little cause for concern. We suspect, however, that the old media's efforts to play a more autonomous role in the campaign had other more subtle consequences, including the erosion of the media's credibility and a heightened sense of public cynicism toward the electoral process.

Most Americans expect the press to remain neutral in its coverage of campaigns. The constant stream of stories designed to instill doubts about candidates' rhetoric provided the public with ample evidence of media bias and hostility toward the candidates. Not surprisingly, the constant stream of "bad news" inflicted damage to the messenger's reputation (for evidence of the high level of negativity in the 1988 and 1992 campaign coverage, see Patterson, 1993). Survey after survey revealed that the credibility accorded the news media reached a nadir in 1992 (Shaw, 1993; Kolbert, 1992). Obviously, credibility is essential if the press is to function as a referee or monitor: If the public is disinclined to believe the news, politicians will not be deterred from making misleading, distorted, or even flatly erroneous claims.

Perhaps the most disturbing (and unintended) consequence of the more critical and interpretive style of news coverage embodied by ad-watches is the risk of eroded public confidence in the political process. Anti-Washington and anti-politician fervor reached a frenzy in 1992. By calling attention to the inadequacies and errors of the candidates' advertising, the press confirmed these negative stereotypes. By doing so, however, the press may also have fostered a more generalized sense of alienation from the system. Negative advertising, for instance, has been found not only to diminish the public's inclination to support the candidate who is the target of the advertisement but also to render people less likely to believe that their opinions matter and less likely to vote (see Ansolabehere, Iyengar, and Valentino, 1993). Negative news coverage may engender a similar "demobilizing" effect.

Granted, the new style of interpretive and adversarial campaign journalism was motivated by lofty objectives. And one can hardly argue with the idea that the news media should deter candidates from misleading the electorate. In practice, however, media scrutiny may contribute to the very syndrome it was designed to combat—candidate control over the flow of information, and the use of news coverage to boost the candidates' stock with voters.

NOTES

1. Antecedents of the agenda-setting argument can be found in the works of the great American journalist Walter Lippmann, who suggested that the press's job was to "signalize" events and who warned of the impossibility of the news and reality being one and the same.

2. See Iyengar and Kinder, 1987. Early agenda-setting studies were plagued by a number of methodological difficulties—most notably, confusion between cause and effect. Did the correlation between newspaper readers' political concerns and the content of the news mean that news coverage had set the audience agenda? Or did it mean instead that newspaper editors had tailored their coverage of issues to suit the concerns and interests of

their readers? Concerns such as these led to the use of experimental designs in agenda-setting research.

3. *New York Times,* November 7, 1991, p. B17.

4. For a review of message-related research, see Petty and Cacioppo, 1981.

5. Pioneering efforts at scrutinizing televised spots were made during the 1990 Texas gubernatorial campaign between Ann Richards and Clayton Williams. KVUE, an Austin television station, broadcast a series of highly critical reports on the content of both candidates' advertisements.

6. Due to a variety of unusual circumstances, both of the state's senate seats were contested in 1992.

7. Roger Ailes, quoted in Runkel, 1990: 142. For further discussion of the audience reaction to news stories on advertisements, see Jamieson, 1992.

8. In this study, we used a Bush advertisement that described Clinton as an advocate of higher taxes. We also used two different Clinton advertisements. The first of these was a positive advertisement in which Clinton's accomplishments as governor were outlined; the second was a negative advertisement condemning President Bush's performance on the economy. All three ad-watches were reported by Brooks Jackson of CNN. The advertisements, the ad-watch reports, and the design and methodology of this study are described in detail in Ansolabehere and Iyengar, 1993b.

9. The control variables were obtained during the pretest and included whether and how the respondents voted in the 1988 presidential election, self-reported party identifications, and gender.

10. The argument here is that negative messages about political candidates work well because most voters hold negative stereotypes about politicians.

11. The videotape of the newscast included no other campaign advertisements, and none of the news stories in that program referred to the presidential race.

12. Both performance advertisements focused on the state of the economy, whereas the character spots dealt primarily with integrity. The Bush positive advertisements concerned the potential for future economic growth (performance) and included a message highlighting his integrity. The Bush negative advertisement dealing with performance detailed the "Arkansas debacle," and his character attack was the infamous "*Time* magazine" spot. The Clinton positive advertisement on performance described Clinton and Gore as a "new breed" of Democrats. The Clinton positive advertisement on character featured was "The Man from Hope." Clinton's negative advertisements included a spot featuring Bush sound-bites concerning the economy (performance) as well as a spot suggesting Bush's involvement in the Iran/Contra affair.

13. James Carville was the architect of Clinton's 1992 campaign strategy.

14. We were able to demonstrate the overriding concern with problem solving as opposed to morality and trust by using our performance and character index to predict voting intention. After adjusting for the effects of party identification, we found that the effects of the performance index were four times as large as the effects of the character index. Clinton's disadvantage on the character dimension was thus largely neutralized.

4

The 1992 Elections and "Minority" Politics: A Perspective

RODNEY HERO

Although the United States has long been an ethnically and racially diverse society, that diversity has not only increased but, in significant respects, has also changed in character over the last generation. Population growth, including immigration, is no longer a primarily European phenomenon but has for some time occurred predominantly in Latin America and Asia. Indeed, the 1980s were touted as the "decade of the Hispanics," suggesting that this group was emerging as a significant social and political force. The overall growth and change in the United States has occurred in the context of an already sizable "minority" presence of more than 20 percent, with African Americans/blacks constituting about 12 percent and Latinos/Hispanics from 8 to 10 percent of the population. Projections suggest that the Latino and Asian populations will be the fastest-growing segments in the foreseeable future as well. This context is one in which the 1992 elections and their aftermath can and should be considered.

The 1992 U.S. election was distinctive in several respects—both generally and with specific reference to "minority" politics in the United States. As the "first post–Cold War election," it modified the intensity of and way in which foreign policy issues shaped the electoral process and debates; it was also notable for featuring a strong third-party candidate. The extent to which minority-related issues did—or did not—enter political discussions and influence political processes was also significant. Moreover, the election occurred after a decade that witnessed not only strong general economic growth but also evidence of a growing minority "underclass."

This chapter seeks to highlight certain notable qualities of the 1992 elections and the early months of the Clinton administration, with respect to minorities in the United States. Particular attention is focused on African Americans/blacks and Latinos/Hispanics, the two largest "minority" groups, in the context of what the election and subsequent events suggest about the nature of political and social change and the implications of such change for understanding U.S. politics. The discussion will proceed on the basis of a particular interpretation of the minority situation in the United States—that of "two-tiered pluralism."

TWO-TIERED PLURALISM: A BRIEF DESCRIPTION

In contrast to most standard interpretations of U.S. politics, (e.g., Hero, 1992; cf. Barrera, 1979; and Garcia and de la Garza, 1977), two-tiered pluralism views the situation of ethnic/racial minorities as one in which legal equality coexists with diminished equality in actual practice, despite significant accomplishments made by minority individuals (Stone, 1990; Hochschild, 1984: 169; cf. Wolfinger, 1974). In other words, although guarantees of equality and protection of rights theoretically apply to all Americans, these guarantees are largely procedural or formal, not substantive—in part, because cultural or racial deficiencies are alleged to exist (Barrera, 1979).

Another dichotomy is evident within this framework. On the one hand, minorities are included in most, perhaps all, facets of the contemporary political process—a fact that is touted by those holding "conventional pluralist" outlooks. On the other hand, minority populations remain largely marginal and stigmatized. In short, formal political recognition coexists with connotations of inferiority. As a consequence, both change and stasis occurred at various levels of the political system. The processes and outcomes of two-tiered pluralism seem to leave the subordinate status of minority groups little changed, however (cf. Chavez, 1991).

Two-tiered pluralism has many of the same double-edged qualities as the related concept of equal opportunity. And equal opportunity has been called "the keystone of U.S. liberal democracy" (Hochschild, 1988: 168–169, 189). Two-tiered pluralism acknowledges, even concedes, that the rough-and-tumble character of interest group politics, as generally described by American political scholars, observers, and practitioners, exists in some form. However, it does not fully exist for all groups. Granted, those groups in the "second tier" may have the formal rights of citizens and may be given "special protection" because they belong to "protected classes." But from the standpoint of two-tiered pluralism, the very need for such designation and protection is perceived as indicating a flaw, as being as much a weakness as a strength of conventional pluralism.

Another way of thinking about two-tiered pluralism is to relate it to contemporary liberal-versus-conservative debates regarding minority-related issues. From the viewpoint of two-tiered pluralism the ongoing debate over affirmative action, for instance, is one in which both liberal and conservative assessments are partly incorrect as well as partly correct. It may be that affirmative action programs in some ways help or seek to help minorities, as liberals hope and claim. Yet such policies may also stigmatize minorities, as conservatives commonly assert. Thus change occurs, but to a limited degree and with significant costs (e.g.,

Elling, 1990). Change is limited both legally, under such doctrine,
tiny," and politically or ideologically, owing to the stigmatizatio,
that often result. So the "glass ceiling" is not broken; at best, it may
slightly.

THE 1992 PRESIDENTIAL ELECTION

What are the implications of the 1992 presidential election with respect to minority politics? Did this election point up significant changes, or emerging trends
that might lead to significant changes, in the political and/or social situation for
minorities? Or was it mostly more of the same, thus suggesting a state of equilibrium? Although political and social phenomena seldom lend themselves to easy
summary or "yes"/"no" assessments, these questions can be "disaggregated" by
reference to the processes and outcomes of the election itself.

The 1992 presidential selection process departed from some trends and continued others. On the one hand, the issue of ethnicity/race was less significant, or
at least less directly and obviously raised, than in presidential elections of the recent past. One reason was the fact that the major candidates did not view this as
an issue that would openly divide the electorate. Another reason was the absence
of a major minority candidate in the race. In 1984 and 1988, by contrast, Jesse
Jackson's candidacy loomed large, especially during the nomination processes of
the Democratic Party. And the 1988 election, in particular, was marked by the
now-infamous "Willie Horton" ads aired by the Republican candidate. Many
public figures, including those who benefited from these ads, seemed to find
them embarrassing, at least in retrospect.

On the other hand, there were no Latino/Hispanic presidential candidates in
1992, nor even any names raised in this regard. Neither were the names of any
blacks or Latinos raised as possible vice-presidential candidates. (Recall, however, that in 1984, former San Antonio Mayor Henry Cisneros was apparently
considered a serious prospect for the post of vice-president to Walter Mondale.)
These omissions can be explained, one suspects, by the very small potential pool
of minority candidates for such positions. This absence of minorities from presidential and vice-presidential consideration raises numerous questions about the
political system itself. That this situation is "the norm" and provokes little attention is noteworthy, especially as it underscores the basic continuity with, rather
than departure from, recent national election patterns.

How might this continuity be viewed? On the one hand, it might be seen as a
sign of indifference to minority issues. On the other, it could indicate a tacit understanding that such issues are now sufficiently established within the policy
agenda that they need not be singled out. However, in the aftermath of a decade
often perceived as one in which minorities "lost ground," replete with evidence of
deteriorating social and economic conditions, a need for specific attention can
readily be argued.

In any case, this pattern of low visibility among minority candidacies seems related to other developments. For instance, an effort was made by the Democratic candidates, whose party has more commonly dealt with racial and ethnic issues, to "deracialize" the 1992 election. In response to the belief that the Democratic Party had been hurt by the public's perception of it as "the party of ethnic/racial minorities" and other "interest groups," the Clinton campaign made a conscious effort to frame and discuss minority issues in more general or "universalistic" terms. However, the assumption that direct and explicit concern with minority (i.e., black and Latino) issues is any more or less influenced by "interest groups" than by other types of groups, such as major business interests, says a great deal about how such issues have been framed and perceived in U.S. politics.

The Clinton campaign also included, however, a Latino/Hispanic outreach component, the "Adelante con Clinton" (i.e., "Forward, or Ahead, with Clinton") effort, essentially a contemporary version of the earlier "Viva Kennedy" and similar programs launched by previous Democratic candidates. Yet, in the estimation of most observers, this effort was a relatively minor one. The existence of the Adelante con Clinton program led to African Americans' calls for similar programs targeted to their community and to annoyance when the calls were not heeded, thus suggesting the fragile nature of minority-group relations within the Democratic Party.

The 1992 election also gave rise to the "Sister Souljah" incident. During the presidential campaign Bill Clinton used his appearance at an event organized by Jesse Jackson to criticize one of the event's participants, Sister Souljah, for the alleged harshness and inappropriateness of her music's lyrics. Many observers believed that Clinton's intention was to demonstrate his independence and assertiveness to middle-class voters, particularly whites, thereby strengthening his claim to be a reasonable, and moderate, "new Democrat." In reframing himself and his party, however, he may have implied that only certain forms or articulations of minority-group sentiment were acceptable.

On the whole, the Democratic Party's efforts included "recognition," or symbolic political appeals, ensconced within a broader economic populist appeal along with certain challenges to specific perspectives. The populist appeal was couched in such a way that it could speak to the general concerns of working-class and economically disadvantaged populations, which included blacks and Latinos. By contrast, the Republican appeal could have been characterized as cultural populism, within a larger free-market and equal opportunity ideology. And the Perot candidacy, for all its ostensible impact and success, seemed to make little effort to appeal to minority groups. Indeed, there is little evidence that minorities responded to that campaign. (If anything, Perot's major speech to the African American community, with its references to "you people," offended many in that community.) Based on available evidence, then, the legacy of Perot's 1992 campaign for minorities is ambiguous at best.

Notable in the conventions of both major political parties were the selection of speakers and the public displays of "descriptive representation." One out-growth of the civil rights and minority political movement of the 1960s has been the general acknowledgment that attention should be given to such concerns. The Republican Convention, for instance, arranged for a Hispanic woman (Gloria Gonzales Roemer of Colorado) to second the nomination of George Bush. Various speakers touted the presence of blacks and Hispanics in the Bush administration: Louis Sullivan at Health and Human Services, Manuel Lujan at Agriculture, Antonia Novella at the Surgeon General's office, and so on. And Bush's Hispanic daughter-in-law and eldest grandson were prominent at the end of the convention.

Similarly, the Democratic Convention featured several appearances by promi-nent African Americans, including national party head Ron Brown and Lena Guerrero of Texas, among others. And party nominee Clinton reiterated his oft-made declaration to have an administration that "looks like America," an obvious allusion to descriptive representational concerns. Also notable was the selection of a prominent Latina public official, Los Angeles County Supervisor Gloria Molina, as the Clinton campaign's co-head. In short, the two parties' conventions stressed policy generality or "universalism," deemphasized particular substantive policy concerns, and addressed minority politics through "recognition" or symbols.

The general election campaign, moreover, was reshaped by shifts in the elec-toral college resulting from population growth and change indicated in the 1990 census. Several states with large minority, particularly Latino, populations were major gainers in the electoral college after the 1990 census; most prominent were California, Texas, and Florida, to which an even higher level of attention was now being paid. The Democrats sought to capitalize on the Latino (especially Mex-ican American) tendency to support Democratic Party candidates. Broad eco-nomic appeals, along with campaigning by Latino politicians such as Henry Cis-neros and Federico Peña, were the main tactics employed toward that end. Over the long term, a major strategy of Republicans has been not so much to win a majority of the Latino vote but to lessen its Democratic leanings in such states as California and Texas through appeals to certain social and moral values. As influ-ences on voting behavior, however, economic issues have typically surpassed concerns over such values.

Meanwhile, the heavy Republican affiliation of Cuban Americans in Florida led Clinton to a different strategy. For the first time in several presidential elec-tions, the Democratic candidate made a significant effort to court the Cuban vote in Florida. Clinton's support for the Cuban Democracy Act (also known as the Torricelli Bill), designed to strengthen the existing economic boycott of Cuba, was intended to appeal to the Cuban community in south Florida. As pres-ident, Bush had earlier opposed this legislation; but later, in the wake of Clinton's endorsement of the legislation, Bush signed it.

Not only the growth of population, then, but also its distribution among segments of the society, has shaped, and will continue to shape, presidential electoral outcomes and the significance of minorities to those outcomes. It follows that the governmental system should include mechanisms for political and social "adjustment." Of course, such mechanisms have always been in place regarding national institutions; for instance, the distribution of state seats in Congress and in the electoral college has always been driven by population as determined by the census. However, the impact of redistricting in terms of the specific division of legislative districts within states (i.e., in state legislatures, city councils, and so on) is a newer phenomenon, one that resulted from the "reapportionment revolution" of the 1960s and was magnified by other developments such as voting rights legislation.

These patterns of growth were particularly important in 1992, when the implications of the 1990 census converged with those of the 1982 amendments to the Voting Rights Act (originally enacted in 1965). These 1982 amendments, which represented Congress's efforts to clarify and redirect Supreme Court interpretations of the Voting Rights Act, provided strong tools for drawing legislative districts conducive to the election of minority candidates at all levels of the political system. Indeed, some critics claim that minorities are now extensively, and inappropriately, *advantaged* in legislative elections (e.g., Thernstrom, 1987).

Although the 1992 presidential election did not overtly stress ethnic/racial issues, certain notable background events did. Most obvious were the riots in Los Angeles that occurred in the aftermath of the acquittal of police officers who had beaten Rodney King. Interpreting the implications of that case and the resulting social upheaval would be a major undertaking, one beyond the scope of this chapter. However, two observations may be briefly noted. First, the King beating and the jury acquittal forced a discussion of issues of "institutional" racism or bias, during which explicit questions were raised about the basic procedural and substantive fairness of common structures of the U.S. legal and justice system, including local police practices and the role of juries. In addition, concerns were voiced about the nature and extent of the role of the national government, including, of course, the president and executive branch, in acknowledging, defining, and developing responses to the crisis presented by the social turmoil. Were the beating of Rodney King, the jury's decision, and the subsequent riots to be viewed as social or institutional problems? As aberrations or somewhat predictable outcomes? Such questions might have significantly entered the presidential election debate. However, they seem not to have done so.

Second, the upheaval in Los Angeles may have underscored the limits of formal authority—even the authority held by minority mayors. In particular, the apparent inability of long-term black mayor Tom Bradley either to direct the Los Angeles Police Department or to effectively grapple with the social conditions that created and were exacerbated by the riots suggests the existence of a formidable chasm between formal authority and significant political power within (local) governmental institutions.

VOTING PATTERNS IN THE
1992 PRESIDENTIAL ELECTION

In the aftermath of the recognition politics regarding minorities and other events of the 1992 campaign—a recognition politics that has taken many forms—little change has occurred in the actual voting patterns of minorities. The distribution of the black vote between the two major party candidates was approximately the same as it had been four years earlier, with about 83 percent supporting the Democratic candidate; in addition, 7 percent voted for Perot. The Latino vote in 1992 differed only slightly from that in 1988, due in part to the Perot presence: 62 percent of the overall Latino vote went to Clinton (versus 69 percent to Dukakis in 1988), 24 percent to Bush (versus 30 percent in 1988), and 14 percent to Perot. However, there was much variation *within* the several Latino groups: Initial evidence suggests that about two-thirds of Mexican Americans supported Clinton, whereas only about a quarter of Cuban Americans did so.

About 52 percent of Asian Americans voted for Bush, 32 percent for Clinton, and 17 percent for Perot. The Latino vote seemed to serve as an important base for Democrat Clinton in states, such as Colorado and New Mexico, that had been won by Republican candidates in recent presidential elections. And Bush's win in Florida was largely attributable to the Cuban vote (Moreno and Warren, 1993). One of the biggest changes between the elections of 1984 and 1988 was that white males voted for the Democratic candidate at somewhat higher levels, thus perhaps vindicating that party's "deracialization" strategy.

Lost in the recognition politics of 1992, however, was notice of the *nature* of the ethnic/racial presence in previous presidential administrations. Specifically, whereas the last several administrations have included minority Cabinet members, a person of minority background has yet to serve within the "inner cabinet"—that is, in the Departments of State, Defense, Treasury, or Attorney General (Justice). Instead, all minorities have served in the "outer cabinet," which comprises the Departments of Agriculture, Health and Human Services, Housing and Urban Development, Interior, Labor, Energy, Education, Transportation, and Veterans Affairs. Most commonly, minorities have served as heads of these departments, and their responsibility for "social" and/or urban issues has continued a kind of personnel or appointment "stratification"—a pattern found throughout the American political structure (cf. Elling, 1990).

This pattern was evident during the Bush administration and persisted in the early days of the Clinton administration with the appointments of Ron Brown at Commerce, Mike Espy at Agriculture, Hazel O'Leary at Energy, Henry Cisneros as head of HUD, Federico Peña at Transportation, Joycelyn Elders as Surgeon General, and so on. However, such stratification now seems somewhat less rigid than it once was. Peña and Brown were the first minorities to head their respective agencies, as was Manuel Lujan at Interior under President Bush. Thus, although minority appointments continue to be confined to the "outer cabinet," at least some diversification has taken place in that realm. Moreover, the first year of the Clinton administration witnessed the nomination of substantially higher percentages of Latinos and Blacks to the federal courts than has occurred in recent presidencies.

Two other events of Clinton's first year deserve attention. The first was the aborted nomination of Lani Guinier to head the Justice Department's Civil Rights division. The quality of the arguments made in her law-review articles cannot be discussed here. Notably, however, she was perhaps the only minority person nominated for a major policy position who appeared ideologically "distinct" and outspoken. The numerous other Clinton minority nominees, whatever their merits or demerits, were ideologically unobjectionable. Clinton's decision to withdraw the Guinier nomination underscored the sense that his administration would be treating racial/ethnic issues delicately rather than assertively, and in symbolic rather than more directly threatening ways.

A second noteworthy event was Clinton's speech to a gathering of black clergy toward the end of his first year in office. In that speech, he spoke compassionately of the issues and problems facing the black community. Interestingly, in stressing self-help, individual responsibility, and family as solutions, he echoed another of his campaign themes, one with clear religious allusions: the "new covenant." However compelling, such themes are obviously quite mainstream and palatable. And they are themes unlikely to bring fundamental change, any time soon, to the structurally rooted social and economic inequality facing minority communities.

Indeed, one important question to consider is whether Clinton's major policy initiatives, such as health care, with their emphatically "universalistic" cast, are sufficiently sensitive and responsive to the unique problems and concerns of minority communities. The framing of major policy reforms in broad and nonracial terms may well increase the likelihood of policy enactment by diminishing the perception of such reforms as "minority" programs. At the same time, however, they may not be sufficiently flexible to address the special circumstances of minority populations. One might anticipate, for instance, that the *curanderos* ("faith healers") preferred by some Latinos might not qualify for reimbursement under the health care policies that ultimately emerge.

In any case, the presidency is not the only arena in which sociopolitical change, or continuity, may manifest itself. Other dimensions of the political system merit consideration as well, and to these we now turn.

THE 1992 CONGRESSIONAL ELECTIONS

The congressional elections of 1992 witnessed substantial growth in minority representation; indeed, it is in this context (with respect to the national elections) that the "convergence" of the 1990 census with the amended Voting Rights Acts had a significant impact. The number of Latinos in Congress (with voting power) increased substantially (from ten to seventeen), as did the number of blacks (now totaling thirty-nine in the House and one in the Senate).

This growth in sheer numbers has been accompanied by other developments as well. For instance, the newest black members of Congress are somewhat different from their predecessors. Whereas the earlier generation of black members of Congress were products of the Civil Rights movement, most of the recent members, though beneficiaries of that movement, are not direct products of it. The latter have also had extensive state legislative experience, which, in conjunction with their increased numbers, may lead to heightened influence in Congress.

The increased number of Latino members, meanwhile, is attributable to population growth in several states, leading to additional seats in Congress. At the same time, however, the redistricting—strongly shaped by Voting Rights legislation—led to lost seats in the House. Thus, whereas California gained 7 seats, Texas 3, and Florida 4, New York lost 3 seats, Illinois 2, and New Jersey 1. Yet as many of the newly elected Latino members of Congress came from states that lost seats as from states that gained seats. This was not the case in previous years, when newly elected Latinos invariably occupied new, "open" seats. New Jersey elected its first Latino, as did Illinois, and New York elected its second. Of the five Latinos in Congress from Texas, one occupies a new seat; another is a Republican who defeated an incumbent Democrat. So not only growth in numbers but also increased regional and party diversity now characterize the Latinos in Congress.

Of what significance is the election of more minorities to Congress? Previous analyses suggest that the numbers of minority members of Congress have been too small to produce a significant impact in terms of substantive representation (Welch and Hibbing, 1988; Hero, 1992; Whitby, 1985). Increased numbers may deepen that impact, but not by very much, for Congress remains a large and complex body whose high level of decentralization will likely provide only limited access to minority concerns.

In this connection, one major congressional vote might be noted: the vote on NAFTA in November 1993. This vote was important in many respects, of course, but was thought to be particularly significant for blacks and Latinos because of the concern that low-wage jobs might be threatened by the agreement. Of the seventeen Latinos in Congress, nine voted for NAFTA and eight voted against. Of the fourteen Latino Democrats, eight voted for and six voted against. And of the three Republicans, one from Texas voted for and two from Florida voted against. The blacks in Congress, all but one of whom are Democrats, were more likely to vote against NAFTA than for it, but their support was greater than might have been expected given their congressional voting histories.

These figures suggest that minority voting patterns are becoming more complex and that "new Democrat"/"old Democrat" distinctions as well as traditional party characteristics may be undergoing some change. As the extent of that change and the direction it will take are not yet clear, further research is merited.

SUBNATIONAL ELECTIONS AND DEVELOPMENTS

The vast number of local governments in the United States have often been seen as an arena into which new groups can be incorporated so as to "learn the ways of" U.S. democracy (see Dahl, 1976). The impact of reapportionment and the revised Voting Rights Act would be expected to enhance such learning processes in state and local politics. But this objective has been met only to a degree. The largest numbers of minority elected officials do indeed occur at the state and local levels; but even with steady growth of these numbers over the years, blacks and Latinos (combined) constitute fewer than 5 percent of all state and local officials. Moreover, recent institutional developments in state (and local) politics may have lessened the impact of increased minority presence in elective bodies.

One such development has been increased use of the "initiative" in the states. More and more individuals and groups have used initiative processes to place measures on the ballot in the states, particularly those with large minority populations. Among the heaviest users of the "direct democracy" initiative are California and Colorado; other states, such as Florida and Mississippi, have recently adopted the initiative process. These latter two states have historically been perceived as "traditionalistic" (Elazar, 1984) and, thus, presumably less likely to encourage broad political participation. What might be the significance of increased use of the initiative?

Some scholars, such as Bruce Cain, (1992), suggest that this increased use may not be entirely accidental or coincidental; rather, he suggests, it correlates, at least in California, with the increased influence of minorities within institutions of *representative* democracy. It follows that as minorities, particularly blacks (e.g., Willie Brown), have gained prominent places within the California state legislature, mechanisms of *direct or majoritarian* democracy—what Cain refers to as the "new populism"—may be increasingly used to counter the impact of representative processes and institutions (1992: 273–275).

The purposes for which initiatives have been used in the last few years may also be instructive (cf. Cain, 1992). Consider, for instance, the "Official English" or "English Only" movement. When national representative institutions (which do not, of course, engage in initiative processes) and state legislatures decided against adopting Official English policies, measures were placed on state ballots and passed in a number of instances, often overwhelmingly. Indeed, through use of the initiative, they were passed in California, Colorado, Arizona, and Florida—all states with substantial Latino populations. Some states with few non-English speakers, but without the initiative, also passed measures through state legislatures; these states had a history of significant racial discrimination (see Citrin et al., 1990).

Another institutional development has been the "term-limits" movement. This measure appears to be weakening the power of representative institutions, to which minority officials have increasingly gained access. But the ultimate impact of term limits on this minority presence remains uncertain. In fact, some analysts have argued that term limits will actually improve the chances of minority presence in elective positions because incumbents, who most often are not minorities, will have to leave their positions (Moncrief et al., 1992). That may be so; but minorities, too, will lose incumbency advantages that may be equally important to electoral and governance outcomes. In short, though a direct causal relationship does not necessarily exist, the increased use of initiative processes, along with their specific outcomes, may well diminish the marginal gains made by minorities in the representative institutions of state government.

CONCLUSIONS

Overall, then, how might the 1992 elections be viewed? Two concepts that may appear mutually exclusive suggest an interpretation: "new progressivism" and "retraditionalization." At the turn of the century, the progressive movement sought to remove the corruption associated with patronage and to move away from "parochial" toward more universalistic structures and public policies. Yet, as has often been argued, a major impact of the progressive movement was to weaken ethnic-group access and influence in city governments (e.g., Stone, Whelan, and Murin, 1986: ch. 8). In this connection, contemporary policy debates seem to be premised on the need and desirability of ostensibly universalistic concerns (e.g., Peterson, 1981; Williams, 1990). Nonetheless, the impact of such approaches resembles that of the early progressive efforts. That is, "unitary" or universalistic policies often overlook the concerns of socially and economically disadvantaged groups. There remains a significant, if more subtle and tempered, majority dominance imbedded in policies and in institutional processes and outcomes despite certain important political and institutional changes of the last generation, such as the Civil Rights Act, Affirmative Action, the Voting Rights Act, and so on. But there are serious questions as to whether those policies make much substantive difference in the context of larger bureaucratic and institutional structures and processes, and as to whether unique dimensions of minority-group policy concerns have been adequately considered. "Second-generation discrimination" in education is, I think, one of the most striking examples of such concerns (cf. Meier and Stewart, 1991).

"Retraditionalization" seems an apt description of the contemporary era in that groups traditionally at the center of political and policy processes continue to be so. Thus, although minority groups are now found at all levels of the political system, the extent and potential duration of their impact are not clear. For instance, according to recent research on state politics, whereas there was once an absence, there is now a presence of minority interest groups in the states. But there is little or no evidence of much policy influence (Thomas and Hrebenar, 1990). And although the 1970s and 1980s witnessed the election of minority mayors in a number of American cities, the policy legacy of those mayors remains unclear at best. Indeed, the fact that several of those mayors were succeeded by moderate to conservative mayors (e.g., Richard Daley, Jr., succeeded the late Harold Washington in Chicago, Richard Riordan succeeded Tom Bradley in Los Angeles, and Rudolph Giuliani succeeded David Dinkins in New York City) also suggests retraditionalization.

In short, the new populism (Cain, 1992), the new progressivism, and retraditionalization, along with those aspects of the 1992 election noted earlier, suggest more continuity than change.

These trends, which do little to alter the basic parameters of two-tiered pluralism, will probably continue into the foreseeable future because the "rights-based" approach of minorities is nearing its limits. Yet, although little more is likely to be gained from this approach, it has been successful in removing many impediments, particularly procedural or formal impediments, to minority equal opportunity, political participation, and inclusion (cf. Fraga and Anhalt, 1993). Minorities may now be able to protect themselves from some forms of political and legal discrimination. But they do not necessarily constitute effective interest groups. In any case, an "interest group strategy" as such may not be the most feasible or desirable one, given that rights, though sometimes seen as group-relevant, are most often viewed individualistically in the United States.

To achieve further successes, minorities must have an impact on the majoritarian elements of the political system; they must alter the orientation of American political thinking from one of liberal democracy toward a more communitarian or social democratic approach. But the ostensible shifts that have taken place in state politics toward more populist mechanisms, along with other apparent reactions against minority gains in representative institutions, do not point in that direction. Similarly, further minority advancement would necessitate a willingness within the larger society and political realm to address questions of social structure (e.g., with regard to economic inequality) rather than just the formal institutional mechanisms that have been the focus of most political reform. Such changes may be on the horizon, but they had little visibility and significance in the 1992 elections.

The success of the "new Democrat" in symbolically broadening and diversifying, if not necessarily elevating, minorities in the national government suggests both change and continuity. And the outcomes of new substantive policy initiatives are likely to have mixed consequences for minorities. Equally interesting is the fact that developments in Congress and at the subnational level seem to point in different directions; the former suggests increased diversity and complexity, the latter a "new populism" ostensibly hostile to minority concerns. Overall, however, the essential parameters of U.S. political and social relations, and of two-tiered pluralism, were modified only slightly by the 1992 elections and the first year of the Clinton administration.

5

The Politicization of Gender

BARBARA NORRANDER

The "Year of the Woman," averred journalists, as they discussed the upcoming elections in 1992. Record numbers of women candidates, lingering memories of an all-male Senate Judiciary Committee grilling Anita Hill, women outpacing men in voter turnout,[1] and an expected gender gap in voting preferences—all combined to convince pundits and politicians alike that women had arrived as major players in American politics. Of course, other election years had been similarly hailed; recall 1984, when Geraldine Ferraro was the Democratic party's vice-presidential nominee. Past election outcomes, however, proved the label premature.

The 1992 election did produce significant increases in the number of elected women. But we must ask whether these increases are best described in terms of revolutionary change, as embodied by the phrase the "Year of the Woman," or in terms of evolutionary growth owing to decades of women's involvement in politics. Winning elections only sets the stage for gender to influence politics. It is the *number* of women appointed to executive and judicial positions in the early Clinton administration that must be considered in the context of real political change. The role of Hillary Rodham Clinton as First Lady also needs to be included in our calculations. Ultimately, it is the ability of these women to influence public policy that will have the most enduring effects on the lives of all American citizens. Accordingly, this chapter explores the evidence and speculates on the policy impact of more women in government.

WOMEN CANDIDATES IN 1992

More women candidates ran and won in 1992 than in any previous year. One hundred and six women competed for U.S. House seats, 11 women vied for Senate seats, and 2,373 sought seats in state legislatures (*CAWP Fact Sheet*, 1993). More than half (57 percent) of these women candidates won. Aside from the 54 women in the U.S. Congress and the 1,516 women in state legislatures, 3 serve as governors, 11 occupy the post of lieutenant governor, and 55 hold other statewide offices.

The figures in Table 5.1 reveal the expanded number of women legislators after the 1992 election. Unusually large increases in the number of women representatives occurred at the national level, lending credence to the "Year of the Woman" label. At the state level, however, the 1992 increases reflect a two-decade evolutionary growth in the number of women representatives. Despite this expansion, women still occupy only a small percentage of legislative offices. As women constitute slightly more than half of the American population, equality in representation would require that women hold 50 percent of elective offices rather than their current high of 10 percent of national seats and 20 percent of state legislative seats. Additionally, the new U.S. high for women in Congress still lags behind the world average of 13 percent for women in national legislatures and falls considerably behind the figures for world leaders: In Finland, Sweden, Norway, Cuba, and Denmark, one-third of the representatives are women (*Distribution of Seats Between Men and Women in National Parliaments,* 1991).

To fully understand the change in women's electoral victories in 1992, we need to understand the reasons for lower numbers of women representatives in the past. The lack of women representatives in previous decades was due neither to voter hostility toward women candidates (Darcy, Welch, and Clark, 1987) nor to the inability of women candidates to raise as much money as male candidates (Burrell, 1985; Darcy, Welch, and Clark, 1987; Uhlaner and Schlozman, 1986). Rather, women candidates were scarce (Darcy, Welch, and Clark, 1987). Some women may have been reluctant to run, believing they would have difficulty attracting votes and money. Others who were raising children may have chosen to

TABLE 5.1
Number of Women in Congress and State Legislatures, 1971–1993

Year	U.S. House		U.S. Senate	State Legislatures	
	Number	Percent	Number[a]	Number	Percent
1971	13	3.0	2	344	4.5
1973	16	3.7	0	424	5.6
1975	19	4.4	0	604	8.0
1977	18	4.1	2	388	9.1
1979	16	3.7	1	770	10.3
1981	21	4.8	2	908	12.1
1983	22	5.1	2	991	13.3
1985	23	5.3	2	1103	14.8
1987	23	5.3	2	1170	15.7
1989	29	6.7	2	1270	17.0
1991	28	6.4	3	1368	18.3
1993	47	10.8	6[b]	1516	20.4

[a]In the case of senators, the numbers and percentages are the same.

[b]Kay Bailey Hutchison's victory in a special election in Texas in May 1993 increased the number of female senators to 7 in that year.

SOURCE: *CAWP Fact Sheet* (1993).

delay political careers until their forties (Darcy, Welch, and Clark, 1987: 95). In the past, women may have been less politically ambitious as well, but this attitude is changing (Costantini, 1990). In addition, women historically have been underrepresented in most professional occupations (such as law), from which many political candidates were drawn. Women now enter these occupations in greater numbers but will continue to lag behind males until older generations are replaced fully by newer ones.

Once women became candidates, they faced additional obstacles. Women candidates during the 1980s were hampered by media coverage that centered more on the horse-race aspects of elections, especially on negative stories about deficient campaign resources; and on the whole, their issues received less coverage than did those of male candidates. These male-female differences in media coverage disadvantaged female candidates, as voters perceived male candidates to be stronger, more electable, and more capable of dealing with military issues (Kahn and Goldenberg, 1991).

Finally, the U.S. election system of single-member districts and plurality decisions may work against women's representation. Women candidates fare better in the proportional representation systems used in many European democracies (Darcy, Welch, and Clark, 1987: ch. 6; Duverger, 1955; Norris, 1985; Rule, 1987). In such systems, women are part of a slate of candidates presented by each party. Voters cast ballots for these parties, and each party receives seats in the legislature equivalent to its proportion of the vote. Thus, more women win legislative seats as part of each party's slate of winning candidates.

Despite continuing disadvantages, the number of women in Congress increased substantially in 1993. Some journalists have attributed this increase to Clarence Thomas's Supreme Court confirmation hearing. Anita Hill, having charged that Mr. Thomas sexually harassed her when she worked for him at the Equal Employment Opportunity Commission (EEOC), faced an all-male Senate Judiciary committee. Lynn Yeakel, angered by the tough cross-examination of Ms. Hill by Pennsylvania Senator Arlen Specter, entered and won the Democratic primary in order to face Senator Specter in the fall. Unlike most of the 1992 women candidates, Yeakel did not have a long political career. Still, she lost the election by a very slim margin, despite being outspent two to one. Carol Moseley Braun's entry in the Illinois senatorial contest also was influenced by the Thomas confirmation hearings, as was that of Patty Murray in Washington. Most women candidates in 1992, however, had worked their way up the political career ladder in the 1980s, providing them with the background to seek congressional seats in the 1990s. For instance, both Barbara Feinstein and Barbara Boxer, who won Senate seats from California, previously held elective offices: Boxer with ten years of experience in the U.S. House of Representatives and Feinstein as mayor of San Francisco.

To enhance their competitiveness and thereby win congressional elections in 1992, women candidates needed to raise sufficient funds. Past studies indicate that women candidates eventually raised as much money as male candidates in similar circumstances, but that women candidates had a more difficult route. Women candidates relied on smaller contributions given disproportionately by women until the candidates' election status was ensured. Only when women candidates appeared to be winners did they receive substantial support from male contributors (Donovan, 1992).

To overcome this initial fund-raising gap experienced by many women candidates, Ellen Malcolm established the political action committee (PAC) known as EMILY's List in 1985. (EMILY is an acronym that stands for Early Money Is Like Yeast: Both make the "dough" rise.) EMILY's list makes early contributions to pro-choice Democratic women candidates to help them attain credibility with more traditional donors. In 1992 it contributed $6 million, making it the largest contributor to House and Senate candidates (Dewar, 1993). EMILY's List was joined by forty-one other women's PACs, contributing a total of $11.6 million to female candidates (Baruch and McCormick, 1993). Fund raising by these groups was spurred first by *Webster v. Reproductive Health Services,* the 1989 Supreme Court decision that allowed state restrictions on abortions, and second by the Thomas confirmation hearing (Babcock, 1992). With these additional resources, women candidates in 1992 actually raised more money than did male candidates under similar circumstances (Wilcox, 1993).

Another explanation for women candidates' successes in the 1992 elections points to the growing distrust of politicians by the American public. To some, women candidates appear to be less professional politicians than do male candidates. Given the House banking scandal, the deadlock on reducing the budget deficit, and a stagnant economy, voters were expected to reject Washington incumbents for fresh, new faces. Yet, although voters in fourteen states passed term limitation resolutions, only 6 of the 116 incumbents running in these states lost. Nationwide, women candidates did not do well as challengers. Of the 7 women facing Senate incumbents, only Feinstein won, and she beat John Seymour, who had been appointed to fill a vacant seat. Most women challenging House incumbents also lost; only 2 of the 24 new women House members defeated incumbents.

Women's gains in 1992 came from winning open seats—seats vacated by male incumbents. Fifty-two open seats became available as House members retired due to concerns over redistricting, the House banking scandal, policy gridlock, Congress's unpopularity, and lack of time for families (Katz, 1992). Thirteen members sought other offices, 2 seats were vacated due to deaths, and 19 incumbents lost in primaries. Thus, a combined total of 86 open seats were available in 1992. The lack of open seats in previous elections and the power of incumbency maintained an overwhelmingly male presence in legislatures (Burrell, 1988, 1990; Darcy, Welch, and Clark, 1987: ch. 7).

Incumbents who seek reelection win more than 90 percent of the time. So challengers face tough battles to overcome incumbents' advantages in name recognition and campaign contributions. Since most incumbents in Congress are men, the incumbency advantage has kept men in Congress and hindered women from attaining seats. The large number of vacant seats in 1992 thus opened the door to women (and minorities) to enter Congress in greater numbers. It is unlikely, however, that as many seats will open again in the 1990s, thus leaving fewer opportunities for increases in female representation.

In sum, a revolutionary jump in the number of women legislators at the national level occurred as a result of the 1992 elections. Women took advantage of the unusual circumstances of 1992 to increase their numbers. But the women candidates who won in 1992 often built their political careers in the 1980s through the evolutionary process of moving up from local and state offices. Women candidates have continued this evolutionary process at the state level, where their numbers continue to grow at a steady pace each year. The reaction of women voters to these women candidates can be explained by reference to the voting phenomenon known as the gender gap.

THE POLITICIZATION OF THE GENDER GAP

The fact that men and women vote differently was first widely recognized during the 1980 presidential election, when women were found to be 8 percentage points less likely to vote for Ronald Reagan than were men.[2] In the early 1980s, feminists groups, particularly the National Organization of Women (NOW), recognized that this gap could be used as a tool in their fight for passage of the Equal Rights Amendment (ERA).[3] After quick passage in thirty-two states, the ERA faced tough opposition in the state legislatures of Illinois, Florida, Missouri, North Carolina, Oklahoma, and Virginia. NOW hoped to convince Democratic leaders in these states that a gender gap in voting meant that the Democratic party could benefit from women's votes in future elections if Democratic legislators passed the ERA (Bond, 1988). The ERA ultimately failed to win ratification, but NOW more successfully used the gender gap to lobby for a woman vice-presidential nominee at the 1984 Democratic convention.

The gender gap itself is due more to issues concerning the use of force or compassion than to women's issues. Although men and women hold similar positions on the issues of abortion, the Equal Rights Amendment, and women's role in society, women historically have been less supportive of using force abroad, as in military conflicts, and are more likely than men to oppose capital punishment and to favor gun control. Women, more so than men, also tend to favor social welfare programs, civil rights concerns, and restrictions on social vices such as illegal drugs, pornography, and gambling (Dodson and Carroll, 1991).

The gender gap does not explain most women's votes. Women are generally influenced by the same factors as men in voting. If anything, party identification and candidate evaluations continue to be more important than gender in explaining why people support candidates. Moreover, significant differences exist among women voters. African American women constitute the greatest percentage of female Democratic Party supporters; the next largest group (as of the 1980s) is made up of younger, college-educated women who work outside the home. Conversely, more Republican Party supporters can be found among homemakers, older women, and evangelical Christian women (Bendyna and Lake, 1993).

The gender gap continues to influence politics both because of the attention it receives in the media and because of its impact on party identification. With each election in the 1980s an increasing number of media stories was devoted to male and female differences. Yet many of these reports failed to discuss the reasons for either male-female differences or differences among women voters. Like most media reports, the gender gap stories focused instead on the horse-race aspects of electoral competition by discussing how gender voting would influence outcomes (Borquez, Goldenberg, and Kahn, 1988). Nevertheless, increased coverage of the gender gap "probably created a favorable atmosphere for female candidates and fostered more serious discussion of women's issues" (Kahn and Goldenberg, 1991: 107).

The gender gap also continues to influence elections through its ties to party identification. In 1992, 40 percent of women and 32 percent of men viewed themselves as Democrats whereas 28 percent of men and 23 percent of women identified themselves as Republicans (Bendyna and Lake, 1993). Insofar as party identification remains a major influence on vote choice, the gender gap will continue to affect election outcomes.

The Gender Gap and Women Candidates

In nonpresidential elections from 1980 to 1990, women candidates rarely drew greater support from women voters than from male ones. In 1992 a gender gap of more than 10 percentage points occurred in four of the eleven senate races involving women candidates (recall Barbara Boxer's and Dianne Feinstein's wins in California, Jean Lloyd-Jones's loss in Iowa, and Lynn Yeakel's loss in Pennsylvania). The largest gender gap in three gubernatorial races involving women candidates was brought about by Deborah Arnesen's gain of 9 percentage points among women voters in New Hampshire ("The Gender Gap at the State Level," 1993). Gender voting within Democratic primary elections also helped to produce more women candidates in 1992 (Cook, 1993). In that year, and in previous ones, the largest gender gaps occurred among Democratic women candidates, suggesting that the gender gap in party identification underlies any gender gaps in support for women candidates.

The Gender Gap and the 1992 Presidential Vote

The gender gap in the 1992 presidential vote shrunk to only a 4-point advantage for Clinton, a 1-point disadvantage for Bush, and a 4-point disadvantage for

Perot. In 1988, by contrast, the presidential gender gap was 7 percentage points; in 1984, 4 percentage points; and in 1980, 8 percentage points. Clinton's gender gap was largest among younger voters, those with very low or very high levels of education, single adults, and individuals employed full time ("The Gender Gap," 1993).

The gender gap was widest during the early months of the 1992 campaign, especially in relation to Perot, whom men favored by as many as 14 percentage points over women. By contrast, Clinton held a 9-point advantage among women voters early in the campaign, and Bush's support varied from a 6-point advantage among women voters to a 8-point disadvantage ("The Gender Gap in 1992," 1992). Perot's early rejection by women led to speculations that his language (he referred to women as "girls" and chided men for hiding behind their women's skirts) and his "command and control" leadership style made women uneasy (Grove, 1992; Goodman, 1992).

The gender gap also reflects the difference in decisionmaking style between man and women. In 1992 women voted *for* a particular candidate, whereas men voted *against* a candidate. Women voting for Clinton expressed more interest in health care, education, and abortion, whereas male supporters voiced concerns over the economy and federal deficit. Women voting for Bush approved of the more conservative family issues stressed in his campaign. And Bush's support among men was anchored in his foreign policy successes (Bendyna and Lake, 1993). In short, a small gender gap influenced the outcome in the 1992 presidential race and some congressional elections, but for the most part, both women and men voters brought more women into the legislative arena. President Clinton eventually had to boost the number of women in the executive branch through his appointments, an issue to which we now turn.

WOMEN IN THE EXECUTIVE BRANCH

With most of Bill Clinton's term as president yet to unfold, his record of appointing women to executive positions remains incomplete. We do know, however, that his initial Cabinet contained three women (one an African American), five minority males (three African Americans, two Hispanics), and six white males. In addition, Clinton gave Cabinet designation to two women appointed as ambassador to the United Nations and head of the Environmental Protection Agency, respectively. By contrast, only three women served in Bush's Cabinet. In all other previous administrations, for that matter, only nine women served as Cabinet members (Clark, 1991).

Although subcabinet appointments receive less national attention, these are the slots that Clinton would need to fill with women and minorities in order to fulfill his campaign promise to reflect America's diverse population in his administration. As of the summer of 1993, Clinton had filled 60 percent of the 400 government posts requiring Senate confirmation. Of these appointments, 33 percent went to women, 15 percent to African Americans, 8 percent to Hispanics, and 2 percent to Asians. The first acknowledged lesbian was nominated and confirmed when Roberta Achtenberg became the assistant secretary for Fair Housing and Equal Opportunity in the Department of Housing and Urban Development. Yet, although African Americans, Hispanics, and Asians have been appointed to the Clinton administration in numbers reflecting their percentages in the population, women remain underrepresented by about 15 percent. Still, the Clinton roster contains more women than did those of his predecessors: In the Bush administration, one out of four appointments went to women compared to one out of seven in the Carter administration (Solomon, 1993a). And although Clinton's close White House staff includes more white males than do his Cabinet appointments, it's clear that women play a more important role in his staff than they did in Bush's or Carter's (Solomon, 1993b).

At one point in the appointment process, Clinton grew angry at the "bean counters" who tallied up the gender and racial characteristics of his appointments and demanded greater representation. Such bean counting in presidential appointments is not new, however. As Ellen Goodman pointed out in one of her columns (January 2, 1993), only the beans have changed. Presidential appointments used to be scrutinized along geographic, religious, or European-heritage lines; hence a Texas male would offset a Catholic New Yorker. Often it is the groups seeking to break into political power that are most concerned with symbolic representation in high-level government posts. In the past, these groups comprised Catholics and Jews; today, they are made up of women and racial minorities.

HILLARY RODHAM CLINTON

Much ado accompanied President Clinton's announcement that his wife, Hillary Rodham Clinton, would chair the task force on health care reform in America. Clinton was both hailed and derided for giving an unprecedented base of power to the First Lady. Yet the revolution lies in the openness and breadth of this power, not in its existence. After all, First Ladies since Abigail Adams have influenced their husbands' decisions. Ellen Wilson's project on housing for the poor resulted in new legislation. President's Wilson's second wife, Edith, served as "de facto chief of staff" when Wilson was disabled by a stroke. Eleanor Roosevelt served as deputy director of the Office of Civilian Defense until media and mail pressure forced her resignation, but she remained powerful as Roosevelt's "eyes and ears." And Rosalynn Carter coordinated the work of thirty task forces dealing with mental health and lobbied Congress for the passage of the Mental Health System Act of 1980 (Anthony, 1993).

Hillary Rodham Clinton faces the task of combining the headship of the health policy task force, the ceremonial duties of the First Lady, and the role of general adviser to her husband on domestic issues with being a wife and mother.

Her position as head of the 500-member health task force is certainly the most public departure from the traditional First Lady role. This high-profile policy role has brought Hillary Clinton both praise and criticism from elected officials, the press, and the public. In the fall of 1993, while lobbying Congress for passage of the health care package, she won acclaim from Washington insiders for her expertise. By the fall of 1994, she and her husband were often criticized for mishandling the political maneuvers needed to pass the comprehensive package. The public's reaction to Hillary Clinton's new role has been mixed. American men remain uncertain about this broader role, with only 40 percent approving of Hillary Clinton in the spring of 1993; but American women, especially those working outside the home, recognize that she faces the same problems as they do in balancing career and motherhood. Sixty percent of women have approved of Hillary Clinton's early performance ("Hillary Rodham Clinton," 1993).

As a result of the 1992 election, more women now serve in Congress. President Clinton's initial appointments also brought more women to high executive posts. The influence that this increase in women officials might have on government policies and procedures is the topic of the remainder of this chapter.

THE INFLUENCE OF MORE WOMEN IN GOVERNMENT

We may be able to predict the effects of more women in Congress in the 1990s on the basis of distinctiveness in earlier Congresses and in state and local governments. In the 1970s and 1980s, women in Congress received scores similar to those of their male colleagues on measures of presidential support and party unity (Gehlen, 1977), but they may have been slightly more liberal in some policy areas (Gehlen, 1977; Leader, 1977; Welch, 1985). These differences arose in part because women were more likely to be elected from liberal districts, which generally had more minority constituents or were urban or northern (Welch, 1985). Female Republican members of Congress have tended to be more supportive of abortion rights than male Republican members, but no such differences exist between men and women on the Democratic side of the aisle (Tatalovich and Schier, 1993). And in state legislatures, women match their male colleagues on many issues but have been more supportive of the ERA, women's rights, abortion, and family issues (Leader, 1977; Hill, 1982; Saint-Germain, 1989; Thomas, 1989). These differences persist even when district type and member's party are controlled for (Dodson and Carroll, 1991).

The low number of women in state and national office may compromise their distinctiveness. And as a minority group, women representatives may not have the power to pursue issues they find uniquely relevant. Evidence from state and local offices in the United States and from national offices abroad suggests that as the number of women representatives increases, women feel freer to pursue women's and children's issues (Flammang, 1985; Skard and Haavio-Mannila, 1985; Thomas, 1991). One study of an American state legislature suggests that 15 percent of seats must be held by women before women are no longer treated as tokens, allowing them to have a real impact on shaping the legislature's agenda (Saint-Germain, 1989). Although the national average for women representatives in state legislatures exceeds 15 percent, six states—Kentucky, Alabama, Louisiana, Oklahoma, Arkansas, and Pennsylvania—have fewer than 10 percent (*CAWP Fact Sheet,* 1993). The U.S. Congress, too, has fewer than 15 percent women members.

A second factor, aside from the number of women legislators, concerns the power positions they hold. Two power bases form the structure of American legislatures: party leadership and committee leadership. In state legislatures in 1991, 18 percent of party leadership posts and 14 percent of committee chairs were held by women (Women State Legislators, 1991); but in the U.S. Congress after the 1992 election, no women were committee chairs. Six women chaired subcommittees, and two women held second-tier positions in the party leadership. In general, power in Congress is obtained through longevity, and committee leadership, in particular, is determined by seniority. Newly and recently elected women representatives lack this seniority.

Women's numbers in the federal judiciary are also expected to increase over the next few years. When President Clinton came into office, 99 federal judgeships in U.S. district and appeals courts were vacant. Over his four-year term Clinton should appoint approximately 250 judges, about one-fourth of the federal government's total. Of course, some of Clinton's predecessors augmented the number of women appointed to the judiciary: Whereas Johnson, Nixon, and Ford appointed fewer than 2 percent female judges and Reagan appointed only 8 percent, 16 percent of Carter's judicial appointments and 20 percent of Bush's were women (Idelson, 1993). Clinton also chose Ruth Bader Ginsburg as his first Supreme Court appointment. Joining Sandra Day O'Connor, appointed by Ronald Reagan in 1981, women now hold 22 percent of the seats on the nation's highest court.

The effect of more women judges is not fully understood. One study (Kritzer and Uhlman, 1977) discovered no differences between male and female judges, but another (Gruhl, Spohn, and Welch, 1981) found that women judges treated women and male defendants more equally, whereas male judges often treated women defendants more leniently than male ones. Yet the presence of a female judge on state supreme courts leads to more rulings in favor of women in sex discrimination cases (Gryski, Main, and Dixon, 1986). The same may be true at the national level. One study found that the appointment of Sandra Day O'Connor influenced other U.S. Supreme Court justices, particularly William Rehnquist, to become more supportive of sex discrimination claims (O'Connor and Segal, 1990).

POLICY CHANGE

American women continue to express unique policy interests. Women in the workplace have child care concerns and often feel that a "glass ceiling" prevents

their advancement to top business posts. Every fifteen seconds a woman is battered; every six minutes a woman is raped (Novak, 1993). And the feminization of
poverty has left one-third of female-headed household with incomes below the
poverty line. An active government response in these areas comes close to match-
ing Democratic party positions. Yet women are not a monolithic group. Conservative women may feel that a second Bush term would have best addressed their
concerns. Even so-called women's issues can divide women: Some are pro-choice
whereas others disapprove of abortion. Thus, not every policy the Clinton administration furnishes will be welcomed by all women. Rapid changes did occur
in 1993 in the areas of child care, abortion, and women in the military. But
changes in such issues as health, education, and abortion are likely to take much
longer.

Child Care and Family Issues

Congress quickly passed the Family and Medical Leave Act of 1993, allowing
Clinton to sign the bill into law in February. The bill provides up to twelve weeks
of unpaid leave to employees who need to care for a new child or a sick family
member. It also requires businesses with more than fifty employees to hold open
the employee's position or to provide a similar position when the employee returns. A similar bill had been passed in 1992, but it was vetoed by President Bush,
who preferred a bill giving businesses incentives to provide such leaves rather
than mandating compliance. Clinton's budget, as passed by Congress, provides
additional benefits for poor families in terms of expanding income tax credits,
providing more funding for food stamps and childhood vaccinations, and instituting stronger child support enforcement procedures.

Abortion and Health Care

Two days after taking office, President Clinton, through executive orders, eliminated some of the restrictions the Reagan and Bush administrations had placed
on abortion. Clinton removed the 1988 gag rule, which prohibited physicians and
staff at federally funded women's clinics from counseling patients on abortion.
He also lifted the ban on abortions in oversees military hospitals, restored U.S.
funding to international health agencies that use some of their funds to discuss or
perform abortions, made federal funds available to medical research projects using fetal tissues, and ordered a study of the ban on the importation of RU-486,
the so-called French abortion pill.

The Freedom of Choice Act, which would prohibit states from restricting
abortions, appears unlikely to pass quickly due to divisions among supporters
and concerns over the inclusion of abortion in the president's health care package. Change has also failed to materialize with respect to the Hyde amendment,
which disallows the use of federal medicaid funds for abortions for poor women;
the amendment persists despite Clinton's endorsement of change. Indeed, congressional action has only increased the number of allowable exceptions to in-

clude pregnancies caused by rape or incest, as well as those that threaten the life of the woman. Most Democratic women in Congress voted to remove the ban, whereas most Republican women voted in favor of the Hyde amendment.

Even though U.S. laws allow abortions, access to abortions has become increasingly difficult. The number of clinics providing abortion services has declined over the past five years. And those that remain open face protests by pro-life groups. Nevertheless, Clinton and his attorney general, Janet Reno, have endorsed congressional legislation to ensure access to clinics and to protect medical personnel. This legislation passed despite opponents' fears that such a bill would violate abortion critics' freedom of speech.

American women remain divided over the abortion issue, but all women will benefit from increased research on women's health. In June 1993 Clinton signed the National Institutes of Health Revitalization Act into law. This act provides additional funds for research on breast, cervical, and ovarian cancer, on osteoporosis, and on contraception. Additionally, federally funded research on general health problems must now include women as well as male subjects, so that doctors in the future will better know how to properly treat women patients.

The Military

Women in the U.S. military have found their advancement hindered by restrictions against the notion of females in combat. But modern warfare, especially in Panama and the Persian Gulf, witnessed increasing numbers of female pilots engaged in dangerous missions. In May 1993 President Clinton's Secretary of Defense Les Aspin removed many of the restrictions against female pilots in combat. Aspin also directed the military to propose new laws that would allow women to serve on most combat ships. Gender segregation would remain only in infantry and armored tank units.

Swift action has been possible on issues of child care, abortion, and women in the military for two reasons. First, executive orders alone were capable of making some of these changes. Second, support for changes in some of these areas had already developed within other branches of the government. For instance, Congress had previously passed the Family Leave Bill. And women had already flown military aircraft as flight instructors and in combat support roles. The presence of a Democratic administration allowed for the swift legitimization of these changes. Other issues of concern to women either lack broad support or cannot be changed by executive order. These issues will be resolved by the normal political process of slow compromises. For example, bills guaranteeing educational equality for girls and curbing domestic violence were introduced in Congress in 1993 but were not expected to be passed swiftly.

THE 1994 CONGRESSIONAL ELECTIONS

The 1994 election produced few changes in the number of women office holders. Women will hold on to 11 percent of the seats in the U.S. House of Representatives. Three-quarters of these women were reelected; the remainder will be new members of Congress. One new female senator, Olympia Snowe (R–ME), will increase the total number of women in the Senate to eight. State legislatures will have approximately the same number of women representatives, about 21 percent. Only one governorship remains in the hands of a woman, although a slight increase occurred in women holding other statewide offices. Some political commentators speculated that women candidates did not fare as well in 1994 because they were not viewed as being as strong on crime as men. Yet women candidates suffered or enjoyed the fate of their party's fortune. In the Republican landslide, Republican women shared the advantages of Republican men candidates, and Democratic women lost just as Democratic men candidates did. Republicans gained seats by retaking marginal seats won by Democrats in 1992 and by fielding better-qualified candidates than the Democrats in 1994.

The gender gap in congressional voting increased in 1994. Women were eight percentage points less likely to vote for a Republican candidate than were men, according to the New York Times exit poll. This difference was larger than the three-percentage-point gender gap that appeared in congressional voting in 1990 and 1992. The increase in the gender gap did not occur because women changed their voting habits: 45 to 46 percent of women supported Republican congressional candidates in all three elections. Rather, men became more Republican in their voting patterns, moving from 49 percent Republican vote in 1990 to 54 percent Republican support in 1994. Most commentators ascribed these changes to male voters who were angry: angry that their real wages had not risen in over a decade, angry over taxes, and angry at President Clinton.

The new Congress should see Republican women chairing two congressional committees, whereas no women held such leadership positions in the 103rd Congress. Nancy Landon Kassebaum (KS) will head the Senate Labor and Human Resources Committee. In the House, Jan Meyers (KS) is expected to chair the Committee on Small Business. The one-third of female representatives and the half of female senators who are Republicans will share the powers of the new majority party. This Republican Congress will better represent the concerns of conservative women. The Republican agenda calls for requiring a balanced budget, cutting taxes, revamping the welfare system, restoring school prayer, instituting term limits, and increasing military spending.

CONCLUSIONS

The quick changes of 1993 built upon years of effort. The 1992 elections opened up opportunities for more women to win national office. And the switch from a Republican to a Democratic president allowed for shift changes in national policies concerning abortion, child care, and women's role in the military. Rapid changes also came in areas where President Clinton could use executive orders or where Congress already agreed with the new president's plans. But most major issues still require the development of a consensus between Congress and the president. Never easy, such a process is exacerbated in these times of great budgetary constraints. More women in Congress may shift the legislative agenda, giving increased weight to women's concerns, but men and women legislators and the president need to agree to pass additional policy proposals.

NOTES

1. In 1992, 6.3 million more women than men voted. Women constituted 53 percent of the voting electorate (Bendyna and Lake, 1993).

2. A gender gap first appeared in 1964, when fewer women than men supported Republican presidential candidate Barry Goldwater. It reappeared in the 1972 election (Bendyna and Lake, 1993), but no such gap existed in 1968 or 1976.

3. The term *gender gap* was coined by NOW President Eleanor Smeal (Bond, 1988).

6

Interest Groups and Political Change

FRANK R. BAUMGARTNER
JEFFERY C. TALBERT

Popular commentators often view the interest group system as a conservative force, contributing more to the maintenance of the status quo than to innovation and change. Groups receiving generous governmental subsidies mobilize to protect their privileges even well after the initial justification for such treatment has long disappeared. So we have mohair subsidies, huge stockpiles of helium, and a variety of wasteful policies that periodically are the subjects of journalistic exposé or of complaints by popular commentators. Compounding this image of government beholden to and immobilized by special interests is the perceived role of money in the electoral process. With members of Congress depending so heavily on the contributions of political action committees, it is no wonder that they reciprocate by doling out millions from the public trough for such purposes as maintaining a 100-year supply of helium (see Verhovek, 1993). Clearly, interest groups are seen as the root of government waste by many commentators, and this view is widely shared by the public. President Clinton, like many of his predecessors, has vowed to overcome the inertial forces of the interest group system. His plea for health care reform represents one of the biggest challenges in this regard, as we discuss here.

Political scientists have also often focused on the inherent conservatism of the group system. In this connection, they perceive groups as forces inhibiting change because of their ability to mobilize to protect those advantages that they have been able to gain in the past. The scholarly literature on interest groups reinforces and informs many of the popular complaints about waste and undue influence. From the scholarly point of view, we have simply multiplied our observations of the possibilities of "intensely feeling minorities" to gain advantage over "apathetic majorities," as Madison feared would happen and, indeed, as has happened throughout our history. Sugar-industry representatives, not candy-bar lovers, are present when Congress considers changes in tariff policy; computer-chip makers, not p.c. hackers, intervene when their issues are being considered;

and oil-industry executives, not motorists, dominate discussion with government officials when new regulations are being considered for that industry. Differential intensities of preference naturally and universally lead to important problems in any system of government.

There can be no doubt that an important function of interest groups is to protect themselves. No interest group leader could be considered successful if on her watch a public policy from which her group benefited were taken away. However, change does occur in the American political system. It is not completely paralyzed by groups mobilizing in opposition to every initiative a public official may take. Curiously enough, some bills do make it through the congressional gauntlet, and important policies are adopted, changed, or even discontinued. Further, interest groups are often the major proponents of political change in America. Certainly one cannot argue that the civil rights advances of the 1960s or the tighter environmental policies of the 1970s were evidence of a stranglehold by "special interests" protecting their gains from attacks by others. In those cases, the entrenched interests were utterly unsuccessful in protecting their established positions of advantage. New groups forced their way into the policy process, and the established groups were unable to countermobilize in the face of this change. Given our collective and usual understanding of the politics of entrenched "special interests," established groups benefiting from the status quo should be able to protect themselves, preventing the political system from diverting too seriously from its traditional course. In other words, industry should never have lost out to the diverse collection of environmentalists that challenged it in the 1960s and 1970s, but in fact it did. (For a more extended argument along these lines, tracing the case of nuclear power, see Baumgartner and Jones, 1991.)

A variety of elements in the American political system make it amenable to change and to influence. Yet we concentrate so heavily on the elements of stability or incrementalism in our political system that we often overlook the adaptive characteristics of the government. Frank Baumgartner and Bryan Jones (1993) describe several elements that allow powerful policy subsystems not only to become established but also to be destroyed. Much literature on incrementalism and stability focuses on the habits, patterns, and institutional structures of Congress. According to one study, for instance, even the congressional committee system, often seen as the linchpin of the Washington establishment, can sometimes be at the center of important change (Jones, Baumgartner, and Talbert, 1993).

This chapter focuses on those dynamics of interest group behavior that contribute to political change. As in other areas of policymaking, scholars and commentators have often overemphasized the degree to which interest groups create stability, protect entrenched interests, and cause paralysis in government. In many important instances, however, groups are central to political and policy change. Changes in the representation of interests over time and changes in the alliances among existing interest groups can create new opportunities for political change. When these opportunities are recognized by policymakers in a position to take advantage of them, important policy changes can indeed be adopted. This chapter considers the opportunities for political reform presented by the interest group system, comparing the situation facing President Clinton with that of some of his Democratic predecessors. We will see that opportunities are not lacking. Groups are often at the center of political change, and they are likely to be at the center of change during the Clinton administration.

GROUPS AS FORCES INHIBITING CHANGE

Much popular wisdom holds groups to be among the major forces enforcing deference to the status quo. Academic discourse on this topic has long been dominated by reference to the competing and countervailing forces of pluralism or to the differential access enjoyed by elite special interests. More popular treatments have complained about the ability of "special interests" to protect their lucrative governmental programs and privileges. But political scientists have traditionally not looked to the group system as a source of change; if anything, they see groups as blocking agents.

Pluralist Views of Countermobilization

In short, interest groups have often been seen as forces of stasis. The interactions between the mobilization of one side and the countermobilization of the other lead to relatively stable outcomes. When faced with a threat to their interests, intensely feeling minorities mobilize in order to protect themselves. In this view of the mobilization of the threatened, groups act as a mechanism to ensure equilibrium of political forces. Whenever the political context seems to be veering too far in one direction or another, those adversely affected will most assuredly recognize the threat and mobilize to counterbalance it. Pluralist visions of the group system often emphasize the importance of the potential for even the unmobilized to move into political action if their interests are threatened.

Two related findings, often repeated, combine to reinforce an image of groups as guarantors of stability. The first concerns the ability of those who are threatened with adverse actions to mobilize. The second concerns the devolvement of politics into subgovernments. Where only the self-interested experts have power, they can be counted upon in almost all circumstances to protect their interests. Considering the many opportunities in the American political system to reject change, many policy communities are remarkably efficient at protecting themselves. Each of these findings is well documented.

David Truman has been the most influential writer on interest groups to describe a system of countervailing power based on the notion of "potential groups." In Truman's view, described most eloquently in *The Governmental Process* (1951), latent groups in society will mobilize and become manifest, or active, in response to a threat. At any given time, therefore, the existing group system may demonstrate a marked bias. However, Truman argued, if this system were really harming any group in society, that group would recognize its interest in mobilization and would indeed mobilize. The threat of encouraging the uninvolved to mobilize and become active could be enough to keep politicians and other policymakers from straying too far from the perceived interests of all large potential groups. If the system ever veered too far from this equilibrium, the disaffected would mobilize to correct the course. Truman stated that the creation and growth of interest groups are likely to follow a pattern of waves, whereby each disturbance leads to the growth of certain kinds of groups to protect themselves; yet this new mobilization itself leads to further disturbances, causing further mobilizations by others (1951: 59). In the logic developed by Truman's analysis of potential groups, the continual mobilization and countermobilization of competing groups ensures that the political, economic, or social system will never deviate too far from equilibrium.

In this process, the willingness of groups to mobilize in order to protect themselves appears to be greater than the ability to mobilize in the absence of any threat. Thus groups are likely to become more active in their efforts to maintain the status quo than in any effort to achieve some new benefit. The fear of adversity or the danger of losing a position that groups currently enjoy seems to be a more urgent and powerful motivator than the desire to achieve some new goal, according to many scholars.

For instance, John Mark Hansen (1985), in describing the histories of three groups (the Farm Bureau, the League of Women Voters, and the Home Builders) over a period of more than forty years, has shown clearly that the periods of their most rapid growth and mobilization did indeed correspond to those periods in which they felt threatened. Truman's disequilibrium theory seems well confirmed by this analysis: Individuals do take into account the degree to which they feel threatened by change in deciding whether or not to join a group to protect themselves. During periods of threat, memberships increase. Farmers' groups, in particular, mobilized when they felt threatened by a declining share of the active population and in response to government policies, not when they felt strong or when they wanted to ask for new policy initiatives (Hansen, 1991).

The early Reagan years were a period of great threat to many environmental and social welfare organizations. In response to a dramatic change for the worse in the receptivity of governmental policymakers to their demands, and sometimes in reaction to outright threats to their existence, these groups mobilized massively to generate increased support. Jack Walker and Mark Peterson report, for example, that "the Reagan administration's strategic attack on opposing organizations did almost nothing to reverse the steady expansion of the group system" (Walker, 1991: 143). Even those groups that had once been relatively dependent on government contracts and grants found new sources of funding (1991: 153). Abortion-rights activists mobilized in response to threats posed by the increased activism of anti-abortion organizations and out of a fear of change in the

Supreme Court throughout the 1980s. Alissa Rubin quotes a major figure in the *Webster* case describing this strategy: "'I don't know how many more years we're going to be able to win in the courts. We've got to build a grass-roots movement and motivate millions of Americans'" (Rubin, 1991: 243).

Clearly, groups see threats to their existence or to policies they cherish as powerful mobilizing agents. Group leaders, always concerned about fund raising and membership building, know that a membership appeal that focuses on the successes of a rival group may be particularly effective in convincing potential supporters to send in a check. The ability of groups to use threats as catalysts of mobilization explains much of the ability of groups to protect the status quo. Other elements of the group system that explain this mobilization include grass-roots movements and extensive media campaigns.

In fact, grass-roots movements are much more common now than before. This is especially clear in the case of health care. One analyst has described "a frenetic nationwide effort to mobilize citizens" surrounding the Clinton health plan (Krauss, 1993). Since health care affects such a large percentage of the population, a large-scale grass-roots mobilization would be cost effective. For example, the American Medical Association (AMA) recently sent its member physicians (43 percent of the nation's doctors) instructions on how to answer questions from their patients regarding the proposed changes in the health care system. One answer explains how the proposed "cost controls may decrease your ability to choose and get some kinds of medical services" (Pear, 1993a). These efforts by the AMA are intended to mobilize not only their member physicians but all of those patients seeking health care.

The outside mobilization strategy is a means of recruiting new members; it is also used as part of a coordinated lobbying strategy. Even those groups most entrenched in the Washington beltway establishment commonly adopt such tactics. For example, former Representative Willis Gradison retired from the House of Representatives in 1993 and now directs the Health Insurance Association of America. By using his working knowledge of Congress and his ties to old friends and colleagues, Gradison has led his organization to become a major player in the health care debate. However, this powerful inside player is also behind the now infamous "Harry and Louise" national advertising campaign that depicts a middle-aged couple "fretting about big changes in health care." As Robert Toner (1994b) notes, "Gradison said he 'regrets that it was necessary' to unleash the anxious yuppies, but with a set of 'survival issues' at stake, he argues, his group had no choice." Powerful Washington lobbies are increasingly turning to television and direct-marketing strategies in coordinated efforts not only to raise money but also to enhance their influence in the legislative process.

Aside from the threat of a well-orchestrated media campaign designed to stifle policy changes, one element in the group system that encourages conservatism is its basis in professional communities. Jack Walker (1991) has shown, as have others, that most interest groups in the United States are outgrowths of occupational patterns of interaction. Groups are typically formed not with the intention of lobbying the government but, rather, for much more mundane professional reasons. Once they are formed, however, lobbying becomes significantly easier. Mancur Olson (1965) has termed this phenomenon the "by-product" theory of lobbying; and, indeed, lobbying may be a simple by-product of the formation of groups for wholly nonpolitical reasons.

Whereas the ability of groups to mobilize in response to threats makes clear that policies cannot be pushed too far in any direction before organized interests might object and mobilize, the dependence of groups on their professional or occupational communities underscores a competing element in the interest group literature. Policy communities based on shared professional interests dominate policymaking in most areas of the economy. Their importance has been so great for so long that the literature on issue networks, subgovernments, iron triangles, systems of limited participation, policy whirlpools, and sub-systems has spawned books and articles in every decade of the century (see Bentley [1908] for a good beginning, and Walker [1991] or Petracca [1992] for a review of some of these studies). Political scientists have continually noted the ability of those individuals or groups with a special expertise to dominate policymaking in their area. Since expertise comes with interest, special expertise often implies a more nefarious concept: special interest.

Mancur Olson (1965) made an important contribution to this literature by describing why Truman's idea that any threatened group could be expected to mobilize in its own defense was probably not true. Differential intensities of preference, different group sizes, and different types of group goals make some potential groups much more likely to mobilize than others. In sum, political scientists have not only thought of the group system as a guarantor of some equilibrium; they have also seen that it has inherent biases. The combination of these two traditions in the literature in fact creates a more troubling conclusion: The ability of groups to mobilize and protect their interests, coupled with the greater ability of special interests to mobilize, implies that the political system can never veer too far from its equilibrium output of favors to the "special interests." Indeed, complaints of the group system as a mechanism by which entrenched interests gain special privileges have a long history.

Complaints of Groups as Defenders of Special Privilege

Political commentators such as Ross Perot complain that "special interests" mobilize to protect their privileges and often exert undue influence in their efforts to gain special protections or benefits from the taxpayers. A wide range of scholars have backed up this complaint with studies showing that as the group system grows it can effectively paralyze the government, or rather paralyze society by encouraging an ever-larger set of government programs designed to protect some group or to regulate competition in some area of the economy. As groups make demands for new programs, few old programs are ever taken away. The result is a progressive hardening of the political arteries.

This more academic literature, with strong roots in economics, has been especially influenced by the work of Mancur Olson. The most important insight of Olson's *The Logic of Collective Action* (1965) is essentially that some potential groups have greater potential than others. Small groups seeking gains that can be allocated only to those members who agree to help support the organization can mobilize with much greater efficiency than large groups seeking benefits that will be shared by all, whether or not they have contributed to the organizational maintenance costs of the group. Olson neatly explains, therefore, why sugar manufacturers, not candy-bar lovers, are mobilized to protect their interests before government—to return to an example at the beginning of this chapter. In general, his theory elucidates why, in many industries, producers rather than consumers are likely to be well represented in government policymaking and are therefore able to extract favorable policies such as regulation, tariffs, and other barriers to competition (see also Becker, 1983).

Given this bias so elegantly explained in his 1965 book, Olson goes on to argue in *The Rise and Decline of Nations* (1982) that societies tend to accumulate more and more "special interest" groups over time. As these groups grow, multiply, and demand protection, groups representing positions of the general interest form at a slower rate or are not present at all (1982: chs. 2 and 3). Over time, governments are forced to allocate more and more of their resources to relatively inefficient subsidies, special tariffs, and regulations as a result of this biased lobbying. The net result, Olson argues, is national decline.

Whether or not one adopts the Texas twang of Ross Perot or the economic analysis of Mancur Olson, it seems clear that increasing mobilization of groups in society is a bad thing given the differential propensities of different types of groups to mobilize. Eventually the ever-increasing numbers of "special interest" groups will clog the arteries of the political and economic system, dragging the economy down through ever-increasing demands for preferential treatment.

Groups as Agents for Change

Groups do more than just ask for special treatment. In fact, the growth of the American group system over time has not been characterized by the uniformly increasing dominance of small, selective incentive groups over large, public-goods groups. Further, whatever their motives, groups often seek goals that also benefit others in society. Finally, groups are engaged in a political process whereby issues may be portrayed and understood in different ways. As the group system changes and as existing groups enter into coalitions with different allies, public issues are transformed—and not always in the predictable and selfish ways described earlier. In the following section, we discuss the growth of the group system in general but also more specifically in the areas of environmental protection and health care—two areas in which change is prominent, and in which the Clinton administration has been the most heavily involved.

THE CHANGING STRUCTURE OF THE
AMERICAN GROUP SYSTEM

If either the countermobilization theory or the Olsonian perspective were entirely accurate, we should expect to observe certain patterns in the growth and development of the group system over time. Truman's countermobilization theory calls for waves of mobilization by different types of competing groups; Olson expects more and more "special interest" groups to emerge. The range of data we review in this section shows that neither perspective is on the money.

A look at the growth of the interest group system over time reveals remarkable changes in the nature of the system. Beginning in the 1960s, the interest group system witnessed a virtual explosion of activity (Berry, 1989: 17). Increases in the number of groups, in their memberships, and in their resources have drastically transformed the interest group landscape. For instance, among the Washington organizations in 1980, 40 percent were formed after 1960 and 25 percent after 1970 (Schlozman and Tierney, 1986: 75). Moreover, the number of formal lobbyists registered in Washington has grown by a factor of ten since 1960 (Smith, 1988). In addition to the formal lobbyists on the Washington scene, many lawyers and organizations are actively involved in pressuring the government. The number of attorneys in the Washington area increased from 13,000 in 1961 to more than 51,000 by 1989 (Harris, 1993: 65). These lawyers represented a wide range of interests, from city and state organizations to country delegations, thus adding to an already overcrowded group system.

This growth characterizes not just Washington-based business and trade groups but citizen and nonprofit associations as well. For example, the Sierra Club increased its membership from 180,000 in 1980 to nearly 500,000 by 1990. During the same period Greenpeace USA achieved even greater growth: At a rate of more than 100 percent growth every year, it reached a total of 1.35 million members by 1990 (Mitchell, 1990: 92). And although the greatest number of citizen groups have been founded since 1960, they amounted to about 20 percent of the total interest group population by 1980 (Walker, 1983). This evidence points to a massive change in the group system since 1960. Thus, both the Olson and Truman theories would seem to be accurate, inasmuch as both can explain growth. However, a closer look may indicate otherwise: Neither Olson's thesis nor Truman's can explain the particular patterns of growth and expansion that we document here.

Figure 6.1 shows the growth and division of the types of interest groups in operation from 1960 to 1992, as listed in the *Encyclopedia of Associations*. Beginning with about 8,000 in 1960, the number of groups grows to a high point in 1992 of nearly 25,000. Note that, although this growth represents an overall tri-

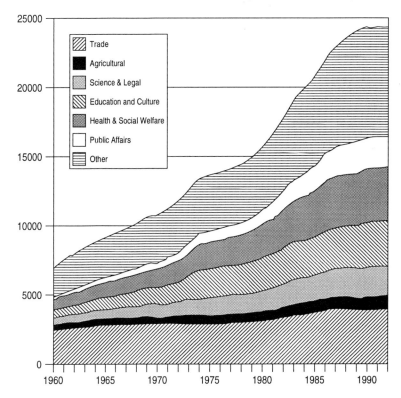

FIGURE 6.1 Growth of Associations by Type. SOURCE: Compiled from *Encyclopedia of Associations* (multiple years).

pling of the number of groups, some parts of the U.S. group system have grown much more quickly than others. Trade groups have traditionally held a position of influence in the group system, accounting for about one-third of all groups in 1960. Other types of groups have grown even faster: As shown in the figure, their absolute numbers increased from 2,400 in 1961 to more than 4,000 by 1990. (In that latter year, trade groups were reduced to only about 20 percent of the total number of groups, a dramatic decline in the relative importance of what was once the predominant type of Washington lobby organization.)

As impressive as the trade groups' growth may have been, it was far outstripped by that of other groups. The largest increases in the number of groups occurred among the health and social welfare groups and the education and culture groups. These groups increased from small numbers in the 1960s (only about 10 percent of the total) to account for about a third of the total groups by 1990. A simple glance at Figure 6.1 shows that two traditionally dominant categories of associations—trade and agriculture—have grown only slowly over the past thirty years. Every other type of association has exhibited much more rapid growth. The American group system is not static. Indeed, the mobilization of bias in the group system appears to have been greatly changed since the presidency of John Kennedy.

As noted earlier, our detailed look at the growth of various types of groups calls into question the fit of both Olson's expansion theory and Truman's countermobilization theory. Olson predicts the emergence of more and more "special interest" groups, but Figure 6.1 shows that although an overall growth of groups occurred, some clearly grew faster than others. Truman calls for waves of mobilizations by different types of groups, but Figure 6.1 indicates a more constant growth. Thus, both perspectives can account for *some* of the changes in the interest group system, but neither can account for all.

What factors could account for such increases in growth? One study suggests that the growth of the middle class in the 1960s, the increasing technology available through the communications industry, and the emergence of interest group patrons can account for some aspects of interest group expansion (Gais, Peterson, and Walker, 1984). In addition, changes in the political system should be considered, along with declining party strength and numerous institutional reforms.

One of the most interesting explanations for the rise in groups is Walker's proposal of the patron. In an attempt to overcome Olson's collective-action dilemma, Walker recommends that patrons provide the spark to mobilize interests. Such policy entrepreneurs may indeed help groups mobilize, but Walker reports that in order to ensure group maintenance, an institutional structure is needed to stabilize the group (Walker, 1991). This conclusion implies an increasing dependence on professionals to organize and operate the group.

An often-studied public-policy case attributed to interest group growth is environmental policy. Around 1970 the federal government's efforts to regulate the environment took a huge step with the enactment of the Federal Environmental Protection Act, the Clean Air Act, the Clean Water Act, the Endangered Species Act, and the Resources Conservation and Recovery Act. Using the *Encyclopedia of Associations,* we have constructed a data set that documents the growth of the interest group system surrounding environmental issues since 1960. First we located all environmental groups in the 1961 edition of the *Encyclopedia.* Then we replicated this search for 1970, 1980, and 1990 to determine how the structure of the group system changed over the thirty-year period (Baumgartner and Jones, 1993, 175–192). As others have found in their studies of environmental groups, the number of such groups more than tripled from 1961 to 1990 (Vig and Kraft, 1990; Bosso, 1987).

Table 6.1 shows this growth in the number of environmental groups. There were 119 environmental groups listed in the 1961 *Encyclopedia of Associations,* compared to 448 groups listed in 1990. The staff resources of these groups exhibit even greater growth. The increasingly professional nature of environmental

TABLE 6.1
Growth in Numbers and Staff Resources of
U.S. Environmental Interest Groups, 1961–1990

	1961	*1970*	*1980*	*1990*
Total number of groups listed in the *Encyclopedia of Associations*	119	219	390	448
Groups with 1 or more staff members	23	36	116	151
Groups with 11 or more staff members	8	16	38	50
Total staff, all groups combined	316	668	1,732	2,917

SOURCE: Data from *Encyclopedia of Associations* (multiple years), adapted by Baumgartner and Jones, 1993.

groups represents a massive mobilization. These groups are not loose coalitions of environmental zealots; rather, they have been transformed into highly professional organizations composed of attorneys, policy analysts, and other professional staff members that directly lobby federal and state policymakers. They testify at congressional hearings, supply members of Congress with valuable information, and file lawsuits against corporations, in addition to the usual grassroots efforts. The number of environmental groups with more than one full-time employee grew from only 23 in 1961 to 151 by 1990, whereas the total number of professional staff employed by environmental groups increased from 316 in 1961 to nearly 3,000 by 1990 (Baumgartner and Jones, 1993: 187). Because of this massive growth, the environmental group system has developed into an influential lobbying force. In fact, environmental groups have become one of the most active sets of interest groups.

As massive as the environmental group system may have become, the growth and size of health and medical groups are even greater. But the shape of the health care group system indicates a different type of mobilization than that of the environmental system. Whereas major changes in the activities of the federal government coincided with a massive mobilization of environmental interests throughout the 1960s and 1970s, the health care arena has long been home to a complex and crowded structure of professional associations (Laumann and Knoke, 1987).

In contrast to the environmental groups, most of which emerged only after 1960, many of the health groups were formed around the time that modern medicine began to thrive in the early twentieth century. The oldest groups, such as the American Medical Association, were founded before the expansion of medicine, but most arose in the early 1900s. For example, the American Cancer Society was founded in 1913, the American Heart Association in 1924, and the National Society to Prevent Blindness in 1908.

Walker describes the growth of various types of organizations at different times in American history. Whereas the growth of citizens' and environmental groups was especially rapid in the post-1960 period, the nonprofit sector grew significantly in the early part of the century, coinciding with the establishment of modern professions and with their national professionalization (Walker, 1983: 1991). Modern medicine was transformed by this transitional period in the early twentieth century (Starr, 1982). Most of the oldest groups—again, such as the AMA—are "professional associations." But the newer groups are more focused on claimants; consider, for example, the Muscular Dystrophy Association (MDA) created in 1950 and the Gay Men's Association created in 1982. In short, health groups encompass a much wider array of issues and types than do the environmental groups. As with the environment in the 1960s, so it is with health care in the 1990s. Changes in the interest group structure are quickly reflected in shifting governmental responses. But health care is much more politicized in the 1990s than it was in the 1960s. Further, the hegemonic position of mainstream professional associations representing physicians and other service providers has been dramatically altered. For example, the Clinton administration's health care team had initially sought the support of the AMA, the nation's largest association of doctors. But support for the AMA now seems to be wavering. Recent AMA announcements have criticized Clinton's plans for the national health spending budget, in which "physicians would be given incentives to produce less care" (Pear, 1993b). However, the power of the AMA has weakened as various medical specialists have concentrated their efforts in their own lobby groups. One of the more fundamental divisions is that between private-practice physicians and members of managed health groups. Even though private-practice physicians argue that managed care entails inferior care, HMOs (health maintenance organizations) have gained in popularity. According to one report, "although doctors worry loudly about the quality of medical care under any new system, their great unspoken concern is money" (Rosenthal, 1993). In any case, health care professionals neither speak with one voice nor are assured of the respect and deference of the public in the 1990s. These changes become clear when we look at the constellation of groups active in the health care arena.

Table 6.2 shows the growth of health groups as presented in the *Encyclopedia of Associations*. For this study, we first identified each health group in the 1990 edition of the *Encyclopedia*, listing 100 or more staff members; we then gathered data concerning their staff in 1980, 1970, and 1961.

Some of the mainstream claimant groups, such as the American Cancer Society, have remained relatively steady with about 300 staff members since 1960, but others have shown dramatic growth. For example, the MDA increased from 80 staff members in 1961 to 1,000 by 1990. This rapid growth may be explained by the MDA's use of a celebrity patron; it was also among the first health organizations to emphasize a direct fund-raising approach based on electronic media. The MDA has mobilized to a greater extent than any other claimant group, thanks to yearly fund-raising drives and to an institutional framework designed

TABLE 6.2
Growth in Staff Resources for Selected Health Care Associations, 1961–1990

Health and Medical Groups	Creation Date	Staff Sizes			
		1961	1970	1980	1990
American Medical Association	1847	700	1025	1000	1200
Muscular Dystrophy Association	1950	80	150	700	1000
American Hospital Association	1898	180	444	665	922
Committee on Accreditating Health Care Organizations	1951	a	a	a	650
Arthritis Foundation	1948	30	55	45	600
Post Graduate Center for Mental Health	1945	130	130	200	400
Jewish Guild for the Blind	1914	300	300	300	382
American Dental Association	1859	189	300	370	380
American Psychological Association	1892	55	110	170	305
American Cancer Society	1913	282	320	300	300
Braille Institute	1919	90	90	150	300
Sister Kenny Institute	1942	a	290	287	287
American Psychiatric Association	1844	40	60	130	270
Commission on Professional and Hospital Activities	1953	42	313	220	250
American Heart Association	1924	150	200	235	240
American Health Foundation	1965	b	a	230	220
American College of Physicians	1915	31	56	100	200
American Nurses Association	1896	111	170	170	186
American Society of Clinical Pathologists	1922	4	30	160	175
American Academy of Pediatrics	1930	16	50	75	172
American College of Surgeons	1913	110	117	132	170
National Board of Medical Examiners	1915	25	50	140	170
American Lung Association	1904	a	a	135	167
Christian Record Services	1899	55	110	140	165
American College of Radiology	1923	10	14	93	150
National Society to Prevent Blindness	1908	54	110	150	150
St. Jude Children's Research Hospital	1957	a	7	55	150
U.S. Pharmacopoeial Convention	1820	a	12	75	135
Helen Keller Society	1969	b	36	a	130
Medic Alert Foundation	1956	25	24	a	130
American Academy of Family Physicians	1947	71	92	115	125
American Dietetic Association	1917	11	18	91	120
National Multiple Sclerosis Society	1946	55	111	132	116
American Diabetes Association	1940	22	22	55	110
American Society of Hospital Pharmacists	1942	a	38	80	110
National Sanitation Foundation	1944	45	45	70	110
American Academy of Ophthalmology	1896	1	5	8	102
Catholic Hospital Association	1915	52	60	65	101
Alzheimer's Association	1980	b	b	a	100
American College of Health Executives	1933	a	a	40	100
Gay Men's Association	1982	b	b	b	100
Total		2966	4964	7083	11150

[a]Missing data.

[b]Association has yet to be created.

SOURCE: This table lists all those health groups reporting 100 or more staff in the *Encyclopedia of Associations* (1990).

to allocate research funding and financial support to patients. This pattern may become more common as groups increasingly take advantage of new communications technologies.

In fact, we can see from the current health care debate just how common these outside strategies have become (Pear, 1993b; Kolbert, 1994; Brinkley, 1993a, 1993b; Toner, 1994b). This debate, according to one observer, has prompted the "largest mobilization [of interest groups] since the establishment of Social Security" (Mankiewicz, quoted in Krauss, 1993). A look at the interest group system in this context shows the enormous resources available, but also the divisions.

Overall, the staff of the large health groups increased from a total of about 3,000 in 1961 to more than 11,000 in 1990. Compared with the environmental groups' total staff of 3,000 for 1990, the health groups' staff seem to have much more lobbying power. Thus, President Clinton faces a group system for health care that has nearly twice the resources than that which faced President Carter. Related to this change is a new definition of the health care problem in the United States: In addition to providing more health benefits, health reform is now aimed at curbing the rising cost of treatment. As new groups mobilize, new definitions of old issues become more convincing. For example, Mark Peterson finds that the once-solidified health care groups have begun to disintegrate due to the increasing pressures of reform (Peterson, 1993: 411). Indeed, old allies have become new competitors as the group system adapts to the changes of the 1990s. The best example of this split is found among insurance groups. The largest insurance companies are in a position to benefit from health care reform, whereas the smaller companies would be put out of business by such reform (Toner, 1994a).

Our evidence has provided a look at the growth of the interest group system since 1960, both overall and in two particular areas of concern. This growth reflects more than just increased membership and numbers; indeed, it represents a change in group structure such that professional employees and organizations are now included.

NEW OPPORTUNITIES FOR POLICY CHANGE

In this chapter we have considered changes in the interest group system over the past thirty years. These changes have been dramatic and far-reaching. They have affected virtually every area of the interest group system and have been noted by a variety of commentators. As we have shown, these changes have affected two important aspects of the political system: Environmental and health care policies are now made in policy networks that feature a great diversity of interests well represented in the Washington corridors of power.

Like every president before him, President Clinton arrived in Washington with a new set of constraints and opportunities presented to him by the interest group system. John Kennedy might not have thought of changing the fees for grazing cattle on public lands in the west, but if he had thought of it, the political power of the 316 staff members of the environmental interest groups present in Washington at the time of his inauguration would have been vastly overtaken by that of the ranching interests. In the period between these two Democratic presidencies, however, many changes have occurred. The growth of the environmental movement has brought many fresh ideas into the political mainstream, along with numerous skilled and knowledgeable environmental staff members and activists.

Similarly, in the area of health, a great variety of interests, not just those representing the major physician groups, are active in promoting some kind of reform. These interests promote, rather than oppose, change in Washington policies by encouraging the exchange of ideas and the building of coalitions with others outside the immediate area. This is particularly true in the area of health care reform. In a policy area as huge and as costly as that of health, issues cannot be said to affect only a single, self-interested, homogeneous group of "special interests." Rather, many different interests are mobilized in competition for public attention and policy influence. The coalitions possible at one point in time depend not only on the existing set of groups in a given area but also on the ability of these groups to define issues in such a way as to appeal to potential allies in related fields. As shown in this chapter, long-term trends have led to important changes in the distribution of interests represented in the nation's interest group system. Far from representing only certain kinds of interests, as might be expected from Olson's analysis, a great variety of groups are present in Washington.

More important, perhaps, than the sheer numbers of interest groups are their coalitional behavior and opportunities. Lobbying on important public issues is not limited to individual groups. Rather, groups form alliances. As one alliance appears to be gaining support, a rival alliance may view it as a threat and mobilize to protect itself. This outcome would be the expected one according to the traditional view of mobilization and countermobilization leading to stability. However, there is another possibility. When making decisions about which issues to work on, groups naturally hope to work on those that promise some chance of success. Then, initial successes beget further successes, as more groups decide that it may be worth their effort to contribute to a joint lobbying effort. If we conceive of groups acting independently, we can see evidence of countermobilization. However, if we add the dynamic by which a group chooses whether to join a particular alliance, then we have a much more plausible explanation for instability and change through the group system. As issues become "hot," many groups enter the fray. These groups are not just trying to halt the potential changes in government policy that they observe; they may be motivated to join in precisely because they see some initial success and want to push the issue even further. Some may prefer to be on the winning side, hoping to be better able to influence the outcome of legislation if they support some kind of reform than if they are labeled obstructionist. There is clear evidence in the health care debate that many groups fear being left behind. Thus, once momentum builds toward reform, the dynamics of interest group lobbying can encourage, rather than discourage, political change. Groups can mobilize to inhibit change or they can mobilize to create further change. Some political scientists have demonstrated the efforts of groups to slow change. In this chapter we have attempted to show how the group system can also encourage change.

PART II

Political Institutions
and Political Change

7

The Return to Unified Party Control Under Clinton: How Much of a Difference in Lawmaking?

DAVID R. MAYHEW

Does American national lawmaking flourish under conditions of unified party control, yet come to a "gridlocked" halt under conditions of divided control?[1] Surprisingly, perhaps, the general answer for modern times is no—at least according to a study I have recently conducted on the post–World War II legislative record from 1946 to 1990 (Mayhew, 1991). The pattern of partisan configurations during those decades allows a convenient test. One party simultaneously controlled the presidency, the House, and the Senate for twenty-six years—under Truman (1949–1952), Eisenhower (1953–1954), Kennedy-Johnson (1961–1968), and Carter (1977–1980). And party control was divided for twenty-six years—under Truman (1947–1948), Eisenhower (1953–1960), Nixon-Ford (1969–1976), Reagan(1981–1988), and Bush (1989–1990). I canvassed the history of those forty-four years from 1946 to 1990 for instances of major legislative initiatives passed by Congress and signed by the president (or, in a few cases, enacted over presidential vetoes or not needing presidential assent—as with constitutional amendments). By "major" legislative initiatives I meant those both innovative and consequential—or at least believed likely, at the time of passage, to be consequential. The evidence was unavoidably rather soft, but I tried to be systematic. The canvass consisted of two independent sweeps through the history of these forty-four years. The first relied on contemporary accounts, chiefly those of journalists writing congressional end-of-session "wrap-up" stories, that cited enactments thought by the Washington community to be major initiatives. The second relied on judgments by specialists in forty-three policy areas, writing chiefly in the 1980s, about which laws enacted in their areas during the preceding decades had proven to be major initiatives (Mayhew, 1991: ch. 3).

The result was a list of 267 arguably major laws—or about 12 per Congress. At the beginning of the list, for example, are the Taft-Hartley Labor-Management Relations Act of 1947, the Water Pollution Control Act of 1948, and the Marshall Plan of 1948; at the end are the Clean Air Act of 1990, the Immigration Act of 1990, and Bush's $482 billion deficit-reduction package of 1990 (Mayhew, 1991: ch. 4).

The twenty-two Congresses varied considerably in their yields of major laws—ranging from, for example, a meager 5 laws during Eisenhower's last Congress of 1959–1960 (an often-analyzed time of divided party control) to a substantial 22 laws during Johnson's Great Society Congress of 1965–1966 (a very-often-analyzed time of unified party control).[2] The latter years were the source of, among other items, the Voting Rights Act of 1965 and Medicare. Overall, however, during these forty-four years, there proved to be a vanishingly small difference— if any at all—in lawmaking yield between the times of unified control and the times of divided control. It was just about a wash (Mayhew, ch. 4 and pp. 175–179).

CONSTANCY AND VARIATION IN LAWMAKING

If one speculates as to *why* the result might have turned out to be a wash, at least two categories of answer seem to apply. First, despite the variation in lawmaking yield among individual Congresses, some factors seem to push toward *constancy* of action across Congresses regardless of conditions of unified or divided control. They help to "even out" lawmaking across those conditions. For one thing, real-world events that occur more or less randomly can quickly trigger such enactments as the Marshall Plan, the Gun Control Act of 1968 (just after the assassinations of Martin Luther King, Jr., and Senator Robert Kennedy), the Coal Mine Safety Act of 1969 (just after a West Virginia mining disaster), and the savings-and-loan bailout of 1989 (Mayhew, 1991: 136–139). For another, public-opinion cleavages that crosscut party lines can foster lawmaking during divided control or suppress it during unified control. Consider, for example, the pattern of civil rights acts passed in 1957, 1960, and 1970 (under divided control) and in 1964, 1965, and 1968 (under unified control); in all six cases, a majority of southern Democrats voted against majorities of both Republicans and northern Democrats on Capitol Hill. That was the underlying politics (Mayhew, 1991: 139–141). Another factor is that largely the same electoral incentives impinge on incumbent members of Congress regardless of conditions of party control. If getting his or her name connected with passing a bill appears likely to help a House or Senate member, then that bill may get passed—regardless of whether the same party holds the White House and Congress (Mayhew, 1991: 102–110). Finally, it is generally difficult, regardless of conditions of party control, to pass laws by narrow congressional majorities; refractory committees, lack of party discipline, presidential veto threats, looming filibusters, or the sheer complexity of Capitol Hill processes can intrude. Such matters as these can put a crimp in "party government" blueprints, even in what would seem to be the most favorable of circumstances—as in 1977–1978, when the Democrats held the White House and immense congressional majorities but faltered at lawmaking anyway (Mayhew, 1991: 119–135).

The second category of answer points to factors causing *alternative variation* in lawmaking results over time—that is, alternative to patterns of results that might stem from changing conditions of party control. Whether one party controls all the elective national institutions at once is not, after all, the only background condition that varies and might count. For one thing, in a pattern that is impressively regular during 1946–1990, even if not of momentous importance, more major lawmaking gets done during the first two years of a four-year presidential term than during the latter two years. The only exception was the period from 1985 to 1988—Reagan's second term—when Democratic House Speaker Jim Wright succeeded in driving a considerable program through Congress in 1987–1988 (Mayhew, 1991: 118–119, 178). In addition, presidents can vary in skill as legislative leaders. During 1946–1990, it is probably no accident that exceptionally ambitious programs were enacted in the mid-1960s under the consummate wheeler-and-dealer Johnson and in 1981 under the unsurpassed popular charmer Reagan. Truman, Kennedy, and Carter enjoyed Democratic congressional majorities—Carter in 1977 had more northern Democrats in the House than Johnson in 1965—but that did not do them much good. As a mobilizer of Congress or the public, none of the three was in Johnson's or Reagan's league (Mayhew, 1991: 112–117). Finally, still under the rubric of alternative variation, nothing stands out more in the postwar record than the surge of hyper-legislating that extended from roughly 1963 through 1975–1976 and is arguably attributable to a "public mood" (though the evidence is wispy). Political, movement-driven activism among the American public during the 1960s and 1970s is sometimes compared to that during the Progressive era or the New Deal.[3] During the most recent of these three putative "moods," a thrust toward increased government spending and regulation went into high gear under Johnson and stayed there under Nixon and Ford, despite a shift to divided party control after the 1968 election. Ambitious laws kept getting passed. Key enactments under Nixon or Ford included the Occupational Safety and Health Act (OSHA) of 1970, the Clean Air Act of 1970, a 23 percent Social Security hike in 1972, the Supplementary Security Income (SSI) program in 1972, the Water Pollution Control Act of 1972, the Federal Election Campaign Act of 1974, and the Housing and Community Development Act of 1974 (Mayhew, 1991: 81–89, 133–174, 177). In short, temporal variations in presidential leadership skill, phases of the presidential election cycle, or the incidence of "public moods" may all occur independent of, and help to "even out," lawmaking across conditions of unified as opposed to divided party control.

The study under discussion, it should be emphasized, concerns legislative motion—namely, the question of whether much notable lawmaking gets done at all. It does not directly address legislative direction—that is, whether the thrust of the laws is toward the left or the right. On the matter of direction, the obvious and conventional view is no doubt correct: that in general, in passing laws, Democrats push to the left and Republicans to the right. But the record of 1946–1990 suggests that this conventional view needs some tailoring also—even if it is generally correct. This is at least because "public moods" can override any predictive arithmetic based on which party holds which offices and on the parties' customary ideological propensities. In the areas of domestic spending and regulation, for example, the legislative initiatives of the Nixon-Ford years decisively surpassed those of the Truman, Kennedy, or Carter years. (It is not enough to denominate an era the "Fair Deal" or the "New Frontier," for the label may not describe very much.) To cite another example, the chief lawmaking theme under Carter, if one looks at measures actually passed, was probably deregulation of industry—the airlines, natural gas prices, the railroads, banking, and trucking. That is an odd emphasis for a Democratic president sharing power with a Democratic Congress, but it evidently responded to a post-mid-1970s "mood" that came into full bloom later under Reagan. The records during these various presidential eras—as well as the transitions between them—offer the lesson that the ideological direction of national lawmaking, like the quantity of it, may not correspond as neatly as we would expect to conventionally posited formulas of party control.

THE CLINTON ERA

With respect to current events, the Clinton era obviously offers an interesting test of whether conditions of party control cause a difference in lawmaking. Not only is unified control back in place, after twelve years, but the currently ruling Democratic party has evolved during the last two decades into an unusually cohesive coalition. With southern blacks enfranchised and southern Republicanism on the rise, the new breed of southern Democrats on Capitol Hill has shifted toward party loyalty. On average they are still Democrats with a difference, but the old days of Mississippi's James O. Eastland and Virginia's Howard Smith seem to have gone forever. Especially since the mid-1980s, the Democratic party has been displaying a level of solidarity on Capitol Hill that we have not seen in decades. Thus, given the Democrats' presidential and congressional victories in November 1992, conditions have seemed auspicious for a notable exercise of "party government."

What has happened early in the Clinton administration—that is, as of this writing in October 1993? Has the unified-party-control variable resurrected itself into significance under Clinton? Not yet. So far, it is hard to see how the Clinton era presents an off-the-charts record of lawmaking either in motion or in direction. Regarding motion pure and simple, four new measures have become law so far that would very likely qualify as notable initiatives using the tests outlined earlier. These are the laws addressing family leave, the "motor voter" measure, national service, and deficit reduction.[4] Journalists have portrayed the first three as genuine innovations, and the last is of course the White House's signal legislative achievement to date. Is this an exceptional record? Not really. It is within the ordinary range—regardless of conditions of party control—for the beginning of a presidential term. It looks good against the last two years of Bush's presidency, but remember that the first halves of presidential terms routinely score higher in legislative productivity than the second halves.[5] We are certainly not witnessing a burst of hyper-lawmaking like those under Franklin Roosevelt in 1933 or 1935 or under Johnson in 1965. And all things considered, given the way Congress watered down Clinton's budget plan, we are not seeing legislative innovation on the order of Reagan's in 1981. The best analogues may be the records under Truman in 1949, Kennedy in 1961, and Carter in 1977. That is, there have been solid achievements but also delays, losses, unhappy compromises, and disappointments. Things have not gone easily. In July 1993, after six months in the White House and frustrated particularly by the treatment of his budget, Clinton assailed a Congress run by his own party for exhibiting legislative "gridlock" (Devroy, 1993).

If we consider ideological direction as well as motion, what seems to stand out in 1993 is the continuity from the Reagan-Bush years demonstrated so far in actual lawmaking under Clinton. To be sure, as under Truman in 1949 and Kennedy in 1961, there has been an expected, detectable drift to the left. The family leave, "motor voter," and national service measures would almost certainly not have passed under a Republican presidency, and high-bracket income taxes would not have gone up so much as they did in the 1993 budget package. But this drift to the left needs to be kept in perspective. For one thing, family leave, looked at from one plausible perspective, is just one more in a sequence of rather strenuous moves to regulate industry that have won enactment in recent years (Weidenbaum, 1991). It joins the Americans with Disabilities Act of 1990, the Clean Air Act of 1990, and the Civil Rights Act of 1991. For whatever reasons, the antiregulatory drive so evident under Carter and Reagan seems to have come to an end in the late 1980s, and the government is enacting regulatory instruments under Bush and Clinton.

For another thing, there exists a class of proposals that were not enactable under Reagan or Bush and that still, despite Democratic control and much early optimism, do not seem to be enactable now—or, at best, are enactable only in quite attenuated form. A Freedom of Choice Act (that is, a proabortion charter) was supposed to be a priority item once the Democrats took over; as of fall 1993, however, it remained a dream owing to a lack of Capitol Hill votes (Clymer, 1993a). It would probably be unwise to bet a great deal that a "striker replacement" bill—a high-priority union aim—will make it through the 103rd Congress. Gays in the military, once that issue reached Congress in 1993, eventuated in a result not to Clinton's liking but rather at the congressional median view; probably the outcome would have been about the same in previous Congresses if the subject had arisen then. Confronted by a sagging economy, both Bush and Clinton asked Congress to enact an economic "stimulus" package; Congress said no both times (in 1992 and 1993, respectively).[6] As for attenuated form, today as under Reagan and Bush, both Congress and the president have to operate under budgetary stringency. In this circumstance, there can be a tendency to enact high-sounding plans and then to underfinance them. This pattern could be sensed in Jim Wright's ample program during 1977–1988 (e.g., in the measures regarding housing, the homeless, and welfare reform), and we are seeing it again with respect to the new national-service program.

Then there is Clinton's 1993 centerpiece—the Deficit-Reduction Act passed in August after months of anxiety, exhortation, and bargaining. From an ideological, programmatic standpoint, this measure originated as a near-counterpart to Reagan's 1981 budget, which drastically sliced taxes and domestic spending. Clinton's budget, like Reagan's, started out as an equally ambitious albeit very different party program. But once shorn by Congress of its innovative energy tax plus much of its "investment" and social-welfare spending, the Clinton plan receded to the status of a more or less ordinary deficit-reduction instrument. It is the fifth such instrument we have seen since 1981 (the earlier ones came in 1982, 1984, 1987, and 1990), or the seventh if we include the measures aimed at balancing the accounts of the Social Security program in 1977 and 1983 (Birnbaum, 1993).

Despite Republican claims, the 1993 Deficit-Reduction Act did not set a record for raising taxes; that distinction, if one calculates in constant dollars, goes to the bipartisan Deficit-Reduction Act of 1982. Despite Democratic claims, the 1993 act stopped well short of setting a record for reducing the deficit. That distinction goes to Bush's deficit-reduction measure of 1990, as amended by congressional Democrats, which took a five-year $482 billion bite. What with inflation, Clinton's measure would have needed a $532 billion reduction to match the 1990 act. In fact, the 1993 instrument seems to have taken a new five-year bite of between $432 billion and $477 billion, depending on assumptions about whether some of its savings had already been included in the 1990 act.[7] In general, there is a striking resemblance between the 1990 and 1993 measures—notwithstanding their differing origins under divided and unified party control.[8] The 1993 act raised the top-bracket income tax rate from 31 percent to 36 percent—with a surcharge on the exceptionally wealthy that pushed the figure to 39.6 percent. But the 1990 act had already reached for the affluent by raising the rate from 28 percent to 31 percent. (In retrospect, it seems clear that the low top-bracket rate proudly established by the Tax Reform Act of 1986 was just sitting there as a target; it survived only four years of real political life.) The 1993 act, like that of 1990, relied heavily on post–Cold War defense cuts. Foreign aid continued to fall off, though Clinton—like Bush, driven by events—has asked for and gotten subsidies for the ex–Soviet Union (Doherty, 1993; Robbins, 1993). In the 1993 act, as in the 1990 one, congressional discretionary spending was capped; Medicare payments to providers (though not to beneficiaries) were slashed; social-welfare sweeteners, notably a hike in the earned income tax credit (EITC) to low-income workers, were included; and the gas tax went up—by 5 cents in 1990 and by another 4.3 cents in 1993. "It tells you a lot about the politics of deficit reduction," former CBO director Rudolph G. Penner remarked. "Regardless of who controls the government, you are pushed in the same direction."[9] Of course, more lawmaking is under way in the 103rd Congress. Parts of the Hatch Act are about to be repealed. Immigration law may be overhauled (as it was in 1986 and 1990). Familiar coalitional churning may yet generate actual results this time in the areas of campaign finance, crime, and education reform. And NAFTA, the North American Free Trade Agreement, remains at this date a pressing agenda item.

Above all, there is Clinton's health plan—which by any standard offers the current Congress its chief opportunity to make a historic legislative breakthrough. This may be an idea whose time has arrived: Virtually everyone, including the business community, has come to agree that runaway medical costs need to be reined in and that health insurance needs to be made portable and universally available. Yet it is hard to watch the politics so far without recalling certain other major legislative enterprises of recent times. Comparably aimed at reorganizing a large sector of the U.S. economy was Carter's ambitious energy plan of 1977—the centerpiece of the early part of his presidency—which fared well on Capitol Hill in its early days but then came apart as a result of ideological and interest group wrangling in a Democratic Senate in 1978. (A much-revised plan did pass.) And there is an ominous possible analogy to Reagan's budget package of 1981—with Ira Magaziner playing the role of David Stockman this time. That is, one way for a president to maneuver through Congress an immense, expensive, and highly popular legislative initiative during a time of budgetary stringency—the tax cut then, health reform now—is to deny that it will cost any money.[10]

The return to unified party control under Clinton, in short, does not seem to be causing more of a difference—at least in lawmaking—than that party configuration has generally caused during recent decades. Some of the likely reasons were suggested earlier. Events can intrude regardless of conditions of party control—as when both Bush and Clinton needed to subsidize the ex–Soviet republics. Crosscutting opinion cleavages can intrude—as do the divisions within the Democratic party that cloud action on NAFTA and abortion. Also, U.S. national institutions do not provide an easy majority-rule system, even if one party seems to be controlling all branches: Much as Republican presidential vetoes (threatened or actual) shaped legislative outcomes under Reagan and Bush, Republican Senate filibusters (threatened or actual) have been shaping results under Clinton. Filibustering killed Clinton's economic stimulus package, forced a revision of the "motor voter" measure, and could yet kill the striker-replacement and campaign-finance measures.

In addition, presidential skill is a scarce commodity: As a manipulator of Congress or the public with the goal of enacting laws, Clinton does not seem to be in a league with Reagan, Johnson, or the Roosevelts. Hence the lack of that kind of exceptional pressure for action in 1993. Another factor is that budget-balancing problems have overhung every presidency and Congress since the mid-1970s, including the current ones, and thus have continually impinged on lawmaking. As much as anything, perhaps, there does not exist right now an activist "public mood" of the sort that has underpinned the major U.S. lawmaking drives of the twentieth century. This is not 1965 or 1970. Across the OECD world today, the only kind of cause that seems to engage the public that intensely is reform of political institutions and processes—as witnessed here in Perot's candidacy and the legislative term-limits drive.

A final idea derives from the pronounced similarity between Clinton's chief legislative victory so far—his deficit-reduction plan, as amended—and other deficit-reduction measures of recent times. Much as we academics like to advance models of politics that posit individuals or groups with fixed, distinctive preferences and then predict outcomes that vector from those preferences, policymaking may not always work that way. There seems to exist a class of policy areas in which, over time, outcomes prove to be more or less constant but their underpinning coalitional structures vary. In these areas, something like a "reason-of-state" frame of mind located in a Washington, D.C., elite seems to override, when necessary, conventional party or constituency preferences. Thus, for example, foreign-aid bills used to attract just Democratic support under Truman, but once Eisenhower took office in 1953, the roll-call basis for foreign aid switched to bipartisan (Kesselman, 1961). A similar story concerns the custom of raising the national-debt ceiling; that looks bad back home, but Congress needs to vote every now and then to do it. In general, to cite one recent span of history, majorities of both Democrats and Republicans backed such debt-ceiling hikes under Eisenhower, just Democrats did it under Kennedy and Johnson, but both Democrats and Republicans did it again under Nixon.[11] For the Republicans, at least, much depended on which party held which offices. Deficit reduction in the 1980s and 1990s looks like a replay of these tendencies. The Senate's Republicans actually took the lead in deficit reduction when they controlled that chamber during 1981–1986.[12] In 1990, under Bush, the coalitional basis for deficit reduction was bipartisan; the White House and Senate Minority Leader Bob Dole cooperated, after a fashion, with Congress's Democratic majority. But in 1993, as with foreign aid and the debt ceiling at earlier junctures of unified party control, the Democrats had to act by themselves. Republican support vanished. Largely the same outcome resulted, but there was a fresh coalitional grounding for it.

CONCLUSIONS: POSTSCRIPT, JANUARY 1994

As of the close of 1993, three measures enacted late in the year seem to merit designation as "major" alongside the four measures already discussed.[13] Revision of the Hatch Act made it easier for federal government employees to participate in politics—an innovation that, like family leave, the "motor voter" measure, and national service, would almost certainly not have come about if Bush had been reelected. After a six-year campaign, the "Brady Bill," which requires a waiting period for handgun purchases, finally passed in November. Critical to this victory—and contributing to the reluctance of the Senate Republicans to wage an all-out blocking filibuster in the glare of the media—was sharply rising public concern about crime in late 1993 (Rogers, 1993).

Most important, NAFTA won House and Senate approval in November 1993 after an intensive drive by the White House, Republican leaders, and many Democrats against an opposition centered in the labor movement and the majority of Democrats on Capitol Hill—including the party's House Majority Leader and Whip. It was a classic bipartisan victory, though with a Republican tinge: Of the 267 major post–World War II enactments referred to earlier,[14] only 2 resembled NAFTA in drawing support for final passage from Republican majorities in both the House and Senate but opposition from Democratic majorities in both chambers. (These were the Twenty-Second Amendment limiting presidents to two terms, approved by Congress in 1947, and the Gramm-Rudman-Hollings Act mandating deficit reduction, enacted in 1985). NAFTA, originated by Bush, supplies an exceptionally clear case of policy continuity across administrations of different parties. It is also a good instance of "reason-of-state": Nearly every president since Hoover, regardless of party, has promoted free-trade policies largely successfully against resistance in Congress, although the resistance in 1993 was unusually spirited. In the area of foreign-trade policy Clinton brings to mind Eisenhower, who during his first term likewise had better luck with the opposition party in Congress than with his own (Bauer, Pool, and Dexter, 1963).

As suggested earlier, the full 1993 legislative year, judged for productivity, seems to belong in a category with the immediate post-presidential-election years under Truman in 1949, Kennedy in 1961, and Carter in 1977—that is, reasonably productive but not in a class with Johnson's year of 1965 or Reagan's of 1981. Like Clinton, Truman in 1949 presided over one particularly important domestic accomplishment (the Housing Act of 1949), one path-breaking foreign policy move (ratification of NATO), and a few lesser though still listable enactments. The 1961 session under Kennedy brought enactments on housing, area redevelopment, minimum wage, Social Security, agriculture, foreign aid, and arms control. Under Carter in 1977 came measures on strip-mining, agriculture, minimum wage, clean air, clean water, Social Security financing, and a tax cut. Inferior to the 1993 record was that under Eisenhower in 1953. Despite recent reports of an all-time "presidential-support-score" peak under Eisenhower that year (Birtel, 1993), virtually no important laws actually passed. That is chiefly because Eisenhower, unlike any other recent president operating under unified party control, passed up advancing a legislative program during his first year after election. Once he settled on one, the results were ample enough in 1954—measures addressing social security, tax revision, housing, atomic energy, agriculture, and the St. Lawrence Seaway (Reichard, 1975).

Reagan's 1981 session aside, the 1993 legislative year cannot easily be compared to post-presidential-election years during circumstances of divided party con-trol—that is, those under Eisenhower in 1957, Nixon in 1969 and 1973, Reagan in 1985, and Bush in 1989. That is because—to add one more statistical wrinkle to all the above—legislative enactments tend to cluster in the *first* year of a post-presi-dential-election Congress under unified party control (Eisenhower in 1953 is the exception) but in the *second* year under divided control (Reagan in 1981 is the exception). This disparity may occur because, under conditions of divided con-trol, an upfront "hundred days" script is harder for presidents to invoke, and also because, under those conditions, Capitol Hill compromises take longer to work out. The pattern of second-year action under divided control is evident in, for example, the Clean Air Act and OSHA in 1970, the Tax Reform Act of 1986, and Bush's omnibus Deficit-Reduction Act of 1990—which took a year longer to ar-range than Clinton's comparable act.

Heading into 1994, the Clinton White House has resolutely set out to break the mold for second-year lawmaking. Since the mid-1930s—a fitting comparison because the "Lameduck" amendment to the Constitution paved the way then for each Congress to meet during the now-familiar two full successive calendar years—no freshly elected Democratic president operating under unified party control has gotten his way with Congress on domestic policy during his *second* postelection year in office—never mind after the midterm. For Franklin Roose-velt, despite huge Democratic congressional majorities, 1938 brought a bitter, los-ing confrontation over executive reorganization. Truman's Fair Deal lost out to McCarthyism and war in 1950. Kennedy's chief domestic aspirations—Medicare, aid to education, civil rights—stayed unaddressed through 1962. The Vietnam War and city rioting hobbled Johnson's Great Society in 1966. And the Senate disassembled Carter's high-priority energy program in 1978. Many kinds of things have gone wrong. The record to date of presidents' second-year program-matic drives is indeed grim, though, to be sure, Clinton enjoys a more unified congressional party than did these earlier Democrats.

NOTES

1. This chapter was adapted from a presentation at a roundtable on "The Causes and Consequences of Divided and Unified Government," at the annual meeting of the Amer-ican Political Science Association, September 2, 1993.

2. See, for example, Sundquist, 1968.

3. See, for example, Schlesinger, 1986: 31–34; and Huntington, 1981: ch. 7 On "public moods needs" during recent decades, see Stimson, 1991.

4. There is a category of acts, nineteen in number, that is given special mention in Mayhew's *Divided We Govern* (1991: 74) because contemporaries seemed to judge them to be not just important but historically important. Clinton's deficit-reduction measure surely belongs in that category—joining Bush's budget-reduction measure of 1990.

5. The second half of Bush's term in 1991–1992 does not figure in *Divided We Govern*'s data for 1946–1990. Yet its lawmaking record is not out of line with the results of the forty-

four-year study. It is about what one would have expected, given that 1991–1992 took place during the second half of a presidential term but not during an activist "public mood."

6. This comparison is drawn in Stein, 1993.

7. These are Congressional Budget Office (CBO) data. At the time of its passage, the 1993 measure was advertised as offering a $496 billion bite. But that figure sagged after later CBO calculations, which allowed for alternative assumptions about whether certain savings specified earlier in 1990 were now being double-counted. See Hager, 1993c; and Rosenbaum, 1993.

8. See Hager, 1993b; Wessel, 1993; Yang, 1993; and *New York Times, 1993.*

9. Penner, quoted in Hager, 1993b: p. 2130.

10. On the economics of the Clinton plan, see Chandler, 1993.

11. Assembled from *Congress and the Nation, 1945–1964,* 1965: 393–395; *Congress and the Nation, 1965–1968,* 1969: 127–140; *Congressional Quarterly Almanac, 1966,* 1967: 714, 886, 953; *Congressional Quarterly Almanac, 1967,* 1968: 316–322, 38-H, 48-H, 28-S, 7-S, S-S, 28-S; *Congress and the Nation, 1969–1972,* 1973: 64–75; *Congressional Quarterly Almanac, 1970,* 1971: 293–295, 30-H, 32-S.

12. See, for example, Hager, 1993a.

13. For assessments of the full 1993 legislative season, see Calmes and Harwood, 1993; Clymer, 1993b, Dewar and Cooper, 1993; and Hook, 1993.

14. To the total of 267 measures listed for 1946–1990 (see Mayhew, 1991: ch. 4), 14 now need to be added, using the same methodology as nearly as possible: 7 measures for Bush's second Congress of 1991–1992 and 7 for Clinton's first year.

8

Political Change in the States: Another Example of Unintended Consequences?

MORRIS P. FIORINA

At first glance the 1992 elections dovetailed nicely with the theme of this collection: political change.[1] According to some, the elections put an end to a quarter-century of Republican presidential dominance, during which Republican candidates were victorious in five of six presidential elections, winning, on average, 55 percent of the two-party popular vote and more than 75 percent of the electoral vote. Against that background Bill Clinton's breaking of the Republican "lock" on the electoral college was the obvious lead story. Others saw a related but broader story in the 1992 outcome. Especially for Democratic politicos, many of whom made it their campaign theme, the elections put an end to "the new era of coalition government" (Sundquist, 1988), during which Republican presidents typically faced Democratic Congresses allegedly producing, in Keith Krehbiel's (1993) pithy summation, "bitter partisanship, poor governmental performance, policy incoherence, nondecisions, showdowns, standoffs, checkmate, stalemate, deadlock, and in the most recent nomenclature, *gridlock*."

Academics have been more hesitant to embrace "change" as the lesson of 1992. Clinton's 43 percent popular vote total was the most obvious and important reason—and the exceptional showing of an independent candidate, Ross Perot, was another significant reason—for reserving judgment on this point. But a more general reason for our uncertainty is simply that a look at the broader picture suggests at most interruption, not change. For one thing, Democrats lost 10 seats in the House of Representatives, a loss that many observers believe would have been larger had not President Bush's poor showing kept the Republicans from realizing some of their expected gains from reapportionment. The 1994 midterm elections will shed empirical light on this belief.

Elections in the states, too, suggest little in the way of systematic change. The era of divided government that has characterized national politics since the 1950s has been equally evident in the states, inasmuch as partisan control of governorships and legislatures grew increasingly disjoint over the same period. The 1992 elections that brought unified control back to Washington changed little in the states. Before the elections, twenty-one states were under unified party control; after the elections, eighteen states were. [Twenty were under unified party control after the 1994 elections.—ed.] The usefulness of that comparison is limited by the fact that only a quarter of the states now hold their gubernatorial elections in presidential years; but even looking only at the dozen states fully exposed to the short-term forces of the national campaign, we find that seven came out of the elections unified (three Republican, four Democratic), whereas the others were divided.[2] Divided government still is common in the states.

In short, change is the implication of the 1992 vote only if we limit our attention to the election for president. Surely that is the most important election in America, and we cannot discount what it reveals. But it is equally certain that looking only at presidential elections—or only at national elections, for that matter—can give us a skewed perspective on American politics. Based on that premise I have concentrated my recent research on state elections. Change is the focus of this research, albeit change over a relatively long period. In seeking to explain some aspects of that change I have become more aware of factors that not only help to explain change at the state level but, ironically, also help to explain stability at the national level—specifically, stability in the partisan composition of the House of Representatives. Moreover, some of the factors underlying electoral change in the states are "nonpolitical" in the usual partisan or ideological sense, reminding us that political change may have its roots in nonpolitical processes that are indirect and subtle in their operation and therefore easy for us to overlook.

AN ERA OF DIVIDED GOVERNMENT IN THE STATES

Background

As Jerome Clubb, William Flanigan, and Nancy Zingale (1990) have observed, divided government in the states historically occurs in the decomposition phases of partisan realignments, whereas unified government characterizes the stable phases. By the late 1940s, the New Deal realignment was consolidated in most states and regions, and, as one might expect, unified state government was the rule, occurring in three-quarters or more of the states (see Figure 8.1). From that high point, however, the proportion of states with single-party government began a sharp decline that bottomed out in the 1980s at a bit above 40 percent. Some argue that the 1964 and/or 1968 elections were realigning, in the sense that they marked a change between two (differing) stable levels along many indicators (Aldrich and Niemi, forthcoming). Although I am inclined to agree, other than a small and temporary uptick in unified state government, there is no suggestion of a realignment in this particular indicator—only a trend.

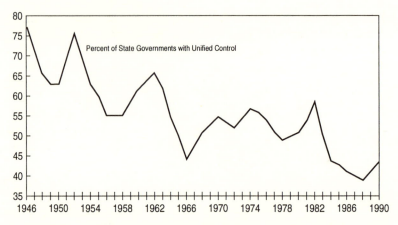

FIGURE 8.1   State Governments with Unified Control. SOURCE: Data calculated from *Book of the States* (multiple years).

As shown elsewhere (Fiorina, 1991), the sources of the decline in unified state government can be located more precisely in two senses. First, in a partisan sense, the decline was one in unified *Republican* state government. Democratic fortunes have fluctuated considerably, but there is no trend across the period from 1946 to 1990. Republicans have not been so fortunate. In the early postwar period they were able to capture a majority of the nonsouthern states in several elections, but by the 1990s their stronghold could be measured in the low single digits—only three states in 1990 and 1992.

The sources of decline in unified state government can be located even more precisely in a second, institutional sense. There has been no apparent erosion in the Republican capacity to contest gubernatorial elections. In fact, given aggregate party identification estimates for the states compiled by Robert Erikson, John McIver, and Gerald Wright (1987), it appears that Republican gubernatorial candidates have enjoyed success disproportionate to the percentage of Republican identifiers in their state electorates. It is in the *legislatures* that Republican fortunes have eroded. From control in a majority of states in the early postwar period, they have declined to single-digit levels today—five state legislatures in 1990, eight in 1992 [but up to seventeen in 1994.—ed.]

Patterns of national government during the past half-century resemble these state patterns writ large. Not since 1952 have the Republicans captured the House of Representatives, and they have controlled the Senate for only six years since then. But Republican presidential candidates have done exceptionally well, certainly far better than the proportion of Republican party identifiers in the national electorate would suggest. Combined, the two patterns yield divided government with Republican presidents and Democratic Congresses; the analogous pattern in the states shows an increase from less than a tenth of the states in the early postwar period to about a third in the past decade—the second most common pattern after unified Democratic.

Explanations

In seeking to explain electoral developments in the states that are roughly analogous to those at the national level, one naturally turns to explanations that have been offered for national developments. However, as explained elsewhere (Fiorina, 1992), little help is to be found in such explanations. The advantage of incumbency enjoyed by U.S. representatives is much less common in the states and, at any rate, is not a sufficient explanation of Democratic dominance of the U.S. House (Jacobson, 1991). A Democratic nomination process consisting of a long sequence of fractious caucuses and primaries (Wattenberg, 1991) does not seem very promising as an explanation of state developments. Issue-ownership explanations (Jacobson, 1991; Petrocik, 1991), according to which voters prefer budget-balancing, saber-rattling Republican presidents and Santa Claus Democratic Congresses, have little to say about states that regularly elect Democratic governors and Republican legislatures. And, finally, gerrymandering has little explanatory potential at either the state or national level.

In seeking new explanations for partisan change in state legislatures, I turned to discussions of what Gary Jacobson (1991) calls *structural* changes in state legislatures that might have had indirect partisan impacts. The most obvious structural hypotheses for divided government at the national level—gerrymandering, campaign finance, incumbency—have been persuasively eliminated by Jacobson. But one structural change in state legislatures, increasing professionalism, appears to have not only an indirect link to partisan change in the states but also a (doubly) indirect link to partisan stability in the U.S. House.

Professionalism in State Legislatures

The U.S. Congress is the world's foremost example of a professionalized legislature. Nelson Polsby (1968) describes the "institutionalization" of the House, a process that has eventuated in the contemporary professionalized body. Numerous others (e.g., Polsby, Gallagher, and Rundquist, 1969; Cooper, 1970; Gamm and Shepsle, 1988; Stewart, 1989) have traced the development of leadership and committee structures. In this chapter I use the term *professionalism* in the more limited sense of "careerism" (Price, 1975; Ehrenhalt, 1991: 35). A professionalized legislature is one in which service is a full-time occupation and members serve for relatively long periods.

In the early postwar period, most state legislatures were what legislative scholars call "amateur" legislatures. State constitutions often limited them to meeting biennially rather than annually and severely constrained the term during which they might sit. A forty-to-sixty-day session limit was not uncommon, and even a legislature permitted to meet annually was sometimes constrained to a short (e.g., twenty-day) session every second year. Legislative compensation was commensurate with these modest responsibilities. Not surprisingly, given such conditions, turnover was often as high as 50 percent per election; it was also more a product of voluntary retirement than of electoral competition.

During the past forty years, many state legislatures have moved away from such an "amateur" concept toward the "professional" model represented by Congress (Kurtz, 1991). Few state legislatures can match the standard offered by Congress, but legislatures in a number of larger states are clearly professional bodies, and in many states there are currently far more professional legislators than before.[3] More than three quarters of the state legislatures now meet annually, session lengths have lengthened significantly (see Figure 8.2), compensation has increased dramatically, especially during the 1960s (see Figure 8.3), and turnover has declined.

The professionalization movement is in some ways the reverse of the currently popular term-limitation movement. A generation ago the widespread perception was that membership stability in state legislatures was too low, not too high (Hyneman, 1938). Many felt that the demands of the modern age required that legislatures attract a higher-quality legislator, who would serve long enough to accrue the knowledge and experience conducive to effective lawmaking. Hence, it was believed, legislatures should be made into full-time bodies with compensation sufficient to attract "professional" legislators. Appropriate reforms were proposed by good government groups like the National Municipal League, the League of Women Voters, and the Citizens Conference on State Legislatures; expert political scientists contributed their recommendations (Heard, 1966); and like others before and after, this "innovation" moved across the states (Walker, 1969).

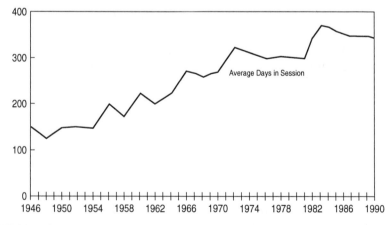

FIGURE 8.2   Average Number of Days in Session in 31 Nonsouthern Legislatures. SOURCE: Data calculated from *Book of the States* (multiple years).

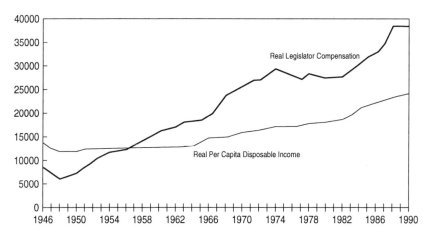

FIGURE 8.3   Average Biennial Compensation Versus Per Capita Disposable Income in 31 Nonsouthern States (1980 Dollars). SOURCE: Data calculated from *Book of the States* (multiple years).

Professionalism and Partisan Advantage

My current research (Fiorina, 1994) suggests that the development of legislative professionalism has contributed significantly to the demise of Republican control in the state legislatures. Specifically, controlling statistically for state electoral histories, temporal trends, national economic conditions, presidential and gubernatorial coattails, and the obvious sociodemographic variables, each $10,000 increase in real biennial legislator compensation is associated with about a 1 percent increase in Democratic representatives in the nonsouthern states.[4] That is the direct contribution; but there is an additional indirect contribution accounted for by the increase over time in the size of the Democratic base. To mention a specific example, real legislator compensation in California has increased ninefold in the postwar period, an expansion that translates directly into a 9 percent increase in the size of the Democratic House contingent.

Why should legislative professionalism give a relative advantage to Democrats over Republicans? I argue that this effect occurs through self-selection, the decisions made by individual candidates who opt in and out of the electoral arena.

Service in an amateur legislature presumes another, primary source of income. Moreover, that livelihood must be one that is not jeopardized by serving one to three months a year in government. In short, professionals and proprietors with flexible schedules, farmers and ranchers with little to do in the winter, and the spouses of same are likely candidates for service in amateur legislatures. In contrast, those whose livelihoods depend on wages and salaries for fixed hours worked are effectively precluded from service. Amateur legislatures advantage those whose occupations allow them to combine public service and private careers—people in Republican-leaning occupational categories.

In professional legislatures, a reverse logic operates. Professional legislatures require an individual to give up outside occupations, become a full-time legislator, and live on the associated compensation. For many Republicans, the "opportunity costs" of abandoning lucrative outside careers are higher than the benefits of legislative service. In contrast, a professional legislature may be an attractive alternative for individuals employed in the lower-salaried public and nonprofit sectors—people in Democratic-leaning occupational groups.[5]

Thus, as legislative session lengths rise, potential Republican candidates find the prospect of service less attractive. Though compensation rises simultaneously, it is not sufficient to replace income from their outside occupations. Conversely, as compensation rises, prospective Democratic candidates regard legislative service as an increasingly attractive prospect; on average, the returns from their outside occupations are not so generous as those enjoyed by Republicans. There is no need to argue that public service is simply a matter of wages and hours; rather, my point is that, at the margins, wages and hours do affect the political calculations of prospective candidates. The most public-spirited Democrat may be financially unable to make it on the compensation provided by an amateur legislature, just as the most public-spirited Republican may be unwilling to make the sacrifice required by a professional legislature.

The argument is completed by reference to the old saw that "you can't beat somebody with nobody" or, more academically, to work like Fenno's (1978), which notes constituents' desire to vote for qualified representatives. Over time, constituents find themselves faced with more numerous and more attractive Democratic candidates, and with fewer and less attractive Republican candidates. The result is more Democratic legislators, even if constituents do not change their partisan or ideological sentiments. I have no direct evidence regarding the hypothesized candidate calculations, but the predicted result is consistent with the empirical facts.[6]

PARTISAN ADVANTAGE IN THE
U.S. HOUSE OF REPRESENTATIVES

What of the persisting Democratic majorities in the U.S. House of Representatives?[7] The New Deal realignment and resulting distribution of party identification provides an adequate explanation for Democratic majorities from 1932 to the mid-1960s. The more interesting question is why Republican House candidates did not do better after their presidential counterparts began winning regularly. Relative to personal income, congressional compensation has been lower since the mid-1970s than at anytime since the 1920s and, in real terms, actually fell between 1972 and 1984 (see Figure 8.4), so some potential Republican candidates for Congress may have been discouraged in exactly the same way as were their counterparts in state legislatures.

But I suspect that legislative professionalism has contributed to the Democratic majorities in the House of Representatives through a process that is one

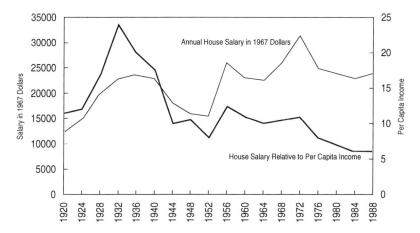

FIGURE 8.4   Congressional Compensation. SOURCES: *Congressional Quarterly Weekly Report,* February 4, 1989, p. 210; *Economic Report of the President* (multiple years), *Statistical Abstract of the United States* (1992), p. 469; and *Historical Statistics of the U.S.: Colonial Times to 1970,* Part 1 (1976), p. E135.

stage more indirect than in the state legislatures. By contributing to the decline in Republican fortunes in state legislative elections, legislative professionalism may simultaneously have contributed to the stability of the Democratic majorities in the U.S. House. The state legislatures have long been jumping-off points for House candidacies, and according to David Canon (1990), state legislative experience became an even more common precursor of House candidacies in the 1980s. Thus, if fewer Republicans serve in state legislatures, and those who do generally find themselves in the minority, one would expect a decline in the size and quality of the Republican congressional candidate pool.

This implication matches up nicely with Jacobson's (1991) explanation for the lack of Republican congressional success during a period when national issues seemed to favor the Republicans and their presidential candidates enjoyed considerable electoral success. Jacobson reports that despite being better funded, Republican candidates in the 1980s were not as qualified as Democrats, if qualifications are measured simply by whether candidates have previously won elected office. An obvious hypothesis is that in the past two decades the nonsouthern states where Democrats have made the greatest state legislative gains are those that have produced the Democratic U.S. representatives who have offset the Republican congressional gains in the South.

CONCLUSIONS

When political scientists study political change, we have a natural tendency to look first for political causes or sources of that change—after all, we are *political* scientists. Accordingly, electoral realignment with its image of massive shifts in voter sentiments grips our imagination.[8] Sharp changes in public policy set us to searching for the proximate political causes—effective leadership, new constituencies and coalitions, and so forth. Changes in the way an institution like Congress operates lead us to study associated changes in rules and procedures. This political focus is natural, and quite often appropriate.

Especially in the last decade or so, as the study of American politics has become more dynamically oriented, more analysts have become aware of the social origins of political change: the movement of African Americans from the South to the urban north, the migration of urban dwellers to the suburbs, the growth of the Sunbelt, the rise of a "new class," the decline of unions, the resurgence of religion, the changing American family, and numerous others. The social and economic world is dynamic, and socioeconomic changes often alter political preferences and political resources in obvious ways.

But there are other sources of political change that work in more subtle ways—in particular, by changing the personal calculations of political actors. For instance, increased media influence in nomination politics may "select for" a different kind of candidate, one with the right look, sound, and manner. (Any number of commentators have wondered whether someone who looked and talked like Abraham Lincoln would stand a chance in today's presidential primary process.) If arguments like these are correct, then technological changes may have produced a shift of political emphasis from substance to style, and from anonymous "team" players to visible "lone ranger" types.

Another example of a hypothesized selection effect is the membership change that accompanies changes in the conditions of congressional service. By the early 1970s, constituents had begun to expect members to come home every week, and changes in journalistic standards had stripped much of the privacy from political life. Perhaps as a consequence, the number of congressional retirements soared. When they settled down again (at least until the scandal-plagued 102nd Congress), some saw their having done so as evidence that a new kind of member—better able to tolerate life in a fishbowl and a frenetic pace—had been attracted to the institution.

As such examples suggest, arguments based on selection effects are not at all uncommon in discussions of candidate emergence. Moreover, such arguments are often associated with observations about "unintended consequences," as is the case with the professionalism argument offered here. If the growth of legislative professionalism has indeed worked against Republicans in legislatures, then we have another classic "unintended" consequence of political reform.[9] Seemingly "nonpolitical" changes, made with the best of intentions, may have created marginal selection effects that cumulated over time into important political changes. More generous legislative compensation may well have attracted a higher caliber of individuals to run for office, as intended; but those higher-caliber individuals have political views different from those they replaced.

The more general point, however, is that political change in the partisan or ideological sense may be a result of seemingly marginal changes in institutions or procedures that are not directly partisan or ideological and that to most observers would not appear to have even indirectly partisan or ideological implications. The study of such indirect relationships, though more difficult than the study of more direct cause-and-effect relationships, is equally deserving of our efforts.

NOTES

1. I wish to thank James Alt for contributing helpful conversations on the subject of this chapter.

2. The following states held gubernatorial elections in 1992: Delaware, Indiana, Missouri, Montana, New Hampshire, North Carolina, North Dakota, Rhode Island, Utah, Vermont, Washington, and West Virginia.

3. For example, Beth Bazar (1987) notes that in the Middle Atlantic states, more than half the legislators were self-designated full-timers by the mid-1980s.

4. During the period of this study (1946–1990) the Republicans never captured a legislative chamber in the southern or border states; their losses occurred exclusively in the non-South. Legislator compensation includes salaries, per diems, and other allowances—anything that could be reliably calculated. Session lengths also were included in the statistical analysis, but real compensation proved to be the much stronger indicator. Of course, session lengths are related to compensation. See Fiorina (1994) for details.

5. The usual objection at this point is that many state legislators in both parties are lawyers—generally high-status, well-paid professionals with flexible schedules. It has been suggested that Democratic lawyers have lower incomes and come from less prestigious law schools than do Republican lawyers, but I have found little in the way of systematic evidence. Interestingly, the National Conference of State Legislatures reports that "the most dramatic change in legislators' occupations nationwide has been the decline in attorneys." (Bazar, 1987: 3) The implication is that lawyers are increasingly finding the opportunity costs of full-time legislative service too high to bear. Presumably, higher-income Republican lawyers would opt out faster than lower-income Democrats.

6. Although it would entail quite a bit of work, state specialists could, in principle, gather more direct evidence about the hypothesized intervening mechanisms. Other things being equal, do Republican primaries become less contested over time and Democratic primaries more contested? Do Republican incumbents have fewer uncontested races over time and Democratic incumbents more? Such trends would be expected if the logic discussed in the text were operating.

7. I will say nothing of the Senate. As this chamber is the second most prestigious elective office, with only two seats per state, finding two willing and qualified candidates is a problem only under extreme one-party conditions.

8. Yet this image of large-scale change is probably inaccurate (Brady, 1988).

9. Republicans understandably may wonder whether this consequence was indeed so "unintended." Although there is some evidence that Democratic legislative strength is positively associated with subsequent increases in session length and compensation, I am inclined to believe that this finding reflects simple self-interest (Democrats are more in need of income) more than a conscious attempt to "do in" the Republican opposition. At any rate, the matter is subject to empirical examination. In the debates and votes (both popular and legislative) that have accompanied initiatives and constitutional amendments, is there evidence of systematic partisan opposition, with Republicans opposing professionalization and Democrats supporting it?

9

Committed Majorities and Policy Change in the U.S. Supreme Court

LAWRENCE BAUM

The U.S. Supreme Court is the object of intense interest in American society, and much of that interest centers on change. It is the Court's departures from past legal positions that generally attract the most attention. The selection of new justices now receives enormous publicity, chiefly because a new justice might help to change the Court's policies.

Scholars have extensively analyzed change in the Supreme Court, offering a considerable understanding of the process of change. This book's theme provides a useful means of pulling together and extending those insights by raising an important set of questions: To what extent is policy change in the Court incremental, to what extent is it sudden and sharp, and how do we explain the balance between the two?

Most of the time, policy change in the Supreme Court is slow and incremental. But the Court also undergoes episodes of sharp and sudden policy change. The classic example came in the late 1930s and early 1940s, when the Court abruptly abandoned its position that the Constitution seriously limits government power to regulate the economy.

Such episodes are exceptional because the Court—like other institutions—operates under basic conditions that favor slow and limited change. But these episodes are not rare; indeed, they account for a large share of policy change in the Court.

What causes the Supreme Court to depart from its usual incremental pace of change? Probably the best simple answer is that the Court sometimes has an effective majority of justices who are committed to sharp change in its policy positions. In this respect the Court is similar to Congress. But change in the Court operates differently from congressional change in certain other respects.

Policy change comes in many forms. The most important aspect of Supreme Court policy is the Court's legal rules or doctrines, as opposed to the outcomes of specific cases, so I will focus on doctrinal change. My concern is doctrinal change across a broad field such as civil liberties, a type of change with an enormous potential impact. As broad doctrinal change is difficult to measure precisely, however, caution needs to be exercised when analyzing it.

CHANGE PROCESSES IN THE SUPREME COURT

Change in the policies of a government institution can result from a variety of sources, which generally fall into two categories: turnover in the membership of the institution and shifts in the positions taken by those who continue as members (Baum, 1992).[1] These two general sources of change are often interwoven, because they may reflect the same forces and affect each other (Burstein, 1980; Brady, 1988). In general, however, it is turnover in membership that provides the necessary impetus to overcome incrementalism. In this section I will examine why policy change is incremental under most circumstances and then describe the conditions required for more decisive change.

Incrementalism as the Ordinary Course of Events

Incremental change tends to be dominant for several reasons. First, the policies of an institution at any given time are likely to reflect what its members think is desirable or advantageous for them to do. A big and speedy change would usually move the institution either toward policies that its members like less in themselves or toward policies that would damage their personal interests. This is why membership change is so critical to major policy change; as long as the same people continue to make policy, they generally adhere to the same positions (Asher and Weisberg, 1978).

Second, change carries costs that increase with its extent and speed (Braybrooke and Lindblom, 1963). Perhaps the most important of these costs is risk. It is relatively easy to assess the impact of a little change, and the chances of truly disastrous consequences are minimal. But sharp and sudden changes are more likely to produce serious negative effects, and decisionmakers have more limited ability to predict the impact of such changes. This difficulty in prediction also increases the costs—in time, effort, and often money—of decisionmaking itself.

Finally, institutional rules and structures often work against sharp change. Most important, the existence of difficult requirements for enacting new policies favors small-scale changes over bigger ones. And seniority rules may concentrate power in the hands of people who strongly support the status quo.

All of these forces operate in Congress. The long sequence of roadblocks that legislation must surmount works strongly against success for proposals containing major policy change (see Herzberg, 1986). The hierarchical structure of each house and the central role of specialized committees give considerable weight to seniority and thus to the continuation of existing policy. Similarly, the basic pattern of current policy tends to reflect the balance of power among major interest groups, whose influence in the legislative process gives them substantial capacity to defend gains won in the past. And elected legislators have a powerful personal incentive to steer away from the criticism that major policy change might entail (see Asher and Weisberg, 1978: 393–394). Indeed, R. Kent Weaver (1986) has suggested that "blame avoidance" is a major goal for members of Congress, who want to minimize the possibility of arousing opposition to their reelection.

The courts have their own special force for incrementalism: the rule of *stare decisis*, which strongly favors adherence to existing legal rules or precedents. Under this rule, the Supreme Court is generally expected to adhere to its past interpretations of the law. The Court is always free to depart from this expectation, and, indeed, it has done so with some frequency in the past three decades.[2] Still, the general injunction to follow precedent creates an additional barrier to big policy change, because most justices and most of their audience in the legal community would find it inappropriate for the Court to abandon precedent in wholesale fashion.[3]

The Supreme Court also has political audiences, among which Congress is especially important because of its powers over the Court (Keynes and Miller, 1989). These audiences sometimes criticize the Court when it changes policy too little for their taste, but they are far more likely to castigate the Court for major policy changes that they dislike. The Court best protects itself from attack when it only modifies existing legal doctrines and policy positions rather than striking out boldly in a new direction.

But in several respects, constraints against sharp policy change are weaker in the Court than in Congress. The justices hold lifetime terms, and few seek other jobs. Primarily for these reasons, the justices are less concerned than legislators about avoiding blame; they thereby gain greater (though still partial) freedom to make big changes in policy. The Court also features greater equality of power and far simpler procedures for action than Congress. And the Court's smaller size means that significant change in its collective viewpoint can come with relative ease: Change in a single justice's point of view or the replacement of a liberal justice by a conservative has a proportionate impact similar to eleven such changes in the Senate or nearly fifty in the House.

Arguably, then, the Supreme Court is more likely than Congress to transcend incrementalism and undertake sudden and sharp policy changes. Yet, because of the fundamental forces that favor incrementalism, it is clearly the normal pattern in the Court as well.

Transcending Incremental Change

As suggested earlier, we can think of major policy change as arising when Congress or the Court has an effective majority of members who are committed to major change. (By *effective majority,* I mean a majority with sufficient numbers and power to enact substantial policy changes in a limited period of time.) Such a committed majority does not appear spontaneously but, rather, develops through interaction between an institution and its environment.

I have already pointed to the strong forces that work against sharp policy change in Congress. When these forces are overcome, it is almost always through change in the political environment and usually through elections that shift the ideological makeup in Congress (Wright, 1986; but see also Sinclair, 1982).

Sometimes short-term political conditions strongly favor one party, tipping the balance in a divided Congress and signaling to continuing members that public expectations have shifted (Brady and Sinclair, 1984). But major policy change in Congress often arises from political realignments, sets of events in which new political issues become dominant, the positions of the Republican and Democratic parties change, and the balance of voter support shifts between the parties (Burnham, 1970; Sundquist, 1983). As described by David Brady (1988), realignments bring to Congress large numbers of new members who carry a strong commitment to major policy change. Their numbers are sufficient to change the balance of views on committees and even in the House and Senate leadership. Moreover, the political forces that they reflect sweep along other members and leaders.

The link between the Supreme Court and its political environment is weaker, so it operates differently in policy change.[4] I have already noted a central element of that weakness: the justices' relative freedom from concerns about maintaining public support. Because of this freedom, the justices have more leeway than members of Congress to undertake or refrain from major policy change in opposition to public opinion or the other branches of government.

Two additional, and related, factors attenuate the role of the Supreme Court's environment in major policy change: the Court's small size and the rules for selecting justices. If fifty new people join the House of Representatives, with policy views that differ greatly from those of the members they replace, their election must reflect general political tides. But differences between the views of a new justice and those of a predecessor, producing the same proportionate change in the Supreme Court's collective viewpoint, can reflect idiosyncrasy more than systematic political forces.

Moreover, the lifetime terms of justices and the uneven pace of retirements weaken—and certainly make less systematic—the impact of general political trends on the Court. Some presidents have replaced several justices with people far more sympathetic to their own views, whereas Jimmy Carter made no appointments at all. And because realignments have no direct effects on its membership, the Court may retard policy change in the federal government (and come into conflict with the other branches) by maintaining the policies of the preceding era. More generally, realignments and other broad political forces are less critical to policy change on the Court than they are to policy change in Congress (see Gates, 1992: 182–183).[5]

Of course, policy change on the Court does reflect its political environment in significant ways. Political tides that affect partisan control of the presidency usually affect the Court's membership as well (see Dahl, 1957). Most justices care about the Court's public standing and about compliance with its rulings, so they have good reason to avoid policies that garner little support. And interest groups influence the Court through the cases they sponsor and the arguments they present (Epstein and Kobylka, 1992). Still, the link between Court and environment is a relatively loose one.

Patterns of Change

This discussion suggests a general scenario for policy change in the Supreme Court. Most of the time, change is slow and limited. If the Court has a liberal majority during a particular period, it overturns some conservative precedents and moves doctrine on some issues in a liberal direction, but the changes are not sweeping. If new appointments create a conservative majority, the direction of change usually reverses, but the new changes also are limited.

Some justices, however, favor sharp changes in the Court's legal doctrines. Their numbers are usually too small for their positions to prevail. But by some combination of presidential design and happenstance, new appointments sometimes produce an effective majority of justices who are committed to sweeping change. If those justices find adequate support in the Court's political environment, such that it is safe to break with the past, they are likely to act on their shared preferences.

Once such a break has begun, strong negative reactions may cause the Court to retreat. If it continues, however, the break may develop a momentum of its own. Interest groups bring new cases that provide an opportunity to sustain the Court's new course. And after old doctrines have been discarded, their replacements stand as precedents supported by *stare decisis* and their own logic, ready for further extensions in the same issue areas and in related areas.[6]

Eventually the pace of change slows or halts altogether. The Court may move on to more "difficult" issues on which the committed majority begins to splinter, or it might begin to exhaust the possibilities of major change in a field. And, of course, the committed majority may break up with new changes in the Court's membership. Before this happens, however, the Court may make fundamental changes in its policies.

TWO EPISODES OF CHANGE

Processes of change in the Supreme Court can be examined more concretely if we look at the Court's policies on civil liberties over the past three decades. During the 1960s the Court revolutionized the law of civil liberties, expanding legal protections for freedom of expression, the rights of criminal defendants, and racial equality. But from the 1970s through the early 1990s, the Court halted its liberal direction and eventually reversed it, narrowing the scope of legal protections for rights in important respects. This trend was slow and uneven, however, and the conservative change in policy over more than twenty years was more limited in extent than the liberal change that had occurred during the 1960s. The contrast between these two periods helps to illustrate the conditions under which sharp and sudden change does and does not occur.

The Late Warren Court

For most of its history, the Supreme Court showed little interest in the civil liberties of individuals, except for their right to participate in economic activity. The Court's support for civil liberties grew during the twentieth century, especially after Franklin Roosevelt appointed several liberal justices. But until the 1950s, the Court took only limited steps to protect individual rights under the Constitution.

President Dwight Eisenhower appointed to the Court two justices who developed a strong commitment to expanded legal protections for civil liberties: Earl Warren in 1953 (as chief justice) and William Brennan in 1956.[7] These appointments did not reflect a policy goal on Eisenhower's part; both were made for other reasons (Katcher, 1967: 295–306; Hentoff, 1990: 48, 52). Joining two Roosevelt appointees with a similar commitment (William O. Douglas and Hugo Black), Warren and Brennan proved to be effective leaders within the Court. In the 1950s they helped secure decisions that established new protections for civil liberties. Most noteworthy was *Brown v. Board of Education* (1954), in which Warren moved a divided Court to a unanimous ruling that state-mandated racial segregation in public schools was unconstitutional (Kluger, 1976).

But the pace of change in the 1950s was limited and uneven. The four justices who supported major expansions in civil liberties remained a minority, and congressional attacks on the Supreme Court for some of its decisions made some justices cautious (Murphy, 1962). Certainly the Court did not make a sharp break with its past during this decade.

Yet such a break did occur in the 1960s. It was then that the Court undertook a concerted expansion of civil liberties that was extraordinary in its breadth and depth (Levy, 1972; B. Schwartz, 1983). In expanding the rights of criminal defendants, it held, among other things, that illegally seized evidence could not be used against a defendant in state court (*Mapp v. Ohio*, 1961) and that indigent defendants must be provided with attorneys in felony cases (*Gideon v. Wainwright*, 1963). It issued major decisions limiting the use of libel and obscenity laws to narrow freedom of expression (*New York Times v. Sullivan*, 1964; *Memoirs v. Massachusetts*, 1966). It strengthened constitutional guarantees of racial equality and acted to protect the civil rights movement against attacks by southern officials. And these were just the highlights of a speedy revolution in the law of civil liberties.

This era illustrated the momentum that helps to sustain judicial revolutions (see Pacelle, 1991). In fields such as criminal procedure and racial equality, landmark decisions created a base from which the Court could work in expanding rights. Further, expansions of rights in one area provided a logic that the Court could employ to take similar actions in other areas. Interest groups such as the NAACP Legal Defense Fund and the American Civil Liberties Union played an important part in this process, bringing cases that asked for extensions of favorable precedents and newly created rights.

The primary trigger for this revolution was probably the two appointments made by President John Kennedy in 1962, particularly that of Arthur Goldberg (Posner, 1990; but see also Segal and Spaeth, 1989). With Goldberg, the Court now had five justices who strongly supported broad interpretations of legal protections for civil liberties, and those justices were eager to act on their commitment.

The civil liberties revolution of the 1960s did not lack critics. The Court was attacked sharply for many of its decisions, particularly its expansions of rights for criminal defendants. Yet on the whole, the Court's environment was unusually supportive of civil liberties. This was a liberal era, during which popular backing for individual rights and equality was relatively strong. In this context, justices with highly liberal points of view had a good deal of freedom to act on their view.

Thus the Court's departure from incrementalism in the 1960s was a product of interaction between the lineup of justices and conditions in the Court's environment. Clearly, however, it was the justices who constituted the critical factor. Although conditions around the Court facilitated a civil liberties revolution, they hardly ensured one. Had Eisenhower appointed different justices, had Richard Nixon won the presidency in 1960 rather than losing by a narrow margin, the sharp and sudden changes of the 1960s could never have occurred. In short, this episode suggests that change in the political system as a whole is less critical to the Supreme Court than it is to Congress.

The Burger and Rehnquist Courts

Nixon was among the critics of the Warren Court. Elected president in 1968, he had the opportunity to select Chief Justice Warren Burger in 1969 and then three associate justices in subsequent years. And as it turned out, every appointment to the Court between 1969 and 1992 was made by a conservative Republican president. By 1991 the only justice left from the Warren Court was Byron White, who offered only limited support for the civil liberties revolution of the 1960s.

During this period, the Court's civil liberties policies became distinctly more conservative. Most notably, the Court was far less sympathetic to procedural claims by criminal defendants (see, for instance, *Harris v. New York,* 1971; and *United States v. Leon,* 1984). It limited protections for freedom of expression in areas such as obscenity and public speech (*Miller v. California,* 1973; *Hudgens v. National Labor Relations Board,* 1976). And increasingly, it gave narrow interpretations to federal laws against discrimination (*Wards Cove Packing Co. v. Atonio,* 1989; *St. Mary's Honor Center v. Hicks,* 1993). Cumulating across fields and over time, these changes made a considerable difference for the law of civil liberties. The break with the Warren Court was sharpest under Chief Justice William Rehnquist (elevated to that position in 1986), when the Reagan and Bush appointments were having their impact (Savage, 1992).

Yet the process of change was undramatic, and it added up to something less than the counterrevolution that many observers had expected as early as 1968 (Blasi, 1982; H. Schwartz, 1987; B. Schwartz, 1990). The early Burger Court actually engaged in some major expansions of civil liberties, striking down existing death penalty laws and state prohibitions of abortion (*Furman v. Georgia,* 1972;

Roe v. Wade, 1973). And even as the Court's conservative majority strengthened, it issued surprisingly few landmark decisions limiting legal protections of rights, and none of the Warren Court's own landmarks were overturned.[8]

The Court did not move further and more quickly in a conservative direction because there was never a majority of justices who were committed to that path.[9] William Rehnquist, Antonin Scalia, and Clarence Thomas seem to share that commitment; to a lesser degree, the same was true of Warren Burger and perhaps now Anthony Kennedy. But these justices have never held even a narrow majority. As late as 1993, with only one Democratic appointee left on the Court, its ideological center was controlled by justices whose positions are best described as moderately conservative. Thus, even when Republican presidents had the extraordinary good fortune to make ten consecutive appointments, their choices did not create a Court of strongly committed conservatives.

In turn, the ideological mix of justices reflected the appointment process. Except for Gerald Ford, who chose moderate liberal John Paul Stevens, the Republican presidents from 1969 through 1992 sought to appoint justices with distinctly conservative views on civil liberties. In the case of Harry Blackmun, whose views became increasingly liberal after his selection ("The Changing Social Vision of Justice Blackmun," 1983), Nixon eventually suffered a failure. More noteworthy are the Republican appointees who took primarily conservative positions but showed little support for a full counterrevolution against the Warren Court: Lewis Powell, Sandra Day O'Connor, and David Souter.

Why did conservative Republican presidents select several justices who then took relatively moderate positions in civil liberties? In each instance, with the possible exception of Blackmun,[10] circumstances worked against choosing someone with a clear record of strong conservatism. For electoral reasons Richard Nixon wanted to put a southerner on the Court, but his first two southern nominees were defeated in the Senate. Meanwhile, Powell was a Virginia Democrat with a relatively moderate record who could be expected to gain easy confirmation. For similar reasons Ronald Reagan wanted to choose a woman, and there were few Republican women on appellate courts. O'Connor stood out as a potential justice despite her moderate conservatism. Seeking an uncontroversial nominee, George Bush deliberately chose Souter as a relatively new federal judge whose record in the New Hampshire courts gave few clues to his policy preferences.

These developments were not unprecedented. Like Blackmun, many earlier justices surprised the presidents who selected them (Scigliano, 1971: 147–148). Gerald Ford was not the first president to nominate a justice with little concern for the nominee's policy views. And presidents have often chosen people with relatively moderate records as a means to advance other goals. From this perspective, the failure of ten consecutive Republican appointments to create a strongly conservative Court is not surprising. Ideological transformation of the Court is even less likely under normal circumstances, when appointments alternate between political parties more often.

The Court's political environment has also worked against drastic policy change in recent years. Although the past quarter-century has been a relatively conservative period in the United States, some of the Court's moves to the right have aroused considerable opposition. Notably, Congress has overturned several narrow interpretations of civil rights statutes (Eskridge, 1991). And in a country deeply divided over abortion, some conservative justices fear the consequences for the Court if it should eliminate constitutional protections for abortion rights. That fear was expressed explicitly in the unusual joint opinion by O'Connor, Kennedy, and Souter in *Planned Parenthood v. Casey* (1992), which reaffirmed the basic tenets of *Roe v. Wade* at a time when the Court seemed ready to overturn that decision. Significantly, the joint opinion emphasized the need to adhere to precedent in order to maintain public support for the Court. And the maintenance of liberal landmarks such as *Roe* slowed and limited the process of change in civil liberties policy.

The Supreme Court's course over the past quarter-century underlines the dominance of incrementalism. Even when one party monopolized appointments to the Court for the whole period from 1969 to 1992, the forces that usually prevent sharp and sudden change continued to exert an impact. Conservative "control" of the Court dates back to 1971, but that control has produced only a moderate shift in the Court's civil liberties doctrines—in contrast with the more radical shift that took place during the 1960s. It is that radical shift which stands out as an exception to the usual pace of change on the Court.

BILL CLINTON AND THE SUPREME COURT

The election of Bill Clinton in 1992 meant a likely interruption in the Supreme Court's shift to the right. Now, for at least four years, the president who fills any vacancies on the Court will not be someone seeking to create a more conservative institution. As in the past, alternation in party control of the presidency was working against sharp ideological change in the Supreme Court. And when Byron White retired from the Court in 1993, the extraordinary streak of appointments by Republican presidents came to an end.

What else does a Clinton presidency mean for the Supreme Court? Past experience cautions against confident predictions. We do not know whether Bill Clinton will serve one term or two, how many and which vacancies on the Court he will fill, and what will be the political circumstances under which he makes appointments. And we certainly cannot predict the kinds of idiosyncratic developments that have shaped the Court's history in the past. Still, events early in Clinton's tenure provide some guides to his potential impact on the Court.

To begin with, any administration has a marginal impact on the Court through its participation in cases. The solicitor general, legal representative of the federal executive branch in the Supreme Court, enjoys a very high rate of success in getting the Court to hear cases (see Salokar, 1992). Partly as a result, a large minority of the cases that the Court actually decides on the merits involve the federal government as a litigant. In many others, the federal government participates as an *amicus curiae,* submitting a brief and often taking part in oral argument.

Although the solicitor general's office has a degree of independence, its positions in litigation inevitably reflect the orientation of the administration. Under Drew Days, Clinton's appointee as solicitor general, the office in 1993 changed positions in four cases from those it had taken at the end of the Bush administration (Biskupic, 1993). More broadly, in the Clinton administration the solicitor general can be expected to support a relatively liberal agenda on issues such as abortion and racial discrimination. The result will be to shift slightly the balance of external influences on the Court.

Of course, if Bill Clinton has a more fundamental impact on the Court, that impact will depend on appointments. It is impossible to predict how many and which vacancies he will fill, but the prospects for a set of appointments that transform the Court are quite limited in any case. When Clinton became president, only two sitting justices (Harry Blackmun and John Paul Stevens) could be described as more liberal than conservative; one of the two, Blackmun, was 84 years old on Inauguration Day, and he retired a year later. Unless several of the Court's conservatives leave the Court during his time in office, even a series of appointments by Clinton could do no more than move the Court closer to the ideological center. The result probably would be to increase the proportion of liberal victories in specific cases and to move the Court's doctrinal positions somewhat to the left; on some specific issues, the Court's doctrines might change considerably. But nothing even vaguely resembling a judicial revolution would occur.

Moreover, it is already clear that Clinton's appointments will have less than the maximum ideological impact on the Court. Clinton was fortunate to have two vacancies to fill in his first eighteen months in office. His choices of Ruth Bader Ginsburg (to succeed White) and Stephen Breyer (to succeed Blackmun) were similar, in that both Ginsburg and Breyer were perceived as moderate rather than strong liberals. Ginsburg was expected to take more liberal positions than White, and her early record meets that expectation. But at least some observers predicted that Breyer would be a more conservative justice than Blackmun. If so—and there has been a good deal of disagreement about Breyer's likely course—the net effect would be to leave the Court's ideological balance about where it had been when Clinton took office.

It is noteworthy that Clinton did not select nominees with more liberal reputations, especially because some interest groups that are important to the Democratic party strongly prefer such candidates. One reason surely is Clinton's own ideological position, a more moderate one than that of most Democratic presidents. Given their views as Clinton perceives them, Ginsburg and Breyer may reflect his preferences fairly well.

Furthermore, political considerations favored the selection of relatively moderate nominees. Clinton has demonstrated a distaste for confrontations, and he has been especially unwilling to engage in conflict over appointments. With Republican senators and conservative interest groups ready to oppose a strongly liberal Supreme Court nominee in 1993, Clinton apparently was more comfortable in choosing a candidate who was acceptable to the Republicans. A year later, he seemed to retreat more directly from confrontation: He apparently passed over Interior Secretary Bruce Babbitt because Republican senators threatened to oppose Babbitt, primarily on the basis of his policies toward federal lands in the west. Barring unforeseen circumstances, Babbitt would have been confirmed by a wide margin, but the opposition in itself might have produced negative political consequences for Clinton, both directly and indirectly.

Clinton's caution resulted in part from his political weakness at the time of the two nominations. In 1994 he also wanted to avoid any conflicts that would detract from his effort to win congressional approval for his health care legislation. But a president inclined toward compromise will always have good reasons to avoid conflicts on matters that are not central to the administration's goals. And if the Republicans gain Senate seats in the 1994 election, especially if they achieve a majority, Clinton will have even more reason to select moderates to fill any future vacancies on the Supreme Court.

This is not to say that Clinton would never name a strong liberal to the Court. Senate Majority Leader George Mitchell probably fits that description, and it appears that he would have won a nomination in 1994 if he had wanted it. In ideological terms, however, a Mitchell nomination would have run counter to Clinton's strongest inclinations.

Clinton's preference for moderate nominees does not represent a sharp departure from the past. Other presidents frequently have taken a similar path, both because of their own views and because of political considerations. This pattern in appointments is one of the forces that limit the speed and extent of ideological change in the Supreme Court. But the Court's history makes it clear that even a president who sought to produce fundamental change in the Court through appointments would be battling against the odds.

CONCLUSIONS

Membership change creates the potential for fundamental change in Supreme Court policies. The Court's relative insulation from its political environment makes its members' preferences the primary basis for collective policy choices; because those preferences tend to be stable, turnover of members is usually required for something more than incremental policy change. Even so, substantial change in the Court's collective views of policy issues is not always enough to produce fundamental change in its doctrinal positions.

It is exceedingly difficult to forecast when the Court will depart from incrementalism. The process for selection of justices and the Court's insulation introduce an unusually large element of chance into the pace of policy change. The role of chance is suggested by what did and did not happen in the Court during the past half-century. A moderately conservative Republican president unintentionally set the stage for a liberal revolution on civil liberties in the 1960s, whereas a series of Republican presidents from the 1960s to the 1990s failed to secure the conservative counterrevolution that most of them wanted.

Even if the Court's course at any given time is determined partly by chance, general patterns of change are more systematic. Like other organizations, the Court is subject to strong forces that favor incremental change, and incrementalism is the dominant form of change in Supreme Court policies. Strong as those forces are, however, they exert a weaker hold on the Court than on institutions such as Congress. As a result, periods of sharp and sudden changes are probably more common in the Court. Ironically, then, the branch of government that seems most wedded to the past through the rule of precedent may have the greatest potential to escape the limits of incrementalism.

NOTES

1. For some related formulations, see Asher and Weisberg (1978), Rowland and Carp (1983), and Segal (1985).

2. Up to 1960, the Court had overturned its own precedents 96 times; between 1961 and 1990, it did so 100 times (Congressional Research Service, 1987, 1991).

3. For a differing view, see Segal and Spaeth (1993: 44–52). Martin Shapiro (1965) suggests that *stare decisis* can be interpreted largely as a means to avoid the costs of major policy change; to the extent that this is the case, *stare decisis* adds little to other forces for incrementalism.

4. My concern is with broad policy change, yet the same is true of change in specific policy areas. Baumgartner and Jones (1993) demonstrate the importance of the congressional environment for such specific change, whereas similar change in the Supreme Court is linked more weakly to the Court's political environment.

5. Ackerman (1988) takes a different view of critical appointments to the Court; Schubert (1970) sees a more systematic link between the Court's environment and policy change.

6. Baumgartner and Jones (1993: 16–17) discuss a related type of momentum in policy change.

7. For a good overview of circumstances surrounding these and later appointments to the Court, see Abraham (1992).

8. Some decisions of the late Burger and early Rehnquist Courts actually expanded civil liberties in significant ways. One example was the line of decisions prohibiting the use of peremptory challenges to eliminate prospective jurors for racial reasons (see *Batson v. Kentucky*, 1986; and *Georgia v. McCollum*, 1992). Also striking were the two Rehnquist Court decisions striking down criminal laws against flag desecration (*Texas v. Johnson*, 1989; *United States v. Eichman*, 1990).

9. On the positions of the Burger Court justices, see Lamb and Halpern (1991).

10. Even in Blackmun's case, circumstances worked in favor of a relatively moderate appointee: Nixon's first two nominees for this seat (Clement Haynsworth and G. Harrold Carswell) failed to win Senate confirmation, so Nixon had reason to avoid a nominee with extreme views that would arouse Senate opposition.

10

The Federal Executive:
Equilibrium and Change

BERT A. ROCKMAN

THE SEPARATION OF POWERS AND
THE ADMINISTRATIVE STATE

In virtually every democratic political system, there is an expectation that the bureaucracy provides ballast and stability to the ostensible changes wrought through the electoral process. New political leadership energizes the policy process by bringing into play different ideas, people, and directions (Bunce, 1980). Bureaucracy stabilizes the process by building political support systems to bolster the programs it maintains, such that, regardless of who is in power, it will produce fairly predictable responses. The practice of building a network of support around programs is a means of institutionalizing the programs. Precisely because political leaders want to institutionalize their preferences over time but also to be left with a minimum of institutionalization by their predecessors (Moe, 1988, 1990), one should expect that at the outset of any new presidential administration there will be tension between the newly elected political leadership and the established bureaucracy (Aberbach and Rockman, 1976). The newly arrived executive leadership wants maximum discretion and minimum restriction by the past. The bureaucracy, in turn, wants stability produced by institutionalizing the past. The newly arrived political leadership in the executive may wish to overturn apple carts, but that is not such an easy matter because the programs administered by the bureaucracy have their own network of political alliances. These alliances are usually centered in Congress and backed by interest groups representing constituencies affected by the programs or at least by advocates of them.

In every political setting, change creates some unease between political leaders and public servants. No one can be fully certain how leadership styles will mesh and how priorities will change. Nonetheless, in most political settings senior civil servants and political leaders are not complete strangers to one another. The role of the civil service as a policy player is better established in most other democratic settings than it is in the United States. Indeed, in most such settings the civil service has a ready-made access to the political leadership, an access that it lacks in this country (Heclo, 1977; Aberbach and Rockman, 1985). Because there is no independent legislature competing for political power with the executive in these other countries, the senior civil service and the political leadership in the executive typically deal with one another more directly and certainly more intimately than they do in the United States. The advantage for these civil servants is that they get to advise political leaders directly; the cost to them, however, is that they are in a lesser position to appeal or expose unpalatable decisions than are their American counterparts.

One peculiarity of the American political process, then, is that relatively little can be taken for granted when presidential administrations change. Although there are numerous organizations in the Executive Office of the Presidency (EOP) such as the Council of Economic Advisers, the National Security Council staff, and others big and small, important and marginal (Burke, 1992), it is debatable as to whether these White House organizations are institutionalized in the sense that they are likely to operate predictably regardless of who is president (Rockman, 1990).

The relative unpredictability of changes across presidential administrations certainly has a lot to do with the large number of positions to be filled by an incoming administration, some of which require confirmation by the Senate. In most other democratic political systems, senior civil servants are perched near the apex of political power. In the United States, they are lodged somewhat lower. Because of their proximity to political power, civil servants elsewhere are positioned perfectly to give policy advice—a function they prize more than management (Wilson, 1993). Because of their relative distance from political power in the United States, civil servants are largely seen as managers or even technicians but not as advisers (Rockman, 1993). They may not be in a position to influence, but they are superbly positioned to impede, obstruct, and delay if they are so inclined.

Moreover, the constitutional structure of the American political system feeds exactly this sort of "bureaucratic cornerfighting" (Campbell and Peters, 1988). In the American system, bureaucrats are not often in a position to advance an agenda of their own. Usually, however, they are sufficiently well connected to ensure that agendas they find distasteful can be prematurely exposed and thus often blocked. The separation-of-powers system gives Congress, and especially the key authorizing and appropriating subcommittees and committees, both a stake and a share in the administrative agencies of the executive branch. The agencies are therefore responsible to Congress as well as to the White House and its appointed officials. The fact that American bureaucrats are the agents not of a single branch but potentially of all three branches of government makes their existence less predictable and more conflictual than that of their counterparts in most other democratic settings (Aberbach and Rockman, 1985). Inevitably, this simple but important fact generates a certain amount of distrust and struggle between the politicians in the executive branch and those in Congress. And because the congressional committees that have jurisdiction over an agency's programs often tend to be supporters of those programs, they are likely to strike up alliances at the staff level with civil servants who administer the programs and often serve as advocates for them (Aberbach, 1990). The politicians in the executive branch, by contrast, tend to have a lesser stake in the programs and are more cognizant of their budgetary implications. Also, presidents often come to office advocating broad changes. Whether their motives are programmatic or purely taken up with public relations, presidents are apt to be less reticent than other political actors on the scene about uprooting the past. The implication is that presidents are more likely to come to office with the view that the permanent bureaucracy is part of the problem, not part of the solution.

To be sure, few presidents think a great deal about the anonymous officials far removed from their line of sight. Presidents usually cannot even know most of their own appointees. Sometimes, as in the case of Ronald Reagan, they can misidentify their own Cabinet members. But this not to say that they are generally unaware of the forces that are reputed to generate obstacles for them. For many recent presidents, the anonymous officialdom of senior civil servants has been one source of those obstacles; and thus these presidents, in varying degrees, have sought to gain control of what they misperceived as their "own" branch of government.

Of course, civil service systems are designed to frustrate wholesale changes of personnel in order to provide continuity to government. The American system does give presidents more discretionary appointments than most other democratic systems give their executive leaders, but it also increases the difficulty of moving government in a clear direction across its various departments. Unlike Cabinet systems, American government possesses no central decisionmaking forum in which the department heads and the president come together to make decisions. In the United States, cabinet meetings are pro forma; in parliamentary systems, they are not.

The president comes to rely, therefore, on central agencies to do for him what the Cabinet cannot. Among these are the White House personnel office for selecting political appointees, the Office of Personnel Administration for selecting career officials, and the Office of Management and Budget for directing budgetary resources (more frequently subtracting them) as well as for regulating the workings of the agencies. In addition, presidents have built numerous staff devices over the years to coordinate policy and programs.

The limits of and possibilities for presidential control of the executive branch rest essentially on the ability of presidents to influence how programs are administered, how budgetary resources are allocated, and which people are chosen to administer the government. Programs, money, and people may be said, therefore, to constitute the holy trinity of administration. To what extent are these three elements stable or variable over time? How much do (and can) they change along with changes in presidential administrations?

CHANGE AND RESISTANCE: THE CLINTON ADMINISTRATION MEETS WASHINGTON

Against the backdrop of recent American history, a relatively rare thing happened in the 1992 election. The same party took control of both the White House and the two chambers of Congress. Unified government in the United States is, of course, something of a misnomer. It is not at all equivalent to a majority party government because the two chambers of the legislature have their own party leadership. More important, the chambers' work units, committees, and subcommittees remain powerful, as do the leaders of those units. The crucial point here is that Congress and the bureaucracy are each sources of ballast against the designs (or improvisations) of any new presidency, regardless of whether there is nominal partisan unity or difference across the branches.

Presidents seem to have a desire or a political need (or both) to demonstrate their proficiency in the management of the federal government. They want to be perceived as attacking waste, inefficiency, and irrationality. Jimmy Carter, for example, seemed to have a penchant for root-and-branch methods of evaluating programs (such as zero-based budgeting) and linking them to budgets. Carter also thought that reorganization was a means of taming the federal beast. Members of Congress, especially those on the appropriate jurisdictional committees, were less inclined to accept such premises. Even the much ballyhooed Civil Service Reform Act (CSRA) of 1978 met with some congressional resistance, especially since the relevant committees in both chambers were tilted a bit toward members with districts abutting Washington. Some members of Congress also believed that the CSRA would diminish congressional influence over the management of programs.

Like most recent presidents before him—Bush being a recent exception (Aberbach, 1991)—Clinton made a commitment to run the federal government more efficiently and intelligently, and to produce savings as a result. The major impetus here was the reinventing-government theme sounded by two public-management consultants, David Osborne and Ted Gaebler (1992). The Clinton administration, hungry for issues that would make it less vulnerable to charges that it was building up the federal bureaucracy through its program proposals, found the idea of reinventing government attractive. It therefore echoed this theme in an omnibus performance review of the federal executive chaired by Vice-President Albert Gore (Report of the National Performance Review, 1993). Like the Grace Commission report that preceded it in the Reagan administration, Gore's performance review promises budgetary savings ($108 billion over five years) and exceeds the range, strictly speaking, of pure managerial reform by recommending program cuts. Although the performance review emphasizes the value of bottom-up management, it is clear that some of its recommendations, whatever their merits, necessarily give the political leadership in the executive more freedom from congressional accountability.

In sum, the White House is typically motivated by two factors regardless of its own political complexion or that of the Congress. The first is that it desires *political payoff* from talking about or even doing something about management reform. Efficiency, cost cutting, and responsiveness are perceived as public totems, whereas bureaucracy, bureaucrats, and overregulation (by definition) are common taboos. Management reform is basically a valence issue (except for the affected interests), but a valence issue of relatively low political yield. It is a subject on which editorialists may ooze but on which the public is more likely to snooze. However, the second factor that motivates presidential efforts to achieve management reform is that managerial rationality provides a means for helping the administration *achieve its goals,* partly by lessening the capacity for Congress to successfully intervene and, thus, lessening the capacity of bureaucrats to effectively utilize the congressional arena.

There is an inherent tension between management rationality as the executive is likely to see it and political accountability as Congress is likely to see it. These differing outlooks are formed in part by the different roles that Congress and the president play in the system of separated powers and in part by their different political needs. Presidents need to give the appearance of attacking big problems and to signal that prospective efficiency gains are also large. Moreover, presidents want to maximize discretion over the executive, an objective they try to promote under the guise of managerial reform. Congress, alternatively, wants to protect key constituencies and to keep itself involved as a player in the administration of programs. It sometimes wants a shorter leash—but it always wants to make sure that it has some control over the process even if that process is ex post facto (McCubbins, 1985).

These differences of perspective are at least as institutional in nature as they are partisan. Of course, partisan differences, manifested through divided government, contribute strongly to perceptions of distrust between the branches. But the separation of powers has its own logic. This logic ensures that concurrent party control of the two branches does not translate into unified party control of them. Accordingly, the bureaucracy remains contested turf between the branches whether or not they are both controlled by the same party, although the terms on which the contest is waged are normally harsher under divided government. Moves to bring about change in the executive are often countermanded elsewhere in the system. But such moves do not always succeed, nor are they always undertaken.

In short, both change and stability characterize the executive branch. The support systems built around bureaucracies and their programs are not ironclad. Nor are they completely resistant to powerful political forces or policy currents. The budget-deficit problem that has afflicted the federal government since the early days of the Reagan administration has a way of focusing attention on what needs to be changed. But a paradox of the American political system is thereby engendered: When attention is focused on the specifics of change, the greater is the ability of resisting forces to mobilize support on behalf of their interests. Hence, the interplay of change and stability in programs, funding, and personnel, to which subject we now turn.

PROGRAMMATIC CHANGE AND STABILITY

Macro-Program Change

Carriers and whales, the saying goes, do not turn around on a dime. In other words, the bigger the object to be changed, the slower and more incremental the change. The same applies to programs, and the reason is evident: The larger a program, the greater the number of stakeholders in the program and the more resistance there is to change.

Big programs may acquire a lot of interest groups as stakeholders. But they are even more likely to acquire large sectors of the population as constituencies. Universal entitlements are of this nature. One very important reason they are so difficult (though by no means impossible) to change is that everyone is a recipient or prospective recipient. No population group can be isolated for cuts (Pierson and Weaver, 1993; Pierson, 1994). Although universal programs for the elderly certainly have a number of important interest groups connected to them, it is the capacity of the elderly to concentrate on their interests (income and health care security) that makes it dangerous for politicians to consider changes that in the short run adversely affect the beneficiaries of these programs. Furthermore, since people get older, not younger, they are more likely to be concerned with the benefits package that awaits them in their retirement. The potential population to be mobilized is thus quite large.

It would be incorrect, however, to assume that these programs are immunized from change. Changes that incur costs have been undertaken (Pierson and Weaver, 1993). But the immediate bearers of those costs are rarely the present generation of recipients. The crisis in the liquidity of the Old Age Survivors and Pension fund that occurred early in Reagan's term was initially confronted by the administration in the form of cutting cost-of-living adjustments. Having been defeated by a 99–0 vote in the Senate, the Reagan administration retreated to higher ground, setting up a bipartisan commission with House Speaker Tip O'Neil to make recommendations for the fund's solvency (Light, 1985). The effect, aside from increasing payroll taxes (a matter affecting donors to the fund rather than recipients of it), was to defer benefit reductions approximately two generations into the future—largely by hiding them (e.g., by increasing the age at which existing benefits can be taken).

Similarly, the Clinton administration's budget package of 1993 proposed to increase the percentage of Social Security income to become taxable in relation to an individual's or household's income. It also proposed some modest cuts in Medicare, among other things. Although the percentage of Social Security income subject to taxation was modified by congressional action, there was still some increase. And in regard to Medicare—whose costs, along with those of health care generally, have skyrocketed—Congress actually required more cuts in the prospective costs over the next five years than the administration had proposed. But these costs do not directly affect the beneficiaries. Rather, they are imposed upon the suppliers—namely, hospitals and doctors—who then charge third-party insurance carriers more to compensate for the cutbacks from the federal government. The third-party carriers, in turn, charge employers more for their policies.

There are several morals to the big-program story. The first moral is that big programs typically are redistributive, and that interest groups serve mainly to mobilize populations targeted to lose from alterations in the status quo. The second moral is that politicians are normally reluctant to tamper with the benefits received through universal programs except to take credit for ratcheting the benefits upward. The third moral is that when crisis requires action that imposes costs on beneficiaries, politicians will seek to hide the costs and defer them from present beneficiaries to future ones. The fourth moral is that when crisis and an accepted explanation for the crisis coincide, politicians will be moved to impose costs—as indirectly as they can, but directly if they must. By 1993 it had become clear that however much Democrats wanted to blame the combination of Reagan's defense-spending increases and tax decreases for the budget deficit, the main culprit for the large structural deficit lay in entitlement programs, especially the popular ones. By this time it was common knowledge that the big dollars needed to patch the budget-deficit problem were to be found in such entitlement programs rather than in those targeted to specific populations such as the unemployed or Aid for Families with Dependent Children (AFDC) mothers (despite the burgeoning costs of the latter program) or in discretionary programs. Cuts in programs for the elderly were not popular, but neither was the budget deficit. Consequently, it became difficult for politicians to support cutting the budget deficit without making a move on Social Security pensions and Medicare costs. The move they did make, however, was indirect. Rather than cutting cost-of-living adjustments in Old Age Survivors and Pension benefits, they increased the proportion of those benefits to be taxed, pegged to the beneficiaries' income. And rather than increasing premiums on Medicare for the recipients (though they had earlier done exactly this), they specified that most of the direct cost would be borne by health care suppliers.

One element that helps to bring about big-program change is a sense of crisis. In health care, the crisis is cost. Another element is the prominence of a set of ideas that have come to legitimize a set of solutions. The seeming acceptance of a connection between universalized coverage and cost controls, and of a connection between cost controls and budget deficits, provided the basis for the administration's health care reform effort in the 103rd Congress. The failure of that effort showed that another important idea essential to any new program of health care cost containment is that health care will be rationed. For now, this idea remains illegitimate in spite of its inevitability. Rationing is being implemented in the private sector through managed care programs in states such as Oregon and Hawaii, which have instituted a schedule of priorities for various procedures and therapies. Policy ideas are important, but they depend upon circumstances to push them forward. Indeed, they depend upon the existence of a propitious political moment—a so-called window of opportunity (Kingdon, 1984; Baumgartner and Jones, 1991; 1993). That window narrowed appreciably in 1994 after two years of widening.

This window of opportunity opened modestly in the last year of the Bush administration at a time when health care was becoming well advertised as a major problem and as proposals were beginning to flow through Congress. The continued rise in health care costs, the growing difficulty of corporations in financing these costs, the insecurities of people concerning their coverage, and the unexpected victory of a Senate candidate (Harris Wofford) who campaigned vigorously on the issue of a universal health care entitlement—all contributed to setting the stage for the health care issue. At this point, the Bush administration put forth its own plan. But the proposals contained in this plan were consumed by election-year maneuvering in which the parties were more interested in creating an issue than in finding a solution (Gilmour, forthcoming). The election of Clinton in 1992, however, ensured that this issue would become a centerpiece of the new administration's policy proposals. It further forced many Democrats (especially those who stood to Clinton's left) to coalesce behind the administration's proposal in the event of their inability to obtain majority support for their preferred alternative of a single-payer system.

The window of opportunity that the Clinton administration and its allies perceived to be open when it introduced its health care proposal to Congress closed with remarkable suddenness as opponents of comprehensive reform, or at least opponents of the proposed means of financing it, gained the upper hand. The enthusiasm of publics and politicians for reform waned as Clinton's approval ratings fell and as both ideology and interest expressed themselves through the extraordinary blocking capacity of American political institutions.

It is, of course, possible that health reform may not be resuscitated for a long time. Indeed, for now, the idea of universal care is being attacked while costs are mainly being ignored. But health care reform is a problem that cannot go away. It undoubtedly will be revisited again unless ways are found to reduce health care costs, although what the new legitimating ideas for reform will be remain to be seen. From the most recent saga of health care reform, we can conclude that big changes do not occur readily in the American system when they impose costs on targeted populations and appear to threaten the currently prevailing distribution of benefits. The essential fourth moral of big program change—a common belief in a crisis, a common explanation for it, and a common commitment to impose costs for its alleviation—were, in the end, absent.

Micro-Program Change

Not all program change is legislated, of course. New administrative interpretations of existing programs are frequently brought about by executive order or administrative regulation. The implications of these actions are narrower than those of statutory change. Yet such actions have vitally important consequences for the actors who are directly affected and may have larger indirect consequences for the society or its economy. Congress is potentially involved in the issuance of all administrative regulations or executive orders, in the sense that it may respond to the executive's actions by changing the law on which those actions are based. An important U.S. Supreme Court decision taken in 1984 (*U.S. v. Chevron*), however, gives ample latitude to the executive to issue administrative regulations so long as they are not inconsistent with the underlying statute.

All administrations tend to put a particular gloss on legislative intent to fit their political and policy needs or desires. The presidential administration always has the power of initiative to issue new guidelines to which Congress or the courts (or both) must react. Both the Reagan and Bush administrations made significant use of administrative regulations to pursue their policy objectives by taking, as presidents are inclined to do, an especially grand interpretation of executive discretion (Sanders, 1990; Tiefer, 1994). As a consequence, Congress was forced to react to executive initiative by amending the relevant statute in order to overturn the executive interpretation. But congressional action is subject to a presidential veto, requiring two-thirds of each chamber to override an executive initiative. In essence, unless super-majorities in both chambers of Congress vote otherwise, the executive interpretation has the force of law. The Reagan and Bush presidencies thus seemed to have perfected a strategy of executive governance tried earlier but less successfully during the Nixon administration (Nathan, 1983; Tiefer, 1994).

Presidential administrations are free to change the administrative regulations or executive orders of other presidents so long as these do not acquire statutory status. With a Democratic majority in Congress, Clinton sought to make a fast start by using his executive powers to overturn the orders of the Reagan and Bush administrations. For instance, two days after being inaugurated, he signed a series of executive orders that overturned the "gag rule" placed on abortion counseling as an option at federally funded family-planning agencies; eliminated the ban on the use of fetal tissue for medical research; canceled the alert set against RU-486, the French "morning-after" birth control drug; lifted the directive against abortions at overseas military medical facilities; and overturned the ban against aid to international organizations that "actively promote abortion" (Donovan, 1993: 182). That constitutes a lot of policy change. More would follow later. However, when congressional majorities were stacked against him on an is-sue such as nondiscrimination against gays in the military, Clinton could do little since he would be facing off against members of his own party whose support he would need on other matters of greater urgency to the fate of his administration.

In sum, presidential change often brings a flurry of executive orders and ad-ministrative regulations. These, in turn, provide an avenue through which presi-dents can influence programs without hurdling Congress (at least not immedi-ately). Big-program changes are a different matter. They require congressional action and a great deal of bargaining. They require the general recognition of a problem, the emergence of a set of ideas as to how to deal with it, and both the political entrepreneurship to push a proposed solution and the political oppor-tunity that allows for the possibility of success.

Without the fuel of money, however, programs cannot hope to have much impact. We now turn, therefore, to another element of executive change—money.

BUDGETARY CHANGE AND STABILITY

Virtually all executive leaders come to office sobered by the realization of how constrained their degrees of freedom are. Campaigns are giddy with talk of change. Governing is another matter. Presidents discover that the federal budget is heavily mandated and not discretionary. Enormous sums of money are dedi-cated to obligations such as pension benefits (civilian and military), health care entitlements, and payments to manage the costs of the deficit. The former two obligations are affected by demographics, previously agreed upon payment for-mulas, and the costs of health care. The latter obligation is naturally affected by the size of the deficit and by the cost of borrowing (i.e., interest rates). The fact is that four basic categories drive the federal budget, accounting for a minimum of three-fourths and closer to four-fifths of all federal outlays. These categories are defense (including military pension obligations), Social Security and Medicare, income security programs (welfare), and interest on the deficit (see Table 10.1). In short, the room for maneuver is limited, though not nonexistent.

President Reagan came to office determined to achieve substantial cuts in fed-eral spending overall, while also substantially increasing spending for defense. By packaging a number of discretionary program cuts into a reconciliation bill in 1981, he was able to achieve close to a 4 percent cut in the first fiscal-year federal budget of his administration, a feat that has not been achieved since.

Political choices constitute just one among the many factors that drive bud-gets. Such choices are typically more important at the level of programs than at that of raw expenditure categories or department budgets (Natchez and Bupp, 1973). Despite the enormous complexities involved in achieving nonincremental change in expenditures—inflation rates, interest rates, demographics, crises, events, and so on—political choices, when persistently followed, do matter. And

TABLE 10.1
Percentage of Total Federal Outlays Accounted
for by Defense, Entitlements, and Interest
Payments: 1981, 1988, 1992, and 1994

Function	Percent of Total Outlays			
	FY 1981	FY 1988	FY 1992	FY 1994
Defense	23.2	27.3	21.6	18.3
Social Security and Medicare	26.4	28.0	29.5	30.9
Income Security (Welfare)	14.7	12.1	14.3	14.2
Interest on the Deficit	10.1	14.2	14.4	14.0
Total	74.4	81.6	79.8	77.4

SOURCES: Office of Management and Budget, *Budget of the United States Government,* Table 20 (FY 1986), Table 18 (FY 1987), Table 16 (1990), Table G-1 (FY 1991), Table A-2 (FY 1992), and Table 1-2 (FY 1993). The percentages in the first three columns were calculated from GNP deflator tables in the appendix to the *Economic Report of the President* (January 1993). Those in the fourth column are estimates based on President Clinton's fiscal 1994 budget, as reported in *Congressional Quarterly,* April 10, 1993.

yet, as Table 10.2 demonstrates, there are limits as to what these choices can control.

The data in this table can be viewed in several different ways. Looking at the Reagan years (1981–1988), we do indeed see the impact of political choices. More than half the categories of federal expenditure exhibit sustained negative growth rates or no growth. The implication of this finding is obvious: Reagan's goal of cutting discretionary expenditures was generally successful. Outlays for his two principal spending priorities, defense and law enforcement, significantly increased. One (defense) cost a lot, the other (law enforcement) relatively little. Overall, then, the Reagan administration achieved its goals of reordering the priorities of governmental expenditure at the federal level. It also seemed to be successful at holding in check programs of income support other than those of universal entitlements. Nevertheless, the Reagan administration was actually less successful than its successor at holding down the growth of governmental expenditures generally. Why?

The answer to this puzzle appears to lie in the fact that the big-ticket items generally increased in cost more rapidly under the Reagan administration than under the Bush administration. Clearly, the relaxation of relations with the Soviet Union and the end of the Cold War (and of the Soviet Union) allowed defense expenditures to decline after their mammoth rise in the first of Reagan's terms in office. Social Security and Medicare expenditure growth also declined on average by about 20 percent during the Bush years compared to the Reagan years. Moreover, the Bush administration was advantaged by the lower interest rates that prevailed as the economy stagnated during the 1990s. Thus, the growth rate of interest payments on the deficit declined dramatically. It is likely, of course, that this economic stagnation stimulated counteractive expenditure forces for income security (especially in the form of unemployment compensation) and job training, thus causing these expenditures to rise.

The 1990 budget deal struck between President Bush and the Democratic congressional leadership also imposed caps on, and walls between, various expenditure categories, forcing these categories to borrow against themselves (other programs within the same cap) rather than against general expenditures. The budget deal of 1990 helped slow some of the general growth in government expenditures, as (most likely) did the less successful overall ceilings imposed by the Gramm-Rudman-Hollings legislation passed in 1986. As noted earlier, the tumbling of defense expenditures was mainly driven by the ending of the Cold War. Actually, the rapidity of its rise in the first term of the Reagan administration was arrested in its second term by a Congress that chose to meet the Gramm-Rudman ceilings by pinching the defense department rather than domestic discretionary programs.

TABLE 10.2
Per Annum Change in Real Budget Outlays Between
1981–1988 and 1988–1992, by Category
(in percentages)

	Per Annum Change	
Category	1981–1988	1988–1992
Defense	6.1	−3.6
Social Security and Medicare	4.2	3.4
Agriculture	2.6	−6.7
Law Enforcement/Justice	7.1	7.8
Science, Space, and Technology	4.3	6.7
International Affairs	−5.4	6.8
Energy	−12.6	16.7
Natural Resources and Environment	−2.4	3.6
Commerce and Mortgage Credit	11.2	−3.8
Transportation	−1.4	1.0
Community and Regional Development	−8.7	1.8
Education, Job Training, and Social Services	−3.8	4.7
Health: Services, Research, and Regulation	4.1	16.8
Income Security (Welfare)	0.1	6.8
Veterans	−0.1	−1.0
General Government	4.8	5.0
Revenue Sharing/General Block Grants	−11.5	−2.8
Interest	10.2	2.4
Total Outlays	3.1	2.0
Negative or No-Growth Categories (minus interest payments)	9	5

SOURCES: Office of Management and Budget, *Budget of the United States Government* (multiple years); *Congressional Quarterly*, April 10, 1993.

The sharp fall-off in interest rates also helped to slow down the pace of expenditure growth. But this outcome, as discussed, was a double-edged sword. The fall in interest rates was a response to the fall in the nation's economic prospects. The economic slowdown did little for the deficit since it decreased cyclically the flow of revenues to the government and increased spending needs for compensatory measures such as unemployment insurance. Nevertheless, the picture is clear. Fall-off in the large categories of expenditure rather than fall-off in more categories of expenditure is what slowed the overall rate of spending growth. From a macro standpoint, Bush (and various congressional decisionmakers) achieved Reagan's objectives of slowing governmental spending better than Reagan had done. But from a sectoral standpoint, budget outlays during the Reagan administration tended to reflect its priorities.

The Clinton administration marched into Washington as the first Democratic administration in twelve years. It is fair to say that many Democrats were eager to promote what they believed were concerns ignored during the Reagan and Bush years. In general, the Clinton administration appears to be more favorably disposed toward discretionary spending in human and social capital development (particularly education and community programs) and health care services. It also seems to emphasize infrastructural developments. In short, the Clinton administration wants to put its own stamp and priorities on the federal budget. But its progress toward this end will be limited by budgetary realities, by the prominence of the budget deficit on the public agenda (partly as a consequence of Clinton's having put it there), and by the actions Congress has taken to respond to the problem.

The data in Table 10.3, unfortunately, cannot be directly compared with the figures pertaining to the Reagan and Bush years in Table 10.2, because Table 10.3 is based on estimated rather than actual outlays and because unadjusted dollars had to be used for these estimates. Still, this latter table is instructive. Compared to the Reagan and Bush presidencies, Clinton's is characterized by fewer negatively signed categories of expenditure—in fact, by only two. But we must be cautious in our interpretations here: When expenditures are adjusted, the expected growth rates are likely to decline. Furthermore, given congressional action on President Clinton's budget bill during 1993, negative signs must be placed on many categories largely composed of discretionary expenditures. The reason is that one of the concessions extracted by Congress in the 1993 budget bill was placement of an unadjusted ceiling on discretionary spending (programs with annual appropriations) at $550 billion. The clear implication is that total discretionary spending must decline for the five-year life of the budget bill. Undoubtedly, this restriction places the Clinton administration in a difficult quandary (Ifill, 1993). After all, this administration came into office with a dual agenda—to cut the federal deficit and to rearrange spending priorities. But its propensities for public investments have tangled with powerful budget constraints and a congressional coalition that has invoked these constraints. Although the Clinton ad-

TABLE 10.3
Estimated Per Annum Change in Unadjusted Outlays
Between 1992 and 1994 (in percentages)

Category	Estimated Per Annum Change[a]
Defense	−3.6
Social Security and Medicare	7.6
Agriculture	6.4
Law Enforcement/Justice	6.1
Science, Space, and Technology	4.1
International Affairs	8.9
Energy	−6.6
Natural Resources and Environment	1.9
Commerce and Mortgage Credit	15.1
Transportation	10.1
Community and Regional Development	23.7
Education, Job Training, and Social Services	9.2
Health: Services, Research, and Regulation	15.8
Income Security (Welfare)	4.6
Veterans	5.5
General Government	4.9
Interest	3.2
Total Outlays	4.9

[a]Based on unadjusted dollars.
SOURCE: *Congressional Quarterly,* April 10, 1993, pp. 900–901.

ministration has largely succeeded in increasing the flow of revenue to the government by increasing taxes, the budget bill also requires the administration to cut prospective increases in medicare payments to health care providers more substantially than it originally had proposed.

Budget outlays, however, are imperfect indicators of any administration's effort to place its mark on the priorities of government. In the first place, the president is obviously not in sole control of this process, even when it comes to political choices. The choices are shared whether a president likes that or not. Congress has its say, and its say is not a modest one. But fundamental forces influence and constrain the degrees of freedom allowable for any set of political leaders. Past program expenditures heavily influence present ones. Unexpected events—the savings and loan crisis or natural disasters—cause plans and budgets to go awry. Formulas set expenditure patterns. And the cost of crucial commodities—money, health services, and so on—profoundly affect the rate of budgetary growth. Indeed, demographics often became budgetary destiny. Older populations require more money in the aggregate to be devoted to health care and to pensions, in spite of the fact that elderly individuals receiving both now pay more for them. Similarly, the massive rise in numbers of dependent children increases in the aggregate the amount of money devoted to income security in spite of the stable or declining amounts received per dependent child. Budgets remind us that there are limits upon political choices, but also that there are political choices to be made. The Reagan administration helped narrow the parameters of future administrations' choices without eliminating them altogether.

PERSONNEL CHANGE AND STABILITY

The third element in the executive triad is personnel. The existence of a civil service is designed to institutionalize the personnel system, thus making it difficult for any particular set of political leaders to radically alter administrative personnel exclusively to their own tastes. A civil service system, in theory at least, prizes two ideas—the competence of those who achieve status within it and the continuity of the system above and beyond changes in the rulers.

In most modern democracies, senior career officials sit cheek to jowl with their reputed political masters. It is more or less expected that politicians will seek advice from civil servants who, themselves, are often the savviest political actors at the table. Here, as in many respects, the United States is different. American politicians, certainly including the president, come into office rarely if ever having dealt directly with a civil servant. In theory, though hardly in reality (Aberbach, Putnam, and Rockman, 1981), the distinction between policy and administration is thus made far more sharply in the United States than elsewhere (Rockman, 1993). The consequence is that a president must fill numerous positions in order to create a "team." A new administration may have as many as 3,000 discretionary appointments, approximately 625 of whom require Senate confirmation (Healey, 1993a). Close to 350 (about 55 percent) of these serve in the Cabinet departments. The actual figures vary from one administration to another. The people appointed to these discretionary positions are called "political appointees," but many are only peripherally political. Some are highly experienced in government; others are neophytes. A few, especially in the State and Defense departments, have come up through the ranks of the career service. Who these appointees are, and what a president expects of them, varies considerably from one president to another. But one thing is certain: No president can possibly know all of them. Furthermore, no president is likely to be interested in knowing any beyond those with whom he deals directly, unless, of course, they embarrass him or otherwise create trouble for his administration.

Subcabinet political appointees, usually at the assistant secretary level, are often the point of executive contact with the senior career officials, who, in the United States, are usually members of the Senior Executive Service (SES). The SES was designed as an elite corps of civil servants—much like the British administrative class or the French *grands corps*—whose members would be portable. The status of each SES official would inhere in the person holding the position rather than in the particular position being held.

A seasoned observer of presidential transitions, whereby the new meets the continuous, has noted that such circumstances lead appointees and civil servants to suspiciously sniff each other like dogs (Stanley, 1965: 87). How quickly and how completely a presidential administration wants to make its mark on the bureaucracy depends a great deal on what it wants to do. Most administrations, surprisingly, have difficulty defining just what that is. Not so with the Reagan administration. It came to office with a strategy designed to "hit the ground running" (Pfiffner, 1988) and wanted to bend the bureaucracy to its design—but only those parts essential to its goals (Maranto, 1993). Other, less goal-directed presidencies may find themselves the object being bent.

Immediately, the following questions arise: How quickly can the presidential administration move its people into place? To what extent are its people selected as a team designed to foster the administration's goals? And to what extent can the administration influence the senior civil servants to support it?

Beginning with the first of these questions, we find that presidential administrations clearly vary in the speed with which they bring in "their" people. In the second year of the Nixon administration, for example, only about two-thirds of Nixon's appointees even identified themselves as Republicans, although the figure was considerably higher for appointments requiring Senate confirmation (Aberbach and Rockman, 1976). This early inattentiveness to departmental staffing may have reflected Nixon's disinterest in the operations of the government, as opposed to those of the White House. Of the past four presidents, Jimmy Carter was the pacesetter in terms of making nominations and getting them confirmed by the Senate. By the end of April of his first term, Carter had nominated 215 individuals and had 72 percent confirmed. Clinton is actually next with 177 nominations, but after his first three months in office only 29 percent of his nominees were confirmed. Bush nominated the fewest individuals—96 total—but had more than half of them confirmed, and Reagan had about 55 percent of his 152 nominees approved by the Senate. As of the August 1993 recess, Clinton had placed only 7 more people in nomination, and his confirmation rate was still below 50 percent—that is, 48 percent (Healey, 1993b).

"Vacant" is a more acceptable name for offices in Republican administrations than in Democratic ones because Republican administrations are not anxious to have someone occupying a role demanding more resources or policy attention. This disinterest in filling positions was notable during the Bush administration, which could be seen as a more mellow version of the Reagan administration entering its ninth year. Having vacancies in office is not a handicap for any administration desiring to do little policy. It is only a problem for an administration that wants to make policy.

The buildup of ethics laws and dirt-digging slows the process. So, too, does the effort to find diversity. In addition, use of the "hold" in the Senate (a senator's use of personal privilege to delay hearings on an individual) has increased massively and can keep appointments tied up for a long time. All of these factors undoubtedly slacken the pace of nomination and, especially, confirmation.

If the process has become more cumbersome, can presidents find a team with which they are satisfied? Whether they can or not depends partly on what they want a team for and partly on their style of relating to the executive branch. Diversity, by definition, impedes a team concept, whether the diversity is genetic, gender-based, or ideological. Carter sought to build an adversarial process over which he would reign as chief magistrate, but the diversity was excessive and could not be digested in the form of coherent policy. By contrast, Reagan's delegation style of dealing with the executive branch fit well with the idea of bringing in people who were ideologically dedicated to the administration's goals. Indeed, at the outset, the Reagan administration filled many of its subcabinet posts before its Cabinet ones. The Cabinet officers provided the administration's public face, but the subcabinet officials in particular were chosen for their commitment to the goals of the White House. In short, the Reagan White House was organized to make an early impact (Pfiffner, 1988).

In the Nixon White House, parallel posts in the White House were designed to monitor their counterparts in the departments. But this apparatus proved unworkable. As Nixon's concerns about the loyalty of his appointees mounted, a new strategy was developed for the second term. The new strategy was to replace public faces in the Cabinet with faceless individuals who had no independent political clout of their own. The administration's strategy also included planting a Nixon White House operative within each department at a high level in order to monitor the department for the White House (Nathan, 1983). The Watergate crisis, of course, brought this and other plans of the second Nixon administration to an ineffective conclusion.

The Clinton administration began with a situation exactly in reverse of that facing the Bush administration. The Bush White House was in a position to take advantage of years of experience staffing the executive branch. It was mainly interested in preserving the equilibrium it had inherited, and it had lots of people available to do just that. The Democrats, however, were out for twelve years. Stocking the Clinton administration with Carter leftovers would have made it vulnerable to the criticism that it was merely a retread of Carter's less-than-widely acclaimed presidency. Given the coalition that produced the nomination for Clinton, about the only theme that his administration could count on in staffing was diversity—again, whether genetic, gender-based, or ideological. This diversity may have reflected America (or some provinces thereof), as Clinton liked to say, but it was no basis for building a team founded on clear and coherent directions. Certainly, it provided no basis on which to put people speedily in place. If Clinton's personnel strategy provided a kind of "punctuation" to the existing equilibrium, it took the form of a question mark in contrast to Reagan's exclamation point.

No matter how much effort may be devoted to selecting appointees as a team responsive to the presidential administration (on those occasions when it knows what it wants), all administrations inherit a corps of senior civil servants. The civil servants, to some degree, dampen any administration's ambitions toward change, especially if the change is unsettling. Alternatively, the civil service is frequently able to guide a presidential administration through its policy course if it is granted the opportunity to do so. Unlike the corps of political appointees who are meant to reflect the presidential administration's political tendencies and, presumably, its policy priorities, the civil service is organized in such a way as to provide continuity and, through the process of career tenure, to be immunized from political tampering. There are limits, however, both to the neutrality of the civil service and to its immunity from political selection.

In 1970, 1986–1987, and 1991–1992, extensive interviews were undertaken both with political appointees and with senior civil servants under the direction of Joel D. Aberbach and myself. Table 10.4 notes the relationship between political party affiliation and the job status of our respondents. The job status category is broken down into the following subcategories: political appointees who require confirmation by the Senate (high-level political appointees with a "passed with the advice of the Senate" [PAS] designation); political appointees who do not require Senate confirmation (middle-level appointees with a "Non-Career Executive Assignment" [NEA] or Schedule C designation); and career officials, who in 1986–1987 and 1991–1992 were divided between those SES career officials who were the top career officials in their organizational hierarchy (meaning that they reported to a political appointee) and other SES career officials (who typically reported to another SES career official). The SES was created by the 1978 Civil Service Reform Act to replace the system of career supergrade positions. A key distinction between the two systems is that SES confers rank in the person (emphasizing mobility of position) whereas the old supergrade system conferred it in the position. In 1970 the supergrade career officials we interviewed were the top career officials in their organizational hierarchy and, therefore, are most comparable to the group we call Career I in sections B and C of Table 10.4. The SES, in turn, is composed of two lists: a reserve list that in theory comprises positions sufficiently technical that they cannot be filled by political appointees, and a general list of positions that in theory are permitted to be filled by political appointees (up to 10 percent of the total SES general list and 25 percent within any particular department). The SES officials represented in Table 10.4 are drawn from the general list. Although no system is immune to dedicated political tinkerers, the SES appears to be somewhat more susceptible to political manipulation than the old career supergrade system. Needless to say, political manipulation rarely announces itself so overtly. Rather, it comes disguised in the form of management flexibility.

In short, Table 10.4 reflects both continuity and change. With respect to continuity, no matter how much more Republican the appointees *and* the civil servants became over time, the differences between them remained relatively constant. And as the appointees became more partisan, consistent with the Republican administrations they were serving, the civil servants (especially the Career I group) became more Republican in their sympathies too, but considerably

TABLE 10.4
Party Affiliation by Job Status

Formal Job Designation[b]	Party Affiliation[a]			(N) Totals
	Republican	Independent	Democrat	
A. 1970				
High-Level Political Appointees (with PAS designation)	81%	6	13	100% (16)
	65%	11	25	
Middle Level Appointees (with NEA or Schedule C designation)	59%	12	29	100% (41)
Supergrade Career Officials	17%	36	47	100% (58)
		Gamma = .58		(N = 115)
B. 1986–1987				
High-Level Political Appointees (with PAS designation)	94%	6	0	100% (18)
	97%	3	0	
Middle-Level Appointees (SES-NA)	98%	2	0	100% (44)
Career I (SES-CA-I)	45%	17	38	100% (64)
Career II (SES-CA-II)	27%	19	54	100% (63)
		Gamma = .74		(N = 189)
	(Gamma = .91 excluding CA-IIs; N = 126)			
C. 1991–1992				
High-Level Political Appointee (with PAS designation)	100%	0	0	100% (21)
	100%	0	0	
Middle-Level Appointee (SES-NA)	100%	0	0	100% (24)
Career I (SES-CA-I)	42%	27	31	100% (52)
Career II (SES-CA-II)	42%	19	40	100% (53)
		Gamma = .64		(N = 150)
	(Gamma = 1.00 excluding CA-IIs; N = 97)			

[a]I measured party affiliation by asking the administrators whether they normally vote for one party or the other. Those who said that they did not normally vote for one party or the other were coded as Independents.

[b]Because of the small number of PAS-designated appointees in our samples, analyses involving the job-status variable will hereafter collapse political appointees into a single category.

SOURCE: Data compiled by the author and Joel D. Aberbach.

less so than did the appointees. The element of change is equally apparent: Overall, the career officials substantially shifted in a Republican direction, just as presidential appointees had done, from the early Nixon period to the later stages of the Reagan and Bush administrations.

One interpretation we might glean from this evidence is that by remaining at some partisan distance from the appointees, the career officials are in a good position to serve any administration that comes into being. Alternatively, the data suggest that, perhaps inevitably, politics has been at play in the selection of top career officials, especially among those who must deal directly with an administration's political appointees. At this point, there are a number of possible explanations for the changes we see in the political profile of America's top federal career officials. One thing, though, is certain: For whatever reason, civil servants do not present an immutable obstacle to long-run changes in the political direction of the system they serve. They can, however, blunt the political directions of any particular administration, especially in its early days. The SES seems to make it at least marginally easier for a presidential administration so inclined to transfer those whom it regards as its most unresponsive careerists in the bureaucracy. Exactly how the Clinton administration views the career SES officials is as yet unclear, but it would not be surprising after twelve years of Republican administrations for the new administration, whether warranted or not, to infer that the top layers of the career service are skeptical toward it.

CONCLUSIONS

The saga told in these pages is one of both change and stability. The president may be a chief executive but the Congress is the board of directors. Their joint territory is the executive branch. The executive is designed to provide stability and continuity across presidential administrations. Each administration institutionalizes programs. It cannot unilaterally change the legislative status of those programs, though it can use administrative means to alter their workings. At the same time, presidents of a mind to do so, and available opportunities, can impose change on the executive. (It is probably the case that leaders of a mind to make things happen also tend to perceive more opportunities than do their more risk-averse counterparts.) This chapter has discussed three areas in which the tension between change and stability exists in the executive branch—programs, budgets, and people. In no case is the president a free agent to shape matters to his liking. But neither is he incapable of generating change. Although the system is designed to stymie the unilateral exercise of presidential will, this story suggests that where there is powerful presidential will there is often a way. Yet the effort to find a way may trigger intense conflict in the U.S. political system between different authorities, each of whom has a legitimate claim on the executive.

Most presidents with intense ambitions to shape the executive branch to their desires will no doubt experience frustration over their seeming inability to make it happen all at once. This frustration may lead, as in Nixon's case, to behavior that in turn leads to impeachable abuses of executive authority. Over the longer haul, the executive branch appears to reach a new equilibrium when it has been subjected to repeated political and policy change in the same direction. However, on those rare occasions when powerful presidential will is congruent with ample opportunity, as in the early Reagan years when the Republicans controlled the

Senate and thus confirmation of the administration's appointments, the prevailing equilibrium is jolted more than it is adjusted.

Despite some large-scale program changes desired by the Clinton administration, especially its health care program and welfare reforms, it is limited by the cumulative impacts of the federal government's deficits. It is also limited by its own priorities in cutting prospective deficits and by the congressional response that produced the 1993 budget bill. There is precious little margin within which a president of Clinton's programmatic ambitions can maneuver, especially given the existing discretionary spending caps. Until concerns with budget deficits are reduced and the present budget legislation is altered, the Clinton presidency's punctuation of the status quo may look more like an ellipsis than an exclamation mark.

NOTES

I am greatly indebted to Paul Goren for his able research assistance.

PART III

The Policy Process

11

Foreign Policy, the End of the Cold War, and the 1992 Election

WILLIAM R. THOMPSON

As commander-in-chief of the U.S. Armed Forces, George Bush presided over a short war in the Middle East in which surprisingly few American lives were lost and in which the enemy was evicted unequivocally from its occupation of Kuwait. Although American troops constituted the bulk of the expeditionary force, the Iraqis were confronted by an impressively large coalition of states organized to demonstrate the illegitimacy of the Iraqi invasion and the righteousness of the U.S.-led coalition. The successful organization, care, and feeding of this winning coalition represented a clear public-relations victory in its own right. President Bush's leadership image was a clear beneficiary of these dramatic developments in the Middle East. Indeed, one obvious political by-product of the Gulf War was the new record high in presidential approval ratings that he enjoyed as a consequence.

On an even wider front, another former enemy's territorial empire crumbled almost as quickly as the Iraqi army disintegrated as a fighting force. The Union of Soviet Socialist Republics, long the fixation of American foreign and defense policy, was no more. It had broken up into a number of smaller states—with the ultimate number still to be determined—and its dual status as the primary enemy of the United States and the world's only other superpower had simply evaporated. The successors to the Soviet Union no longer seemed very threatening. Russian military capability had been exposed as an emperor with no clothes. Even the rhetoric changed as the population and decisionmakers of Russia began to transform the basic operating principles of their state and economy so that they more closely resembled those of Western societies characterized by political democracy and market competition. The Cold War was finally over and the West, led by the United States, had won. A "new world order" was proclaimed by the surviving superpower. President Bush could and did also claim some portion of this victory as well.

Yet the titular victor of the Gulf and Cold Wars was defeated in the 1992 election, and not all that long after his ostensible victories. How is it possible that someone with such impressive foreign policy laurels could lose the presidential election to the young governor of a relatively poor southern state with little, if any, experience in global politics? The simple answer, courtesy of the Clinton campaign, points to the economy as the reason and suggests that little else mattered. There is a great deal of truth in this simple answer, but the corollary that nothing else mattered is not quite accurate. At the very least, foreign policy considerations played important facilitative roles in the defeat of President Bush and the triumph of Governor Clinton.

This chapter is structured around four partial explanations of the 1992 outcome: (1) the "its the economy, stupid!" hypothesis, (2) the "rally 'round the flag" hypothesis, (3) the "electoral punishment for war" hypothesis, and (4) the "end of the Cold War" hypothesis. By no means do these four exhaust the full set of possible explanations for the Bush defeat. They are meant only to highlight some of the leading external or "foreign policy" hypotheses regarding the recent American electoral outcome.

The electoral salience of economic problems cannot be denied. But these economic problems are less clearly "domestic" in nature than is often assumed. Indeed, the domestic/foreign distinction tends to fade once one moves beyond short-term economic problems. A second type of fading, the predictable decay of the Gulf War's rally effect, and the strong tendency for American electorates to punish incumbent parties for initiating wars also shed light on former President Bush's political problems in 1992. Finally, the end of the Cold War seems to have played only a very indirect role. At best, it facilitated the election of a candidate with very strong foreign policy negatives within a context of popular perceptions of greatly diminished external threat. It may also have encouraged the initial complacency and slow-to-start campaign of the incumbent.

THE "IT'S THE ECONOMY, STUPID!"
HYPOTHESIS

The most popular explanation of the Clinton victory—that only the state of the economy mattered to voters—is well supported by the evidence. Table 11.1 contains two types of pertinent information. The first half of the table lists the amount of public-opinion support that President Bush was able to generate between March 1989 and May 1992. Support for presidential handling of the economy declined between 1989 and late 1990/early 1991 before returning to the level at which it had been in early 1989. Then, after February 1991, the erosion of support was steady and devastating. In marked contrast, the level of support for the Bush administration's foreign policies was fairly stable through April 1992. It rose in February 1991, but only halfway through 1992 did it ever drop below 60 percent.

The second half of Table 11.1 provides opinion data on registered voters' pref-

TABLE 11.1

Bush and Clinton on Economic and Foreign Policy

Approval of the way President Bush is handling economic conditions and foreign policy:

	Economic Conditions	Foreign Policy
March 1989	52	62
November 1989	40	65
July 1990	40	62
October 1990	30	61
February 1991	51	84
March 1991	37	79
June 1991	36	64
July 1991	34	71
August 1991	33	68
August 1991	36	68
September 1991	32	70
October 1991	29	70
October 1991	28	68
December 1991	22	64
January 1992	24	64
February 1992	22	65
April 1992	22	60
May 1992	20	52

Question: Regardless of which presidential candidate you support, please tell me whether you think George Bush or Bill Clinton would better handle each of the following issues:

	Bush	Clinton	No preference
A. Foreign affairs			
March 20–22	70	22	8
July 17–18	64	25	11
August 10–12	62	30	8
August 21–22	73	19	8
August 31–September 2	67	24	9
September 11–15	73	20	7
B. Economy			
March 20–22	37	49	14
July 17–18	24	58	18
August 10–12	30	60	10
August 21–22	37	52	11
August 31–September 2	34	55	11
September 11–15	36	52	12

SOURCES: Gallup, 1991, 1992.

erences between Bush and Clinton with respect to the two principal policy areas. By a ratio of 2 or 3 to 1, voters preferred Bush to Clinton as the manager of foreign policy. But a roughly 2-to-1 margin favored Clinton on economic issues. Given the electoral outcome, it seems reasonable to infer that foreign policy questions were not all that salient in voters' minds and that economic issues were.

Public-opinion pollsters (Gallup, 1992: 188–189) believe that a fairly consistent pattern has characterized the dimensions of peace and prosperity, at least for the last ten elections. Immediately before each of these elections, the party that preferred to keep the country out of war and/or prosperous has tended to win. Table 11.2 tallies the party preference/electoral outcome data for the period between Eisenhower and Clinton. There are exceptions, to be sure; but in most cases, they are related to differential weights bestowed on peace and prosperity. In some years, one issue or the other has seemed more important. In 1968, for example, the Democrats enjoyed a slight preference margin over the Republicans on the prosperity dimension but trailed considerably on the peace issue. In the midst of an unpopular war, it was more critical to lead on this aspect of voter expectations.

At other times, peace has seemed much less salient. The winning party in 1960 and 1980 trailed considerably on the peace question. In 1960 the barely winning side led on the prosperity question in an economic climate characterized by recession in the late 1950s. Yet in the 1980s the winners and losers were almost evenly split on the prosperity issue. In this case, it could be said that peace was somewhat devalued, or perhaps simply represented the wrong question to pose, after the intensification of Cold War antagonisms over Afghanistan and the embarrassment over the inability to gain the release of the American hostages in Iran. Accordingly, the exception denoted by the 1980 election reminds us that electoral outcomes cannot be reduced solely to a question of who looks better on the peace and prosperity themes. The Republicans did not have a clear lock on either category, yet they managed to win the election with a nearly 10 percent edge in the popular vote. The relative and absolute values placed on peace and

TABLE 11.2
Peace and Prosperity Candidates

Question: Which political party do you think would (a) be more likely to keep the United States out of war, and (b) do a better job of keeping the country prosperous?

Date of Opinion Poll	Out of War		Prosperous		Winner
	Party	% edge	Party	% edge	
October 1956	R	30	R/D	0	R
October 1960	R	15	D	15	D
October 1964	D	23	D	32	D
October 1968	R	13	D	3	R
September 1972	R	4	R	3	R
August 1976	D	3	D	24	D
September 1980	D	17	D	1	R
September 1984	R	3	R	16	R
October 1988	R	16	R	16	R
October 1992	D	4	D	9	D

SOURCE: Gallup, 1992: 188–189.

prosperity are not constants. Their weights depend in part on what is taking place in the external environment and in part on the state of the economy. Therefore, their predictive capabilities are imperfect.

At the same time, there is something akin to a contextual seasonality for the relative weights given economic and foreign policy concerns. The seasonality I have in mind is not on the order of a few months, as observed in patterns of weather or Christmas shopping. Rather, the general primacy of one type of concern over the other appears to have had a run of two to three decades in the American political system. Figure 11.1 graphically displays this propensity over the last fifty to sixty years.[1] The American public has been asked to identify the most important types of policy problems since 1935. The specific problems vary somewhat from year to year, but if we aggregate the problems that relate to foreign policy concerns and those pertaining to economic concerns, the appearance of cyclicality is quite pronounced.[2]

Although the data are largely nonexistent, it is not difficult to imagine the primacy of economic concerns in the period between World Wars I and II. In the late 1930s, foreign policy concerns became increasingly paramount. The peak values recorded for foreign policy concerns during World War II would, no doubt, have persisted a bit longer than those shown in Figure 11.1 if the nature of the question had not been changed in the early 1940s. Some of the evident increase in the relative salience of economic concerns of the early 1940s was due to the poller's assumption that the ongoing war was clearly the most important problem. Thus respondents were asked to put aside their war concerns and to identify their next most pressing problems.

The economic constraints of wartime shortages and postwar demobilization,

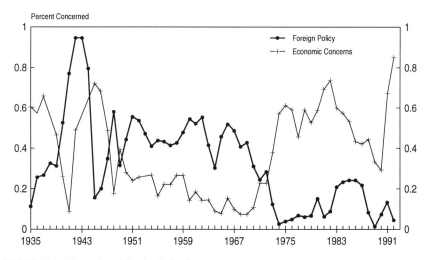

FIGURE 11.1   Economic and Foreign Policy Concerns

as well as the changes in question format, boosted economic policy concerns to first place briefly in the middle to late 1940s. The Cold War crises of 1948 and then the outbreak of the Korean War restored the hegemony of foreign policy concerns—a hegemony that was to persist into the early 1970s. Economic concerns drifted downward with some short-term fluctuations until 1970. In 1973 economic policy problems predominated over foreign policy issues for the first time since 1949. That predominance has been maintained ever since. The end of American participation in the Vietnam War and the first oil price shocks provide one way to account for the switch in respective priorities in 1973. Some gradual diminishment in Cold War antagonisms in the late 1960s and 1970s is also suggested by the fact that foreign policy issues did not return to first place in the early 1980s, despite a number of external shocks (Afghanistan, the Iranian hostages, Beirut, and the Soviet destruction of a Korean airliner) and the emergence of official rhetoric about evil empires and a "return" to early Cold War rollback policies in places such as Nicaragua and Grenada. Foreign policy concerns became relatively more salient in the 1980s, but not to the point that they threatened to dislodge the overriding primacy of economic concerns.

The respective priorities assigned to foreign and economic policy issues are long term in nature and, as such, cannot be explained by short-run shocks. The latter can help to account for small blips in the year-to-year oscillations of the expression of public priorities. But it would be highly erroneous to give credit to the short-run shocks for the primacy of one concern over the other for several decades.

There are various ways to explain the long-term staying power of the fluctuating priorities. Analysts have stressed ideological swings, isolationist/expansionist propensities, the alternating salience of political and economic problems, long waves of rapid and slow economic growth, and generational changes (see Schlesinger, 1949; Schlesinger, 1986; Modelski, 1981; Klingberg, 1952, 1983; Holmes, 1985; Namenwirth and Weber, 1987). Space considerations limit the evaluation of these emphases; but what does seem clear is that the long-term state of the economy is a critical factor. When the economy performs consistently poorly (in terms of growth, productivity, employment levels, and/or inflation), as in the years preceding World War II and after 1973, economic concerns become paramount. When the economy performs reasonably well, as in the 1950s and 1960s, economic concerns do not disappear, but their importance is much less significant.

The waging of World War II, of course, was critical to the postwar reemergence of foreign policy concerns as primary. The United States emerged from the war as the world's leading military and economic power. Indeed, it had no economic rival, and only the Soviet Union was perceived as posing a military threat. The ensuing Cold War, from the American perspective, was waged to contain that military threat. Some thirteen years of warfare in the Eurasian periphery (Korea and Vietnam) were viewed as manifestations of this Cold War containment effort. The specter of nuclear war was omnipresent. Not surprisingly, the clearest threat to many individuals' way of life was seen as originating from the external realm.

The interesting question that must remain unanswered at this time is whether economic concerns are capable of suppressing foreign policy concerns. Do these respective priorities have a zero-sum quality? When one is relatively high in salience, must the other type of concern be relatively low? Or is it simply a coincidence that these priorities have alternated over at least the past sixty years?

Coincidence is difficult to rule out completely, but it is doubtful that the apparent long-term tendency for foreign and economic concerns to switch positions is purely a function of chance. One simple explanation lies in the cyclicality of long-term economic growth (Modelski and Thompson, 1995). Periods of high growth are followed by periods of low growth, which are then followed by periods of high growth. High-growth phases, in turn, are keyed to surges in the appearance of radical technological innovation as exemplified by railroads in the midnineteenth century, electricity in the early twentieth century, and semiconductors in the midtwentieth century.

A long-wave approach to economic growth is hardly a mainstream position. Nor is this the best place to elaborate its explanatory power. The reason I raise the issue at all has to do with the central question of this chapter: What role did foreign policy concerns play in the 1992 election? If we decide that economic concerns dominated the 1992 election, as suggested by most commentators and by Table 11.1, are we to conclude that the influence of foreign policy concerns is negligible? I would suggest that the appropriate answer is negative, for several reasons. Explicit foreign policy considerations did play a role in the electoral outcome of November 1992. And, in any case, it is a highly dubious proposition to assume that American economic problems are inherently domestic in origin. To the extent that long waves in technologically induced growth fit the American case and have something to do with cyclical fluctuations in economic concerns, American economic problems have been increasingly internationalized. Accordingly, the differentiation between internal and external problems has been increasingly breaking down.

Technological growth surges are initially concentrated in space and time. One country—for example, Britain in the late eighteenth and early nineteenth countries and the United States in the late nineteenth and much of the twentieth centuries—leads the rest of the world in producing technological innovations, which are then gradually diffused, if not everywhere, then at least to other parts of the world economy. Then the leader's economic growth slows down as competitors catch up and reduce the leader's pioneering edge. And everybody's growth slows down in the troughs between the innovation peaks.

In short, there are three interrelated economic dynamics at work here: (1) the oscillation of growth phases based on (2) intermittent surges in radical technological innovations and (3) the ascent and relative decline of the lead economy. The development of the system's lead economy provides a resource foundation for subsequent foreign policy leadership initiatives. It also gives the lead economy's decisionmakers powerful incentives for attempting to preserve the stability of the world's political economy. It is the coming together of these dynamics that explains the twentieth-century tendency for the primacy of economic and foreign policy concerns in American politics to fluctuate. Periods of low economic growth and/or relative economic decline encourage the popular salience of economic issues, whereas periods of high economic growth and extensive foreign policy activity permit the elevation of foreign policy issues.

The discussion of these dynamics does not lend itself very well to the maintenance of rigid lines of division between what is internal and domestic and what is external and foreign. U.S. economic growth patterns in the twentieth century are at the very heart of world economic growth patterns. So, too, are the ascent and relative decline of the American economic hierarchical position in contrast to that of its competitors. The very nature of long-term economic growth problems, especially in the United States, is Janus-faced. What seem to be conventional domestic problems (e.g., unemployment) are actually problems of worldwide scope and vice versa. In this context, then, we should be careful not to rule out "foreign policy" problems solely because economic issues appear to be predominant. Those same economic issues are linked inevitably to foreign policy issues, whether or not decisionmakers choose to acknowledge them publicly.

In the 1992 election, the winning side came as close to acknowledging the linkages among economic problems, long-term economic growth, and foreign policy concerns as did any previous campaign. One of the reasons the Democrats won is not because they offered a concrete solution to these problems, but rather, because they were seen as visibly struggling with the linkages while their Republican opposition was arguing that there were no long-term problems that required attention.[3]

THE "RALLY 'ROUND THE FLAG" HYPOTHESIS

The "rally 'round the flag" hypothesis stipulates that public opinion will shift positively in support of leaders when their country is confronted with the abrupt appearance of an external attack or threat.[4] This hypothesis assumes that a public will be quite likely to perceive dramatic changes in the external environment that are well covered by the media, interpret attacks on or threats to their country as personal attacks or threats, and bestow support on one of the primary political symbols of the country, the principal leader. It further assumes that the principal leader will react in a manner that is perceived as appropriate and that opinion leaders will be supportive of the reaction. Still another underlying assumption is that the political opposition will be reluctant to voice open criticism during a period of crisis. Either the opposition will genuinely support the leader's response or it will fear being scapegoated if things should go badly. The 1941 Japanese attack on Pearl Harbor is an excellent example. President Roosevelt's approval ratings were already fairly high prior to this event. Nevertheless, his popularity increased by 12 percent. Numerous other examples, all of which meet the minimum threshold of a 5 percent increase in approval, are listed chronologically in Table 11.3.[5]

Table 11.3 ends with five rally events linked to the Gulf War. Bush's approval ratings benefited first from the crisis over the initial Iraqi occupation of Kuwait, and then from the fact that various institutions (the UN Security Council and the U.S. Congress) ratified the president's opposition to the Iraqi attack. Additional approval was gained when the allied attack on Iraqi positions began, and then when they ended with the rout of the Iraqi armed forces. The last four rallies suggest a particularly unusual cumulative or compound rally effect. In November 1990 the approval rating increased 7 points from 54 to 61 percent. Two months later 3 percentage points had slipped away, but the congressional approval generated another 6 percent increase. During the same month, the outbreak of war contributed another 18 points. The brevity of the war and the successful avoidance of much loss of American lives earned another 9 points, setting a record high for presidential approval in the process. The four-month net increase of 45 percent (54 to 89 percent) in the approval ratings must also have established a record for the rate of increase.

Table 11.3 underscores how unusual this compounding effect really is. To begin with, rally events are not all that common. Only thirty-two events credited with 5 percent increases took place between May 1940 and February 1991. On average, then, a significant rally occurs only once every 1.6 years. Bush experienced four in as many months. Not only the timing was unusual but so, too, was the number. The twenty-five qualifying events between Roosevelt and Reagan average to about three per president. But this calculation ignores how many terms (thirteen) were involved in the tenures of Bush's immediate eight predecessors. The average number of rallies per four-year term is slightly less than two. President Bush managed to come up with six.

Of course, there need not be a very precise relationship between a presidential approval rating and the voting decision. Whether an individual approves, disapproves, or has no opinion of an incumbent president is a different situation than choosing among two or more candidates for the presidential office. Still, one would expect that establishing a record-high approval rating would benefit an incumbent in the next election. For instance, most recently reelected incumbents (Eisenhower, Johnson, Nixon, and Reagan) enjoyed 50 percent or better approval ratings during their reelection years. Recall, too, that the Gulf War ended about ten months before the next reelection year began. Moreover, the timing of the Gulf War rallies made Bush the first president since the late 1950s with a more favorable rating in the third year of his term than in the first year. Yet as indicated in Figure 11.2, a year after the Gulf War, Bush's presidential approval had declined to less than 50 percent, and more of the public disapproved than approved of his performance.[6]

TABLE 11.3
Selected Rally Events and Changes in Presidential Approval

Event	Approval Pre- Post- Event Change			Duration in Weeks
Roosevelt				
Hitler invades Low Countries (May 1940)	58	66	+8	4
Pearl Harbor (December 1941)	72	84	+12	30
Truman				
Truman Doctrine proposed (March 1947)	48	60	+12	a
South Korea invaded (June 1950)	37	46	+9	10
Eisenhower				
Bermuda Conference/UN Atom Pool Speech (December 1953)	59	69	+10	20
Indochina Truce signed (July 1954)	65	75	+10	6
Marines sent to Lebanon (July 1958)	52	58	+6	8
Goodwill Trip (December 1959)	67	77	+10	5
Kennedy				
Bay of Pigs Invasion (April 1961)	78	83	+5	1
Cuban Missile Crisis (October/November 1962)	61	74	+13	31
Johnson				
Marines sent to Santo Domingo (April 1965)	64	70	+6	8
First bombing of Hanoi/Haiphong (June 1966)	48	56	+8	6
Glassboro Summit (June 1967)	44	52	+8	6
Halt of bombing of North Vietnam (March 1968)	36	50	+14	19
Nixon				
Vietnamization Speech (November 1969)	56	67	+11	15
Warning of USSR on Mideast (July 1970)	55	61	+6	3
Vietnam Ceasefire Proposal (October 1970)	51	58	+7	10
Moscow Summit (May 1972)	54	62	+8	4
Vietnam Peace Agreement (January 1973)	51	67	+16	15
Ford				
Mayaguez Incident (May 1975)	40	51	+11	25
Carter				
Camp David Accords (September 1978)	43	48	+5	17
Hostages seized in Iran (November 1979)	32	51	+19	30
Reagan				
Beirut bombing/Grenada Invasion (October 1983)	45	53	+8	b
TWA Hostage Crisis (June 1985)	58	63	+5	5
First Reagan/Gorbachev Summit (November 1985)	62	69	+7	4
Air Strikes against Libya (April 1986)	62	68	+6	3
Bush				
Panama Invasion/Capture of Noriega (December 1989–January 1990)	71	80	+9	5
Iraqi Invasion of Kuwait (August 1990)	60	74	+14	9
UN Security Council approves use of force against Iraq (November 1990)	54	61	+7	c
Congress approves use of force against Iraq (January 1991)	58	64	+6	c
Desert Storm begins (January 1991)	64	82	+18	c
Desert Storm ends (February 1991)	80	89	+9	4

[a]No data were available between September 1947 and April 1948.
[b]The timing of the event corresponded with an economic recovery.
[c]The timing of the event overlapped with other rally events.
SOURCE: Hugick and Gallup, 1991.

How can we account for this outcome? Table 11.3 suggests just how limited the longevity of rally effects are. Only three (Pearl Harbor, the Cuban Missile Crisis, and the seizure of hostages in Iran) out of thirty-one events had effects that were estimated as lasting as long as thirty to thirty-one weeks, or less than eight months. (The average duration was apparently eleven and a half weeks.) Clearly, American rally effects come and go and can be subject to quite rapid decay. In this respect, the evaporation of the Bush rally effects was not unusual.

One of the earliest systematic students of rally effects, J. E. Mueller (1973), introduced rally effects as a way of accounting for some of the upward bumps in the anticipated progressive decline of each president's popularity. In particular, Mueller argued that each president comes to power supported by a coalition of people with diverse interests and expectations. Each time a president acts, he is apt to satisfy some of his supporters but not all of them. Those whose expectations are disappointed are apt to move from the approval to the disapproval categories. The longer into a presidential term (and, therefore, the more opportunities to act and to disappoint), the lower the level of approval we should expect. Rallies have thus been seen as events that slowed or temporarily interrupted the general tendency toward approval decay.

If we add to this argument the finding that new ralliers tend to come from the ranks of the opposition, rather than from the neutral/no-opinion column (Edwards with Gallup, 1991), we have all the more reason to anticipate the rapid erosion of rally effects. These new ralliers are the most likely group to revert to the opposition ranks and the disapproval category after an international crisis has

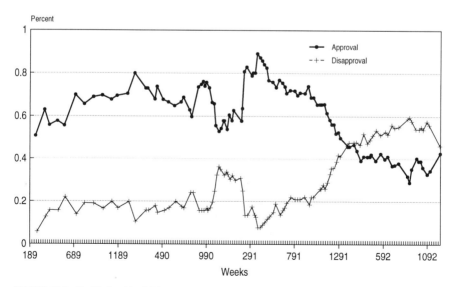

FIGURE 11.2 Bush's Presidential Approval Ratings

settled down. An external, threat-induced, rapid increase in presidential approval, therefore, is most likely to be followed by a not quite equally rapid decrease in approval, accelerated by some normal rate of decay. Other things being equal, we should have expected Bush's spectacular rise in the polls to have been followed by a more gradual but equally spectacular fall. The only question should have been over what rate of decay was most likely.

However, other things were not equal. Bush's economic problems have been mentioned already. His foreign policy problems were complicated by, among other events, postwar developments in the Gulf region. His emphasis on maintaining the allied coalition and avoiding the loss of allied lives led to his eagerness to disengage from further combat once Kuwait had been liberated. Saddam Hussein remained in power and, given the absence of continued allied intervention, in a position to punish revolts in southern and northern Iraq that had been encouraged by the United States. These postwar ambiguities permitted what was initially viewed as a successful victory to become something much less.

In addition, doubts were voiced about American policies prior to the war. To what extent were Iraqi military prowess and territorial ambitions related to U.S. encouragement of the Iraqis' side in the long war with the Iranians? For that matter, was the U.S. warning to Iraq not to invade Kuwait delivered clearly enough? In short, not only was the victory questioned but some voters also blamed the Bush administration for encouraging Saddam Hussein in the first place.

The relevant opinion data on these questions are awkward because they lack specificity. In addition, there were major changes in the way the most pertinent question was asked. (I am referring here to the question in which respondents were asked essentially whether they approved of U.S. policy in the Persian Gulf conflict.) But the data do suggest that an increasing number of people were dissatisfied by the Gulf War outcome. Table 11.4 provides responses to three questions of interest that were posed between August 1990 and August 1992.

In contrast to the findings as to what category new ralliers came from, the initial increase in support for Bush's Kuwaiti policy clearly came from the no-opinion column. The initial August rally decayed subsequently, with some approvers shifting to the disapproval column (but without much movement back to the neutral response). The missing data between January and April 1991, given what happened to presidential approval in general, presumably mask more movement from the disapproval and no-opinion categories to the approval side of the ledger. When the question shifted from general approval or disapproval to the much more focused reaction to what exactly constitutes victory, a different image of public sentiment emerged. Almost immediately after the war's end, 55 percent of those surveyed regarded the outcome as a victory. In less than five months, and especially after the Iraqi repression of the Kurdish rebellion in April, only 25 percent still regarded the outcome as a victory. Sixty-nine percent did not.

The point here is that American presidents can usually expect "rally 'round the flag" support when they are visibly confronting an external threat.[7] The 11-point

TABLE 11.4
Evaluation of American Foreign Policy in the Persian Gulf

	Favorable Response	Unfavorable Response	No Opinion
Question One			
August 3–4, 1990	52	16	32
August 9–12, 1990	80	12	8
August 30–September 2, 1990	74	18	8
October 3–4, 1990	69	25	6
November 1–4, 1990	61	29	10
December 6–9, 1990	57	36	7
January 3–6, 1991	60	34	6
January 11–13, 1991	62	28	10
Question Two			
February 1, 1991	37	60	3
February 22, 1991	29	68	3
March 1, 1991	29	68	3
March 14–15, 1991	55	38	7
April 4–5, 1991	46	45	9
April 18–19, 1991	36	55	9
Question Three			
July 31–August 2, 1992	25	69	6

Question One: Do you approve or disapprove of the way George Bush is handling the current situation in the Middle East involving Iraq and Kuwait?
Question Two: Last year Saddam Hussein withdrew from Kuwait, but he remains in power in Iraq. Do you think this was a victory for U.S. and allied forces in the Persian Gulf region or not?
Question Three: Indicate whether you agree or disagree with the following statement: If Saddam Hussein withdraws from Kuwait but remains in power in Iraq, this will be a victory for the U.S. and allied forces.

SOURCES: Gallup, 1991, 1992.

rally for President Ford during the 1975 Mayaguez Incident is a reminder that the external threat need not be all that great.[8] The outbreak of war or near-war, however, is almost guaranteed to increase presidential approval. World War II, the Korean War, the Vietnam War, and the Gulf War were all good for 9 or more points at the outset. Win or lose, the increase in approval has been temporary. But when a president is perceived as losing or not handling a war crisis very well, the increase in approval is even more transitory than might otherwise be the case. Truman and Johnson were wounded greatly by their respective wars. Carter's ratings improved dramatically at the beginning of the Iranian hostage drama, only to fall as the crisis dragged on without resolution. A lack of success tends to be punished at the polls. Bush's case may have been complicated by the state of the economy and by his main opponent's unusual negatives in the foreign policy realm. If the prevailing economic grievances somehow had not been present, Bush might conceivably have won reelection, but probably not on the basis of his having presided over the Gulf War.

THE "ELECTORAL PUNISHMENT
FOR WAR" HYPOTHESIS

Another pertinent hypothesis is that in the American political system, and perhaps elsewhere as well, it does not really matter whether a war is won or lost. Wars are expensive. They cause suffering and inconvenience. They invariably generate opposition and discontent—whether over the idea of war itself or over the tactics being applied. Even though a conflict may ultimately be reckoned a win, victory may not have come fast enough or as decisively as all might prefer. The outcome is often a loss of popular support for governmental decisionmakers during and immediately after a war.

The strongest version of this interpretation has been advanced by A. Stein (1980), who contends that the longer and more costly a war is, the more probable it is that a society will be mobilized to fight the war. Moreover, the greater the costs of mobilization, the more likely the integrative effect of an external threat will be overwhelmed by tendencies toward societal disintegration. Depending on the levels and length of the mobilization, the disintegrative tendencies may be manifested in a variety of ways, ranging from violent protest to electoral punishment.

Stein applied his theory of war consequences to America's twentieth-century experience and found considerable general support for his argument. T.Y.C. Cotton (1986) utilized the same argument more specifically in an analysis of electoral punishment in five American wars since the late nineteenth century (the Spanish-American War, World War I, World War II, the Korean War, and the Vietnam War). He, too, found strong empirical support for the mobilization-punishment argument. Cotton concluded that elected leaders, particularly presidents, who were associated with American entries into war were likely to lose electoral support both during and after the wars in question. These losses in support were most closely linked to increases in military spending. The greater the spending increase, the greater was the consequent loss in support. Over the time period examined by Cotton, a 100 percent increase in wartime military spending led to a loss of 2.65 percent of the vote for the incumbent party in the next presidential election.

Several studies have traced the loss of support for American presidents during the Korean and Vietnam Wars. In both cases, popular support for the president increased at the beginning of the conflicts and then gradually eroded until only a core of supporters remained. Mueller (1973: 60) argues that the pace of this erosion was tied closely to battle deaths. Every tenfold increase in American battle deaths translated into a 15 percent loss of support.[9]

Table 11.5 provides illustrative support for the general contention that one of the costs of fighting American wars is a loss of votes. All of the major U.S. wars, beginning with the War of 1812 and extending through the 1991 Gulf War, are included in this table. Depending on whether a presidential election was held dur-

TABLE 11.5
The Pattern of Incumbency and the Suggestion of
Electoral Punishment for War Initiation, 1788–1992

War	Incumbent Party[a]		Vote Proportions[b]			Did Incumbent Party Initiate War?	Electoral Punishment Suggested?
1812	DR		1808	1812	1816		
		E	69.7	59.0	84.3	yes	mixed
Mexican-American War	D		1844	1848			
		P	49.5	43.8			
		E	61.8	42.5		yes	yes
Civil War	R		1860	1864	1868		
		P	39.8	55.0	52.7		
		E	59.4	91.0	76.5	yes	mixed
Spanish-American War	R		1896	1900			
		P	51.0	51.7			
		E	51.1	65.3		yes	no
World War I	D		1916	1920			
		P	49.2	34.2			
		E	52.2	23.9		yes	yes
World War II	D		1940	1944	1948		
		P	54.7	53.4	49.5		
		E	84.6	81.4	57.1	yes	yes
Korean War	D		1948	1952			
		P	49.5	44.4			
		E	57.1	16.8		yes	yes
	R		1952	1956			
		P	55.1	57.4			
		E	83.2	86.1		no	no
Vietnam War	D		1964	1968			
		P	61.1	42.7			
		E	90.3	35.5		yes	yes
	R		1968	1972			
		P	43.4	60.7			
		E	55.9	96.7		no	no
Gulf War	R		1988	1992			
		P	53.3	37.4			
		E	79.2	38.4		yes	yes

[a]Party symbols: DR = Democratic Republican, D = Democrat, R = Republican.
[b]Vote-proportion symbols: P = popular vote, E = electoral college.
SOURCES: Data on vote proportions were taken from Mackie and Rose, 1991; Stanley and Niemi, 1992; and Pomper, 1993.

ing the war or after its end, the incumbent party's prewar, wartime, and postwar proportions of the popular and electoral-college votes are listed. The basic question is whether there is any evidence of electoral punishment, which in this case, means simply any decline in the votes received.

In six out of nine cases (the Mexican-American Wars, World War I, World War

II, the Korean War, the Vietnam War, and the Gulf War), the incumbent party suffered some decline at the polls if it was associated with an entry into war. The extent of decline varies considerably. The 1968 and 1992 cases are at one end of the continuum. The very slight loss suffered by Franklin Roosevelt during World War II, 1.3 percent between 1940 and 1944, is at the other end. In two cases, the War of 1812 and the Civil War, the outcome was mixed. During the War of 1812, the Democratic Republican Party lost support but regained it quite dramatically in the postwar election. Although the War of 1812 can hardly be counted as an American success, it was not considered a defeat at the time. That war ended with American victories on the battlefield and no loss of territory, despite the asymmetry of power inherent in the British-American confrontation. During the American Civil War, Abraham Lincoln generated more electoral support during the war than just before it broke out. Of course, it helped that a large number of his opponents in 1864 resided in states attempting to secede and were therefore ineligible to cast dissenting ballots. The 1868 election gave the Republican candidate (Grant) proportionally more votes than the Republicans had gained in 1860 but not as many as in 1864.

Two additional cases in Table 11.5, 1956 and 1972, represent wartime or postwar elections in which the incumbent party was not associated with the war-entry decision. In these cases, neither Eisenhower nor Nixon appeared to suffer at the polls. The third clear clase of nonpunishment was the 1900 election, in which the Republicans did about as well as or slightly better than they had done in 1896. The Spanish-American War was short, inexpensive, and clearly successful.

In sum, we have six clear cases of apparent electoral punishment and only one clear exception. That would suggest a rather strong tendency in support of the electoral-punishment hypothesis. The problem is that it is not uncommon for incumbent parties to lose support in subsequent presidential elections. In fact, this outcome is the norm. Since 1832 the average incumbent party's popular vote change from election to election has been −3.3 percent. It is also possible to slip at the polls and still win the election. So we need to ask the question in a more systematic fashion if we want to be sure of the answer.

Table 11.6 supplies two more systematic answers in the form of cross-tabulations. Regarding the first of these, respondents were asked whether there is a relationship between an incumbent party that had initiated a war and subsequent electoral punishment. The evidence for punishment is quite strong. Eight of ten cases since 1832 (with 1864 and 1900 being the two exceptions) demonstrate some decline in support, as compared to only eighteen of thirty-one cases (58 percent) in situations not involving incumbent war initiations. The average incumbent party's vote change after a war initiation is −5.3 percent, or about 60 percent greater than the general average change.

What does this finding mean in terms of who wins or loses elections? The second cross tabulation in Table 11.6 addresses this question. In only half of the cases (five out of ten) did war-initiating incumbent parties lose power. In nonwar-ini-

TABLE 11.6
Electoral Punishment and Defeat Due to War Initiations

		Incumbent Party Initiated War	
		Yes	No
Apparent	Yes	8	18
electoral		(80.0)	(58.0)
punishment	No	2	13
		(20.0)	(42.0)
		Incumbent Party Initiated War	
		Yes	No
Incumbent	Yes	5	13
defeated		(50.0)	(42.0)
in election	No	5	18
		(50.0)	(58.0)

SOURCE: Data compiled by the author.

tiating situations, incumbent parties lost 42 percent of the time. Thus a war initiation improves the odds of losing the next election, but not by all that much.

THE "END OF THE COLD WAR" HYPOTHESIS

Having discussed American shooting wars both in general and in particular, I now turn to one other type of war that deserves further attention—the Soviet-American Cold War. Exactly when this Cold War began is debatable; the range of years falls between 1917 and 1950. Precisely when it ended will also continue to be debated for some time to come. However, the 1988–1992 Bush administration can make some claim to having presided over a segment of the end phase. The Berlin Wall came down in 1989. The Soviet Union disintegrated into a number of large and small states. And the Russian reform movement, if not Gorbachev as well, survived the attempted August 1990 coup by hardliners. Between May and September 1990, a majority of the American public came to believe that the Cold War was truly over. By May, that figure had declined to 40 percent. By September, only 40 percent thought the Cold War even existed (Gallup, 1991: 52).

Prior to President Bush's record-high approval rating at the conclusion of the Gulf War, the record (87 percent) had been established by President Truman at the surrender of Germany in World War II. For that matter, Eisenhower benefited from the signing of the Indochina Truce in 1954 (+10 percent), and Nixon's approval ratings were enhanced by 16 points after the signing of the 1973 Vietnam Peace Agreement. The rule, at least since 1945, seems to be that ending wars results in political reward. Why shouldn't this rule apply to the end of the Cold War as well? In particular, why didn't Bush receive some electoral credit for the termination of the Cold War?

At least two interrelated answers come to mind. The Cold War was neither a shooting war nor one being intensely waged in the late 1980s. The euphoric ending of a shooting war means that combatants come home and are no longer in harm's way in foreign lands, and that the inconvenience of any domestic restrictions on consumption and normal life are relaxed. But as the Cold War continues to wind down—though American bases overseas will be closed, some troops will be rotated home, and the size of the military will be scaled down—the effect will be gradual. Except for those people employed by a firm heavily dependent upon military contracts and/or located in Southern California, the domestic economic reverberations are likely to be both incremental and subtle. The effects are also likely to span several presidential administrations.

Additional evidence for the lack of intensity of the Cold War is provided in Figures 11.3 and 11.4. Figure 11.3 plots U.S. defense spending as a proportion of gross national product against the proportion of the public who favor greater defense spending.[10] Controlling for inflation, we can see defense spending as decreasing ever since the Korean War, with brief upturns during the Vietnam War and the Reagan administration. Public demand for increased defense spending is partially a function of how much is being spent on defense. For instance, increases in military preparation were desired prior to World War II and immediately after its conclusion. And spikes of sentiment for more spending occurred in the late 1950s when the public expressed alarm over Sputnik and alleged missile/bomber gaps; in the 1960s, during the Vietnam War; and in the reintensified segment of the Cold War in the late 1970s and early 1980s. Since about 1983 or 1984, however, the interest in increased defense spending has been markedly stable and very much a minority position, reaching a low of 10 percent in 1991. Both defense

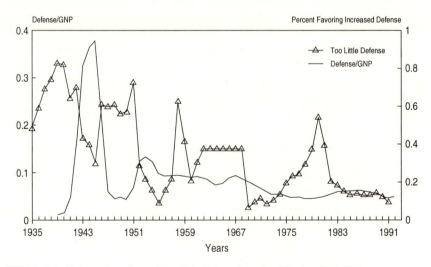

FIGURE 11.3   Defense-Spending and Too-Little-Defense-Spending Attitudes, 1935–1991

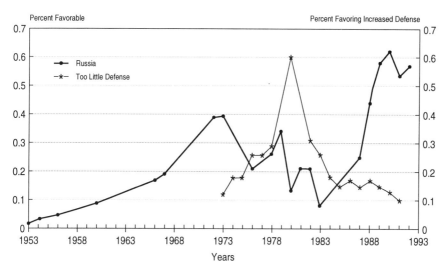

FIGURE 11.4   Perceptions of the Soviet Union and Too-Little-Defense-Spending Attitudes

spending and the demand for increased defense spending can be viewed as indicators of perceived external threat. Both indicators give credence to the notion that the Cold War has been winding down for some time and certainly before 1988. After all, Bush's predecessor also claimed credit for the triumph over Soviet communism.

The demand for increased defense spending demonstrated in Figure 11.3 was not always oriented toward a perceived Soviet threat. German, Japanese, North Korean, and North Vietnamese threats, to mention some of the more obvious sources, were also involved. Some might argue, then, that the picture painted by this figure is too general to serve as an adequate representation of the intensity of the Cold War. Figure 11.4 helps close the gap by suggesting that there is a roughly negative relationship, especially after the Vietnam War, between popular perceptions of the Soviet Union/Russia and the desire for increased defense spending. Favorable perceptions of the former Soviet Union reached new highs in the middle to late 1980s and early 1990s.[11] Of course, there are countries that fare better in public popularity than did the former Soviet Union—Canada and Germany, to name two. But in early 1992, the former Soviet Union outscored two other states, Japan and Israel, considered to be tied closely to the American-led coalition in the Cold War. As depicted in Figure 11.4, this turnabout of popular attitudes toward the principal Cold War threat has been emerging or reemerging since the early 1980s. Overall, but without getting into the controversy over the multiple sources responsible for ending or reducing Soviet-American antagonisms, the Cold War probably wound down too gradually and too subtly for any American president to earn much electoral credit for its decline.

Moreover, some of the good feeling toward the former Soviet Union must be due to the highly visible roles played by Gorbachev and Yeltsin in deescalating the Cold War. But if the "other side" deserves some proportion of the credit for ending the Cold War, there is less reason to congratulate one's own leaders unless it can be claimed convincingly that the other side quit only because of unrelenting American pressure to do so. That claim has been advanced by recent Republican presidents, though in a less than convincing way (see Deudney and Ikenberry, 1992; Schneider, Widmer, and Ruloff, 1993).

Does this conclusion imply that the Cold War played little or no role in the 1992 election? If our argument is that it had been winding down throughout the 1980s, we would be hard-pressed to give the Cold War much direct electoral impact. Its indirect impact may have been a different matter. It is difficult to dismiss Clinton's adverse evaluations on foreign policy issues during the campaign (see Table 11.1) as simply irrelevant in light of the great dissatisfaction that exists over questions of economic growth. Indeed, it is more likely that the perceived demise of the Cold War contributed to the deemphasis of the significance of Clinton's strikingly negative evaluations on foreign policy issues.

One of Bush's successful campaign strategies in 1988 was his emphasis on his advantages in foreign policy experience over Dukakis. Similar assertions were tried in 1992 against a candidate whose background made him seem even more vulnerable than Dukakis. Table 11.1 suggests that Clinton was unable to evade this vulnerability, but it was obviously not important enough to cost him the election. The significance of foreign policy experience and the "soft on defense" attack had clearly depreciated between 1988 and 1992. How much one wishes to attribute this depreciation to the economy, to the nature of the Gulf War outcome, to lingering doubts about Bush's role in the Iran/Contra affair, or to the end of the Cold War is an open question. Suffice it to say that it is hard to imagine someone with no military or foreign policy experience, someone accused of draft evasion and even of collaborating with the KGB in organizing antiwar protests as a student, defeating Bush and Perot during an era of intense Cold War antagonisms. It is much easier to conceive of the election of such a candidate during a period in which one's Cold War stance is no longer a significant litmus test to be passed in order to achieve at least minimal credibility as a presidential candidate. In this respect it is possible to surmise, but difficult to prove, that the demise of the Cold War indirectly facilitated the 1992 defeat of George Bush.

Two or three other indirect roles for the end of the Cold War can at least be suggested. On the one hand, it seems improbable that the Gulf War would have taken place if the Cold War had continued. The Iraqis might have been more cautious or restrained as Soviet clients. On the other hand, the Western/Arab opposing coalition might have been much more difficult to assemble and maintain in the face of potential Soviet involvement. If the Gulf War had not taken place on Bush's watch, the electoral implications would be difficult to specify with certainty—but certainly different scenarios are imaginable.

Focusing instead on the Gulf War's aftermath, we find that President Bush seemed undefeatable eighteen months before the 1992 election. The Cold War was over. The latest American shooting war had just ended handily. Bush's image of undefeatability probably had some influence on potential opponents. It was not inevitable that Clinton would become the Democratic standard-bearer. Some potential candidates chose not to enter the race—in part, presumably, because the odds of winning seemed poor.[12] In short, a different slate of candidates in the primaries might have produced a different winner at the Democratic National Convention. And a different Democratic opponent might have fared differently at the polls.

On the Republican side of the equation, Bush's initial image of undefeatability must also have encouraged a fair amount of complacency and confidence. When it is difficult to imagine being defeated, one has much less incentive to engage in strenuous campaigning or worrying about winning policy positions.[13]

Many of the elements emphasized in this chapter may strike readers as difficult for policymakers and incumbents to manipulate. Long-term economic growth problems, the decay of rally effects, and electoral punishment for war initiations all have a deterministic flavor. Yet what incumbents can choose is whether they will acknowledge the existence of long-term economic growth problems. If they choose to ignore them when voters are having difficulties ignoring them, the opposition's economic policies are apt to seem all the more credible. Incumbents also have to decide how comfortable their leads really are. If incumbents come to believe they will be difficult to defeat, a certain complacency about the ensuing campaign should not be too surprising, even though elections can be won or lost on the strength of respective campaign strategies. Again, it is difficult to determine how much, if any, credit for incumbent complacency should be given to the ending of either shooting wars or the Cold War. Nonetheless, some influence remains plausible and deserves further study.

CONCLUSIONS

With the advantage of hindsight, the defeat of George Bush and the victory of William Clinton seem almost overdetermined. That economic problems were quite salient is not at issue. The only real question is whether these problems should be counted as genuinely domestic in nature. My response is that it is difficult to sustain the domestic/foreign accounting scheme given the structural roots of the economic problems. Moreover, Bush's preelection position in the polls was quite unusual. He had set a new record high for public approval, and his average rating was better in his third year than in the two preceding years. Yet though his seemingly invulnerable position was unusual, the disintegration of that same position was quite predictable. Rallies induced by foreign threats and confrontations are, without exception, short-lived. Also quite probable is some level of electoral punishment for war initiations—regardless of how the war turns out, but especially if what seemed to be an initial victory quickly turns sour by subsequent developments. Even the demise of the Cold War, though it does not seem to have played a direct role in the 1992 election, may have contributed in several indirect ways to the electoral outcome. Thus, there are few reasons to minimize the 1992 role of "foreign policy" issues and several very concrete reasons for crediting them with a significant influence.

But what of the prospects for significant changes in American politics? Are the factors that have been discussed in this chapter the harbingers of a new external environment for domestic politics? A focus on the foreign policy aspects of the 1992 election highlights elements of continuity and at least some potential for discontinuity. The historical syndromes concerning "rally 'round the flag" and electoral punishments for war initiations underline the elements of continuity in the Bush defeat. The interpretation of American economic problems as structurally long term in nature as well as the various hypothesized effects of the end of the Cold War suggest areas in which substantial discontinuities may be revealed.

If the American economy has indeed been experiencing a long-run downswing since about 1973, two immediate future possibilities can be conjectured. The downswing may continue and even accelerate, as in the nineteenth-century British case of relative decline as the world economy's lead unit. In that event, American politicians would find it increasingly difficult to mobilize the resources necessary to deal with domestic and foreign policy problems. Alternatively, we may see a revival of American economic growth and leadership. Although outcomes lying between these two possibilities are certainly imaginable, the basic point is that long-run economic growth is an inherently discontinuous process. The precise location of the American economy in its long-run growth trajectory will have profound implications not only for economic performance but also for electoral behavior and attempts at the management of policy problems.

The end of the Cold War suggests a different type of discontinuity. Unless a new primary enemy promising intense global rivalry emerges to replace the one that has recently disintegrated (a development that is not impossible in light of ongoing economic challenges primarily emanating from Japan), American politics should no longer be quite as subject to the political constraints imposed by the old obsession with the nation's principal enduring rivalry and the attendant security implications. In effect, the Cold War acted as a filter screening which politicians, issues, and policies could rise to prominence and survive in the American political arena. That filter is presumably no more. Its demise contributed to the Clinton victory. Whether a new foreign policy filter on domestic political behavior will emerge to replace it remains to be seen. Even so, it seems unlikely that the domestic effects of any new external security constraints will soon approximate the earlier political impact of perceptions and interpretations of the Soviet threat.

NOTES

1. These data are based on information reported in Smith (1985) and updated with information found in Gallup (multiple years).

2. This rather dramatic switch in priorities would appear to contradict Stimson (1991:3), who argues that public opinion is rarely subject to discontinuous change that is either nontrivial or unrelated to differences in the way one asks questions.

3. This type of policy issue could conceivably lead to a realignment of voting patterns. But it is too soon to tell whether the Clinton victory is the harbinger of a new era of Democratic political hegemony. It may simply represent more of the same dealignment fluctuations of the past two or so decades in which different parties have controlled different institutions (to varying degrees) and no single party has exercised political dominance over the country's agenda for very long.

4. The rally argument is developed and examined in Waltz (1967); Mueller (1970, 1973); Lee (1977); Kernell (1978); Sigelman and Conover (1981); Stoll (1987); Brody (1984, 1991); Wittkopf and Dehaven (1987); Edwards with Gallup (1991); Russett (1990b); and Liam and Oneal (1993). A related literature on presidential uses of force in order to improve their poll standings and electoral chances also exists: See Stoll (1984); Ostrom and Simon (1985); Ostrom and Job (1986); Morgan and Bickers (1992); and Russett (1990a, 1990b).

5. The list of rally events in Table 11.3 is based on the following definition (Hugick and Gallup, 1991: 16): Rally points are associated with events that are connected with foreign affairs, diplomacy, and military operations; directly involve the United States and the president; and are specific, dramatic, sharply focused, and highly salient to the public. In comparing the levels of approval in the polls immediately before and after the event, I utilized a 3 percent increase in presidential approval as a minimal threshold. In Table 11.3, I restrict the criterion for rating improvement to 5 percent, following Edwards with Gallup (1991), who suggest that a 5 percent change is necessary in order to have 95 percent confidence that the change is statistically significant when approval ratings approximate 50 percent.

6. The Bush approval ratings are taken from the *Gallup Poll Monthly* (1992). Sigelman (1979) and Brody (1991) report formulas for translating presidential approval into electoral outcomes.

7. Keep in mind that the impact of a potential rally event is not all that predictable. Some rally events have little, if any, discernible impact, whereas a variety of noncrisis events (presidential speeches, summit meetings, health reports) can actually have positive effects.

8. The Mayaguez Incident involved a merchant marine ship seized by the Cambodian navy. The crew were in the process of being released just as American military forces attacked to secure their rescue.

9. Other writers on the "electoral punishment for war" hypothesis include Stein and Russett (1980), Russett (1990b), and Bueno de Mesquita, Siverson, and Woller (1992).

10. The defense-spending data in Figure 11.3 are taken from U.S. Department of Commerce (multiple years). The opinion data on defense spending are based on information reported in Abolfathi (1980), Wood (1990), Mayer (1992), and Gallup (multiple years).

11. This information on attitudes toward the Soviet Union and its successors is taken from Mayer (1992) and Gallup (multiple years).

12. Baker (1993: 44) attributes the noncandidacies of several Democrats to this image of undefeatability, although he links the image exclusively to the Gulf War. Barilleaux and Adkins (1993: 37) suggest that Gore was not a presidential candidate because of Bush's "new world order" popularity.

13. Atherton (1993: 80) suggests that Republican campaign strategists were confident throughout much of the election that they could repeat the 1988 outcome with similar tactics predicated on attacking Clinton's credibility.

12

Issue Expansion in the Early Clinton Administration: Health Care and Deficit Reduction

BRYAN D. JONES
BILLY HALL

Often we think of democracy as a form of government that responds to the preferences of popular majorities. It seems so simple: People have concerns, and representative government enacts policies that deal with those concerns. What actually happens most of the time, however, belies this description of democratic governance. More typically, politicians present ideas to the public and try to convince people that their proposed policies are good ones. And the public—again, for the most part—is asked to react to the policies presented to them by politicians.

Because this pattern of activity on the part of political leaders and publics is so typical in forging the linkage between people and their representatives, it is important to try to understand, first, where the ideas come from and, second, how they get "expanded" to include the public's support. After all, lots of political leaders float "trial balloons" to garner public reaction, and only a few of their ideas survive.

In this chapter, we examine two of the three major domestic initiatives of the first year of the Clinton presidency and show how neither of them was responsive to the *major* concerns of the public. The three issues are Clinton's "investment and jobs" package (which met defeat at the hands of Congress), his deficit-reduction bill, and his health care initiative, of which the latter two will be examined here. The deficit-reduction bill was narrowly approved by Congress in August 1993, and in September of that year the president introduced his health care initiative. All three issues are prime cases of how presidents must present issues to the public, how they must deal with the concerns of other political elites, such as members of Congress and interest groups, and how they must successfully engage the public—even though the issues of deficit reduction and health care were not at the top of the list of concerns expressed by the public over the last several years. Ironically, these latter two issues were not primary themes of Clinton's campaign, although he did discuss both in response to the actions of other candidates, and he embraced both with gusto very early in his presidency. Meanwhile, the issue dearest to his heart, the use of government to promote human capital investment, turned out not to be a "winner" even though it was closest to the primary concerns of citizens. In the end, we show just how complex democratic government is, and how limited the idea of "responding to public preferences" is in explaining what is going on.

WHAT DO PEOPLE WANT?

Public-opinion polling is now a mature art. Political scientists and professional public-opinion pollsters not only have good polls from more than forty years ago to the present, but they also have good ways of telling poor polls from good ones. Several studies have been made of the history of public opinion since World War II, and the best of these have carefully examined the reliability of the polling techniques used.[1] If we examine the proportion of Americans in favor of (1) more government action to improve health care, (2) more government action to promote jobs and economic growth, and (3) more government action to reduce the deficit, we find large majorities in each case. For example, from 1965 through 1990, the percentage of Americans favoring more government spending on health care never dropped below 55 percent and sometimes rose well above 80 percent (Page and Shapiro, 1992: 130; Mayer, 1992: 455).[2] Large majorities of Americans have long favored a balanced-budget amendment to the Constitution, a measure that would prohibit deficit financing under normal circumstances. The lowest percentage recorded in reliable national polls was around 63 percent and often went above 80 percent (Mayer, 1992: 468; Page and Shapiro, 1992: 148–149). Finally, most Americans strongly support government policies to help provide employment. Again, majorities over time are large: Between 1966 and 1982, more than 60 percent of Americans favored the passage of a "full employment bill" that guaranteed jobs to everyone (Page and Shapiro, 1992: 121).

Now these are unqualified opinions; that is, they are not tied to a specific plan to provide jobs or spend more on health care. When real policies with real costs are proposed, the outcome may be different. But it is abundantly clear from years of public polling that large majorities want government to provide better health care, more jobs, and lower deficits. They also want more crime control, more spending on education, more money for improving the environment, more control over guns, and lower taxes. It would not be correct to say that everyone just wants more services for less taxes, however. Majorities are against more "welfare" spending, and most people think spending on the problems of cities is "about right." Neither are Americans very supportive of antitrust activities, and support for energy policies to increase supplies has declined since the 1970s (Page and Shapiro, 1992: ch. 4).

Put directly, the American public harbors complex and occasionally contra-dictory preferences about public policies. This is not to imply any kind of "irra-tionality." Almost all people hold contradictory preferences; the limits on human wants are set by context, not by the structure of the preferences themselves. In the private sector, prices cause us to choose among competing priorities. We compare what we want with what we can pay. And in the public sector, it is *atten-tion* that allocates among priorities. There are many worthy objectives govern-ment could accomplish (from limiting its intrusiveness to "doing more"). But what it ends up actually doing is dependent on what problems policymakers think are important at the time. Often this connection is not evident from what the people "want"; we have seen, people want lots of things from government. Accordingly, it is in the nature of democratic governance that political leaders must convince the public that the problems they want to work on are the impor-tant ones to address.

Public preferences are extraordinarily insensitive to changes in administration and even to changes in policies that are enacted—primarily because what people want out of life is pretty fundamental. Mass preferences do change, but they tend to change gradually, over decades rather than years. But what people view as an important problem for government to address is extremely sensitive to changes in political context (Jones, 1994). Fortunately, polls do measure this attentiveness to problems; indeed, the Gallup polls have regularly asked citizens what they consider to be the major problem facing the United States. By studying these polls, we have found that Americans are primarily concerned with two major issues—the state of the economy and social order. By *state of the economy* we mean issues such as inflation, unemployment, and jobs. By *social order* we mean crime, drug use, civil disorder, and (in earlier times) strikes and civil disobedi-ence. Although other issues occasionally intrude, the "big two" have basically dominated public concern since World War II. Neither health care (and other social welfare issues) nor the deficit has received much attention by the public (Jones, 1994). This is not to say that people do not want these problems ad-dressed. Public-opinion polling indicates that they clearly do. It's just that these are not the problems that concern citizens most. On the contrary, deficit reduc-tion and health care have generally been of relatively low priority during the last quarter-century.[3]

Campaign Appeals and Public Responses

Recent Gallup polls on the "most important problem" were useful in our exami-nation of public perceptions of problems as the Clinton administration came to power.[4] Figure 12.1 shows the distribution of popular opinion on issues that arose during September 1991, before the presidential campaign had really gotten under way. The economy was emerging from recession, but the full effects of the reces-

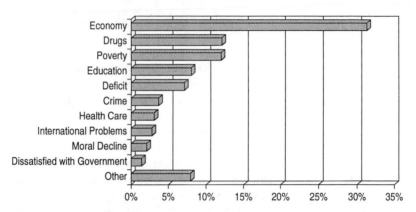

FIGURE 12.1   Most Important Problem Facing the United States (September 5, 1991). SOURCE: Gallup poll, September 5, 1991.

sion had not yet dawned on the public. At that time, the economy was rated as the most important problem facing the American public, cited by about a third of American citizens. Another 12 percent cited "poverty," so we can conclude that around 45 percent of the public put general economic matters at the top of their list of concerns. Of the other problems cited in the survey, only drugs reached a 10 percent level of concern. Crime and drugs, taken together, reached a level of somewhat over 15 percent. It is noteworthy that the issue of foreign affairs was almost absent from the minds of Americans at the time, even with the recent Gulf War triumph of President Bush. By the fall of 1992, the economy was still the number-one concern of the public—and now by a wide margin. It is little wonder that Clinton's campaign strategists kept a sign at headquarters that reminded the staff (and the candidate): "It's the economy, stupid." Indeed, the Clinton campaign's most important asset in 1992 was the weak state of the economy, which was heavily on the mind of the public.

It has been said that election campaigns amplify and clarify issues for the public. If that is true, the 1992 campaign was about the economy. No issues changed in relative salience during the period between the fall of 1991 and the fall of 1992; the economy was overwhelmingly on people's minds at both times.[5] Granted, the candidates did emphasize other issues. President Bush reiterated his "no new taxes pledge," but taxes were of scant concern to the public (taxation ranked eleventh as a concern in the fall of 1992). Similarly, Governor Clinton promised a tax cut for middle-income Americans, but this prospect, too, did not strike a responsive chord. Independent candidate Ross Perot made the deficit the centerpiece of his campaign, with more success than the major-party candidates. The deficit was of concern to Americans, but it took a back seat to economic worries.

It would be a mistake to assume that the public failed to respond to the appeals of the campaign. Rather, it would seem that the issues raised by the election

just needed a period of digestion. Figure 12.2 shows the "most important problem" tabulation for three issues—the economy, health care, and the deficit—the
period extending from the summer of 1990 to the winter of 1994. Just prior to
Clinton's inauguration in January 1993, the economy was still number one; but
now the deficit was most important to over 11 percent of the public, and health
care was the third most mentioned problem facing the country, noted by around
8 percent of respondents. Conditions had changed somewhat; the economy was
improving, albeit at a snail's pace. For this reason the public may have had more
freedom to focus on other issues. But the choice of those issues seems to have
been influenced very heavily by the campaign and the period between the election and the inauguration, as the news media and policy elites speculated on the
new directions that the president-elect would adopt.

It was clear between the election and the inauguration that Clinton would
make two pieces of legislation the focal points of the early part of his administration: a program of public spending designed to stimulate the economy, and a
health care plan designed to provide universal coverage and cost control. With
the success of Perot, who received around 20 percent of the total vote, it had also
become clear that President-elect Clinton could not afford to ignore the problem
of the burgeoning federal deficit. His domestic agenda was set: public investment, health care, and deficit reduction.

Of these three issues, only public investment responded to the most critical
concern of the public: economics. Large and growing deficits were thought by
many economists to harbor long-term corrosive effects on the economy; but in
the short run, they believed, a strong deficit-reduction package would actually
hurt the economic recovery by limiting government spending as a stimulus.
Many economists had thought that large government deficits were inflationary,
because government borrowing would cause the cost of money (reflected in interest rates) to go up. However, as the deficit skyrocketed during the first Reagan
administration, and again in the late Bush years, inflation and interest rates declined. And an increase in spending driven by Clinton's investment program ac-

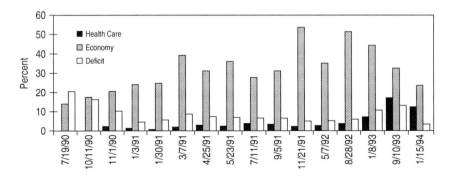

FIGURE 12.2   Most Important Problem Facing the United States. SOURCE: Gallup polls (multiple years).

tually added to the deficit. Hence these two factors were in conflict. Clinton's solution was to propose immediate spending increases, with longer-run deficit reduction; in the lingo of Washington, the deficit reduction was to occur in the "out
years." The "selling" of health care was also affected by the fiscal situation of the
government; Clinton spokespersons claimed again and again that controlling
health care costs was the key to deficit reduction, because the fastest-growing segments of the federal budget were Medicare (health insurance for the elderly) and
Medicaid (health insurance for the poor).

By late September 1993, just after Clinton presented the outlines of his health
care plan, health care was second only to the economy as "the most important
problem facing the country" (Toner, 1993). It is clear that this rise in the public's
perceptions of problems had nothing to do with changing objective circumstances. The health care situation was essentially the same as it had been a year
earlier, when virtually no one indicated that health care was a major issue for the
country. These changes in issue salience constitute strong evidence of the ability
of political actors to *activate* policy preferences in the mass public. That is, policy
elites do not merely respond to the policy wishes of the mass public; they go out
and try to mobilize the public behind their ideas. This mobilization occurs
through the activation of previously latent preferences.

Parallel Publics

Political scientists Ben Page and Robert Shapiro (1992) have developed the notion of "parallel publics"—namely, subgroups of the public that may respond
differently to public issues. For example, an examination of concern with the deficit during the Bush administration yields the finding that men and college-
educated people are far more attentive to deficit problems than are women and
high school–educated citizens. Similarly, women and minorities are considerably
more concerned with the issue of poverty than are white males (Jones, 1994; ch.
5). The working poor are especially worried about health care; among citizens
with less than $20,000 in annual income, more than 18 percent reported having a
problem paying health bills during the previous year—a higher percentage than
for other category of problems. Conversely, among the segment of the population receiving government welfare (AFDC) payments, health concerns take a
back seat to buying clothing, paying utilities, and finding a job. Medicaid recipients worry about their health and about buying prescription drugs, but they do
not report problems with paying health and doctor bills (James, 1993). In short,
the very poor, those receiving government aid, are not very concerned with
health care in comparison to the working poor. The reason is that the Medicaid
program is designed to aid the very destitute but leaves the working poor to fend
for themselves. As employers of low-wage individuals often do not provide coverage, it is not surprising that this segment of the public is concerned with health-
related issues. The general conclusion is that some segments of the public may
well be very concerned about an issue even if the general public, which in effect
constitutes an "average," is not so concerned.

CONGRESSIONAL PRIORITIES

Whatever was happening in Washington regarding the particulars of public policy was only tangentially related to the concerns of most Americans. As we have shown, the public has consistently supported more government involvement in health care, deficit control, and spending for jobs and economic growth. But during the 1992 campaign, people were concerned almost exclusively with only one of these issues: spending for economic growth. To the extent that Clinton chose to focus on the other two aspects of policymaking, he was responding less to explicit concerns of the mass public and more to his own set of priorities and to the discussions of policy elites—members of Congress, interest groups, and the media. The classic pattern of *issue expansion* was emerging: Policy elites debated the policy options and tried to engage the public as allies on the matter.

It is important in the documentation of the issue expansion process to garner some evidence about the priorities of elites. Presidents make their priorities clear, but Congress can sometimes be inscrutable. We are fortunate that in January 1993 a consulting group, Bonner and Associates, commissioned the Gallup Polling Organization to undertake a survey of the new Congress—and billed it as the most comprehensive survey of members of Congress ever undertaken. Gallup polled 149 new and returning members on the issues facing the 103rd Congress (1993–1995), asking which issues would be "critical" legislatively. The results of this survey are presented in Figure 12.3. The questions posed by Gallup to the senators and representatives are different in form from those posed to the public. In effect, members of Congress could list as many priorities as they saw fit, rather than being limited to the "*most* important problem" as the public was. Nevertheless, if appropriate caution is exercised, some comparisons between congressional priorities and public priorities can be made.

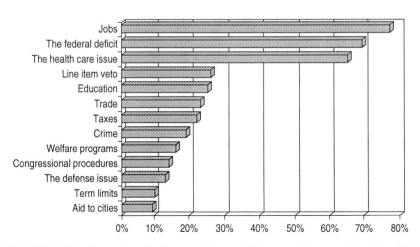

FIGURE 12.3   Critical Issues Viewed by Congress (January 1993). SOURCE: Bonner and Associates (1993).

Like the public, members of Congress rate the economy ("jobs") as more critical than any other issue. Very close behind, however, are health care and the deficit. Other issues, including taxes, environmental concerns, and political reforms such as term limitations and campaign financing, fall far lower in terms of the percentage of legislators rating the issue as critical. It is hard to escape the conclusion that Congress reflects a kind of "inside the beltway" understanding of issues—one that, though not really remote from the public, simply does not reflect public preferences. So a key question involves just how Congress comes to focus on the issues that it does, given that a panoply of problems face the nation.

PUBLIC PROBLEMS AND POLICY HISTORIES

Having explored the idea that the president and Congress simply reflect mass preferences in the policymaking process, we have found it wanting. We cannot say that this view of democratic policymaking is untrue, for both the president and Congress knew that the economy has been of serious concern to Americans. But we can say that such a view is limited, because both the president and Congress have defined two other problems, of more limited interest to the public, as critical legislative objectives: health care and the deficit. One possibility is that policymakers in Washington are responding to the nature of the problems, regardless of whether mass publics currently view them as critical. In effect, democratic policymakers are anticipating problems that might become of critical concern to the public in the future.

The problems that political leaders try to solve today are very much affected by what past policymakers tried to do in the area. In late-twentieth-century America, policymakers almost never work on policies anew; rather, they work on policies that have been dealt with in the past. Those past policies alleviated past problems, but they almost always have generated new "spillover" problems as well; now government must deal with those new problems. The problem of health costs would be less thorny today if the government had not intervened in the provision of health insurance for the elderly and the poor in the 1960s: By stimulating demand for care, the federal government inadvertently increased the price of care. So in order to examine the early Clinton administration's focus on the problems of health and the deficit, we now turn to a brief review of the historical development of health and budget policies in the twentieth century.

Health Care

In this century, medical practice has risen from a beleaguered profession to an enormous community of specialists that commands the attention of political elites. The early thrust, during which insurance for health care was advocated, came from reformers outside of government rather than from political leaders (Starr, 1982: 243). Government attention to developing national policy began with the Flexner report in 1914, which recommended that medical education be transformed. As a consequence, several medical schools were closed, whereas others were revitalized (Brown, 1978: 9).

Health care as a public-policy issue stems from the peculiarities of labor-management relations in the United States. In contrast to Europe's class-based political parties and centralized states, U.S. political parties have been "umbrella-style," each incorporating broad and occasionally shifting coalitions of groups operating at various levels of government. By the late nineteenth century, organized labor, lacking a firm party base and chastened by the strike-breaking activities of both state and federal governments, called for a hands-off relationship with government. Labor would thus rely on collective bargaining to bring about gains in health and other benefits for workers. The result was that health care became a national issue much later in the United States than in other industrial countries.

Health policies were of two types in the 1900s: public-health initiatives, designed to stem the spillover effects of urban epidemics of typhoid, tuberculosis, and dysentery; and health insurance schemes, designed to protect workers. The former issues were addressed as cities began building infrastructure in the early twentieth century. The latter policies were an outgrowth of efforts to enact workers' compensation laws in a majority of states. During the period from 1915 to 1919, several states considered compulsory state health insurance (Weeks and Berman, 1985: 250). Some even set up commissions to review health-related issues.

In the 1920s, America experienced unprecedented prosperity. Americans began to experiment with private health insurance, including prepaid group hospitalization (Weeks and Berman, 1985). At the same time, costs emerged as an issue: The Committee on the Costs of Medical Care reviewed some twenty-five different plans and experiments in medical care and health insurance in progress. The private nonprofit insurer known as Blue Cross made the first major attempt at insurance of groups in 1930 (Brown, 1978: 10).

Federal government activity took on a whole new perspective in the 1930s. The Depression created conditions ripe for the passing of compulsory health insurance. Economic upheaval revived the social insurance movement and gained the support of a larger, more organized collection of reformists. Although President Roosevelt did not respond to this movement directly, on several occasions he showed interest in some sort of national health insurance plan (Weeks and Berman, 1985: 253). In June 1934 he created the Committee on Economic Security to explore concerns later tagged as "cradle to grave" ideas. And in 1937 a Roosevelt-appointed Interdepartmental Committee to Coordinate Health and Welfare Activities began a comprehensive survey designed to explore health needs.

It was in 1939 that Senator Robert Wagner (D–NY) introduced his national health services plan in Congress. The plan, which called for federal aid to medical care in the states, did not pass in that year, but Wagner was hopeful for 1940 (Weeks and Berman, 1985: 257). President Roosevelt slowed the momentum, however, by saying that he favored an experiment with one phase of the bill. As a result, nothing of substance happened, and health-related issues stood on the perimeter of national politics throughout the New Deal. They were "omitted from Social Security and never fully backed by the president" (Starr, 1982: 280). The few instances that Roosevelt did address were subordinated to other programs.

When Senator Wagner introduced a second health bill, usually referred to as the Wagner-Murray-Dingell bill, President Roosevelt gave consent but little direct support. As a result, it lay in Congress for two years without coming to a vote. Nevertheless, this was "the first major legislative proposal in which there was a decided shift from state action to federal action in the health field" (Weeks and Berman, 1985: 259). The year 1944 witnessed a historic fourth-term victory for Roosevelt; the end of the war was foreseeable. Domestic initiatives to prepare the nation for a return to peacetime were necessary. But when it seemed that Roosevelt was at last ready to promote a national health program, he died. The president had planned to deliver his health message in the spring 1945.

President Truman made health care a major item on his domestic agenda. Many of the recommendations in the Truman health care message to Congress on November 19, 1945—the first to be delivered on this topic—were similar to those of the Wagner bills (Weeks and Berman, 1985: 260). Although the message drew support, it also aroused the opposition of the American Medical Association (AMA) to any health insurance program not under the control of state and county medical societies. The AMA's opposition also hampered the Hill-Burton Act. In fact, its intense opposition to compulsory hospital insurance continued until after the Medicare and Medicaid legislation was passed in 1965 (Berlant, 1975).

World War II, even more than the New Deal, underscored a great expansion in the federal government's support of medicine. Before the war, American scientists had generally opposed "any large-scale federal financing or coordination of research" (Starr, 1982). A shift in population from the farms to the industrial cities of the Northeast and the Midwest—as well as to California, where unions had long supported health care reform—buttressed organized demands for initiatives (Weeks and Berman, 1985: 257). The end of the war also brought breakthroughs in medical technology that shaped the health industry. Modern medicine now included anesthesia, aseptic surgery, insulin, and antibiotics (Renn, 1987: 10). But though the "capacity and capability of clinical medicine advanced, the capacity and capability of the domestic hospital system languished" (Weeks and Berman, 1985: 257). The Hill-Burton program, begun in 1946, provided massive infusion of federal and state governmental money and helped construct more than half of the hospital beds in use today (Renn, 1987: 10). This legislation marked the beginning of hospital construction in rural areas to supply much-needed clinical care (Brown, 1978: 10).

President Truman continued to speak in support of health insurance while in office, but nothing substantial came of it. The election of Dwight D. Eisenhower ushered in a quieter period for national health concerns. Eisenhower's ideas were not innovative. He principally supported a conservative progression of existing programs (Weeks and Berman, 1985: 262). It is worth noting, however, that the Salk polio vaccine was developed and dispensed during this administration. And on the legislative front, the Forand bill, a labor-backed effort calling for health insurance for Social Security beneficiaries, was introduced in 1957.

The liberal agenda in the mid-1960s "brought a new generation of programs and policies in health care" (Starr, 1982: 363). Democratic presidents meant activity and increased responsibility for government. President John F. Kennedy sent a special message to Congress about a month after his inauguration advocating health insurance under Social Security. Soon after, the King-Anderson bill (referred to as "Medicare") was introduced. Although it did not pass in Kennedy's first congressional session, the momentum it generated helped carry it through under the guidance of Lyndon B. Johnson (Weeks and Berman, 1985: 264).

Johnson was able to pass much of the social legislation initiated by Kennedy. The Social Security amendments 1965 (Titles XVIII and XIX) enacted Medicare and Medicaid and represented the first major thrust of the federal government toward insurance (Brown, 1978: 10). These programs changed the American health care world forever. The elderly and needy gained new access to care. Hospitals found themselves with a new but restricted source of revenues. Physicians, once opposed to "socialized medicine," quickly recognized that the government programs meant higher demand for their services and, hence, higher incomes for themselves. Federal and state governments (Medicaid was administered and partially funded by the states) now "were faced with health care demands and costs beyond the imagination" (Weeks and Berman, 1985: 264).

Many of the developments that have occurred since the inception of Medicare and Medicaid can be explained as attempts to adjust to the Social Security amendments of 1965 and accompanying events, which revolutionized the practice of health care. These amendments were largely responsible for the recent spurts of growth of the health sector. Although their specific effects are debatable, James Blumstein and Michael Zubkoff argue that the Medicare and Medicaid approach "expanded the effective demand for medical services, but did not simultaneously spur short-run increases in supply" (1981: 56).

The 1970s opened with foreboding signs of a "crisis" in health care. For years, liberals had been trying to persuade Americans to recognize a health care breakdown in order to open the way for reforms beyond Medicare (Starr, 1982: 380). Upon assuming office, Nixon's administration confronted rapidly mounting costs and adopted a rhetoric of crisis to convey concern for the problem.

In retrospect, we must ask, do the data support the conclusion that health care in the 1970s reached crisis proportions? Blumstein and Zubkoff (1981) point out that national health outlays expanded during this decade in both absolute and relative terms at a staggering pace. In fiscal 1972 "national health expenditures amounted to $83.4 billion, an increase of $7.8 billion above the previous year and a rise of 10.3 percent, yet the rate of increase in health expenditures in fiscal 1972 was the lowest incremental rise since fiscal 1966" (Blumstein and Zubkoff, 1981: 56). In addition, Louise B. Russell (1981) notes that price increases in health grew rapidly after the middle 1960s. From 1965 to 1974, "physicians' fees rose 5.7 percent per year on the average" (Russell, 1981: 120). Cost per hospital day climbed at an annual 12.1 percent; about half this increase was due to higher levels of inputs per hospital day, putting the rate of pure price inflation at just over 6 percent per year (Russell, 1981). During the same period the Consumer Price Index rose at a more modest 4.5 percent annually (Russell, 1981: 120). However, economist William Baumol argues that inflation in the service sectors, such as health care, is structurally "built in." In comparison to the production of goods, health care is resistant to automation. Moreover, as William Baumol points out, quality is "inescapably correlated with the amount of labor expended on their [the service's] production. Doctors who speed up their practices . . . are held to be shortchanging those they serve" (1993: 17). Baumol believes that increases in manufacturing productivity make possible quality gains in health and other services.

Nevertheless, inflation of medical services affected government expenditures in this period, whereas productivity gains in manufacturing did not. The rapid inflation paralleled an enormous expansion in federal health services. In 1965 federal health outlays amounted to $5.2 billion (Office of Management and Budget, 1974). Then, by 1969, "a swarm of new programs, of which Medicare and Medicaid were the largest, had brought the total to $16.7 billion. By 1974 that amount nearly doubled again, to about $32 billion" (Russell, 1981: 120). A trend toward greater federal involvement in health care was clearly established during this period. The proportion of total medical expenditures paid for by government programs increased just over 10 percent in 1965 to around 33 percent today (Thompson, 1981; Brewster and Brown, 1994). This increase helped fuel a rise in the proportion of the gross national product devoted to health from roughly 6 percent in 1965 to more than 9 percent in 1978, and to 13 percent currently (Thompson, 1981; Brewster and Brown, 1994).

The federal government, meanwhile, moved toward greater regulation of factors related to health. Between 1971 and 1974, Congress passed a plethora of elaborate legislation. But when "the blizzard of regulation stopped, the federal government found itself snowed in" (Starr, 1982: 405). This legislation was remarkably detailed, chiefly because the Democratic members of Congress were reluctant to give the Nixon administration much discretion—a scenario repeated during the Reagan and Bush administrations.

As Congress struggled with the problems of cost and access, it devoted more and more time to the health care issue. Figure 12.4 shows the number of House and Senate committee hearings that were devoted to health. First there was a brief spurt in hearings during the 1960s associated with the passage of Medicaid and Medicare. Then, beginning in 1970, a steep and continual rise in the number of hearings on health care occurred. In 1970 Congress held 10 hearings on health. In

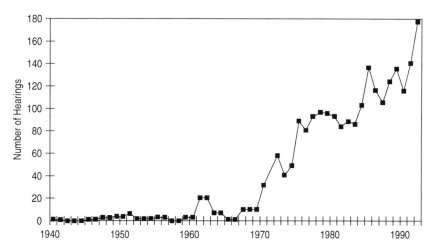

FIGURE 12.4 Congressional Hearings on Health Care. SOURCE: *Congressional Information Service* (multiple years).

1990, it held 180. As noted earlier, in intervening in the health care system via Medicare and Medicaid, the federal government made big waves, affecting almost every aspect of health care either directly or indirectly. To describe the process by which government attacks a problem, causing more problems for itself as it deals with "spillovers," Aaron Wildavsky has used the phrase "policy as its own cause." Health care politics in the United States is a prime example.

In the 1980s national health expenditures continued to rise at a rate "that surpassed the increase in the Gross National Product, the growth of expenditures for education and defense, and even the total federal, state, and local government increase in expenditures for all nonhealth purposes" (Checkoway, 1981: 1). Medical fees increased faster than at any other time in history, at a rate consistently higher than that of other components of the Consumer Price Index (Checkoway, 1981). Health expenses consumed even larger shares of income, forcing people to spend greater portions of their income for health care. The "average expenditure on health care was $943 per person in 1979, representing more than ten times the level for 1950" (Checkoway, 1981). And health care was being organized differently as independent, nonprofit hospitals consolidated into multi-institutional systems designed to deliver health care for profit (Renn, 1987: 12).

The substantial increase in demand and the increasing pace of development of expensive medical technology placed momentous strain on the system (Blumstein and Zubkoff, 1981: 56), owing in part to the importance that people placed on medical care and in part to the fact that most people had either government or private health insurance that moved cost from them to "third-party payers." Hence, in the short run at least, people tended to ignore the cost of treatment. As a result, the federal government came under great political pressure to solve the problems it had helped create.

The disadvantages of this complex mixed system are graphically illustrated in Figure 12.5. Note that the per capita health care expenditures of various countries are plotted against the percentage of public financing of health programs. As the figure makes clear, no major industrial country has a health care system as privatized—or as expensive—as that in the United States.

As the federal government has become increasingly enmeshed in health services, the politics of health care has became national in scope. Leading members of Congress report that they are swamped with conflicting messages from a growing number of lobbyists and lawyers representing all facets of the health care industry (*New York Times*, 1992). The number of national health groups that have offices in Washington or employ Washington representatives has increased dramatically: from 502 in 1986 and 117 in 1979 to 741 in 1992.[6] Health care groups frequently try to influence legislation by making sizable donations to lawmakers' reelection campaigns. For instance, data compiled by Common Cause (the citizens' lobby) show that health and medical organizations have contributed $60 million to candidates for Congress in the last decade, including $19 million from January 1989 to January 1992. And in a separate study, the Center for Responsive Politics, a nonpartisan research group, reveals that the health and insurance industries gave $19 million to congressional candidates in the 1990 election, as

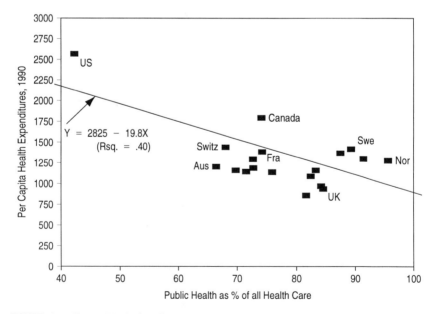

FIGURE 12.5   National Health Care Expenses, 1990. SOURCE: Data compiled by authors.

weighed against $14 million from agricultural interests and $8 million from military contractors.

Yet despite these reports of political and economic trauma, Americans are healthier now than ever. Norma K. Raffel (1984), for example, points to such indicators as life expectancy, mortality rates, the occurrence and prevalence of diseases, the amount of disability, and people's assessments of their own health. Life expectancy was only 47 years in 1900; today it is in the 70s (75 for women, 72 for men).

Three issues of health care reform have dominated public debate since at least the turn of the century: cost, access, and quality. The cost of health care is higher in the United States than in other countries; moreover, it has been growing rapidly in comparison to that of other economic sectors. Access is a problem, particularly for the "working poor" (poor people on welfare are covered by Medicaid). And, for those who can pay (or have insurance plans that will pay), quality is high. At the same time, there is no evidence that the number of uninsured is growing, although the "crisis mentality" associated with Clinton's introduction of health care reform has suggested a burgeoning number of unprotected individuals.

At any rate, the preceding overview of the development of health care policies in the United States should elucidate Clinton's focus on the issue to a greater extent than would a simple examination of the preferences of the public alone. Indeed, a complex dynamic has emerged in which activities by government have raised expectations and led to various questions (such as What happened when the federal government solved the problem of elderly health insurance, only to face steeply increasing costs associated with the newly created demand for services?). Because segments of the public are affected by an issue in different ways (the poor and the wealthy receive good health care relative to the near-poor), demands may come disproportionately from these segments or from organized interests. As Frank Baumgartner and Jeffrey Talbert show in Chapter 6 of this book, the number of health care interest groups has grown phenomenally since the late 1960s (compare this finding to Figure 12.4). Accordingly, the development of policy can be explained by the activities of members of the health policy community, but major changes are a function of the actions of presidents when they attempt to mobilize opinion on the issue.

The Federal Deficit

The issue of the federal deficit has a policy history as tortured as that of health care. Donald Kettl (1992) describes the course of federal budgeting through three distinct stages in U.S. history. The first period, approximately 1789 to 1933, was marked by a "norm of balance." Although neither the president nor Congress balanced the federal budget every year, there was "the clear expectation that the budget should be balanced, and that a deficit ought to be the rare exception" (Kettl, 1992: 15). This standard was so ingrained that when the economy crumbled during the Great Depression, President Herbert Hoover proposed a tax increase to lower the deficit and bring the budget back into balance (Kettl, 1992: 17).

During this interval Congress was the clear center of the budgetary process. In actuality, there was no "budget" in the modern sense. Individual agencies "submitted their spending requests directly to Congress, which decided agency by agency how much to approve" (Kettl, 1992: 124). The final budget was the accumulation of all individual congressional decisions. As the country grew and demands on government increased, however, congressional budgeting lost its effectiveness. Congress moved toward a more diverse committee system, which was further broken down by subcommittees. In short, America's budget "was becoming too complicated and its programs too important to operate without effective coordination" (Kettl, 1992: 124).

The executive branch rose to dominance during the second budgetary era, which stretched from 1933 to the late 1970s. The impetus for such a shift was the Budget and Accounting Act of 1921. This act created the General Accounting Office, an arm of Congress; established the Bureau of the Budget in the executive branch; and empowered the president to submit an annual budget to Congress. For the first time, there was to be a truly federal budget in the American system, "a coordinated plan of spending and a statement of how revenues and spending would be related" (Kettl, 1992: 126).

By the time Franklin D. Roosevelt took office in March 1933, the American economy was devastated. President Roosevelt advocated that government "could and should use its ability to borrow money to launch new employment programs" (Kettl, 1992: 18), thereby stimulating the economy in accordance with the theories of British economist John Maynard Keynes. The lessons policymakers drew from the 1930s guided public budgeting for generations. The norm of budgetary balance slid from its central place, and a new era tolerant of budgetary deficits replaced it. As a consequence, the federal budget has been in deficit in all but eight of the sixty-two years from 1931 through 1993 (Eisner, 1986: 78). Only once (in 1969) in the thirty-two years since 1960 has there been no deficit. In these early years, however, deficits were quite modest when measured against the size of the economy. The Keynesian approach reached its high-water mark during the administrations of John Kennedy and Lyndon Johnson (Kettl, 1992: 21). The economy was booming, with high growth and low inflation. Economists talked of using federal spending to "fine-tune" the economy. Budget deficits were manageable. But 1970 brought a sharp recession, inaugurating a decade of lackluster economic performance and high inflation.

In particular, the 1970s witnessed a troublesome span of persistent federal deficits. Economic data from this period support those observers, such as Robert Eisner, who saw deficits "as evidence of unbridled government spending contributing to inflation" (1986: 85). Inflation rose throughout the 1970s, peaking in 1981. But then, as deficits reached unprecedented heights in 1982, inflation rates suddenly plunged. The persistently high deficits of the 1980s and early 1990s were associated not with increasing inflation, as had been claimed for generations, but with moderating inflation and good economic performance.

The stagflation of the early 1970s had sown the seeds for the ultimate decline of Keynesianism (Kettl, 1992: 22). But the economic policymakers of the decade were not quick to see this decline. The deficits continued to be perceived as evidence of expansionist fiscal policy. Even President Richard Nixon, a long-time fiscal conservative, felt compelled to announce his allegiance. In 1972 he said, "We are all Keynesians now" (Eisner, 1986: 85). President Jimmy Carter and his advisers, in early 1977, had considered a tax-rebate plan to pump up the economy (Kettl, 1992: 22). The Carter proposal is the last time policymakers would employ the Keynesian apparatus to diagnose policy problems—until President Clinton proposed doing so in his "jobs and investment" program of 1993. The quick failure of this approach in Congress emphasizes the rejection of Keynesianism as a political doctrine.

Two persistent trends have made it harder to propose workable theories and formulate budget decisions. First, the deficit became "stubbornly large and resisted the efforts of Republicans and Democrats, presidents and Congresses, to reduce it" (Kettl, 1992: 25). Second, the budget itself changed, thus leaving decisionmakers with much less discretion (Kettl, 1992: 26). As the new Reagan administration took office in 1981, the economy fell into recession, and "unemployment rose to a post–World War II record of 10.7 percent of the labor force" (Eisner, 1986: 2). The administration responded by running huge budget deficits through tax cuts and defense-spending increases, and the economy recovered sharply. A new "Reaganomics" was born, and "supply-side" economists flocked to claim credit (Eisner, 1986).

The Reagan era was marked by dramatic increases in the deficit, increases that did not abate as the economy improved (Friedman, 1988). The deficit was no longer associated with business slowdowns; it also grew during the long expansion of the middle to late 1980s. As Benjamin Friedman has noted, "From 1984 onward, more than three fourths of each year's deficit has reflected the gap between revenues and spending *that would have occurred even at full employment*" (1988: 171; italics added). According to James Clayton, "This massive government demand for credit crowds out competing business and individual credit needs by absorbing private savings. Furthermore, it reduces the rate of capital formation, raises interest rates, and tempts the Federal Reserve to monetize the debt" (1984: 6). But none of this came to pass, allowing supply-side economists to claim that the deficit did not matter very much. Mainstream economists fell back to a more modest claim: that the deficit would cause lower growth than otherwise.

Members of Congress soon realized how disorganized their role in the budget had become. The president, though strong, was certainly not independent of the constraints of Congress. What resulted was a relationship that Donald Kettl describes as "the era of stalemate," lasting from 1974 to 1990 (1992: 129). The "stalemate" was broken with a budget accord between congressional Democrats and

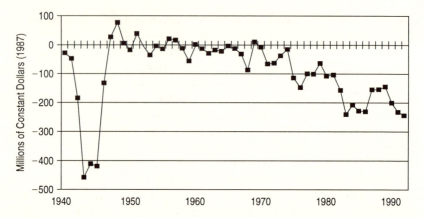

FIGURE 12.6   Surplus or Deficit: Budget of the U.S. Government 1940–1990. SOURCE: *Statistical Abstract* (multiple years).

President Bush, an accord that raised taxes, capped spending, and provided that any new government spending in the future must be offset with taxes or cuts elsewhere, so as not to add to the budget deficit. Conservative Republicans attacked Bush for "raising taxes," conveniently ignoring the constraints on the growth of government that the accord enforced. The pressure was so great that Bush apologized at the 1992 Republican National Convention for the accord.

The struggle with the federal deficit is graphically depicted in Figure 12.6. This figure depicts the U.S. deficit in constant dollars. As indicated, the great deficit of World War II was replaced with an era of stability and almost balanced budgets, lasting until the early 1970s. After that, the deficit grew, especially after 1981. Figure 12.7 shows the growth of the federal debt as a percentage of the size of the

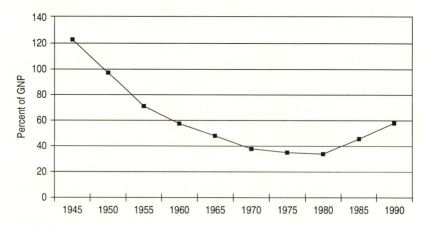

FIGURE 12.7   Gross Federal Debt. SOURCE: *Statistical Abstract* (multiple years).

economy. Note that relative debt declined until the early 1980s, when the unbalanced Reagan budgets began to take effect.

CONCLUSIONS: WHY THESE? WHY NOW?

The French mathematician Blaise Pascal claimed that "there is no reason why here rather than there, why now rather than then." That is the lesson of our brief examination of the background of President Clinton's domestic policy initiatives during the early part of his administration.

Our reviews of health care and deficit policies have highlighted the independent life that policies lead in American politics. What governments do today in trying to solve problems is very much affected by what they did in the past. Policies become their "own cause," in Aaron Wildavsky's (1979) words, and they generate policy communities as the action gravitates toward Washington. Accordingly, any model of representation *must* take policy history into consideration. Indeed, we have shown that the two domestic issues facing Clinton in his first year were important problems, and that governments at least since the New Deal have struggled with both in one form or another. But these problems are no more important objectively than numerous others, including crime, the breakdown of family life, the degradation of the environment, the deterioration of cities, racial discrimination, and structural economic changes. *In short, objective conditions cannot explain Clinton's policy choices because numerous problems of co-equal objective status are pressing government. Neither can most choices be explained by citizen preferences, as we have shown, because citizens want many things from government, several of which are in competition with one another.*

We have also shown that citizens harbor complex and not infrequently conflicting preferences about the role of government in modern society. Proponents of various policy proposals often point to public-opinion polls that suggest the American public "overwhelmingly supports" this or that, often claiming that there is a "crisis" and that "the public demands action." This state of affairs has characterized President Clinton's health initiative, for example. Numerous polls commissioned by the media have purportedly found public sentiment to be in favor of action. Yet the proponents of action often fail to note that there is nothing new about these circumstances: The public has wanted action ever since the advent of careful polls; and it has wanted even more action in the face of considerable government initiatives (in the case of health care) during the last quarter-century. A better model of democratic representation, then, would include the concept of *preference activation:* the idea that unless people pay attention to a particular want, it is not relevant to their political decisionmaking. Hence public officials are often in the position of trying to activate the public on issues for which the direction of opinion is already crystal clear.

Therefore, we must ask why a president (or any politician) would emphasize one issue over another in the struggle to activate public preferences. We propose that three conditions must be present for an issue to rise high on a president's agenda. First, there must really *be* a problem, both objectively and in the mind of the public. Second, government must be perceived as a potential solution to the problem. This criterion is easier to meet when government has been part of the problem, as is clearly the case with health care and the deficit. Policy communities have emerged, making demands for solutions to the problems they perceive. Finally, the president must perceive some political advantage from attacking the problem. That problem may be forced on him, as was Ross Perot's pursuit of the deficit. Or it may be a conscious and deliberate choice by the president, as health care was for Clinton. But in any case, the president has substantial leeway to choose what problems he will emphasize during his presidency. A simple "thought experiment" will verify this claim: Would health care be at the very top of the domestic agenda if George Bush had been reelected president? Would the deficit problem be as severe if Jimmy Carter had been reelected, or if Gerald Ford had served two full terms?

Of course, events have a way of interfering with the president's attempts to control the national agenda. After the introduction of his health care legislation (in November 1993, almost two months after the fanfare in September), President Clinton strove to keep the issue before the public. But issues of foreign affairs, including the dramatic NAFTA vote (see Chapter 7 in this book), the Whitewater investigation, and mounting public concern with crime, caused major distractions from the main presidential domestic agenda. While Whitewater persisted as distraction, Clinton treated NAFTA and crime as major opportunities.

The crime situation is particularly instructive. In September 1991 crime ranked sixth in concern among Americans, behind the economy, the related issues of drugs, poverty, education, and the deficit (see Figure 12.1). By January 1994, it ranked first. Later in 1994, Clinton introduced a major crime bill, which he pushed very actively, leading some Republicans to complain that the Democrats had "stolen" their issue. In this case, we might view the president as simply responding to the changing concerns of the public; in reality, however, the situation is more complicated. It would be more correct to see the mounting concern with crime as an opportunity for action that may or may not be grasped. And any opportunity carries with it the possibility of redefining the manner in which the issue has traditionally been viewed. In the case of Clinton's crime bill, traditional concerns are addressed: more prisons, more police officers, longer sentences. But Clinton has also supported the gun control initiative (the Brady Bill) as a *crime-control* measure.

For the most part, there is nothing inevitable about politics and the policies that come from the pursuit of politics in the United States. Historical approaches to *any* problem not only constrain what can be done today but also generate powerful associations of interests. Calculations of political opportunity color what issues are seen as critical. And so the public waits, full of wants, wishes, hopes, and dreams, for political leaders to activate preferences for particular policies.

NOTES

1. The studies referred to here are Page and Shapiro, 1992; and Mayer, 1992.

2. The wording of questions affects the size of majorities, as in all polling exercises. For example, "Do more in health" garners more support from the public than "Spend more on health," even though the two phrases mean the same thing (Page and Shapiro, 1992: 130).

3. The fact that people hold numerous and often contradictory preferences about government policies leads to an interesting phenomenon: that of "finding a majority." It works like this: An issue comes to be addressed by policymakers. Public-opinion polls are commissioned. Then, lo and behold, the media report that a majority of citizens supports action in the area.

4. We thank the Center for Presidential Studies at Texas A&M University for making these data available.

5. These measures were taken in September 1991 and September 1992. Early November assessments would have been better, but Gallup asked the "most important problem" question only in polls taken in September.

6. These figures were reported by the National Health Council, a Washington forum for health care advocates.

13

Cities, Political Representation, and the Dynamics of American Federalism

DENNIS JUDD

FEDERALISM AND THE CITIES

It has often been asserted that the structure of American federalism simultaneously exaggerates urban problems and makes it more difficult to design effective policies to solve them (Judd and Robertson, 1988). Moreover, scholars strongly agree that the political subordination of cities to the states has frequently had the effect of spawning systems of local government that are dysfunctional in important respects (Newton, 1984). In addition to limiting the authority of local governments to spend and borrow, the states have facilitated the governmental fragmentation of metropolitan areas—a fragmentation that has brought with it a variety of consequences ranging from fiscal and service disparities among governments to the absence of regional planning and land-use policies (Blakely and Ames, 1993). These effects have long occupied urban scholars.

Unfortunately, the scholarly literature has almost completely ignored one of the most far-reaching consequences of federalism: the absence of a coherent national urban policy. In the literature on federalism and cities, far too much has been made of the legal and political subordination of the cities to the states. Despite their constitutionally subordinate status, cities in the United States have operated with a high degree of autonomy, and they have long exercised their autonomy to undertake a range of important and expensive policies. In his comparative study of local government in Europe, Edward Page has noted that "by definition . . . the constitutional status of local government is subordinate" in all countries, and superior governments uniformly dictate governmental structures, specify service and other responsibilities, and impose debt limitations (Page, 1991: 22). It is difficult, perhaps impossible, to measure the degree of autonomy that cities possess in different nations because the degree of centralization, level of grants, and general fiscal arrangements are extremely complex in their structure and effects, and in any case are mediated politically (Page, 1991: 34–40).

However much autonomy cities seem to possess in different national contexts, and whether they are mandated to do so or not, local governments everywhere in the developed nations supply a similar bundle of basic services.

Noting that in the United States President Reagan pursued decentralization as a way of forcing cities to independently promote economic growth and that in Britain Prime Minister Thatcher sought centralization to accomplish the same goal, Edmond Preteceille has cautioned against "explanations too dependent on one country's political history and institutions" (Preteceille, 1991: 123). Indeed, the recent experience of cities in several nations ought to make us cautious about blaming urban problems or the lack of effective solutions on the system of federalism per se. Over the past two decades, older cities in all Western nations have been experiencing remarkably similar problems of physical decay, economic decline, and rising inequality. These problems are hardly unique to American cities. The retreat from national policies designed to save declining cities and regions is also not a peculiarly American phenomenon. All of the advanced Western nations have stopped trying to protect their cities from the effects of global economic change and have encouraged urban elites to seek local economic growth as a substitute for previous programs of governmental assistance (Judd and Parkinson, 1990). Only in the United States, however, have cities been essentially cut off from formal relationships to national government. The American federal structure has made this possible.

Federalism has exerted a fundamental influence on urban development in the United States, but its effects have often been misunderstood. Despite being creatures of the states, cities have been able to wield significant authority and have had access to considerable resources. Federalism has not greatly hindered cities in their exercise of formal governmental authority. Rather, cities and urban populations have long been disadvantaged by the political dynamics of the federal system. These dynamics have had three fundamentally important effects. First, over the long term they have worked in such a way as to underrepresent urban interests in the American political system. Second, they have exacerbated and exaggerated the segregation and inequality of various groups making up urban areas. Third—and crucial to the central theme of this chapter—the structure of federalism has decoupled local government from national power and public policy making. In Europe, cities have been integral to national political systems, with the result that urban policy has been embedded within national public policy. In the United States, cities have never been integrated into national policy structures. For cities, the effects have indeed been far-reaching.

CITIES AS CREATURES OF THE STATES

The Legal Position of Cities

Almost every analysis of the impact of federalism on American cities begins with a commentary on the fact that cities are creatures of the states. Though the right of cities to control their own destinies may have remained somewhat ambiguous for several decades after the constitutional period, in the nineteenth century the absolute authority of the states to control the cities within their boundaries became firmly established in American law. In the Dartmouth College case of 1819, the U.S. Supreme Court ruled that cities were corporations created by the states and that the states were legally empowered to dictate the terms and purposes of these public corporations (*Dartmouth College v. Woodward*, 1819). The decision in this case did not, however, stop cities from challenging (or, more often, ignoring) the restrictions placed upon them. When confronted by one such challenge in 1868, Judge John F. Dillon, then chief justice of the Iowa Supreme Court, handed down his famous dictum that states held absolute legal jurisdiction over cities. In a passage by now quoted in generations of textbooks on city politics, Dillon tried to lay to rest any doubt about their legal rights and governmental status:

> Municipal corporations owe their origin to, and derive their powers and rights wholly from, the legislature. It breathes into them the breath of life without which they cannot exist. As it creates so may it destroy. If it may destroy, it may abridge and control. Unless there is some constitutional limitation on the right, the legislature might, by a single act . . . sweep from existence all of the municipal corporations of the state, and the corporations cannot prevent it. We know of no limitation on the right so far as the corporations themselves are concerned. They are, so to phrase it, the mere tenants at will of the legislature. (*City of Clinton v. Cedar Rapids,* 1868)

Not always appreciated is the fact that Judge Dillon was motivated to issue his decision because cities in Iowa, like their counterparts elsewhere, were engaging in a frenzied competition for railway connections. The states imposed few limitations on what the cities could do to subsidize railroads and other private undertakings. As a result, cities gave away land, bought railroad bonds, and sometimes helped finance construction. Until 1861, cities supplied $300 million in railroad subsidies, compared to $229 million from the states and $65 million from the federal government (Chalmers, 1976: 4). And in the years from 1866 to 1873, the legislatures of twenty-nine states granted more than 800 authorizations for aid by local governments to railroad projects (Goodrich, 1960: 266–267). Cities went heavily into debt, so much so that hundreds of cities and towns were forced into default on bonds by the depression of the 1870s (which was triggered, in part, by railroad overbuilding and the overvaluation of stock in railroads and real estate). An estimated $100 million to $150 million of municipal debt was involved in railroad defaults in 1873—one-fifth of all the debt held by municipalities in the nation (Hillhouse, 1936: 39). From 1864 to 1888, the most common category of case before the U.S. Supreme Court involved railroad bonds (Sbragia, 1990: ch. 5, p. 4). It is hardly surprising, given this record of local government recklessness, that state legislatures reacted by imposing restrictions on local debt and limiting the aid that cities could provide for private undertakings (Goodrich, 1960: 145–169; Sbragia, 1990: ch. 5).

Dillon's enthusiasm for the principle that states absolutely controlled the cities was fired by the cases that came before him, which revealed not only pervasive corruption in city politics but also a frequent disregard for any limitations imposed by the state (Schultz, 1989: 73). In 1872 Dillon, by then a U.S. circuit judge, distilled his crusade into the famous principle that became known as "Dillon's rule." His Treatise on the Law of Municipal Corporations was originally 800 pages long, and by the time the fifth edition was published in 1911 it had grown to five thick volumes (Schultz, 1989: 73). By tirelessly speaking and writing on behalf of his cause, Dillon helped enshrine his obsession as the law of the land.

Dillon's rule is associated with extreme restrictions on the autonomy and power of American cities. In fact, however, city governments continued to wield significant powers, and urban elites were not stopped from using local governments to promote growth and prosperity. Despite newly imposed state restrictions, city borrowing continued to climb all through the 1870s, leveled out in the 1880s (Sbragia, 1990: ch. 4, p. 25), then skyrocketed during the 1890s. Restrained from investing in private undertakings, the cities in this round of activism "carried out huge capital projects, requiring sophisticated mobilization of financial, technical, and administrative resources" (Sbragia, 1990: ch. 4, p. 4). Cities paved streets, built bridges, and presided over the construction of complicated waterworks and sewer systems—and built an administrative apparatus capable of initiating and overseeing these activities. By the end of the century, American cities were supplying a greater volume of clean water to a higher proportion of urban residents, providing more complete and better sewer systems, running a greater number of public libraries, and constructing more basic infrastructure than were cities in Europe (Teaford, 1984).

Throughout much of the nineteenth century, state legislatures meddled in the internal affairs of cities. Legislative committees sometimes exercised detailed oversight of budgets, named streets, and appointed various public officials. It should be pointed out, however, that the capacity for close oversight was limited by the amateur status of the legislatures themselves. Most of them met every other year for brief sessions and conducted their business with practically no professional or administrative staff. The fact that state capitals were typically located in backwater towns at some distance from the major cities also handicapped state legislators who wanted to exercise close oversight.

The legislative meddling that occurred in the latter quarter of the century was prompted mainly by the intense lobbying of urban interests (Teaford, 1984). Arguing that elections were controlled by ignorant immigrants and their corrupt political representatives, upper- and upper-middle-class reformers beseeched legislatures to take authority from aldermen and city councils and place more control in the hands of mayors and budget comptrollers (Klebanow, Jonas, and Leonard, 1977). To fight patronage and spoils politics, they also asked legislatures to amend city charters so that the administration of essential city services would be placed under the supervision of boards and committees, whose members would be appointed by mayors, governors, or state legislative committees. It is true that the reformers were preaching to the converted. State legislators were already alarmed that the riffraff seemed to have taken over the cities. John Dillon articulated the prevailing sentiment when he observed that "men the best fitted by their intelligence, business experience, capacity and moral character, for local governors and counsellors are not always, it is feared—it might be added, are not generally—chosen" (Schultz, 1989: 69).

Thus, state legislatures intruded themselves into city affairs, not so much to curb the power of cities as to rearrange their internal governance. Legislatures in New York, Boston, Indiana, Ohio, Maryland, Louisiana, and other states granted more power to mayors to control budgets and to veto legislation. They placed the administration of services such as public works, education, libraries, and health in the hands of independent, specialized boards and commissions whose members were appointed rather than elected. The members of these boards tended to come from the "bastions of the city's elite"; likewise, mayors, because they represented entire cities and not single wards, and because most of them had to finance their own campaigns, tended to come from prominent, wealthy backgrounds (Teaford, 1984).

With the granting of more authority to mayors and administrative bodies, a significant proportion of city budgets and services was removed from the control and oversight of aldermen and city councillors. The separation of day-to-day city affairs from the immediate influence of elected representatives, it could be argued, compromised local democracy. According to Teaford, however, this arrangement amounted to an "unheralded triumph" because it allowed city governments in the late nineteenth century to accomplish two contradictory but essential tasks. The first task was that of brokering among contending political interests; that is, cities still had to engage in the job of governance. Thus, the spoils system connected to ward-based political organizations remained intact, even though large areas of the cities' budgets and business were removed from this arena. The second task was the building of a local administrative state with the capacity to run a panoply of services and amenities.

This history is worth noting because the era of legislative interference immediately preceded and indeed generally overlapped the granting of home-rule charters in the early years of the twentieth century. By granting home rule, state legislatures legitimated the recently expanded responsibilities that cities had assumed. Home-rule charters codified the principle that cities were obligated to provide an array of public services to citizens, depending on their size, and that they were expected to do so using their own resources. Later responding to the municipal reform movement, many states further encouraged or required all but the larger (and smallest) cities to hire professional city managers. In all of these ways states were urging—even requiring—cities to build a minimum level of administrative capacity.

In addition to encouraging the building of local administrative capacity, states significantly changed local political processes during the Progressive Era. (Indeed, there can be little doubt that these reforms gave legislatures the confidence to loosen their control over cities through home-rule charters.) To combat corruption, the states required voter registration and the use of the Australian ballot. By 1905 voter registration laws had been placed on the books in most states (Griffith, 1974: 71), and in the ensuing years states set up election boards to oversee local elections. Prosecution for fraud became an ever-present threat for local politicians. All throughout the Progressive era, states implemented components of the evolving agenda of the municipal reform movement by requiring nonpartisan and at-large elections and civil service hiring procedures. Except for the states along the eastern board, most states began to require their cities to run nonpartisan elections, so that by 1929, 57 percent of cities with populations above 30,000 had them (Hawley, 1973: 14). In most cases, a nonpartisan charter replaced wards with at-large elections.

The fact that states controlled the cities provided the means by which the political systems of cities could be changed, but was state control the cause of these changes? It should be kept in mind that the reforms were not being forced upon cities. Instead, they were responses to a well-organized nationwide campaign initiated by political elites in the cities. It is important to note, as well, that the Progressive reformers launched campaigns to reform government at all levels of the federal system. Election reform and civil service systems were adopted in Washington, D.C., as well as in Springfield, Albany, and Chicago. The belief that efficient, honest government could solve all public problems not only led to the growth of organization charts and public bureaucracies at all governmental levels but also became the reigning ideology of modern liberalism in the United States (Lowi, 1979). It is hard to see how the governmental structures of cities would have evolved much differently even if they had been more independent of the states.

Municipal reform did not curb the cities' ability or willingness to take on new responsibilities. In the 1920s counties and municipalities spent 55 to 60 percent of all public funds in the nation (Patterson, 1969: 26). From 1923 to 1927, the largest 145 cities increased their spending by 79 percent, at a time when state spending had risen by 43 percent (Maxwell, 1952: 23). This spurt in public spending followed the cities' earlier investment in basic infrastructure. This time around, the cities were responding to the demands of the automobile, as well as to middle-class demands for improvements in services and amenities. Cities invested in traffic lights, police cars, garbage trucks, school buses, snowplows, roads, and bus and airline terminals, and dramatically increased spending for parks and stadiums. They also took on social welfare responsibilities. In the nine years from 1923 to 1932, the states increased relief spending by 63 percent, but the thirteen cities with populations above 100,000 increased the money budgeted for public works and relief by 391 percent. In the last year of the Hoover administration, these same cities spent $53 million more for public welfare than all the states combined. Toward this end, they incurred a 50 percent increase in public debt in the 1920s (Gelfand, 1975: 49).

Contemporary cities demonstrate a similar capacity and penchant for major new undertakings. Despite (or because of) the withdrawal of federal grants, since the early 1980s cities all over the nation have helped to underwrite riverfront development projects, festival malls, convention centers, stadiums, and other ambitious projects. To support the dramatic remaking of their downtown areas, they have invested heavily in public infrastructure (Frieden and Sagalyn, 1989; Teaford, 1990). All through this latest period of local activism, they have been able to regularly escape state borrowing restrictions and recalcitrant electorates by freely issuing revenue bonds.

This does not add up to a portrait of cities cripplingly constrained by the structure of the federal system. The status of cities as creatures of the states has not robbed cities of the capacity to expand services and undertake ambitious projects. But it is also not the case that American cities evolved in the same way as cities in more centralized systems, such as those in Europe, where they became the implementors of a variety of national policies. Occupying the middle tier of the federal system as they do, the states, from the New Deal on, became the level of government that administered grants programs in social welfare, job training, transportation (highways), the environment, and other policy areas. As a consequence, cities lost control over policies of great importance to local constituencies. For example, state highway department engineers planned the freeway systems that slashed through urban areas in the 1950s and 1960s, and city officials and neighborhood leaders gained a voice only after protest activities stopped some of the highway projects (Mollenkopf, 1978).

Even this intermediate administrative role of the states should not be overemphasized, however. Beginning with the Housing Act of 1937, federal agencies established direct links with the cities. In the 1950s local housing and urban renewal authorities received federal dollars with scarcely any oversight by the states. In administering these programs they regularly bent federal rules to fit their own political needs and policy agendas. Then, in the 1960s, City Hall found that its direct relationship to the federal government could be far more traumatic than its worse fears about state interference. Partly in order to shake up local power structures, federal administrators bypassed city government in favor of nonprofit, neighborhood, and newly created independent agencies. In this instance, city officials might have preferred that the states rather than the federal government meddle in their affairs!

FOUR CONSEQUENTIAL EFFECTS OF FEDERALISM

The states' control over the cities has not restrained the cities from gaining substantially autonomous control over their affairs. Nor has it constrained the cities from taking on new responsibilities over time. Nevertheless, the cities' subordinate status in the federal system has profoundly affected not only the cities them-selves but American politics generally. The most important effects of federalism on cities can be discovered in legal and structural relationships, as well as in the political dynamics that characterize the federal system.

I will label the first (and perhaps most consequential) effect of federalism the *representation effect*. For most of the nation's history, the political influence of cities and metropolitan areas in the politics of the state and nation was irretriev-ably compromised by the cities' subordinate position in the federal system. By ensuring that urban populations would be underrepresented in party organiza-tions and legislative districts, the states were able to reduce the influence of the cities both in states and in national institutions. The systematic underrepresenta-tion of urban populations was not ended until the 1960s, a fact that has had an immense, though generally overlooked, impact on the balance of power in the states and across the nation.

The second consequential effect of the cities' dependency on the states has been expressed in the political dynamics associated with the fragmentation of governments in metropolitan areas. Local political boundaries have evolved to closely mirror the fracturing of urban populations along the dimensions of class, race, and ethnicity. My argument is that political fragmentation has exaggerated and amplified the segregation and inequalities that have characterized the Ameri-can pattern of urban development. I label this the *equity effect*.

The fragmention of urban governments has also made it nearly impossible for America's urban areas to devise or implement metropolitan planning, land-use, or economic development policies. Instead, governments compete with one an-other in a "beggar thy neighbor" style of politics wherein every local government tries to maximize its economic advantage and unload undesirable land uses or social problems onto other jurisdictions. I call this the *governance effect*.

These previous "effects" are outcomes of federalism. It is important to note that all three interact in complex ways to make it impossible for urban areas to become integrated into the American system of government. In the United States, there is essentially no "urban" interest but, rather, a cacophony of con-tending political interests. I label this characteristic of federalism the *political structure effect*.

The Representation Effect

Since the first state constitutional conventions and ever thereafter, rural legisla-tors have ensured that they would continue to control state political institutions. Maine's constitutional convention of 1819 established a ceiling on the number of representatives allowed to sit in the legislature on behalf of the state's towns. And in 1845, at a time when New Orleans accounted for 20 percent of the state's popu-lation, the Louisiana legislature limited the city to 12.5 percent of the state's sena-tors and 10 percent of the state's assemblymen (Gelfand, 1975: 11). Eventually this formula gave way to another that was equally effective, when it was decided that each parish would have at least one representative in the state senate and house, no matter what its population. Georgia applied this standard to each county; and Rhode Island, to each town (Dixon, 1968: 174). And so on, from state to state. Every state in the Union presided over a system of representation that kept the political influence of urban populations in check.

The underrepresentation of cities had profound and enduring consequences, in both state and national politics. Within the states, the fact that legislatures were controlled by rural interests meant that problems such as traffic congestion, slum housing, overcrowding, disease, joblessness, and poverty would be neglected, simply because rural and small-town legislators lived at a far remove from both the problems and the constituency groups that might have demanded some action. At the national level, these effects were amplified. Through the same devices that limited urban representation in state legislatures, rural elites firmly controlled the party caucuses that nominated governors, congressional representatives, senators, and presidents. Thus, urban constituencies were effectively silenced at the national level, thereby undercutting the populist and labor movements that swept the country in the decades after the Civil War.

The indifference of the states in the early years of the Great Depression illustrates how the underrepresentation of the cities reverberated through the political system. When Franklin D. Roosevelt assumed the presidency in 1933, only eight states provided any money at all for relief (Brown, 1940: 72–96). When local officials pleaded for assistance, they were ignored. At their national conference in 1930, the governors took up such topics as the essential components of a model state constitution, constitutional versus legislative home rule for the cities, and the proper extent of state legislative control of city governments (Patterson, 1969: 45). The economic and social problems of the depression did not make it into the program. Reflecting such lethargy, many states tried to keep their budgets balanced by cutting spending, thus contributing to destitution and high unemployment.

The effects of urban underrepresentation were substantially overcome, at least in national politics, when city officials began to organize lobbying organizations, and when Democratic presidents began to identify their political prospects with the urban electorate. One feature of federalism, the electoral college, amplified rather than reduced the influence of urban constituencies. The heavy Democratic majorities in cities could tip the scales and deliver a state's entire slate of electors into the Democratic column. Winning enough of the industrial states in just this way put John F. Kennedy into the White House in 1960. And realizing the pivotal position of urban voters, Lyndon Johnson crafted his Great Society programs to keep urban voters within the party's embrace (Piven and Cloward, 1971). Since the 1960s cities have lost their status as powerbrokers in the Democratic party because central-city voters now constitute a small proportion of the electorate even in the key industrial states.

For a time, the voting strength of urban blacks, ethnic groups, and labor unions in the industrial states gave cities a voice in national politics. The big-city vote was decisive in every one of FDR's four presidential election campaigns. The nation's eleven largest cities provided more than 27 percent of his national vote in 1932 (Eldersveld, 1949: 1200), along with a much larger proportion of the vote cast in pivotal industrial states with big blocs of electoral votes. Roosevelt would have lost the presidency in 1940 and 1944 without overwhelming pluralities in the cities. The urban vote continued to be important to Democratic candidates after World War II. Big-city pluralities put both Truman and Kennedy over the top. And in 1964, although Lyndon Johnson would have won anyway, the cities topped the national margin of victory by 10 percent or more.

If their party continued to rely on voters in the older industrial cities disproportionately, the Democrats were bound to find it harder and harder to win the presidency simply because the populations of those cities declined rapidly after the 1950s. In contrast, the Republicans were strongest in the suburbs, the West, and the South, exactly those areas where the reapportionment following every census was, decade by decade, redistributing congressional seats and electoral college votes. Actually, the industrial states and their cities had been losing their share of national representation beginning with the 1930 census. The number of House members representing six older cities—Boston, New York, Philadelphia, Baltimore, Detroit, and Chicago—fell from fifty-two in the 1920s to thirty-three by the 1980s (Bradley, 1983). Within the industrial states the proportion of central-city voters likewise declined. In the 1952 presidential election, for example, New York City cast almost half the total votes in the state of New York (48 percent), but by 1992 the city's share of the statewide vote had fallen to less than a third (31 percent). This has been the experience of other cities as well: Chicago's share of the popular vote in Illinois fell from 41 percent in 1952 to 22 percent in 1992, and St. Louis's share of Missouri's vote fell from 20 percent to just 6 percent over the same forty-year period.

As the central cities have lost population and representation, their voters, predictably, have lost influence with the White House, Congress, and state capitals. This is a principal reason why the New Deal coalition fell apart in the 1970s, and why presidents of both parties began to abandon urban policies. After the 1990 census, media commentators often noted that a majority of the nation's voters were, for the first time, suburban (Schneider, 1992). The census showed that 48 percent of Americans lived in metropolitan areas but outside of the central cities. Moreover, suburbanites cast a majority of the votes in the 1992 presidential election. In 1992 fifteen congressional seats were reapportioned to the South and West from northern states. Also as a result of reapportionment, more congressional districts were dominated by suburban majorities than by any other voting bloc. The number of states with suburban majorities increased from three after 1980 to fourteen after 1990, and most of these were the most populous states.

The rising influence of cities in national politics was not matched, in most of the states, by increasing influence in state legislatures. The reason is simple: The system of malapportionment remained in place. The federal courts finally moved against legislative malapportionment in the 1960s. In the 1962 case of *Baker v. Carr*, a group of Knoxville residents challenged the fact that the Tennessee legislature had not reapportioned since 1901. Their lawyers argued that citizens living in urban areas were being deprived of the "equal protection of the law," as guaranteed in the Fourteenth Amendment to the U.S. Constitution. The more sweeping decision came on June 15, 1964, when the U.S. Supreme Court, in *Reynolds v. Sims,* ruled that state legislative apportionments must follow a "one man–one vote" standard. Within a few years, state legislative and congressional districts were apportioned to equalize population among legislative districts—for the first time in the nation's history.

The lifting of the artificial restraints on the cities' representation would have fundamentally changed the political dynamics in state houses and also in Congress—if it had come decades earlier. For central-city voters the court's decisions simply came too late. By the mid-1960s white flight to the suburbs had emptied the cities of millions of middle-class voters who, if they had still been dependent on city services and infrastructure, would undoubtedly have pressed hard for state and federal aid. Instead, now living in the suburbs, they became enemies rather than allies of the blacks, Hispanics, and poor who made up an increasing proportion of inner-city populations.

The Equity Effect

In all the industrialized nations, jobs and populations have decentralized. What makes the United States unique is not only the extent of its urban sprawl but, much more important, the fact that an extraordinary proportion of its urban population lives within governmental jurisdictions that are separate from central cities. Throughout the twentieth century, local governments have proliferated as suburbanites formed new towns and cities beyond the boundaries of the old core cities. By 1987, there were 83,237 local governments in the United States (U.S. Bureau of the Census, 1992: 278). As Kenneth Newton has observed, "The degree of local government fragmentation in the United States . . . is unique among the urban-industrial societies" (1984: 350).

Before the turn of the century, suburbanization was the exception rather than the rule; as urban dwellers moved beyond the limits of the cities, they often sought annexation so that they could continue to receive the public services that central cities supplied. Even when they wanted to remain separate, they were often coerced into joining the city by threats that they would lose access to water and sewer networks and other essential urban services.

In the early years of the nineteenth century, the incorporation of local government was regarded as a privilege bestowed by state legislatures. Wealthy people who wanted to separate from the cities claimed that small cities were closer to the people and were therefore the purest expressions of democracy (Syed, 1966). Fighting for separation from Boston, for example, separationists of the 1880s painted a portrait of "the ideal of small town life: the simple informal community, the town meeting, the maintenance of the traditions of rural New England" (Warner, 1962: 164–165). Showing the other side of the coin, they argued that Boston's politics had become corrupted by immigrants and their political representatives. Such an appeal carried a good deal of weight with rural legislators in Massachusetts, who harbored much the same combination of suspicions and ideals. Massachusetts led the way, but before long virtually all the states had made it easy for suburbanites to resist annexation through the simple expedient of incorporation. State legislatures made it so much easier to incorporate new towns and cities that incorporation shifted from a privilege to a right (Teaford, 1979: 6).

The upper- and middle-class people who fled the industrial cities quickly used their new weapon, with the result that "by the early twentieth century suburbanites had begun carving up the metropolis, and the states had handed them the knife" (Teaford, 1979: 31). When the waves of European immigrants were replaced by the great migrations of the twentieth century, the industrial cities soon became surrounded by rings of suburbs that captured a disproportionate share of metropolitan wealth and business activity. The fragmentation that resulted has tended to reflect and accentuate patterns of racial and income segregation by establishing a mechanism whereby the race and incomes of urban residents are related to the fiscal health of the cities they live within.

Racial and economic segregation between cities and suburbs became fixed in the 1950s, a decade when suburban populations in metropolitan areas grew by 19 million people. Since 1950 the median incomes of central-city populations have lagged further and further behind the incomes of suburbanites, and since the 1960s pockets of concentrated poverty within the central cities have rapidly expanded. The fact that income, ethnic, and racial groups are segregated is certainly not unique to the United States. But two characteristics make the U.S. pattern different: the extreme concentration of the poor in the metropolitan center, and the close relationship between patterns of segregation and political boundaries.

In the United States, governmental fragmentation has nurtured an "enclave consciousness" that is expressed in efforts to withdraw from the larger urban community (Plotkin, 1991: 5–26). Suburban jurisdictions assume that they have a right to withdraw from the surrounding urban society. The ease with which suburbanites have been able to express their desire to escape has become represented on the urban landscape by the complex mosaic of governments. The proliferation of local governments has not been neutral. Instead, political boundaries have had the effect of exaggerating economic inequalities among ethnic and racial groups by separating the fiscal resources of governments from public needs. In light of the differences in income levels, it is hardly surprising that per capita taxes are higher in central cities than in suburbs—or that the per capita amount of tax raised also heavily favors the suburbs. Of course, the suburbs also differ greatly among themselves in fiscal resources, and to the same effect: Those with wealthier residents and healthy business activity can tax themselves less and yet raise more money than jurisdictions with lower property values and poorer residents.

The fiscal resources of urban governments are matched closely to patterns of social class and of ethnic and racial segregation, but it clear that lower-income African Americans are affected by these patterns far more than are lower-income whites. African Americans disproportionately live in central cities and, as a result, pay higher taxes and gain less from property ownership. In 1981 per capita taxes were 37 percent higher in central cities than in suburbs (Advisory Commission on Intergovernmental Relations, 1981: 23); nevertheless, it is clear that the public services they receive are often inferior. In addition, central-city homeowners benefit less from the dynamics of the private housing market than do homeowners in the suburbs (Edel, 1975: 366–387; Swanstrom, 1985: 69–70; Hill and Bier, 1989: 140). It could be argued that this difference has nothing to do with fragmentation per se, since home values obviously vary because of lot sizes, the age of the housing, and the bundle of services and amenities that wealthier people are able to afford. But such an argument makes sense only if one ignores the complex interaction between housing values and the fiscal health of local government. Obviously, when wealthier residents are able to isolate themselves within a governmental jurisdiction, with modest tax efforts they are able to support superior schools and other governmental services that make one area a more desirable place than another.

African Americans are systematically disadvantaged because they disproportionately reside within poorer governmental jurisdictions. Even suburban blacks are disadvantaged in this way. Suburbs tend to fall into "black" and "white" jurisdictions, a pattern so systematic that most suburban whites have little contact with blacks: 86 percent of suburban whites live in jurisdictions with a black population of less than 1 percent (Logan and Molotch, 1987: 194). Older, inner-ring suburbs also hold a disproportionate share of blacks. Thus, the suburbanization of blacks has resulted not so much in a breakdown of segregation as in the replication of the patterns of neighborhood segregation found within the central cities (Logan and Molotch, 1987: 195).

These patterns of racial segregation matter because most suburban blacks live within political jurisdictions that have many of the same fiscal problems as the central cities. A study of Philadelphia's suburbs for the period from 1977 to 1982 found that predominantly black suburbs had a per capita tax base that averaged 30 percent less than the average for white or mixed suburbs; in addition, municipal debt per capita in African American suburbs is often twice that of mixed and white suburbs. In general, black suburbs tend to have lower tax bases, higher debts, and poorer municipal services, as well as lower socioeconomic status and higher population densities, than suburbs that are predominantly white (Massey and Denton, 1988: 595–596).

It would be extremely difficult for the fragmentation of governments to persist in metropolitan areas if it disadvantaged wealthier, politically influential elites. It continues to exist precisely because the spatial patterning of governments materially benefits the privileged, and because those who benefit from fragmentation are able to use their governments to preserve the existing governmental arrangements.

The Governance Effect

For some time a debate has raged between those who advocate the consolidation of governments in metropolitan areas and a group of scholars who claim that fragmentation gives consumers the ability to shop around among jurisdictions for a preferred bundle of taxes and services. In the 1980s the Advisory Commission on Intergovernmental Relations, which had traditionally represented a reformer's perspective, turned a sudden about-face in favor of the public-choice perspective. Without attempting to comment on this debate as it relates to the provision of municipal services, I suggest that fragmentation has made it nearly impossible for metropolitan areas to be governed as regions in three important respects: They are unable to engage in regional planning, to coordinate land-use policies, or to implement regional economic development strategies. No matter how thoroughly the consumer of governmental services may shop around within a fragmented metropolitan area, this particular bundle of services is unavailable.

In the United States, comprehensive regional planning simply does not take place on a metropolitanwide basis in any meaningful sense. For that to occur, planners would have to be able to persuade public officials to coordinate land-use activities and public resources. Reflecting decades of attempts by the federal government to promote some degree of regional coordination, there are currently almost six hundred councils of government (COGs). Beginning with Section 701 of the Housing Act of 1954, urban renewal authorities were required to frame their proposals within language about metropolitan planning. In 1965 the Office of Management of Budget issued its famous circulars A-85 and A-95. A-85 required a sign-off from the chief executive of the state or local government from which a grant proposal originated. A-95 went much further, requiring the states to designate clearinghouse agencies for metropolitan regions.

The Reagan administration stopped funding COGs in the early 1980s, and in 1983 it abandoned the A-95 requirement in favor of a policy that entrusted coordination procedures to the states. Even so, most of the states continued the review process because local-government officials found it to be useful for facilitating a continuing exchange of information. A few COGs do much more: Sixteen have some taxing powers, fifteen try to coordinate zoning (though in all cases cooperation is voluntary), and a few coordinate planning for highways, mass transit, and water and wastes (National Association of Regional Councils, 1988: 4). There is even a national organization of regional associations to promote regional approaches.

By no stretch of the imagination, however, can it be said that the presence of COGs signals the dawn of regional planning. They are useful or even necessary because grant proposals for mass transit, solid waste, and a few other activities are just not possible without a regional component to the application. Almost all COGs do little more than coordinate one or two services; their role is basically that of a special district, but one that lacks taxing and actual service-providing responsibilities. Except for grant activity in specified areas involving more than a few governments, and except for their role in facilitating communication, they are legendary for lacking political authority. According to the editors of *Governing* magazine, who have nevertheless expressed optimism about the future of COGs, "most have not proven themselves as political policy makers, especially when the issues are controversial" ("Ready or Not," 1992: 67).

The style of planning that occurs in urban America—deal making—is a product of the competition among cities for economic growth. Cities that can afford to do so hire planners and economic development specialists who act in a mediating capacity between private firms and public agencies, coordinating land acquisition, public subsidies, tax expenditures, and enhanced public services for developers and firms (Fainstein, 1994: 100–102). Thus, within jurisdictions as well as within urban regions, strategic planning is absent. Instead, a piecemeal, project-by-project process occupies both professional bureaucrats and elected officials.

Since land-use policies in urban areas are controlled by local governments, it is difficult to see how these policies could be pried loose and made regional, especially given that land use is a principal means by which privileged communities maintain the character of their communities. With the possible exception of local control of the schools, probably no public policy in America is so identified with local prerogatives. When the Nixon administration tried to involve itself in zoning disputes in the 1970s, it quickly learned that it was treading on sacred ground, and it backed off (Judd and Swanstrom, 1994: 227–233). In 1975 the U.S. Supreme Court took steps to keep zoning off its docket by making it very difficult for litigants to challenge zoning in the courts. The Court ruled that to challenge a zoning ordinance on the grounds that it constituted racial discrimination, a litigant would be required to show "distinct and palpable injury." In other words, it would not be sufficient for the litigant to claim a general injury just because he or she desired to live in a particular community (*Warth v. Seldin,* 1975).

As in the case of zoning, local officials view their control over economic development policies as a fundamental right. Privileged communities use zoning as a growth-control measure, whereas less privileged cities possess a complex arsenal of devices to promote investment within their boundaries. An intense competition among jurisdictions is driven by the most fundamental dynamic set up by local fragmentation—namely, the immediate, intimate connection among jobs, investment, and the tax base. Competing jurisdictions typically try to induce investment in their own as opposed to neighboring jurisdictions by offering tax and financing concessions that run the risk of further impoverishing the local fisc. Central cities have been particularly zealous in this competition; since the 1980s a virtual urban war has been waged involving the construction of new or expanded convention centers, stadiums, and other facilities meant to attract tourists and the middle-class people back to the city.

Despite the obvious advantages that might accrue to regions able to devise comprehensive plans for economic development, it is extremely difficult to persuade local governments to give up their internecine battles. Through the region's Metropolitan Council, cities in the Minneapolis–St. Paul area were able to work out an agreement for limited tax sharing to discourage competition among localities. The agreement reduced per capita tax base disparities among municipalities to a 4-to-1 ratio from the 22-to-1 ratio that had prevailed before the agreement (Shanahan, 1991). Similar arrangements could conceivably be worked out in other metropolitan areas, but they would remain rare because wealthier cities and their residents have no incentives to cooperate.

It is important to emphasize that the fragmentation of governments does not deny most cities the capacity to engage in activist, even aggressive policies. As I indicated earlier, central cities have recently been engaged in a competition for growth, and there are considerable weapons at their disposal. Indeed, it might be useful to compare the railroad wars of a century and a half ago with the tourist and office-tower wars today. In both cases, city governments seem to be remarkably unrestrained by the states. It would be incorrect, then, to conclude that fragmentation has robbed most cities of the resources or capacity to govern their own affairs. Undeniably, however, fragmentation has made it impossible for most metropolitan areas to be governed, except in their divisible parts.

This situation matters, in part, because urban regions have interests that transcend their constituent parts. Cities and suburbs share a closely symbiotic relationship. Not only do a large proportion of suburbanites work in the cities, but the economic vitality of cities helps determine the economic health of suburban economies (Savitch et al., 1993). Cities and suburbs share common fates in a political sense as well, such that their inability to cooperate weakens both. State legislatures represent, and respond to, three seemingly separate constituency groups: rural, suburban, and what is typically labeled "urban," as if the suburbs were not also urban. Missouri supplies a ready example of the costs of fragmenting urban interests into contending constituencies in this way. In 1985 the city of St. Louis and St. Louis County (which is geographically separate from the city) became locked in a virtual war when the owner of the St. Louis Cardinals threatened to leave the region if a new stadium was not constructed to house the team. The battle for the team raged on through 1986, with both the city and the county promising to build new stadiums. In 1988 the Cardinals moved to Phoenix, Arizona. Finally, in 1990 the city and county presented a united front, and in the first such instance in anyone's memory, the mayor and county supervisor organized a joint lobbying effort in Jefferson City. Ultimately, the governor, a conservative, downstate Republican, agreed to sign a bill to float $100 million in bonds to help build a stadium—in the city. In the absence of cooperation, such a breakthrough in state assistance would never have been forthcoming. And it is certain that if urban constituencies were able to speak with a unified voice on more policy issues, the state legislature would respond earlier, and more frequently, to the urban constituencies within the state.

The Political Structure Effect:
Federalism and National Urban Policy

Unlike the European nations, the United States has never implemented a coherent set of urban policies. There can be little doubt that the incoherence of past programs in the United States often reflected the complexity of the federal system. Federal programs composed a complex matrix, often contradicting one another in their purposes and exacerbating the disparities that already existed among governments (Kantor, 1993: 237). Programs flowed to a multitude of local governments or were passed through the states, a step that added complexity and political intrigue. In contrast, urban policy in Europe tended to be quite comprehensive; in addition, local governments were called upon to administer policies that made up the national welfare state. National governments relied on cities to implement a variety of policies, and the grants that flowed to cities for other purposes tended to equalize fiscal resources and to give cities considerable autonomy in using and administering funds (Heidenheimer, Heclo, and Adams, 1983: 274–304).

All Western nations have fundamentally revised their urban policies. National governments everywhere have turned away from policies intended to protect cities and urban areas from the consequences of economic transformation and decline. Instead, cities have been forced to adjust to global economic change by becoming entrepreneurial; in particular, urban leaders have been compelled to learn how to use public powers and resources to underwrite private investment (Judd and Parkinson, 1990). The method for accomplishing this shift in local policy priorities was, however, starkly different in the United States as compared to Europe. In the United States, grants-in-aid were drastically cut, and cities were instructed to adopt policies to replace the lost federal money. Some cuts also occurred in Europe during this period, but a disconnection between national governments and cities would have been almost unthinkable because cities there are essential components of national systems of governance. Aside from being responsible for a wide range of public services, cities in Europe administer national policies in health, housing, and income maintenance. As a consequence, unlike the American case, "the degree to which [local] government is really 'local' cannot be . . . easily assessed (Page, 1991: 1).

In the United States, the underrepresentation of urban populations in both state and national legislative bodies became a fundamental structural characteristic of the federal system. By the time this system was finally changed in the 1960s, it was impossible for urban issues to be kept on the national political agenda for long because urban areas had become irretrievably fractured into a multitude of governments, each representing narrow political constituencies. Since no one could speak for urban areas as regions, there could be no "urban" interest, only a multitude of voices.

Federalism has facilitated the containment of the central cities within a ring of politically independent suburbs. As a result, discourse about urban problems in the United States "bisects the world into two polar opposites" (Beauregard, 1993: 218). The extreme political isolation of the cities, which is peculiar to the United States, may also have produced a peculiar way of thinking about urban problems: In America, decline happens to inner cities but not to suburbs; cities house minorities, suburbs the white majority. In the nineteenth century, the great cultural divide pitted immigrants against "natives," cities against rural areas. These images became represented in a political structure that artificially preserved the political hegemony of people who lived outside the cities. In the twentieth century, the great divide has pitted cities against suburbs, and in this case too, the structure of the federal system has set in motion political dynamics that are hardly neutral.

At the time the 1990 census was conducted, central cities of 50,000 or more people held 29 percent of the nation's population. Political commentators and the media characterized the 1992 presidential election as a contest for the "swing" white working-class voters who had become disaffected from Democratic policies targeted to central cities, the poor, and blacks (Edsall and Edsall, 1991; Schneider, 1992). Bill Clinton made an effort to appeal to suburban voters. He distanced himself from Jesse Jackson and the urban wing of his party. He called for a get-tough approach to welfare reform. His bus tours with Hillary and Albert Gore and his wife were replete with suburban and small-town imagery. Clinton's claim that he represented a new Democratic party that would pay attention to the concerns of the middle class was politically shrewd. Republicans had been effective at driving a wedge between suburban (white) and central-city (minority) voters. Clinton's victory, in turn, was generally credited to his success in reaching the suburban middle class.

During the 1992 campaign, Clinton promised big-city mayors a $20-billion-a-year infrastructure investment program that would link the physical revitalization of the cities to national economic revitalization (Ayres, 1992). And in the wake of the Los Angeles riots of late April and early May 1992, he supported aid to the cities. Then, in April 1993, Congress defeated a modest package of urban aid. But an urban program was salvaged when the administration incorporated "empowerment zones" into the Omnibus Budget Reconciliation Act of 1993, which passed the House by two votes and the Senate by a vice-presidential tie-breaker. This legislation made $3.5 billion available for enterprise and empowerment zones in seventy-two urban and thirty-three rural communities.

The passage of a modest urban program demonstrates that some urban (meaning central-city) programs can still be gotten through Congress, despite the decades-long movement of people to the suburbs and the Sunbelt. The fact remains, however, that because cities do not implement national programs in the United States, as they do in Europe, they can be abandoned when it is politically advantageous for politicians to ignore them. In the American political system, those who would speak for central cities are one voice among the many contending interests that originate in urban regions. Since, in the American political system, "urban" has come to mean "central city," the near absence of urban policy is hardly surprising.

14

The Evolution of Environmentalism: From Elitism to Participatory Democracy?

JAMES P. LESTER
W. DOUGLAS COSTAIN

Environmental advocates had great expectations for the presidency of Bill Clinton. The return of one-party government after twelve years of divided government was expected to be especially rewarding for those seeking more aggressive federal leadership to protect the ecological systems of the nation and the world. During the 1980s environmental groups grew increasingly supportive of the Democratic Party, an alliance that was cemented by the rhetorical attacks on environmentalists coming from President Reagan's administration. This environmentalist partisanship continued through the Bush presidency, despite conciliatory gestures by the Bush administration toward mainstream ecology groups. After a decade of defending the breakthrough legislation of the early 1970s from political threats, environmentalists hoped to address the global environmental challenges that had been raised at the Rio ("Earth") Summit in June 1992. Vice-President Al Gore was a particular object of hope for those seeking a "green government" based on the agenda laid out in his 1992 book, *Earth in the Balance.*

The end of Republican control of the executive branch removed major barriers to the enactment of environmental policies. Under Presidents Reagan and Bush, business interests and economic conservatives had been able to use their access to the Office of Management and Budget (OMB) and the Council on Competitiveness (chaired by Vice-President Quayle) to gain delays or to weaken regulations implementing environmental and natural resource protection laws. To counter these tactics, lawmakers and environmental groups tried to limit administrative discretion by writing detailed specifications into the laws themselves, mandating the timely issuance of implementation regulations by executive agencies. Although William Reilly, who headed the Environmental Protection Agency (EPA) during the Bush years, was a tireless advocate for environmental causes within the administration, he was often unsuccessful, especially in his efforts to have the United States play a leadership role in the creation of global institutions for environmental protection. A Democratic executive was also expected to work more harmoniously with Democratic congressional leaders to strengthen and speed up the reauthorization of several major environmental laws, including the Safe Drinking Water Act, the Clean Water Act, and Superfund.

Yet the national political climate for an ambitious environmental agenda was less hospitable after the 1992 election than it had been four years earlier. In contrast to the 1988 campaign, which saw candidate Bush proclaim himself an environmentalist and attack Michael Dukakis for neglecting the cleanup of Boston harbor, little attention was paid to environmental issues during the 1992 race. The Clinton campaign stayed with its strategy of emphasizing the weakness of the economy, particularly unemployment, and downplayed the implications of some of the ideas in Al Gore's book. The Bush campaign attempted to deflect public concern about jobs by raising the specter of the Democrats as environmental extremists, more concerned with saving spotted owls than with saving jobs. Gore did attempt to reconcile job creation with environmental protection through his vision of the United States as an exporter of high-tech environmental protection and restoration products and services to the world. Economic growth was the issue that overshadowed all others in the political debate and among most voters. President Clinton promised in the campaign to "focus like a laser beam" on the economy, a concentration that offered little attention to issues such as the environment.

The transition in environmental policies from the Bush to the Clinton administrations offers an opportunity to test not only explanations of the evolution of environmental policy but also several broader theories of policy change in America. Have the first two years of President Clinton's presidency illustrated incremental or discontinuous policy change in this case? Is there a larger evolutionary pattern that allows us to understand environmental policy change not just over two years but over perhaps several decades? We suggest that the evolution of environmentalism over the past hundred years illustrates a number of important changes in the nature of public policy, in the nature of policymaking, in the scope of the issues considered, in the level of governmental responses, and in patterns of participation. Specifically, we have witnessed an evolution from a concern over preservation of natural resources to a concern over "third-generation" environmental issues such as acid rain, global warming, and desertification. We have also observed a number of policy changes (e.g., from the "wise use" of natural resources to pollution prevention and waste minimization); indeed, patterns of participation have evolved from a largely elitist style in the late 1890s to "participatory democracy" in the 1990s. Similarly, the emphasis in environmental policymaking has evolved from a concern about adding to the agenda to policy implementation and evaluation. Meanwhile, other scholars have noted that innovation in environmental policymaking shifted from the national level to the state and local levels in the 1980s and the 1990s; and that concern over "environmental science" in the late 1800s evolved into a concern over "environmental ethics" in the 1990s.

All these changes, taken together, suggest that the nature of environmentalism has greatly expanded over the past hundred years to include more issues, more participants, greater awareness, and greater attention to the environment. They also suggest a number of trends for the 1990s and beyond. If these past hundred years are any guide to the future, then we will likely observe the emergence of strong democracy, local activism, and significantly new approaches to dealing with environmental problems yet to come. Some scholars have made similar arguments (e.g., Inglehart, 1989; Milbrath, 1984).

We begin by presenting three very different explanations of changes in American public policy over time. One explanation has been proposed by Arthur Schlesinger (1987), who suggests that public policy in America is patterned around a "policy cycle" in which thirty-year periods of conservatism alternate with thirty-year periods of liberalism. A second explanation of policy change is offered by Paul Sabatier (1987), who argues that "policy learning" plays a major role. Finally, Edwin Amenta and Theda Skocpol (1989) have proposed that American public policy follows a zig-zag pattern in which different groups are offered patronage that produces a backlash in public policy over time. After evaluating the utility of these three explanations in terms of the evolution of environmentalism, we incorporate the first year of the Clinton administration's policies into our analysis.

ALTERNATIVE ANALYTIC FRAMEWORKS: ANALYZING POLICY CHANGE OVER TIME

The Cyclical Thesis

According to the "cyclical thesis" offered by Arthur Schlesinger, there is a continuing shift in national involvement between public purpose and private interest. (See Schlesinger, 1986, 1987; and Burnham, 1970. See also Huntington, 1981, who presents a more sophisticated version of the cycles approach.) More specifically, Schlesinger argues that American politics follows a fairly regular cyclical alternation between conservatism and liberalism in our national moods. In other words, there are swings back and forth between eras when the nation is committed to private interest as the best means of meeting our national problems and eras when the nation is committed to public purpose. At roughly thirty-year intervals, Schlesinger further argues, the nation turns to reform and affirmative government as the best way of dealing with our troubles. For example, Theodore Roosevelt ushered in the Progressive period in 1901, Franklin Roosevelt brought in the New Deal during the 1930s, and John Kennedy introduced the New Frontier in the 1960s. Alternatively, Ronald Reagan ushered in a conservative era in the 1980s, which was a replay of the conservative 1950s and the Harding-Coolidge era of the 1920s.

Schlesinger claims that there is nothing mystical about the thirty-year cycle. After all, thirty years constitute the span of a generation. And people tend to be formed politically by the ideals that are dominant in the years during which they attain political consciousness: roughly between the ages of 17 and 25. When their own generation's turn in power comes thirty years later, they tend to carry forward the ideals they imbibed when young. Over time, each phase tends to run its natural course. The season of idealism and reform, when strong presidents call for active public interest in national affairs and invoke government as a means of promoting the general welfare, eventually leaves an electorate exhausted by the process and disenchanted with the results. People eventually become attuned to a "new" message that tells them that private action and self-interest in an unregulated market will solve the nation's problems. This mood eventually runs its course, too, as problems become acute, threaten to become unmanageable, and demand remedies by governmental actors. The change in public mood thus ushers in a new era of reform and governmental intervention.

According to Schlesinger, then, the evolution of environmentalism over the past hundred years would suggest the following proposition.

Proposition 1: The evolution of environmentalism follows a fairly predictable pattern in which a thirty-year period of private remedies (and minimal governmental intervention) will be followed by a thirty-year period of significant governmental intervention and reform.

Moreover, Schlesinger predicts that the 1990s will usher in a new era of political liberalism and governmental intervention in public policy. "Shortly before or after the year 1990," he notes, "there should come a sharp change in the national mood and direction—a change comparable to those bursts of innovation and reform that followed the accessions to office of Theodore Roosevelt in 1901, of Franklin Roosevelt in 1933 and of John Kennedy in 1961" (Schlesinger, 1986: 47).

Samuel Huntington's elaboration of the cyclical thesis also emphasizes the power of ideas in shaping public policy and institutions. Huntington argues that periods of "creedal passion," or intense and widespread debate over the gap between the ideals and the actual performance of the American government, lead to major bursts of institutional reforms. The enactment and implementation of these reforms serve to channel and control the debate over fundamental values and usher in an era of relative calm. In time, the shortcomings of the reforms will become increasingly obvious, triggering another period of controversy and another attempt to bring America's political system closer to its mythic ideals. Paradoxically, the reforms of one generation create the vested interests of the next generation.

The Policy-Learning Thesis

A second explanation comes, as noted, from a recent work by Paul A. Sabatier (1987). He offers a conceptual framework of policy evolution and learning based on a policy subsystem of competing coalitions (mediated by policy brokers) and two broad types of variables that affect policy learning. According to Sabatier, policy change is the product of both (1) changes in systemwide events, such as socioeconomic perturbations or outputs from other subsystems, and (2) the striving of competing advocacy coalitions within the subsystem to realize their core beliefs over time as they seek to increase their resource bases, to respond to opportunities provided by external events, and to learn more about the policy problem(s) of interest to them. On the basis both of perceptions of the adequacy of governmental units and/or the resultant impacts, and of new information arising from search processes and external dynamics, each advocacy coalition may revise its beliefs and/or alter its strategy. The latter course may involve seeking major institutional revisions at the collective-choice level and more minor revisions at the operational level, or even going outside the subsystem, for example, by seeking changes in the dominant electoral coalition at the systemic level (Sabatier, 1987: 653).

This framework has special significance for the study of policy-oriented learning, which entails relatively enduring alterations of behavioral intentions that result from experience and are concerned with the attainment or revision of public policy (Heclo, 1977: 306). Specifically, within this framework the core aspects of a governmental action program—and the relative strength of competing advocacy coalitions within a policy subsystem—will typically remain rather stable over periods of a decade or more. Major alterations in the policy core will normally be the product of changes external to the subsystem—particularly large-scale socioeconomic conditions or changes in the systemwide governing coalition. Whereas changes in the policy core are usually the result of external perturbations, changes in the secondary aspects of a governmental action program are often the result of policy-oriented learning by various coalitions or policy brokers. Policy learning involves the feedback loops depicted in Figure 14.1, as well as increased knowledge of the state of the problem and the factors affecting them. It is here that Sabatier's framework is presented, along with the factors that condition public-policy change over time.

Proposition 2: The evolution of environmentalism is explained by an extended period of policy change in which governmental actors repeatedly revise policy on the basis of "policy learning" brought on by events external to subsystem politics. More specifically:

Proposition 2a: Policy-oriented learning across dual belief systems is most likely when there is an intermediate level of informed conflict between the two. The requirement is that (a) each has the technical resources to engage in such a debate and that (b) the conflict is between secondary aspects of one belief system

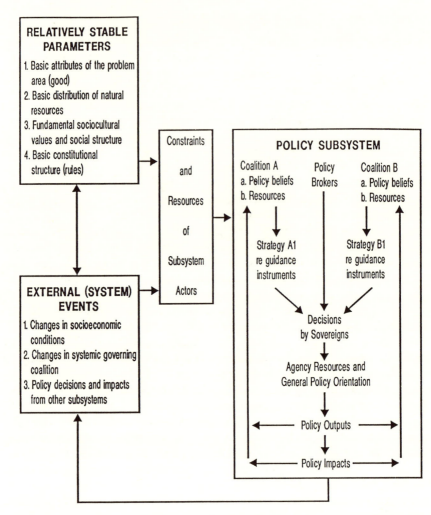

FIGURE 14.1   Overview of Sabatier's Conceptual Framework of Policy Change. SOURCE: Compiled from Sabatier (1987).

and core elements of the other or, alternatively, between important secondary aspects of the two belief systems.

Proposition 2b: Policy-oriented learning across belief systems is most likely when there exists a forum that is (a) prestigious enough to force professionals from different coalitions to participate and (b) dominated by professional norms.

The Backlash or Zig-Zag Thesis

Still another explanation of changes in public policy over time comes from the work of Edwin Amenta and Theda Skocpol (1989). They argue that there is an erratic pattern in the history of American public policies characterized by a "zig-zag effect" or a backlash stimulus (i.e., a stimulus and response). It is not so much a shift from liberal to conservative as from policy that benefits first one group, then another as a backlash to the first group. The concept of "class struggle" or competing societal coalitions comes to mind as a useful way to explain this shift. For example, the late nineteenth century was characterized by high levels of spending and by a distributive character and patronage for *white men.* Specifically, this patronage was devised by the "radical Republicans" and included a Civil War pension system in which benefits were distributed in a partisan way. Pensions went to Northerners who could make a plausible case for their role in preserving the Union. Political affiliation to Republicans was a major criterion for the pension. What resulted was a backlash against the "radical Republicans" in the southern states—a backlash that persists to this day. There were also federal jobs for those with suitable party connections. Indeed, the federal bureaucracy could be seen as largely an employment program for the "right people" (i.e., northern and midwestern Republicans).

This was followed by the Progressive era (1900–1930), during which an attempt was made to eliminate political machines and patronage from the previous era. Civil service reforms, including the merit hiring system, were instituted. There was a movement away from direct election of administrative officials. And child labor laws emerged, along with legislation limiting women's working hours. A variety of public health and safety laws were passed, as was workers' compensation. Gradually, Democrats became more powerful as a consequence of their southern and western bases of support. Individual and corporate income taxes were established. Democrats became known as the reform party due to their attempt to replace the radical Republicans with their own members. By the end of the 1920s, Democrats were allied with the labor movement and threw their support behind social spending. It was at this time that they more or less established themselves as a "social democratic" party.

This was followed by the New Deal period, (1930–1950), during which many of the social insurance programs and welfare programs were enacted. These initiatives were propelled by the Great Depression. Meanwhile, Democrats continued their domination of the public-policy debate. Legislation included the 1935 Social Security Act (the centerpiece of the New Deal). According to this model, the United States adopted Keynesian economics and used the federal government as an agency for massive redistribution of wealth through the creation of large social spending programs and direct intervention in the economy. Politically, these events encouraged deficit spending rather than balanced budgets. As for social spending policy, veterans of World War II and retired veterans of wage-earning employment and their survivors were advantaged relative to other social groups.

Finally, we can designate a postwar period (1950–1980s), during which the country experienced a reaction to the free spending of the previous period of Democratic administrations. In particular, the "new federalism" of the 1970s and 1980s represented a backlash against large federal welfare programs. Later cuts deeply reduced the growth in Great Society programs enacted in the late 1960s. (Note that recent economic policies have relied on fiscal stimulation rather than New Deal liberalism—for example, on tax reduction rather than spending programs to stimulate the economy.) In addition, heavy investments were made in military spending (in fact, jobs in the military were the counterpart to employment in the civilian bureaucracy during the late nineteenth century). Patronage today exists in terms of military employment and old-age assistance. In effect, this model finds that policies today are very similar to those of the first period of the late nineteenth century.

The following proposition is derived from the argument by Amenta and Skocpol.

Proposition 3: The evolution of environmentalism during the period from 1890 to the present is best explained by a "zig-zag" pattern in which the environmental policies of one era provide the stimulus for a reaction in the next era. In other words, the policies undergo drastic changes as a reaction to a previous policy; for example, policies that favor one group (e.g., the preservationists) in one era are replaced by policies that favor other groups (e.g., the corporate sector) in the next era.

In the following two sections, we describe the evolution of environmental policies during the 1890–1990 period and then examine the extent to which any (or all) of the above propositions explain this phenomenon.

THE EVOLUTION OF ENVIRONMENTALISM, 1890 TO THE PRESENT

The history of environmental politics and policy may be roughly divided into four periods. These four periods are the "conservation-efficiency movement" from about 1890 to 1920; the "conservation-preservation movement" from about 1920 to 1960; the "environmental movement" from about 1960 to 1980; and the contemporary period of "participatory environmentalism" starting in the 1980s.[1] However, we can identify earlier attempts to protect the environment as well. For example, during the first part of the nineteenth century, the federal government took a number of actions to preserve good mast timber for ships, and the administration of President John Quincy Adams went so far as to establish a program of sustained yield operations on some forest reservations in 1827 (Engelbert, 1961: 226). However, environmental protection received relatively little attention until after the Civil War. With the exception of the Adams administration, no other presidential administration from Washington to Buchanan revealed any foresight in planning for the nation's future natural resource needs (Englebert, 1961: 233).

Essentially, the years between 1865 and 1890 may be characterized as a period of resource exploitation by a rising industry, during which time natural resources were subordinated to the political objectives of industrial development, homestead settlement, and the promotion of free enterprise (Englebert, 1961: 227). During the reconstruction era after the Civil War, it was necessary to rebuild the South and to develop the American West, both of which required the use of resources rather than their conservation. Nevertheless, by the late 1800s serious efforts were being made to protect the nation's natural resources.

The Conservation-Efficiency Movement, 1890–1920: Elitism in Policymaking

The years from 1890 to 1920 saw some of the nation's most bitter conservation battles as Republicans and Democrats began to take firm positions on the environment. The essence of the "conservation movement" was rational planning *by government* to promote efficient development and use of all natural resources (Hays, 1959: 2). According to historian Samuel P. Hays, "The modern American conservation movement grew out of the firsthand experience of federal administrators and political leaders with problems of Western economic growth, especially Western water development"(Hays, 1959: 5). Later, federal forestry officials joined hydrographers and campaigned for more rational and efficient use of timber resources. During the 1890s the organized forestry movement in the United States shifted its emphasis from saving trees to promoting sustained-yield forest management (Hays, 1959: 28). In 1891 the executive branch took the lead in setting aside "forest reserves" within the federal domain, and in 1897 it authorized selective cutting and marketing of timber (Caulfield, 1989: 16).

A number of individuals, including W. J. McGee, Gifford Pinchot, John Wesley Powell, Frederick Newell, George Maxwell, and others, were concerned about the short-sighted commercial exploitation of the nation's natural resources. Many were employed by the federal government in the late 1800s, especially by the U.S. Geological Survey. Together, they formulated four basic doctrines for what later became the creed of the conservation movement. These doctrines were as follows: (1) Conservation is not the locking up of resources; it is their development and wise use. (2) Conservation is the greatest good for the greatest number, for the longest time. (3) The federal public lands belong to all the people. And (4) comprehensive, multiple-purpose river basin planning and development should be utilized with respect to the nation's water resources (Caulfield, 1989: 20–21).

Gifford Pinchot became an important link between the intellectual and scientific founders of the conservation movement, on the one hand, and President Theodore Roosevelt, a Republican, on the other. Indeed, the Roosevelt administration is as noteworthy for the drive and support it gave the conservation movement as for its initiation of new policies and legislative enactments. A new spirit of law enforcement pervaded the once-corrupt land management departments, as dramatized to the country at large by the influence of Gifford Pinchot and his role as adviser to President Roosevelt (Englebert, 1961: 245) Under Pinchot's guidance, the Roosevelt administration greatly enlarged the area of the national forests from 41 to 159 national reserves (Hays, 1959: 47). Pinchot, who studied forest management in France and Germany, completely reorganized the Forest Service and infused it with a new spirit of public responsibility (Hays, 1959: 28–46).

The period from 1908 to 1920 saw numerous conflicts over conservation policy. For example, much of the Western livestock industry depended for its forage upon the "open range," which was owned by the federal government but free for anyone to use. Soon, however, the public domain became stocked with more animals than the range could support. Chaos, violence, and destruction of property were typical of the times. Range wars developed between Western cattlemen and sheep operators, as well as between both of these groups and farmers, as all struggled for control of the public grazing lands (Hays, 1959: 53).

Nevertheless, the deepest significance of the conservation movement, according to Samuel Hays, "lay in its political implications: how should resource decisions be made and by whom?" Should conflicts be resolved through partisan politics, by compromise among various interest groups, or through the courts? (Hays, 1959: 271). To the conservationists, politics was anathema; instead, they believed, scientific experts should decide all matters of development and use of natural resources together with the allocation of public funds (Hays, 1959: 271). The crux of the gospel of efficiency, then, "lay in a rational and scientific method of making basic technological decisions through a single, central authority" (Hays, 1959: 271). The inevitable tension that developed between those "grassroots" interests and the technocratic elites of this conservation-efficiency era raised a question that was to be addressed by future conservationists: How can large-scale government programs be effective and at the same time fulfill the desire for significant grass-roots participation?

Another branch of the Progressive movement, the urban public-health and sanitation groups, also shared this respect for experts as policymakers. The idea of a central role for government in promoting and protecting the health of people, rather than relying on market forces or voluntarism, emerged during the Progressive period. Health was not simply a private decision. It was also a public concern, because diseases spread by inadequate sanitation or impure water seemed to call for communitywide solutions. Just as foresters decried the loss of natural resources resulting from private management of land, so early public-health advocates saw the need for government to assume responsibility for the prevention of communicable diseases in crowded cities. As the germ theory of disease became accepted among health experts, it was increasingly clear that individuals acting alone could not protect their own health, because each was vulnerable to exposure to germs carried by others. Thus policies such as mass vaccinations, nutrition education, purified drinking-water supplies, and municipal sewer systems were believed to be justified. The idea that experts, working through governments, could identify and protect the interests of the community was common to the Progressives. The recognition that an individual's health could be put at risk by the actions of others, whether by infection from a contagious disease (in the early 1900s) or by toxic emissions from industrial smokestacks (in the 1970s), unites the public-health Progressives with modern environmentalism. The latter owes much of its public support and political influence to its public-health content. Indeed, many current environmental laws are concerned with human health as well as with the preservation of nature.

The Conservation-Preservation Movement, 1920–1960: The Growth of Subgovernments

The second form of conservationism, the preservationist movement, was very similar to the efficiency movement, except that it was more concerned with *habitat* than with sustenance (Engelbert, 1961: 380). That is, the preservationist movement developed largely under the pressures of increased leisure and affluence and the growth of outdoor recreation. It garnered support from the upper-middle class and also from hunting and fishing groups drawn from the working classes. Although there were conflicts over natural resource policy, these were largely confined to struggles between those who favored "multiple use" of public lands versus those who favored "pure preservation" (Schnaiberg, 1980: 386). Whereas the earlier conservation movement was often characterized by conflicts between extractive industries in the West and manufacturing industries in the East, the preservationist movement often included capitalist sponsors, such as Laurence Rockefeller, who facilitated the preservation of major tracts of land surrounding the hotels that he built (Schnaiberg, 1980: 386).

Beginning in 1920 water power, coal, flood control, and even wildlife were given special attention in the major party platforms. Much of the emphasis on natural resources was shifted from conservation of public lands to programs of conservation under private ownership (Engelbert, 1961: 240). Another major difference between the conservation and preservationist movements was that conservation-efficiency concerns resided with corporations and national and state agencies, whereas conservation-preservationist concerns resided in local and especially national voluntary organizations, such as the Sierra Club, the National Wildlife Federation, and the Wilderness Society.

The period from 1921 to 1950 took on a different character as much of the federal legislation for natural resources became associated with broad social and economic objectives such as the Agricultural Adjustment Act of 1938, which was passed to control agricultural production. Similarly, the job-creating agencies of the New Deal often undertook major environmental protection responsibilities. The Civilian Conservation Corps (CCC) not only planted millions of trees in the Dust Bowl states but also upgraded many of the national parks. The legislative history of environmental and natural resource issues suggests that Democrats attained a much better voting record than their Republican counterparts during 1921–1950 (Engelbert, 1961: 244). In the 1960s, however, the movement began to change dramatically as environmental concern was broadened to include many new issues involving groups that had previously been inactive.

The Environmental Movement, 1960–1980:
Pluralism in Policymaking

One prominent scholar of environmental politics argues that the conservation movement was an effort made by leaders in science, technology, and government to bring about more efficient development of natural resources, whereas the environmental movement was a product of a fundamental change in public values in the United States that stressed the quality of the human environment (Hays, 1959: 13). More typically, perhaps, the environmental movement is viewed as a grass-roots or "bottom-up" phenomenon in which environmental objectives arose out of deep-seated changes in values about the use of nature. Conservation, by contrast, is viewed as a "top-down" phenomenon in which technical and political leaders were stirred toward action. Essentially, the environmental movement integrated the habitat and sustainability concerns of the efficiency and preservation movements, but it also encompassed a broader set of ecosystem concerns (Schnaiberg, 1980: 382). New concerns were voiced about the relationship among social welfare issues, growth management, and decisionmaking about the expansion of production. Threats to human health, especially from air and water pollution and more recently from hazardous waste, prompted additional concerns. Although philosophers of environmental ethics and ecology activists talked about the transformation of human values, a much more basic need was often expressed through environmentalism—the need to protect oneself and especially one's children from risks to life and health.

The environmental movement could also be characterized by the breadth of its constituency, as well as by its strategies for political influence. For example, environmental groups used lobbying, litigation, the media, electoral politics, and even civil disobedience in contrast to the more conventional mechanisms used by the conservationists, such as technical negotiations, corporate sponsors, and small pressure groups (Schnaiberg, 1980: 383).

Finally, the base of support for the environmental movement comprised a larger sector of the public, including the middle and working classes. Such broad support attracted the attention of entrepreneurial politicians seeking to attach themselves to popular causes. With the decline of strong programmatic national parties, ad hoc coalitions of opportunistic politicians advanced the issues of the movement. This transitory support became institutionalized in the laws and regulations that were administered by new agencies such as the EPA. The media and ambitious politicians would move on to newer topics, but the environmental groups and the civil servants were firmly rooted in "issue networks" and "policy communities."

The Contemporary Period, 1980 to the Present:
Toward Strong Democracy and the
Environmental Movement

Some recent authors describe a turning away from "representative democracy" toward the direct action associated with "participatory democracy" (Goldsteen and Schorr, 1991). Others describe contemporary environmental politics in terms of "advocacy coalitions," in which groups from federal, state, and local levels form coalitions for the purpose of supporting or opposing major environmental issues (Sabatier and Jenkins-Smith, 1988). Still others argue that we are evolving toward "postenvironmentalism," which calls for the adoption of environmentally sound methods of industrial production, solar technology, recycling, soft transport technology, and sustainable agriculture (Young, 1990).

Table 14.1 describes some of the salient characteristics of each era of the environmental movement from the 1890s to the 1990s.

THE FINDINGS: EXPLAINING ENVIRONMENTAL POLICY CHANGE OVER TIME

In this section we provide data that is suggestive rather than definitive to "test" the three models of policy change. Our composite of several collections of environmental laws, in Table 14.2, does not show the striking cycles of government activity that Schlesinger seems to have predicted. An upsurge of new laws did occur during the New Deal era, as expected, but there was even more legislative activity in the supposedly quiet 1970s and 1980s. Moreover, it is difficult to argue that the *substance* or content of recent laws is less significant than that of the laws

TABLE 14.1
The Evolution of Environmentalism, 1890s–1990s

	1890–1920	1920–1960	1960–1980	1980–1990s
Scope of the Issues	Preservation Issues	Conservation Issues	Second-Generation Issues	Third-Generation Issues
Dominant Policy	Efficient Use of Resources	Multiple Use of Resources	Pollution Abatement	Pollution Prevention
Patterns of Participation	Elite-Dominated	Subgovernments	Pluralism	Advocacy Coalitions
Policy Cycle Stage	Pre-Problem Stage	Agenda-Setting Stage	Policy Formation	Policy Implementation
Level of Action	National Government	National Government	National Government	National, State, and Local Governments
Dominant Concern	Environmental Science	Technology Development	Economics and Politics	Philosophy and Environmental Ethics
Techniques of Power	Technical Negotiations	Corporate Pressure	Middle-Class Politics	Participatory Democracy

SOURCE: Data compiled by the author.

TABLE 14.2
New National Laws for the Environment, 1890–1990

Decade	Number of Laws	Examples
1890s	4	Forest Reserve Act (1891), River and Harbor Act (1899)
1900s	2	Lacey Act (enforcing state hunting laws) (1900), Reclamation Act/ Newlands Act (1902)
1910s	3	National Park Service Act (1916), Migratory Bird Treaty (1918)
1920s	5	Mineral Leasing Act (1920), Oil Pollution Control Act (1924)
1930s	7	CCC, TVA (1933), Taylor Grazing Act (1934)
1940s	1	Federal Water Pollution Control Act (1948)
1950s	1	Water Pollution Control Act (1956)
1960s	7	Multiple Use Sustained Yield Act (1960), Wilderness Act (1964)
1970s	17	NEPA (1970), Clean Air Act (1970, 1977)
1980s	12	CERCLA (Superfund) (1980, 1986), Clean Air Act (1990)

SOURCE: Data compiled by the authors from a variety of sources, especially Nash (1990: xi–xix).

passed in times presided over by activist presidents. Supporters and critics alike concur that the environmental laws passed in the past two decades are of unprecedented scope in terms of their impact on the nation. (Whether these expensive actions have been effective in addressing their problem areas is another question, of course.)

The other two models are less clearly tested on the basis of this evidence. Specialists in particular environmental policies can track the evolution of air or water pollution laws over time, but the aggregation of expert judgments across the range of environmental laws does not clearly refute either the policy-learning or the zig-zag model.

The early emphasis on laws regulating public lands and hunting and fishing has given way to a much broader array of antipollution and preservationist legislation in recent decades. Yet a historic continuity also exists between the wilderness and endangered species laws of the 1970s and 1980s and the forest reserve and wildlife refuge laws of ninety years earlier.

The "zigs and zags" of policy are obvious when we analyze who benefits from the dominant thrust of environmental laws. The single unambiguous trend is away from unlimited private consumptive uses of "public goods," whether they are national forests or air. In the ongoing debate as to which social groups benefit and lose from this redistribution, conservatives argue that upper-class environmental activists are winners and the poor are losers. But even this limited generalization is difficult to sustain when we turn to Sabatier's model. Clearly, the "advocacy coalitions" at work in this policy arena have grown in both number and composition over the decades. There is also evidence of the impact of external events on environmental policies. Consider, for instance, the arrival of two waves of social movements, the progressive and the environmental, as well as the New Deal and its stimulus, the Depression.

Table 14.3, featuring an approximation of the eras during which particular types of groups appeared, provides further evidence of the evolution of this issue area. Early on, both preservationist and hunting and fishing groups emerged and were visible participants in the policy debates of the period. Yet a vast gulf separated the two categories of groups. Audubon and Sierra were tiny in contrast to the mass-membership sportsmen's clubs, but their members were unusually well connected to the nation's political and economic elites, so they exercised an influence far out of proportion to their size.

The groups that were founded during the environmental era were deliberately focused on using the political system to advance environmental protection. They were also membership groups, relying on a broad base of members and donors to fund their advocacy, as well as soliciting larger grants from foundations. The universe of environmental groups has grown to encompass a vast range of organizations from the sedate real-estate brokers in the Nature Conservancy to the theatrical rhetoric of Earth First!

The sheer size and diversity of these groups make the zig-zag model less credible, inasmuch as new participants often carve out new niches rather than directly competing with older groups. Their diversity also suggests an expansion of the issue area, with established issues and groups coexisting with emerging groups and subjects. In short, although we can point to eras in which new groups formed, such as the late 1960s, and to other eras in which they did not, such as the

TABLE 14.3
New National Environmental Organizations, 1890–1990

Decade	Number of New Groups[a]	Examples
1890s	2	Sierra Club (1892), American Scenic and Historic Preservation Society (1895)
1900s	2	National Audubon Society (1905), National Conservation Association (1909)
1910s	3	American Game Protective & Propagation Association (1911), Save the Redwoods League (1918)
1920s	1	Izaak Walton League (1922)
1930s	2	Wilderness Society (1935), National Wildlife Federation (1936)
1940s	1	Soil Conservation Society (1944)
1950s	0	(none found)
1960s	3	Environmental Defense Fund (1967), Friends of the Earth (1969)
1970s	3	Natural Resources Defense Council (1970), League of Conservation Voters (1972)
1980s	1[b]	Earth First! (1981)

[a]The purpose of this table is to illustrate the emergence of groups during particular eras, rather than to offer a precise count of the number of groups.

[b]There are numerous specialized national groups as well as alliances of state and local groups.

SOURCE: Data compiled by the authors.

1950s, there is no direct correspondence between Schlesinger's cycles of government initiative and the formation of new groups.

Even the focus of new groups may not match the new agenda of the government, as suggested by the anomalous appearance of the Wilderness Society during the peak of the New Deal. Sabatier's model pays careful attention to the actual participation of groups in the making of policy, a perspective that Table 14.3 cannot begin to depict. It is worth noting, however, that scholars examining the impact of the environmental movement on policy have pointed to the late 1960s and early 1970s as a time when old and new environmental groups were able to break into the closed circles of policymaking. This was also a time that witnessed the influx of new groups and the revitalization of existing organizations.

Table 14.4 summarizes the coverage of environmental topics in the *New York Times Index* over the full hundred-year period. The subjects of this coverage during the first three decades were the "animals/fish and hunting" category and the "public lands/forests" category. Although it is common for scholars today to speak of this period as encompassing the conservation or progressive conservation movement, very few stories are indexed under that term. The overall low level of environmental coverage supports the common generalization that conservation was of concern to a small elite rather than to the broader public. The contrast between the attention given to environmental topics in the past thirty years and that in prior decades is very striking.

As is evident from our summary of environmental laws and organizations, the range of subjects within this arena has expanded greatly. Coverage of air and water pollution began during the 1930s, but these concerns did not surpass the old focus on animals and forests until the 1950s. According to the *Index*, the dominant environmental topics in the 1990s continue to be air pollution and water pollution.

TABLE 14.4
Space Devoted to Environmental Issues in the *New York Times Index*, 1890–1990

Decade	Average Number of Column Inches Per Year[a]
1890s	3.1
1900s	13.5
1910s	12.6
1920s	36.5
1930s	42.9
1940s	40.1
1950s	110.3
1960s	284.5
1970s	944.7
1980s	688.9

[a]Standardized to reflect varying type fonts and column widths.
SOURCE: Data calculated by the authors.

The same data in Table 14.4 are graphically displayed in Figures 14.2, 14.3, and 14.4 for each year rather than each decade of news coverage. Given the disparity between the space devoted to the environment in recent decades, as compared with the early part of the century, we will focus our analysis on Figures 14.3 and 14.4.

At first glance, Figure 14.3, with its attention to the years prior to 1960, shows signs of Schlesinger's cycles. Indeed, the 1905–1915 peak in news coverage coincides with the height of the Progressive initiatives. Unfortunately, the next cycles are perversely the opposite of the prediction. Media attention to environmental topics boomed during the 1920s and 1930s and grew even more rapidly during the 1950s, when few groups were active and few laws were being passed. Figure 14.4 reveals that the Nixon and Ford presidencies overlapped with the greatest period of news coverage of environmental topics. But again, this is not the cycle we expected to find. (It should be noted that Huntington focuses his analysis on similarities between the Progressive era and the decade from the mid-1960s to the mid-1970s. His concern for the passions stirred by new movements and for their impact on government is more consistent with our limited evidence.)

In analyzing the substance of the news stories in the *New York Times Index*, we distinguished between "conservation" and "environmental" topics, thus allowing a limited "test" of the zig-zag model. As is obvious in Figures 14.3 and 14.4, the older conservation subjects (combining public lands and forests, parks and wilderness, and fish and animal [hunting] regulation) do not disappear as new environmental ones (combining air and water pollution, chemicals and toxins, and oceans) emerge. Until the 1950s about twice as much *Index* space is given to the conservation agenda as to newer issues. In the past thirty years, these older topics were much less visible to the general public, even though they receive *more* attention in the *Index* (note the change in scale, from 0–80 to 0–1600 inches, between Figures 14.3 and 14.4). The dramatic shift in environmental, largely pollution, issues overshadows the rise in conservation topics. The arrival of the environmental movement in the 1960s did not mean that the conservation issues were being ignored. The public agenda of environmentalism, as revealed by the *New York Times Index*, built on the foundation of the conservation movement. Although newer concerns were *added* to the existing agenda, the media attention devoted to environmental topics eventually dwarfs the space given to older issues.

The simple measure of space allotted to each subject also restrains our analysis of the policy-learning model. Certainly the increased complexity of this once-narrow issue area and its scrutiny by the media fell within Sabatier's analysis. Since journalists often define news worth covering in terms of conflict and controversy, it is not surprising that the eras of policy change, such as the early 1970s, are also extensively followed by the *Index*. Events external to the policy subsystem are key impetuses to policy change in this model, and media attention transmits

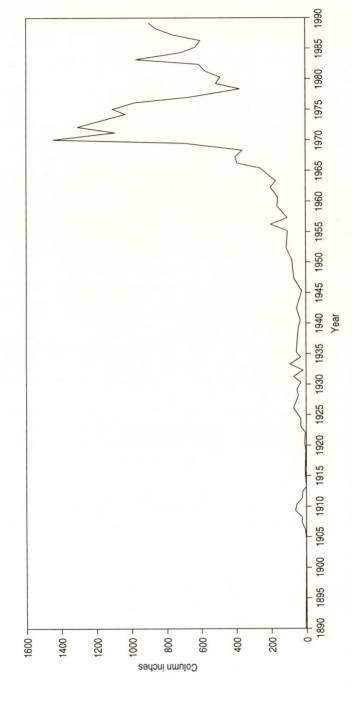

FIGURE 14.2   Space Devoted to Environmental Topics in the *New York Times Index*, 1890–1990. SOURCE: Data compiled by the authors.

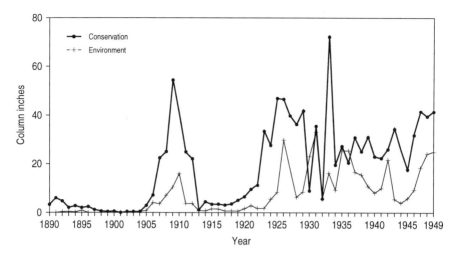

FIGURE 14.3 Space Devoted to Conservation and Environmental Topics in the *New York Times Index,* 1890–1949. SOURCE: Data compiled by the authors.

as well as creates such external pressure. Increased media coverage in the otherwise tranquil 1950s may have been the harbinger of the policy innovations of the early 1970s. The longer time series allows us to see the gradual building of concern a decade *before* the explosion of activity in the late 1960s.

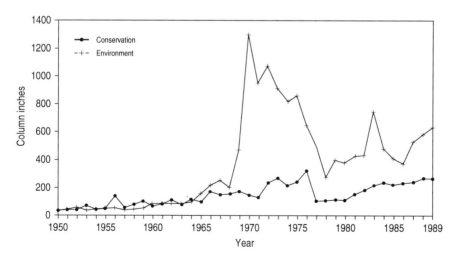

FIGURE 14.4 Space Devoted to Conservation and Environmental Topics in the *New York Times Index,* 1950–1989. SOURCE: Data compiled by the authors.

IMPLICATIONS

From this brief history of the environmental movement, several observations may be drawn. First, we see how the environmental movement has steadily broadened its base of support over the past hundred years from the 1890s to the 1990s. Specifically, it has moved from being largely an elitist concern, involving scientific and government experts, to one with broad-based support from the middle class and even the working class. This broader base of public support has been joined by national environmental groups, ranging from the National Wildlife Federation to the Sierra Club, the Natural Resources Defense Council, Friends of the Earth, Greenpeace, and Earth First! This tendency toward "opening up" the issue to greater and more representative participation is also illustrated by the extant literature that seeks to explain the formulation or implementation of environmental policy. Initially, this literature stressed "subgovernments" as a major explanation for environmental policymaking (Foss, 1960). More recently, it has suggested that "advocacy coalitions," composed of interests from all three levels of government and the private sector, are now involved in environmental policymaking (Sabatier and Jenkins-Smith, 1988). Clearly, the scope of citizen involvement has changed over the past hundred years.

Numerous other changes have occurred in the nature of environmental policy and politics over just the past thirty years. Consider, for example, the ways in which we evaluate the severity of the environmental problem. Specifically, the focus of our concern has evolved from "natural resource issues" to "environmental issues," or from first-generation problems (e.g., public lands, irrigation and water rights, and park management) to second-generation problems (e.g., toxic waste, groundwater protection, and air pollution) to third-generation problems (e.g., global warming, thinning of the ozone layer, tropical deforestation, and acid rain). Along with this change, we have shifted our concern from purely localized issues involving air and water pollution in communities to the realization that an effective response to these second- and third-generation problems requires diverse actions by individuals and institutions at all levels of society (Carroll, 1988; see also Vig and Kraft, 1990: 4).

Moreover, the nature of public opinion on this topic has changed dramatically over the past thirty years. Public opinion in the late 1960s and early 1970s initially reached a high level of support, but it was judged to be "soft support," meaning that it would dissolve in the face of concerns over economic development (i.e., jobs versus the environment). In the late 1980s, however, public opinion was described as both strong and salient (Mitchell, 1984; Dunlap, 1989). The American public has indicated that it wants stringent environmental protection regulations and is willing to pay for it in new taxes.

We have also witnessed the growing involvement of states, cities, and grassroots organizations in environmental management. With the advent of the "New Federalism" in the 1970s and 1980s, states and communities have increasingly been asked to assume more environmental responsibilities that were previously handled by the federal government. Yet it is also clear that not all the states are able to muster the economic and institutional wherewithal to meet their new responsibilities (Lester, 1986; Davis and Lester, 1987; Lester and Lombard, 1990). Indeed, the states vary greatly in terms of their capacities to assume environmental management in the 1990s.

If the present trend continues, then the next few decades will likely be characterized by significantly increased levels of citizen activism or "strong democracy" in the environmental movement. In this new era of environmentalism, we will significantly change the nature of our approach to environmental protection by moving toward "postenvironmentalism," as described by John Young (1990) and others. Increasingly, localism will characterize environmentalism as neighborhood groups and citywide organizations become even more important in affecting the direction and scope of environmental protection.

However, these new local groups will be joining a worldwide network of environmental organizations. Many national and global ecology groups now provide tactical and technical assistance to local citizens groups around the world. Indeed, neighborhood associations in the United States and in developing nations are already participating in "cross-level and cross-national" environmental alliances. These flexible forms of aid will reduce the barriers to broad-scale citizen participation in environmental politics.

LONG-TERM TRENDS AND
CLINTON'S ADMINISTRATION POLICIES

Although long-term trends seem to be moving toward more "bottom-up" and participatory environmental policymaking, the lure of the "top-down" exercise of power is especially tempting during the Clinton presidency. For the first time since the Carter administration, environmentalists have significant power and influence in the executive branch in Washington, D.C. The president, often with strong input from the vice-president, has appointed many environmental advocates to major policy positions. Among the most visible are Carol Browner as head of the EPA and Bruce Babbitt as secretary of the interior, the federal government's major land management agency. Less visible are large numbers of subcabinet and lower-level political appointees with "green" credentials who have moved beyond traditional environmental positions into slots at the White House, Office of Management and Budget, State Department, and National Security Council.

From their positions in the executive branch, these advocates-turned-administrators are involved in an increased number of ecology issues on the legislative agenda. Of note are reauthorizations and major amendments of many important pieces of environmental legislation, including the Clean Water Act, the Safe Drinking Water Act, and the "Superfund" toxic-waste cleanup program. The latter is a highly symbolic law reflecting a high level of public fear and anxiety—a law that is often mobilized by grass-roots citizen groups. Some environmental activists are critical of the administration's willingness to build alliances with industry and insurance groups to reduce legal complexities and costs in order to speed the cleanup of toxic sites. The public debate over revising Superfund will likely provide the clearest recent example of the contrast between the priorities of expert elites and those of local activists.

In the area of public lands, Congress is on the verge of reforming the 1872 mining law, unrevised since the 1920s, which will pass with the administration's support. The updated law will explicitly incorporate environmental protection and royalty payments to the federal government, changes from the old law that encouraged mining as part of nineteenth century policy to develop and populate the West. Secretary Babbitt seems to be involved in a broad effort to increase the economic return on federal investments, and thereby reduce the incentives for users to waste these resources, while at the same time increasing environmental protection. Expansion of federal revenues will also allow the administration some fiscal leeway as it embarks on expensive social programs such as health care reform.

Meanwhile, long-simmering environmental conflicts are emerging now that the time is seen to be politically advantageous. After a controversy arose over the president's 1993 budget plan to raise grazing fees for ranchers using public lands for their livestock, Secretary Babbitt enlarged the debate over higher fees to include the complex issues of quality of public lands and the adequacy of current management to sustain land quality. Interestingly, most major environmental groups *opposed* Babbitt's proposed reforms, which expanded local range management councils to include environmentalists, in favor of centralized control from Washington that would be easier for environmental groups to monitor and influence. Traditional extractive industries using federal lands in the West are politically well organized. And, ironically, president Clinton's political success in 1992 in winning electoral college votes from western states heightened the sensitivity of the political staff in the White House to concerns of western Democrats (governors and senators especially) who have ties to these traditional industries. These Democrats have influence that is disproportionate to their numbers, inasmuch as they are more conservative than some of their colleagues and may be the source of key swing votes on broad issues like the budget and health care reform. Moreover, the mining, timber, and ranching interests have credibility as symbols of the Old West that resonate with newer western urban voters; indeed, these interests can claim that the future of many picturesque small towns continues to rest on traditional livelihoods. The forced resignation of Jim Baca as director of the Bureau of Land Management (BLM) in 1994 has been attributed to the sensitivity of the administration to these interests as expressed through western-state Democrats.

Needless to say, there is no shortage of criticism leveled against Clinton's environmental policies, both from the advocates of a greater federal effort at ecological protection and from business groups and conservatives opposed to new initiatives. The "green" critics see too-frequent compromises on policy and legislation and an unwillingness of the administration to risk heated battles even when the outcome will be successful. This pressure stems from several sources, including the simple observation that it is much easier to be true to one's principles when in opposition, as was the case for environmentalists from 1981 to 1993, than to be uncompromising when leading a legislative coalition to pass a new law.

It is also worth noting that environmental groups, like most social movement organizations, find their fund raising and membership recruitment most difficult when they face a *supportive* government. This "paradox of success" occurred during the Carter years for environmentalist organizations and during the Reagan years for conservative groups. Adversity and perceived threats to deeply held values are powerful mobilizers, and the oft-repeated example that James Watt (Reagan's anti-environmentalist secretary of the interior) was an unsurpassed fund raiser for ecology interests reminds us that uncompromising criticism is a common tool for organizational maintenance. A supporter of an ecology group could well ask: If the Clinton administration is doing a good job, then why do I need to renew my membership? Conversely, if the administration cannot always be counted on to do the right thing, then my check is needed to help apply pressure.

In addition, an important theme among environmental activists adheres to an adversarial view of the proper role of government regulation of pollution originating from private industry. At the extreme are such activists as the "red greens," who see profit-seeking business as inherently untrustworthy and who believe that only vigilant government enforcement of regulations can limit the damage from capitalist by-products such as pollution. Moreover, every effort to introduce market-based environmental protection, along with every negotiation to reach compromises and avoid legislative conflicts, can be criticized as undermining the strict supervision by government agencies. Environmentalism also has elements of a moral crusade, replete with clear villains who are portrayed as the embodiments of evil. For example, the ancient (old-growth) forests of the Pacific Northwest are characterized as "natural" and "good," so President Clinton's compromises in an effort to preserve some jobs in the forest product industry undermine that purity and draw criticism as well as lawsuits.

Although he campaigned as a "new kind of Democrat," President Clinton has become a symbol of traditional "big government" liberalism to many conservative organizations and activists. The religious right is among the most visible of grass-roots opponents of the new administration, but other economic and ideological forces have also been revitalized since the election. Environmental issues for these groups are examples of expansive federal regulation that hamstrings business and reduces individual freedom. In western states, conservatives have allied with traditional economic beneficiaries of pro-development policies to assail the undue influence of eastern environmentalists on federal bureaucrats. For example, the late 1970s saw the rise of a precursor antienvironmentalist movement labeled the "Sagebrush Rebellion" (although it disappeared during the Reagan years). However, the current movement and its environmental opponents have a vested interest in exaggerating the power of each other. The "browns," as some greens call them, provide flamboyant rhetoric that can be used to mobilize complacent donors to ecological causes. The visible presence of environmental groups and their vocal demands on the Clinton administration serve a similar function for "wise use" (pro-development) groups. Both movements claim to be truly representative of the grass roots, and both brand their opponents as tools of elite interests.

A new intellectual perspective on regulation, rooted in conservative legal theory, may have a far-reaching impact on environmental policy. Known as the "takings" doctrine, this argument draws on the language in the Fifth and Fourteenth Amendments requiring governments to compensate people for property "taken" for public use. By extension, any restrictions on the *use* of private property that affect the value of the property are a form of "taking," thus requiring compensation. A particular target of this analysis is the Endangered Species Act, parts of which limit landowners' ability to modify their property in ways that would threaten certain species. Environmental advocates and the Clinton administration are working together to challenge this "takings" doctrine in the courts—as well as in state and local governments in western rural states, where it has some support.

INTERNATIONAL ENVIRONMENTAL ISSUES

The end of the Cold War has diminished the military component of U.S. foreign policy, thereby heightening the visibility of economic and environmental issues. This global agenda includes the unfinished legacy of the 1992 Rio "Earth" Summit. Many environmentalists, including Vice-President Gore, criticized the Bush administration for not asserting U.S. leadership on global environmental issues. The Clinton administration has begun to take advantage of the discretionary foreign policy powers of the presidency, which allow more latitude for action than is the case in most areas of domestic policy. The "top-down" initiatives of this administration coincide with the expanded global agendas of many large environmental groups.

Among the early actions taken was the endorsement of two international agreements, left unsigned by President Bush, on biodiversity and global warming; both were modified slightly and then signed by Clinton. In the meantime, a new emphasis has been placed on "global environmental governance," and new institutions for coordinating national environmental policies have been created. On issues such as population control, there is renewed U.S. leadership—this after a decade during which Republican administrations were swayed by their Christian Right constituency to avoid supporting international family-planning programs. Population planning also has links to another phobia of conservatives, feminism, given that the empowerment of women has been deemed crucial to limiting population growth in developing nations. Note that former Senator Tim Wirth has been given a high-profile State Department position that combines traditional liberal Democratic internationalism with feminist and ecological topics.

But liberal internationalism and environmentalism have come into conflict over efforts to institutionalize and expand free trade. When the Clinton administration finalized the North America Free Trade Agreement (NAFTA), largely negotiated by President Bush, even the addition of two side agreements on labor standards and environment protection failed to end criticism from traditional Democratic party constituencies. Organized labor remained opposed, but environmental groups divided over NAFTA, allowing a narrow Clinton victory in Congress in 1993. The 1994 expansion of the General Agreement on Tariffs and Trade (GATT) has gained less support from environmental groups. Most groups are neutral or opposed; those opposed voice the basic concern that environmental laws are barriers to international trade. Public-health issues—such as those concerning pesticide residues in imported foods, as well as nature concerns, such as those linking tuna imports to dolphin protection—have combined to put environmentalists at odds with free traders. An underlying fear is that freer trade will succeed in stimulating "nonsustainable" economic growth in developing countries, and that growth will come at the expense of environmental quality. In short, although efficient global markets might be created, this new worldwide market may not allow protection for less efficient but less environmentally damaging economic practices.

CONCLUSIONS

Environmental policy in the first two years of the Clinton administration has generally not departed from the long-term trend toward participatory policymaking. Yet, this presidency seems to emphasize substantive outcomes rather than participatory processes. This tendency may be attributable to the influence of policy "wonks," or experts, who are focused largely on the content of policy. There has been a return to the active initiation of new environmental policies, and most environmental groups seem satisfied with sharing executive power and once again shaping policy. Moreover, the renewed government activism is tempered with greater concern for costs and efficiency and with a willingness to compromise and build broader political and legislative coalitions that some activists find unpalatable. It is also worth noting that the Clinton election campaign gave little attention to increased citizen participation. The White House political tacticians have been noted for their attention to the current public-opinion polls and for adjusting their policy announcements to reflect the public's agenda. But this rhetorical flexibility in response to the content of citizen concerns has been accompanied by a continuity of existing structures of policymaking. Public involvement in environmental policy is structured through formal comment periods, public hearings, and government-organized meetings. Thus, although environmentalist perspectives have gained a more sympathetic response from this administration, the role of citizen participation as part of the process has not changed much since preceding Republican administrations.

One exception has been the expansion of mass involvement in the area of environmental racism or environmental justice. This issue concerns the disproportionate impacts of various forms of pollution on minorities and the poor. Most apparent is the frequent siting of hazardous waste disposal or handling facilities in areas populated by such people. The NAACP and local civil rights groups are heavily involved with this issue, and President Clinton has ordered executive agencies to report on the severity of this problem. The civil rights community, with its long tradition of mobilizing citizens and activating its grass-roots supporters, has gained enormous legitimacy through these strategies. Along with growing numbers of local NIMBY ("not in my backyard") groups, which are often made up of white middle-class homeowners, the environmental justice issue has the potential for expanding environmental activism into the minority community and enlarging the policy agenda to include citizen participation as well.

NOTES

1. Not all scholars are in agreement with regard to the exact dates of these movements, but the ones listed here are generally acceptable as benchmarks for each movement. (See Hays, 1959; Schnaiberg, 1980; Caulfield, 1989.)

15

The New American Politics:
Reflections on the Early 1990s

LAWRENCE C. DODD

The great social changes of history are those moments when the attitudes or habits of thought of a citizenry shift in some fundamental fashion (Bateson, 1972). Such moments may not look dramatic in the immediate alterations they produce in political institutions, public policy, or social relations. The shifts in thought may be subtle and elusive to the participants, such obvious responses to historical developments that citizens have difficulty sensing any "shift" at all, much less foreseeing dramatic long-term consequences. But out of the subtle reformulation of attitudes can emerge new mindsets and behavioral patterns that transform a society and its politics.

One such dramatic shift in attitude during the height of the Cold War came when the Russians launched Sputnik into orbit around the earth and thereby convinced the American public that our educational and research institutions lagged behind those of the Soviets. The increased public support for education and research then helped generate the large national research universities that educate so many of our national citizens and that now, with the Soviet menace gone, are increasingly under attack as unnecessary public investments. Another such shift, identified by Morris Fiorina in Chapter 8 of this volume, occurred as the states chose to create professionalized legislatures with substantial salary and retirement benefits for members and inadvertently produced an incentive for working-class Democrats to create long-term legislative careers, an incentive less attractive to middle-class Republicans. The new careerist mindset of Democrats then helped tilt the control of legislatures toward the Democratic Party.

And of course the broadest and most sustained shift in popular mindset in the twentieth century came in the 1930s and 1940s (Lowi, 1979). During that period the depression, World War II, and then the Cold War led citizens to abandon the laissez-faire and isolationist policies of the early twentieth century and to embrace an activist government at home and abroad. Much that modern political scientists treat as "normal politics"—the strong presidency, a powerful bureaucratic state, incumbent advantage, a professionalized Congress preoccupied with processing casework and controlling entitlement programs—derives from the attitudinal shifts and political experiments of the Roosevelt-Truman era.

I raise the issue of shifting mindsets because it is my belief that a new American politics is emerging in the early 1990s, a politics resulting from subtle shifts in contemporary perceptions and political beliefs of the American public. This emerging mindset, though elusive, is evident in the distinctive and unusual behavior of citizens in the early 1990s, particularly in the nature of the candidates, political movements, and issues positions that they supported during the early and mid-1990s. This behavior suggests that the broad historic developments of the late twentieth century—the end of the Cold War and demise of the Soviet state, the coming of information highways and the interactive telecommunications revolution, the emergence of a postindustrial and postmaterial service society—are generating wide-ranging alterations in how Americans think about politics and society. These alterations may not have come in response to such dramatic events as depression or war; yet they have the potential to transform American politics just as fundamentally as did the depression, World War II, and the Cold War two generations ago (Dionne, 1992; Dodd, 1981, 1993; Fowler, 1994; Huntington, 1974; Inglehart, 1989; Mayhew, 1994; Shefter, 1994).

My purpose here is to identify four shifts in the political mindset of the public that I see occurring in the early 1990s and to discuss some of their general implications. These four shifts—in how we think about the presidency, the functions and structure of government, the nature of political representation, and the character of democratic deliberation—involve some extensive transformations in the nature of American politics. These transformations could ultimately be beneficial, adjusting American political practice to the needs of a postindustrial society. Or they could ultimately be harmful, eroding the institutional and participatory foundations of democratic government. What is important at this point is to recognize the potential transformations that may now be under way in our politics and to begin a systematic assessment of their character and long-term consequences.

THE NATURE OF THE AMERICAN PRESIDENCY

Perhaps the most obvious shift during the early 1990s has occurred in the way Americans think about the presidency and current or potential presidents. From the end of World War II onward, the presidency was seen as the institution most responsible for protecting the nation from the onslaught of communism, and the president was the man with his finger on the nuclear button. In this view, candidates for the presidency needed to be tough enough to face down the communists, stable enough to carry the burden of nuclear decisionmaking, and experienced enough in national politics to mind the domestic store while remaining ever attentive to the realities of the Cold War. The presidency was deemed the most powerful office on earth and its occupant thus needed to be an individual of extraordinary character (Barber, 1977; Lowi, 1985; Neustadt, 1960; Rockman, 1984; Schlesinger, 1973; Tiefer, 1994).

In the face of such expectations, candidates for the presidency sought to demonstrate their mettle. Military service, preferably a heroic performance in wartime, became a virtual necessity, such that almost every elected president from Truman through Bush had served in the military, usually with some distinction; the one exception was Ronald Reagan, who made up for this lack of military service by being the greatest Cold Warrior of them all. Potential presidents also sought to demonstrate an incredible capacity for hard work and stamina in the face of adversity, with the country's grueling presidential nomination process often justified as an essential rite of passage that separated the men from the boys; any stumble during the nomination or election process could cast a candidate into oblivion. Personal problems—evident in marital infidelity, divorce, psychological counseling—became stigmas to be avoided or hidden at all costs. And significant symbols of personal success—in national politics, during wartime, or in business—seemed virtually mandatory.

Despite the efforts of candidates and presidents to create heroic images, there was an almost unreal element to these Olympian expectations—expectations that cast presidents as supermen beyond the capacities of ordinary mortals. Their unreality was reinforced by the painful awareness that every president who served out at least one full elective term found himself confronted by scandals, health crises, or misjudgments that brought into question his sufficiency as president. Thus Truman faced charges of corruption among his cronies; Eisenhower confronted heart attacks and accusations of lying to the American public; LBJ faced a credibility gap and the Vietnam fiasco; Nixon, Watergate; Carter, the Iran hostage crisis; Reagan, the Iran/Contra scandal. For his part, George Bush made the mistake of breaking his promise not to raise taxes. Though significant in their own right, each of these problems took on added magnitude because of the exaggerated expectations of postwar presidents and helped produce a growing disillusionment with all aspects of government. Despite the crises, misjudgments, and magnified scandals, the public nevertheless held to an Olympian model of presidents so long as the Cold War continued, the obsession with image over reality most clearly witnessed in the election and reelection of the former actor Ronald Reagan.

With the end of the Cold War and the demise of the Soviet Union in the early 1990s, considerations of the presidency and of presidents are now in transition. The sitting president during the 1992 election, George Bush, fit all the basic characteristics of the postwar expectations. A war hero; a business success during his early years as an oilman; a family man with no evident marital problems; an individual widely experienced in national politics as a member of Congress, a party chairman, a United Nations ambassador, a CIA director and vice-president; the successful commander in chief during the Gulf War—all of these attributes recommended Bush as the epitome of the postwar candidate for reelection. Yet, after flirtations with the unorthodox candidacies of Paul Tsongas, a former senator and cancer survivor, and Jerry Brown, the strange former governor of California, the nation instead focused its prolonged attention on Ross Perot and Bill Clinton.

The candidacies of Perot and Clinton would have been virtually unthinkable during the height of the Cold War. For his part, Perot lacked any major appointed or elected political experience, had a reputation as an eccentric and testy billionaire, was affiliated with no initial political organization, and, during the campaign, exhibited an extraordinarily unstable streak to his personality—entering the campaign on the Larry King talk show, leaving the campaign to avoid complicating his daughter's wedding, reentering the campaign to avoid the appearance of being a quitter. Bill Clinton, in turn, had no military record and was in fact a draft dodger; he had experienced serious marital difficulties and essentially acknowledged his infidelity on national television; he was the governor of a small and historically insignificant state, with very limited business or real-world experience outside of Arkansas politics; and, following his brother's arrest for drug dealing, he had engaged in family counseling with his brother and mother to deal with the consequences of a remarkably dysfunctional early family life. In essence, Clinton entered the race with little that would have recommended him as a man of stature capable of facing down "the evil empire," had the Soviet threat still preoccupied the public. Moreover, like Ross Perot, he possessed a series of shortcomings whose public acknowledgement would have disqualified him in earlier decades. Despite these numerous liabilities, the nation elected Clinton president and gave Perot the largest third-party vote in modern history.

The public fascination with Clinton and Perot, and the rejection of Bush, undoubtedly owes to numerous reasons, including the state of the economy in 1992 and a lackluster Bush campaign; but underlying all such factors, I suggest, was a subtle shift in attitudes about the presidency itself. With the end of the Cold War the public seemed less concerned with the presidency as the most powerful office in a dangerous world, and thus with ascertaining the stable character of potential presidents; citizens seemed more concerned about the presidency as an instrument of change and thus more attentive to candidates' visions of the nation's future. In part, this shift in attitude reflected unhappiness with the nation's economy and a growing concern for domestic policies, with the public anxious to have its president focus attention on the nation's woes. But this shift may well have been more than just a desire to look homeward; it may also have reflected a long-overdue desire on the part of the public to reassess the attributes appropriate to presidents, a reassessment made possible by the end of the Cold War.

In 1992 and thereafter, citizens seemed almost consciously to be scaling down their personal expectations of the president, looking less for blemishes in character than for someone with whom they could personally identify, someone whom they could believe understood them and cared about their real-life problems, someone willing to listen, interact, and empathize, someone for whom health care costs and dysfunctional and violent families were not abstractions but felt realities. It was almost as if the public, soured on supermen, was desperately seeking an everyman who would use the power of the presidency to address the long-neglected problems of real people. In turn, at least during the first two years of Clinton's presidency, the public seemed willing to grant the new president a life, to let him take daily runs in public, to have a strong wife who was clearly his intellectual equal, to protect the privacy of his daughter, to bemoan the unfairness of the Whitewater investigation, and to whine about the suffocating nature of life in the White House. Clinton was permitted to acknowledge publicly that the presidency was a bit daunting, that it took months in office before he became comfortable with the reality that he was the president, that he felt a bit overwhelmed by foreign policy issues and regretted the diversion from domestic policymaking.

The flip side of a more human view of the presidency, ironically, has been a willingness on the part of the public to subject the president as an individual to an extraordinary level of unrestrained personal criticism. Conservative talk-show hosts thus have lambasted Clinton in a more virulent, personal, rapid, and dismissive manner than has affected any other postwar president. Even the attacks on Richard Nixon and the Watergate scandal came slowly and were remarkably restrained for almost a year. By contrast, some widely popular commentators rushed to accuse Clinton of complicity in the suicide of White House aide Vince Foster and of murders in his Arkansas years designed to cover up information about his extramarital affairs, with no evidence to support such accusations. Even the highly visible and hysterical nature of the attacks themselves, however, demonstrates a shifting perception of the presidency—underscoring the point that the office itself is not so critical to world security that criticism must be muted until scandals are far advanced, nor are presidents assumed to be superhuman individuals above the crass motives and behavior of the common citizen. Rather, presidents are flawed individuals like ourselves whom we can assume to be subject to common human frailties and flail accordingly.

Whether such apparent shifts in attitudes, in habitual expectations of the presidency and presidents, are real and permanent only time will tell. Perhaps the early patience with Bill Clinton was a result of the public's simple exhaustion with the nuclear nightmares and magnified scandals of the Cold War era. Perhaps with time the Olympian expectations of presidents will yet return, reinforced by the president's role as head of state and thus by a natural expectation that he or she will represent the nation unblemished. Perhaps the very human frailties and political failings of Bill Clinton himself will end the public experimentation with a less grandiose presidency. Certainly one can imagine that the tepid presidency of George Bush and the vascillations of Bill Clinton could tempt the public to return to early Cold War mythology and seek a strong, flawless, and omniscient president whom citizens could blindly trust to do what's best for America. But maybe not.

Possibly the public has learned that the president must be allowed to be human too; that the Cold War belief in superpresidents was a dangerous illusion that magnified rather than defused the dangers of the past fifty years; that character should be gauged less by the appearance of perfection than by the struggle with the wheelchair, the back brace, or the dysfunctional childhood family. Perhaps after fifty years of flawed supermen the public has decided to let go of the president as Olympian warrior and to embrace a new humanized presidency and a new range of standards for presidents: At best, an empathetic and skilled political leader in close and interactive connection with the public; at worst, an everyman beyond his depth. With such a humanized presidency we then could afford to have more daily and personal attacks on the president and, in the process, could confront potential scandals before they engulf our political system; we could use presidents as instruments of change, and then change presidents as a result of policy choice rather than of domestic or international crisis; and we could encourage presidents to interact closely and honestly with citizens and, by this means, provide the depth of explanation and leadership that will allow the public to understand the societal problems and policy choices of a postindustrial and post–Cold War era.

THE FUNCTIONS AND
STRUCTURE OF GOVERNMENT

The second habit of thought that may now be shifting is the way citizens think about the nature of government (Chubb and Moe, 1990; Dodd and Schott, 1979; Eisenger, 1988; Osborne and Gaebler, 1992). For most of this century, if not longer, the debate over the role and nature of government has divided between liberals who wanted an activist government committed to solving societal problems and conservatives who wanted a limited and largely passive government; liberal activists supported the creation of a large bureaucracy to deliver government services and engineer social change, whereas conservative advocates of a limited government supported a small bureaucracy that primarily served business growth. The debate was complicated by the suggestion on the part of conservatives that the creation of a large service bureaucracy was a backdoor path to socialism and communism, and by the intimations on the part of liberals that adherence to a passive government demonstrated an inhuman insensitivity on the part of conservatives toward their less fortunate fellow citizens. The bitterness of the debate over the role of the government grew out of the social and economic conflicts that attended the industrial revolution, particularly the division of society into an industrial working class and a capitalist entrepreneurial class.

With the late-twentieth-century arrival of postindustrialism—particularly the move away from a mass-production blue-collar economy toward an urban and suburbanized service society—the industrial-era divisions over what government should do and should be now appear to be shifting. In this new world, most citizens are reasonably well educated and accustomed to material well-being; at the same time, virtually all citizens find themselves vulnerable to job insecurity as technological innovations sweep through all employment sectors and threaten the downsizing of corporate executives as well as service and industrial employees. In the face of such circumstances, there is a growing consensus throughout society that the government has a fundamental responsibility to provide basic economic and health security to all citizens, a consensus that can unite such disparate politicians as Edward Kennedy and Dan Quayle in support of job-training programs and convince Bob Dole and Hillary Rodham Clinton to discuss universal health care (Fenno, 1989).

One recent sign of the broadening concern for government activism is the preoccupation on the part of virtually all political sides with the issue of government gridlock—the widespread sense that there are fundamental societal problems that the government is failing to address. The concern with gridlock is voiced by the traditional right in assessments by such politicians as Jack Kemp and Dan Quayle; by the traditional left in comments by Bill Clinton, Al Gore, and Jesse Jackson; by political newcomers such as Ross Perot; and by long-standing political commentators such as David Broder. The concern across the political spectrum with the issue of gridlock is a decided break with the past, when large segments of the nation argued that the best government was no government. Whereas a Coolidge, Hoover, Taft, Eisenhower, or Reagan welcomed government inaction, not only the Kennedys but also the Doles, Kemps, and Quayles today see a need for job training, health care, and urban renewal and lament the gridlock that inhibits their preferred form of action.

The existence of gridlock is attributed most often to divided party government, or to constitutional and congressional arrangements (particularly the existence of bicameralism and the Senate cloture rule) that require super majorities in Congress before united party government can work (Brady, 1995; Fiorina, 1987; Kelly, 1994; Mayhew, 1991; Quirk and Nesmith, 1994). Thus the politicians suggest that the immediate solution is to put their party in power: In 1992 Quayle used the issue of gridlock to call for a Republican takeover of Congress, whereas Clinton and Gore used it to call for a Democratic White House. Behind the politicians' efforts to use the issue of gridlock for partisan advantage, however, there lurks a growing perception across the parties that the real solution to government inaction may lie less in united party government than in a re-creation of the nature of government itself.

A growing number of political analysts argue that perhaps the government is gridlocked and unable to address critical problems because our historic conception of government is inappropriate to the new realities of the postindustrial era. According to this view, which emerged first at the local, county, and state levels, government has so many responsibilities in a postindustrial era, and bureaucracies are such inefficient and costly strategies for problem solution, that a government that relies on a large bureaucracy to solve societal problems will necessarily become overwhelmed and immobilized. The solution is not to forgo activist government but to find new strategies for government action; to reinvent government. In particular, such advocates argue, an activist government must be willing to downsize bureaucracy and rely increasingly on government creation of incentive systems that encourage the private sector to cooperate with public organizations in addressing societal problems. Again, according to this view, the government neither leaves health care issues solely to the private sector, as conservatives once argued, nor creates a huge national bureaucracy to provide health care benefits directly to all Americans, as liberals once envisioned. Rather, it seeks to create a system of managed competition in which the government provides incentives and guidelines for the private sector to provide universal health coverage to citizens, with oversight and assistance from a limited government bureaucracy. Hence the government plays a strong and facilitative role, rather than the limited and passive role espoused in the past by conservatives; yet in so doing it avoids the interventionist and controlling role espoused by traditional liberals.

The discussion of a reinvention of government, the possibility that there is a third way aside from inactive government or large bureaucracies, came to the nation's attention more forcefully than ever before in the 1992 presidential election. Not only Democrats such as Bill Clinton but Republicans such as Jack Kemp made the restructuring of government a centerpiece of their campaigns, with Clinton's victory attributed in part to his ability to convince the public that his activist policy agenda could be accomplished through strategies of managed competition that would avoid the difficulties associated with a large bureaucracy. Once in the White House, Clinton authorized Vice-President Al Gore to lead the effort at reinventing government and used the principles of managed competition as a core elements of his universal health care plan.

Much like the shift in the public's view of the presidency, the move of the citizens to embrace a re-creation of our conception of government—a view often associated with the term *entrepreneurial government* because it combines activist government with the competitive principles of free enterprise—is a subtle and fragile one. Whether this shift actually solidifies and becomes a fundamental component of our postindustrial politics undoubtedly depends on how successful the early federal experiments with managed competition prove to be. Even if entrepreneurial government is successful in limited policy areas, an extensive move to managed competition as a dominant strategy of activist government probably will take at least a quarter of a century or longer, in part because large public bureaucracies have powerful clienteles that will resist the downsizing of existing bureaucratic agencies. The public acceptance of a new form of government activism—social services sans public bureaucracy—could nevertheless have significant consequences for American politics.

A first consequence is already evident and could dramatically increase—namely, a shift in the public willingness to discuss government responsibility for addressing societal problems. For roughly a quarter-century, since Lyndon Johnson's experiments with the Great Society, the nation has been "gun shy" about discussing government responsibility for societal woes lest doing so ignite another round of bureaucratic programs, federal intervention into state and local government, massive federal budgets, and national tax increases. The experience with the Great Society left the public with a widespread sense that an activist government, however well intentioned, may generate problems worse than the initial ills its programs were designed to address. My own belief is that much of the nation's policy gridlock of the past two decades may truly have been tied to the public's fear that however difficult the nation's social problems may be, action by the national government will create bureaucracies whose expense and inefficiencies only make society worse off than it was before, a fear that political leaders were simply unable to overcome as long as discussion of government action centered on bureaucratic programs.

One of the most significant breakthroughs of the early 1990s was the willingness of the public to envision the possibility that an entrepreneurial form of government activism could address societal problems without a massive increase in bureaucracies and taxes. Thus so long as Clinton's discussion of health care in the 1992 election centered on bureaucratic solutions, the public responded coolly. But when Candidate Clinton introduced the idea of managed competition and the possibility that government could truly address deep-seated problems without creating a new large bureaucracy, the health care issue and his candidacy took off.

Insofar as managed competition works both as an idea and as a form of government action, it could provide a strategy whereby the nation moves beyond its fears of state bureaucracy and broadens its debate over the social responsibilities of government. Clearly, as the subsequent history of Clinton's health care proposals during his first two years in office demonstrated, this process of changing perspectives may prove to be a difficult one, with many pitfalls. Leaders must give attention not just to the rhetoric of reinventing government but also to the drafting of legislation that convinces the public that managed competition without a massive new bureaucracy is possible. Otherwise, public fear of government will resurface and cripple even innovative social programs such as national health care that initially enjoy widespread public support. Although national health care floundered at the end of the 103rd Congress as a result of growing public fear that the Clinton plan was more bureaucratic in nature than he had promised, the ultimate consequence of this defeat may be to encourage leaders to give more sustained attention to the genuine reinvention of government, thereby increasing the long-term possibility of successful social activism at the national level once existing public bureaucracies are downsized and entreprenuerial strategies of government activism are perfected (Dionne, 1994).

A second, ironic consequence of the shift toward an entrepreneurial conception of government may come in the nation's electoral and party politics. One of the reasons that Democrats proved so successful in maintaining control of Congress and most state legislatures over the past forty years was that the ideological opposition of the Republicans to a large state bureaucracy deprived them of the opportunity to claim credit for the social services provided to individual constituents by national or state governments. Democratic legislators, seeking long-term political careers and willing to embrace bureaucratic service delivery, could claim credit for service delivery; the result was a vote advantage for the Democrats, particularly in poorer legislative districts reliant on state bureaucratic services. The irony today is that, although it is a Democratic president, Bill Clinton, who has brought the issue of managed competition most forcefully to the public's attention, it could well be the Republican Party, and conservative movements generally, that benefits in legislative elections. The reason is that the move to an entrepreneurial conception of government may liberate Republican candidates to support activist social policies that utilize principles of free-enterprise competition and to highlight the value of business experience in the design of such policies. Democratic candidates, tied to the bureaucratic clienteles, could prove not only less adept in embracing entrepreneurial government but also, in the process, less competitive in legislative elections.

The prospect for such a Republican resurgence was vividly demonstrated in the 1994 general elections, as the Grand Old Party gained control of both houses of Congress for the first time in forty-two years and increased its strength significantly in state legislatures. The immediate and pressing question is whether the Republicans, particularly in the Congress, can find a way to implement a fundamental and fiscally responsible restructuring of government while ensuring the existence and equitable availability of vital social services, perhaps even including national health care. Clinton found this a daunting task as a Democrat, falling prey to divisions within his party between supporters of bureaucratic service delivery and advocates of managed competition. The Republicans likewise may find long-term and sustainable innovation difficult; they will be torn between old-school conservatives who see government as evil and revisionist conservatives who believe government can do good for society if only it will do so in accord with entrepreneurial principles. Should the Republicans succeed in overcoming this division and provide a restructured government that citizens find both fiscally credible and responsive to human needs, then a prolonged era of Republican rule could unfold. In contrast, a Republican failure could set the stage for a fundamental alteration of our electoral and party politics as new or reinvented parties attempt to fill the void, a possibility already evident in the surprising success of the Perot movement in 1992 and the unease among moderate and conservative Democrats, particularly members of the Democratic Leadership Council, following the 1994 elections.

The shifting conceptions of government evident in the early 1990s thus could have some truly profound consequences for the nature of American government in the twenty-first century. Instead of gridlock and divided party government, the central characteristics of our politics in the next quarter-century could be programmatic innovation and a restructuring of our party system. In the gloom of the early 1990s, preoccupied as we have been by gridlock and a party politics grown exceedingly stale, these possibilities have seemed almost unthinkable. But American politics has experienced renewal and restructuring before; the Jacksonian period and the Progressive era are two obvious examples. One should not underestimate the power of new ideas (Kingdon, 1994) and their capacity to generate partisan realignment and political renewal. Indeed, the idea that one can restructure government, marrying principles of free-enterprise competition with committed government activism, could provide a mechanism for fundamental alterations not only in policy strategies but in the distribution of political power itself. Such alterations might include, moreover, not only electoral restructuring but also a devolution of political power to state and local governments should policymakers in Washington choose to mandate only the general national goals of social policies and then empower local and state governments to choose among a broad range of entreprenuerial strategies in pursuit of such goals, supported in the process by federal funds.

THE NATURE OF POLITICAL REPRESENTATION

A third shift in the public mindset, even more elusive and ill defined than the shift in the conception of government, may be an alteration in our conception of legislative representation (Eulau et al., 1959; Eulau and Karps, 1977; Pitkin, 1972; Shepsle, 1988). Early in American history, legislators were expected to be citizens who spoke for their fellow countrymen in the general debates over public policy. The primary issue about representation was whether such legislative spokespersons should be trustees—listening to a debate and using independent judgment in speaking for the issue concerns of citizens—or delegates—articulating positions of the electorate as the members understood those positions.

With the coming of industrialization, and the growth of the service state, the meaning of representation began to shift in America. Increasingly, elected representatives were expected to be professional careerists who would gain clout in the state assembly or on Capitol Hill and use their influence to serve the special and particularized interests of individuals, groups, and the constituency as a whole. Thus in a world of Social Security and veterans' benefits, legislators helped ensure that constituents received their checks on time; in a world of agricultural price supports, legislators gained clout on the agriculture committees and ensured that tobacco or dairy or cotton constituents received their price allotments; in a world of international trade, legislators gained influence on the tax and revenue committees to aid the local manufacturers with special trade or tax benefits; and in a world preoccupied by national security and the building of an invulnerable national defense, legislators served on armed services committees to ensure that their local districts had defense contracts and military installations that would help the local economy while aiding national defense. Legislators came to focus, in other words, less on the major national issues of the day and more on the specific needs of constituency clienteles within a broad industrial-era Cold War agenda that seemed essentially permanent in its general characteristics.

Although legislators certainly have pursued local and particularized interests throughout American history (Swift, 1988), the seemingly permanent emergence of the service state and the defense establishment in the midtwentieth century created such constituent reliance on the national government that service representation came to rival or even surpass spokesperson representation as the basis on which citizens selected their local legislators (Fiorina, 1977; Cain, Ferejohn, and Fiorina, 1987). The public thus focused not so much on the issue disputes among candidates as on which candidate could best serve the particularized interests of constituent clienteles. This focus gave a distinct advantage to incumbent legislators with seniority and expertise, particularly entrenched Democrats who supported the service state and also desired long-term legislative careers.

The irony of contemporary legislative politics, and the dilemma for many legislators, is that the public now increasingly appears to see entrenched legislators and clientele politics as major obstacles that inhibit the nation from addressing the policy problems of the late twentieth century. In other words, just as the public no longer sees a bureaucratic state as the most desirable way to produce activist government, it seemingly no longer sees the election of long-term careerist legislators as the best way to ensure the public interest. The bureaucracy magnifies the problems it is expected to redress because it introduces inefficiency and high costs into our economic and social programs; entrenched legislators reinforce these problems by defending bureaucratic agencies whose existence gives the legislator clout with particular constituencies. Together the bureaucracy and the careerist legislators would appear to be making innovative responses to new policy problems virtually impossible, particularly policy solutions that embrace managed competition and the downsizing of public bureaucracies.

The primary response to this dilemma in the 1990s has been widespread support in the public for the imposition of term limits on all legislators. Referenda and initiatives to impose term limits on state and national legislators have now passed in twenty-two states, with some states such as California also voting to reverse the growth of legislative staffs and resources and to move away from pensions for legislators. The effort to change the nature of legislative politics goes beyond these legislative reforms, however, to include widespread efforts to impose balanced-budget provisions in state and national constitutions and to ensure that chief executives have line-item vetoes to use in budget battles with legislatures. Behind these moves appears to be a public perception that representative decisionmaking is so undisciplined and irresponsible in American politics today that a broad range of constitutional checks must now be imposed on legislators if the fiscal integrity and general interests of society are to be ensured.

At issue in the public assault on legislatures is the conception of political representation that will dominate our legislatures in the nation's third century. It could be, of course, that term limits and balanced-budget movements simply reflect a repudiation of professional legislators and service representation and signify a desire for a return to citizen legislators and spokesperson representation. Alternatively—and more likely, I suspect—these movements reflect public experimentation with new conceptions of legislative representation that are more attuned to a postindustrial society and entrepreneurial government.

It is difficult to say what the essence of this new conception of representation will be. My guess, based on a limited number of interviews with California state legislators who are experiencing the shift to term limits, is that the language of representation may increasingly center on "problem solving," with legislators presenting themselves not solely as issue spokespersons in great debates nor as clientele servants focused on particularized interests but, rather, as troubleshooters with the special knowledge and skills to help address the pressing problems of the moment, after which they will then move on to new political arenas and policy challenges. Underlying this conception of representation is the view that good public policy must be a shifting, fluid, and dynamic response to a rapidly changing, technologically driven society, with today's policy solution potentially becoming tomorrow's policy problem if it becomes entrenched through bureaucratic programs and legislative power structures. Thus long-term entrenched legislators are to be avoided, just as are entrenched bureaucratic agencies, with each generation of new legislators having clear budgetary guidelines spelled out (within which they must address pressing societal dilemmas), and with their political careers in future races for other offices dependent on their ability to demonstrate problem-solving capacities in previous offices. In this model of representation, legislatures are legitimized not solely by the citizen connection of their members nor by the members' careerist clout but by the broad task performance of the legislators in addressing pressing societal dilemmas.

As this discussion indicates, I take the movement for term limits and related reforms seriously. The existence of this movement tells us that something potentially quite significant may be occurring in Americans' attitudes about legislative representation, with real implications for the future of American politics. Perhaps out of this experimentation with a new form of representation will come a more responsive form of legislative decisionmaking attuned to the realities of postindustrialism. Perhaps out of it will come the destruction of legislatures as policymaking institutions, as citizens impose such high levels of turnover, and such tight policymaking constraints, that representative assemblies are unable to sustain their policymaking power. These are issues that require serious assessment and debate, with the results to be shaped not only by the conception of representation that is emerging in America but also by a fourth shift in our attitudes toward politics, to which subject we now turn.

THE CHARACTER OF DEMOCRATIC DELIBERATION

The final and most elusive shift that I see in American politics concerns the way citizens think about deliberative democracy (Dodd, 1993; Fishkin, 1991; Mansbridge, 1980). This is not to suggest that citizens ever really think about deliberative democracy as a philosophical concept or as part of a full-blown theory of democratic politics. But most citizens, I suspect, do have some sense of the character of democracy that they prefer and of the role of public discussion and debate that is part of that democratic vision. Throughout American history, political deliberation and policy choice were expected to occur primarily among elected or appointed government officials who had been selected for their position in a constitutional manner, with some linkage to a public mandate. Moreover, as the foregoing discussion of representation should have indicated, deliberation and policy choice in the twentieth century have focused increasingly not on broad policy issues but on the particularized interests of constituents. As a result, deliberation has been a heavily institutional-based process, centered particularly in the Congress and in congressional-executive interactions; it has also been primarily a strategic choice by executive and legislative officeholders about which particularized interests should be most strongly supported in return for reelection benefits and political power. As with the public conception of representation, this twentieth-century understanding of political deliberation may also be changing.

In many ways the most remarkable aspect of the 1992 election and the two years following it has been the growing involvement of the average citizen with the daily discussion of candidates, politics, and policy. This involvement is seen in a variety of forums and activities—the radio talk shows that involve interactive conversations of the hosts and guests with listeners; the town hall meetings that involve questions from the audience for political candidates; the televised legislative sessions beamed to many living rooms daily; the expanded use of candidate debates in the nomination process as well as in the general election and in local and state as well as national races; instantaneous polls that determine the public sentiment on controversies of the movement; the growing use of citizen initiatives and referenda at the state and local levels; and the emergence of the Perot phenomenon, with all the earmarks of a new social movement. All of these factors, of course, had roots in past forms of political activity. But in 1992 they seemed to come together in full force, playing a decisive role in the Perot candidacy and, one suspects, in the Clinton victory as well. And in 1994 Republicans were so convinced that the radio and television talk shows helped generate their congressional landslide that, following the general elections, they held a public testimonial in Washington for conservative talk-show host Rush Limbaugh and publicly attributed their victory to him. Such developments, of course, might be reflecting only a passing public fancy. Then again, they could be manifestations of a deeper public shift.

What may be at play in the emergence of this new interactive and electronic politics is a shifting conception of democratic deliberation. The postindustrial problems of our society and the electronic revolution of recent years may have joined together in the early 1990s to shake public commitment to institutional deliberation and to stimulate growing appreciation of the role of citizens themselves in policy debate and agenda choice. In other words, we may be witnessing a shift away from reliance on political institutions for deliberative decisionmaking and toward societal deliberation and citizen agenda setting—with public officials left to solve the technical and instrumental problems of implementing the broad agenda and policy directions that emerge from the national interactive dialogue among the citizenry.

Although a move toward societal deliberation may well not replace institutional deliberation in quantitative terms, it could become quite potent in setting the broad directions of policy and in determining the fate of particular public officials and policy issues. Thus citizens would be able to focus on issues of crime so extensively on talk shows and in polls that they could almost overnight push crime to the forefront of the national agenda and force Congress and the president to respond with new legislation. The public could deem Vice-President Gore's defense of NAFTA more persuasive than Ross Perot's attacks and shift the position of Congress decisively toward the passage of NAFTA. Citizens could turn against the nomination of Zoe Baird, insisting through talk-show conversations on new and high standards for attorney-general, and thereby doom a presidential nomination. Likewise, they could tire of entrenched legislators and pass term limits that essentially vote all the rascals out of office. And as happened in the state of Colorado, citizens could fly in the face of virtually all public officials, tire of taxes, and decree that all new state, local, and county taxes must be approved by the voting public.

How deep and long lasting the emergence of societal deliberation will be, only time will tell. Hugh Heclo has suggested that the growth of citizen involvement in political deliberation may well reflect a Tocquevillian need for community (Heclo, 1989). In essence, the mobile citizens of a postindustrial society could be creating a kind of interactive and electronic national community that will bind them together through the airwaves as their ties to local communities disintegrate. If in fact we are witnessing a deep-felt reconstruction of community, then the rise of societal deliberation could be a long-lasting shift indeed. Insofar as the move toward societal deliberation succeeds in creating a sense of national community, it could play a vital role in creating a more cohesive postindustrial nation-state. By contrast, agenda setting through societal deliberation may be inherently prone to simplistic, faddish, and uncompromising policy solutions that exacerbate rather than defuse long-term societal problems; certainly the public imposition of tax limitations in states such as California and Colorado has produced serious long-term consequences, particularly for higher education.

The most explosive consequences of a move toward societal deliberation would seem to occur in interaction with changes in the nature of political representation and thus in the character of our representative assemblies. Reliance on societal deliberation for policy directions, when combined with highly restrictive term limits for legislators (particularly restrictions to three two-year terms or less), could produce revolving legislators who engage in limited institutional deliberation and focus primarily on implementing the policy fad of the moment. Such a development, I fear, would leave public policy and deliberative democracy in a shambles. I say this because of my belief that sound policymaking ultimately requires a balanced and informed awareness of the multiple consequences that policy decisions can have, an awareness that normally requires more time and attentiveness than the average citizen can give to public issues. Thus, for citizen deliberation to work effectively, it needs to be moderated and guided by seasoned legislators who refine the policy moods of the public and bring to final policy debates a long-term and broad vision of the implications of policy decisions. It probably takes eight to ten years for legislators to gain such seasoned awareness (Hibbing, 1993), so a responsible term-limit provision would probably need to allow legislators at least fourteen to sixteen years of service in order to encourage the presence of legislators capable of generating reasoned institutional deliberation.

Should a move toward highly restrictive term limits be combined with a heavy reliance on citizen deliberation, the nation may experience a very painful learning experience indeed, as citizens support and legislators duly implement faddish popular policies only to realize gradually that with such policies come long-term consequences that the citizens abhor. Of course, legislators have always paid close attention to public-opinion polls. But the very entrenched nature of many legislators has meant in past decades that major policies could not be changed rapidly; owing to the protection of key legislators, the entrenchment of legislators thus had the ironic consequence of helping to ensure for some time the assessment of the potential consequences of new policies. In a world of highly restrictive term limits, there may exist few such obstacles to rapid shifts in public policy and thus to the embrace of momentary policy fads, even in areas of complex and critical policymaking such as taxation. Thus, although there is much that is potentially creative and valuable in the move toward citizen deliberation, as in the move toward a problem-solving vision of representation, there is potential danger as well, a danger that requires extensive recognition and public discussion. Whether the public can learn to engage in extensive societal deliberation productively and safely, particularly in conjunction with changes in political representation, is today an open question (Dodd, 1994).

CONCLUSIONS

These, then, are some reflections on changing habits of thought in modern American society and on the ways that they could generate a new American politics. Such shifting attitudes, evident particularly in the distinctive character of the 1992 and 1994 general elections, are made possible by the end of the Cold War and fueled by the coming of postindustrialism and the modern electronic revolution. The single thread running through all four shifts, I suspect, is a broad desire within the citizenry for a more connected and interactive public policymaking than existed during the Cold War era, a new politics in which presidents listen, governments facilitate, legislators problem solve, and citizens are heard.

I share these reflections with a note of caution. Attitudinal shifts that today seem fundamental transformations can easily be seen tomorrow as transient fads. Likewise, unforeseeable world events can engulf what otherwise would be significant political developments, such that very real shifts may in fact leave little lasting trace.

It is important, nevertheless, for students of American politics to grapple with issues of change and transformation and to be attentive to imminent possibilities. In retrospect, it seems inexcusable and virtually inexplicable that contemporary scholars of comparative politics and international relations left largely undiscussed and unforeseen the possibility of broad transformations in Soviet politics and the international world order. Thus the breakup of the Soviet bloc and the end of the Cold War caught virtually the entire political and academic world unawares. Perhaps less attention to the repetitive forms of normal Soviet and Cold War politics—and closer attention to possible shifts in the habits of thought within Soviet society (evident, for example, in the role of public opinion in producing the Soviet withdrawal from Afghanistan)—would have led analysts to more rapidly recognize the weakening of the Soviet state, to foresee the demise of the Soviet Union, and to prepare for the end of the Cold War. Just such attentiveness is needed today with respect to the emerging possibilities of American politics, an attentiveness that requires us not only to examine the predominant and repetitive patterns of politics but also to exercise our intuitive imaginations in assessing its new and unusual manifestations.

I offer here my tentative imagining of how the new, distinctive, and unusual events of the early 1990s in America combine into broader patterns of imminent political transformation: ways in which the emergence of a new American mindset may generate distinctly new forms of governmental and political life. At one level these suggestions are empirical possibilities to be examined through systematic observation and testing: Can we find survey evidence over the next decade, for example, that demonstrates shifts in public understandings of the presidency, the nature of government, political representation, or democratic deliberation? At another level my suggested shifts are dilemmas to be resolved: Each of these political transformations, after all, raises serious issues of statecraft—how best to maintain the authority of the presidency while acknowledging the frailty of presidents; how best to maintain an activist and authoritative state while limiting that aspect of the state—the bureaucracy—that analysts often see as its most critical defining element; how best to sustain the power of legislatures while limiting the entrenched power of legislators; how best to engage the public in serious policy deliberation without turning policymaking into a faddish electronic game show. Most fundamentally, what I offer here is an interpretation of how politics and society may fit together in the postindustrial aftermath of the Cold War. It is only an interpretation, and an early interpretation at that. But then all of science, all of knowledge, is only an interpretation, subject to debate, probing, testing, and reformulation. In the social sciences, moreover, the most compelling and relentless test is the future itself.

NOTES

My thanks go to Leslie Anderson, Bryan Jones, and Jennifer Knerr for their comments and support.

References

Aberbach, Joel D. 1990. *Keeping a Watchful Eye: The Politics of Congressional Oversight.* Washington, D.C.: Brookings Institution.

———. 1991. "The President and the Executive Branch." In Colin Campbell and Bert A. Rockman, eds., *The Bush Presidency: First Appraisals.* Chatham, N.J.: Chatham House.

Aberbach, Joel D., Robert D. Putnam, and Bert A. Rockman. 1981. *Bureaucrats and Politicians in Western Democracies.* Cambridge, Mass.: Harvard University Press.

Aberbach, Joel D., and Bert A. Rockman. 1976. "Clashing Beliefs Within the Executive Branch: The Nixon Administration Bureaucracy." *American Political Science Review* 70: 456–468.

———. 1985. *The Administrative State in Industrialized Democracies.* Washington, D.C.: American Political Science Association.

Abolfathi, F. 1980. "Threats, Public Opinion and Military Spending in the United States, 1930–1990." In P. McGowan and C. W. Kegley, Jr., eds., *Threats, Weapons and Foreign Policy.* Beverly Hills, Calif.: Sage.

Abraham, Henry J. 1992. *Justices and Presidents: A Political History of Appointments to the Supreme Court,* 3rd ed. New York: Oxford University Press.

Ackerman, Bruce A. 1988. "Transformative Appointments." *Harvard Law Review* 101 (April): 1164–1184.

Advisory Commission on Intergovernmental Relations. 1981. *Fiscal Disparities: Central Cities and Suburbs.* Washington, D.C.: U.S. Government Printing Office.

"Airborne Attacks." 1992. National Journal (October 31): 2742–2747.

Aldrich, John, and Richard Niemi. Forthcoming. "The Sixth American Party System: The 1960s Realignment and the Candidate-Centered Parties." Westview Press.

Amenta, Edwin, and Theda Skocpol. 1989. "Taking Exception: Explaining the Distinctiveness of American Public Policies in the Last Century." In F. G. Castles, ed., *The Comparative History of Public Policy.* New York: Oxford University Press.

American Enterprise Institute. 1993. *Monthly Opinion Report* (November/December).

Ansolabehere, Stephen, and Shanto Iyengar. 1993a. "Riding the Wave and Claiming Ownership over Issues: The Joint Effects of Advertising and News Coverage in Campaigns." Unpublished paper, University of California, Los Angeles.

———. 1993b. "Can the Press Monitor Campaign Advertising?" Unpublished paper, University of California, Los Angeles.

Ansolabehere, Stephen, Shanto Iyengar, and Nicholas Valentino. 1993. "The Effects of Campaign Advertising on Voter Turnout." Unpublished paper, University of California, Los Angeles.

Anthony, Carl Sterrazza. 1993. "First Ladylike, After All." *Washington Post,* January 31.

Asher, Herbert B., and Herbert F. Weisberg. 1978. "Voting Change in Congress: Some Dynamic Perspectives on an Evolutionary Process." *American Journal of Political Science* (May 22): 391–425.

Atherton, F. C. 1993. "Campaign '92: Strategies and Tactics of the Candidates." In G. Pomper, ed., *The Election of 1992*. Chatham, N.J.: Chatham House.

Ayres, D. Drummond. 1992. "Mayors Applaud Clinton's Promise to Remake American Economy." *New York Times,* June 23.

Babcock, Charles. 1992. "Woman Are Filling Coffers of Female Candidates." *Washington Post,* October 22.

Baker, R. K. 1993. "Sorting Out and Suiting Up: The Presidential Nominations." In G. Pomper, ed., *The Election of 1992*. Chatham, N.J.: Chatham House.

Barber, James David. 1977. *The Presidential Character.* Englewood Cliffs, N.J.: Prentice-Hall.

Barilleaux, R. J., and R. E. Adkins. 1993. "The Nominations: Process and Patterns." In M. Nelson, ed., *The Elections of 1992*. Washington, D.C.: Congressional Quarterly Press.

Barrera, Mario. 1979. *Race and Class in the Southwest: A Theory of Racial Inequality.* Notre Dame, Ind.: University of Notre Dame Press.

Baruch, Lucy, and Katheryne McCormick. 1993. "Women's PACs Dramatically Increase Their Support in 1992: An Overview. *CAWP News and Notes* 9: 10–11.

Bateson, Gregory. 1972. *Steps to an Ecology of Mind.* New York: Ballantine Books.

Bauer, Raymond A., Ithiel de Sola Pool, and Lewis Anthony Dexter. 1963. *American Business and Public Policy: The Politics of Foreign Trade.* New York: Atherton.

Baum, Lawrence. 1992. "Membership Change and Collective Voting Change in the United States Supreme Court." *Journal of Politics* 54 (February): 3–24.

Baumgartner, Frank R., and Bryan D. Jones. 1991. "Agenda Dynamics and Policy Subsystems." *Journal of Politics* 53: 1044–1074.

———. 1993. *Agendas and Instability in American Politics.* Chicago: University of Chicago Press.

Baumol, William. 1993. "Do Health Care Costs Matter?" *The New Republic* (November 22): 16–18.

Bazar, Beth. 1987. *State Legislators' Occupations: A Decade of Change.* Denver: National Conference of State Legislatures.

Bean, Louis H. 1940. *Ballot Behavior: A Study of Presidential Elections.* Washington, D.C.: American Council on Public Affairs.

Beauregard, Robert A. 1993. "Descendants of Ascendant Cities and Other Urban Dualities." *Journal of Urban Affairs* 15, 3: 217–229.

Becker, Gary. 1983. "A Theory of Competition Among Pressure Groups for Political Influence." Quarterly Journal of Economics 98: 371–400.

Bendyna, Mary E., and Celinda C. Lake. 1993. "Gender and Voting in the 1992 Presidential Election." In Elizabeth Adell Cook, Sue Thomas, and Clyde Wilcox, eds., *The Year of the Woman: Myths and Realities.* Boulder: Westview Press.

Bentley, Arthur F. 1908. *The Process of Government.* Chicago: University of Chicago Press.

Berlant, Jeffrey L. 1975. *Profession and Monopoly: A Study of Medicine in the United States and Great Britain.* Berkeley: University of California Press.

Berry, B.J.L. 1991. *Long-Wave Rhythms in Economic Development and Political Behavior.* Baltimore: Johns Hopkins University Press.

Berry, Jeffrey M. 1989. *The Interest Group Society.* Glenview, Ill.: Scott, Foresman/Little, Brown.

Birnbaum, Jeffrey H. 1993. "Clinton Follows Predecessors' Path in Wrestling with the Demon Deficit." *Wall Street Journal,* May 21, p. A2.

Birtel, Mark. 1993. "Clinton Bested Only by Ike, LBJ." *Congressional Quarterly Weekly* (December 18): 3429.

Biskupic, Joan. 1993. "At the Supreme Court, a New Solicitor General Takes a New Stand." *Washington Post,* October 11, p. A13.

Blakely, Edward J., and David L. Ames. 1993. "Changing Places: American Planning Policy for the 1990s." *Journal of Urban Affairs* 14, 3/4: 423–446.

Blasi, Vincent, ed. 1982. *The Burger Court: The Counter-Revolution That Wasn't.* New Haven: Yale University Press.

Blumstein, James F., and Michael Zubkoff. 1981. "Perspectives on Government Policy in the Health Sector." In John B. McKinlay, ed., *Politics and Health Care.* Cambridge, Mass.: MIT Press.

Bode, Kenneth. 1992. "Pull the Plug, Empower the Voters." *The Quill,* 80: 10–14.

Bond, Kathy. 1988. "The Selling of the 'Gender Gap': The Role of Organized Feminism." In Carol M. Mueller, ed., *The Politics of the Gender Gap.* Beverly Hills, Calif.: Sage.

Bonner and Associates. 1993. *Survey of Congressional Opinions on Business Issues* (conducted by the Gallup Organization). Princeton.

Book of the States. Multiple years. Lexington, Ky.: Council of State Governments.

Borquez, Julio, Edie N. Goldenberg, and Kim Fridkin Kahn. 1988. "Press Portrayals of the Gender Gap." In Carol M. Mueller, ed., *The Politics of the Gender Gap.* Beverly Hills, Calif.: Sage.

Bosso, Christopher, J. 1987. *Pesticides and Politics: The Life Cycle of a Public Issue.* Pittsburgh: University of Pittsburgh Press.

Bradley, Robert B. 1983. "The Changing Political Realities for National Urban Policy in the Eighties." In Donald A. Hicks and Norman J. Glickman, eds., *Transition to the 21st Century: Prospects and Policies for Economics and Urban-Regional Transformation.* Greenwich, Conn.: JAI Press.

Brady, David. 1988. *Critical Elections and Congressional Policy Making.* Stanford: Stanford University Press.

———. 1995. *Unified Gridlock.* Boulder: Westview Press.

Brady, David, and Barbara Sinclair. 1984. "Building Majorities for Policy Changes in the House of Representatives." *Journal of Politics* 46 (November): 1033–1060.

Braybrooke, David, and Charles E. Lindblom. 1963. *A Strategy of Decision: Policy Evaluation as a Social Process.* New York: Free Press.

Brewster, Lawrence G., and Michael E. Brown. 1994. *The Public Agenda: Issues in American Politics,* 3rd ed. New York: St. Martin's.

Brinkley, Joel. 1993a. "Lobbying Rule of 1990s: Show the Most Vulnerable." *New York Times,* June 16.

———. 1993b. "Cultivating the Grass Roots to Reap Legislative Benefits." *New York Times,* November 1.

Broder, David. 1992. "Hit the Streets." *The Quill,* 80: 8–9.

Brody, R. A. 1984. "International Crises: A Rallying Point for the President?" *Public Opinion* 6: 41–43.

———. 1991. *Assessing the President: The Media, Elite Opinion, and Public Support*. Stanford: Stanford University Press.

Brody, Richard, and Lee Sigelman. 1983. "Presidential Popularity and Presidential Elections: An Update and Extension." *Public Opinion Quarterly* 47 (Fall): 325–328.

Brown, Josephine Chapin. 1940. *Public Relief, 1929–1939*. New York: Holt, Rinehart and Winston.

Brown, J.H.U. 1978. *The Politics of Health Care*. Cambridge, Mass.: Ballinger Publishing.

Bueno de Mesquita, B., R. M. Siverson, and G. Woller. 1992. "War and the Fate of Regimes: A Comparative Analysis." *American Political Science Review* 86: 638–646.

Bunce, Valerie. 1980. "Changing Leaders and Changing Policies: The Impact of Elite Succession in Democratic Countries." *American Journal of Political Science* 24: 373–395.

Burke, John P. 1992. *The Institutional Presidency*. Baltimore: Johns Hopkins University Press.

Burnham, W. D. 1970. *Critical Elections and the Mainsprings of American Politics*. New York: W. W. Norton.

———. 1991. "Critical Realignment: Dead or Alive?" In Byron E. Shafer, ed., *The End of Realignment*. Madison: University of Wisconsin Press.

———. 1993. "The Legacy of George Bush: Travails of an Understudy." In G. M. Pomper, ed., *The Election of 1992*. Chatham, N.J.: Chatham House.

Burns, James McGregor. 1963. *The Deadlock of Democracy*. Englewood Cliffs, N.J.: Prentice-Hall.

Burrell, Barbara. 1985. "Women's and Men's Campaigns for the U.S. House of Representatives, 1972–1982: A Finance Gap?" *American Politics Quarterly* 13: 251–272.

———. 1988. "The Political Opportunity of Women Candidates for the U.S. House of Representatives in 1984." *Women and Politics* 8: 51–68.

———. 1990. "The Presence of Women Candidates and the Role of Gender in Campaigns for the State Legislature in an Urban Setting: The Case of Massachusetts." *Women and Politics* 10: 85–102.

Burstein, Paul. 1980. "Attitudinal, Demographic, and Electoral Components of Legislative Change: Senate Voting on Civil Rights." *Sociology and Social Research* 64 (January): 221–235.

Cain, Bruce E. 1992. "Voting Rights and Democratic Theory: Toward a Color-Blind Society?" In Bernard Grofman and Chandler Davison, eds., *Controversies in Minority Voting*. Washington, D.C.: Brookings Institution.

Cain, Bruce, John Ferejohn, and Morris Fiorina. 1987. *The Personal Vote*. Cambridge, Mass.: Harvard University Press.

Calmes, Jackie, and John Harwood. 1993. "Congress Rushes to Close Book in One Busy Year, But Clinton Promises to Apply Spurs in Next." *Wall Street Journal*, November 22, p. A16.

Campbell, Angus, Philip E. Converse, Warren E. Miller, and Donald E. Stokes. 1960. *The American Voter*. New York: Wiley.

Campbell, Colin, and B. Guy Peters. 1988. "The Politics/Administration Dichotomy: Death or Merely Change?" *Governance* 1: 79–99.

Canon, David T. 1990. *Actors, Athletes, and Astronauts*. Chicago: University of Chicago Press.

Carroll, John, ed. 1988. *Environmental Diplomacy: The Management and Resolution of Transfrontier Environmental Problems*. Cambridge, Eng.: Cambridge University Press.

Caulfield, Henry P. 1989. "The Conservation and Environmental Movements: An Historical Analysis." In James P. Lester, ed., *Environmental Politics and Policy: Theories and Evidence*. Durham, N.C.: Duke University Press, 1989.

Cavanagh, Thomas E., and James L. Sundquist. 1985. The New Two-Party System. In John E. Chubb and Paul E. Peterson, eds., *The New Direction in American Politics*. Washington, D.C.: Brookings Institution.

CAWP Fact Sheet. 1993. New Brunswick, N.J.: Center for the American Woman and Politics, Rutgers University.

CAWP News and Notes. 1993. New Brunswick, N.J.: Center for the American Woman and Politics, Rutgers University.

Chalmers, David. 1976. *Neither Socialism Nor Monopoly*. Philadelphia: Lippincott.

Chandler, Clay. 1993. "Health Care Costs a Long-Term Headache: Economists Fear National Program Would Become a Budget Buster." *Washington Post*, October 17, pp. A1, A12.

"The Changing Social Vision of Justice Blackmun." 1983. *Harvard Law Review* 96: 717–736.

Chavez, Linda. 1991. *Out of the Barrio: Toward A New Politics of Hispanic Assimilation*. New York: Basic Books.

Checkoway, Barry. 1981. *Citizens and Health Care: Participation and Planning for Social Change*. New York: Pergamon.

Chubb, John E., and Terry Moe, 1990. *Politics, Markets, and America's Schools*. Washington, D.C.: Brookings Institution.

Chubb, John E., and Paul E. Peterson. 1985. "Realignment and Institutionalization." In John E. Chubb and Paul E. Peterson, eds., *The New Direction in American Politics*. Washington, D.C.: Brookings Institution.

Chubb, John E., and Paul E. Peterson, eds. 1989. *Can the Government Govern?* Washington, D.C.: Brookings Institution.

Citrin, Jack, Beth Reingold, Evelyn Walters, and Donald P. Green. 1990. "The 'Official English' Movement and the Symbolic Politics of Language in the United States." *Western Political Quarterly* 43, 3 (September): 535–560.

Clark, Janet. 1991. "Getting There: Women in Political Office." *The Annals* 515: 63–76.

Clayton, James L. 1984. *On the Brink: Defense, Deficits, and Welfare Spending*. New York: Ramapo.

Clubb, Jerome M., William H. Flanigan, and Nancy H. Zingale. 1990. *Partisan Realignment*. Boulder: Westview Press.

Clymer, Adam. 1993a. "Bill to Prohibit State Restrictions on Abortion Appears to Be Dead." *New York Times*, September 16, p. A1S.

———. 1993b. "Sour End to Strong Year." *New York Times*, November 24, pp. A1, A21.

Congress and the Nation, 1945–1964. 1965. Washington, D.C.: Congressional Quarterly Service.

Congress and the Nation, 1965–1968. 1969. Washington, D.C.: Congressional Quarterly Service.

Congress and the Nation, 1969–1972. 1973. Washington, D.C.: Congressional Quarterly Service.

Congressional Quarterly. 1985. *Guide to U.S. Elections*, 2nd ed. Washington, D.C.: Congressional Quarterly Press.

Congressional Quarterly Almanac, 1966. 1967. Washington, D.C.: Congressional Quarterly Service.

Congressional Quarterly Almanac, 1967. 1968. Washington, D.C.: Congressional Quarterly Service.

Congressional Quarterly Almanac, 1970. 1971. Washington, D.C.: Congressional Quarterly Service.

Congressional Research Service. 1987. *The Constitution of the United States of America: Analysis and Interpretation.* Washington, D.C.: U.S. Government Printing Office.

———. 1991. *The Constitution of the United States of America: Analysis and Interpretation* (1990 Supplement). Washington, D.C.: U.S. Government Printing Office.

Converse, Philip E. 1964. "The Nature of Belief Systems in Mass Publics." In David E. Apter, ed., *Ideology and Discontent.* London: Collier-Macmillan.

———. 1966a. "The Concept of a Normal Vote." In Angus Campbell et al., eds., *Elections and the Political Order.* New York: Wiley.

———. 1966b. "Information Flow and the Stability of Partisan Attitudes." In Angus Campbell et al., eds., *Elections and the Political Order.* New York: Wiley.

Cook, Elizabeth Adell. 1993. "Voter Response to Women Senate Candidates." In Elizabeth Adell Cook, Sue Thomas, and Clyde Wilcox, eds., *The Year of the Woman: Myths and Realities.* Boulder: Westview Press.

Cooper, Joseph. 1970. *The Origins of the Standing Committees and the Development of the Modern House.* Houston: Rice University Studies.

Costantini, Edmond. 1990. "Political Women and Political Ambition: Closing the Gender Gap." *American Journal of Political Science* 34: 741–771.

Cotton, T.Y.C. 1986. "War and American Democracy: Voting Trends in the Last Five American Wars." *Journal of Conflict Resolution* 30: 616–635.

CQ Weekly Report. 1993. "Fiscal 1994 Budget by Function" (April 10): 900–903.

Dahl, Robert A. 1957. "Decision-Making in a Democracy: The Supreme Court as a National Policy-Maker." *Journal of Public Law* 6 (Fall): 279–295.

———. 1976. "The Other Ninety-Thousand Governments." In Samuel Hendel, ed., *Basic Issues of American Democracy.* Englewood Cliffs, N.J.: Prentice-Hall.

Dalton, R., S. Flanagan, and P. A. Beck, eds. 1984. *Electoral Change in Advanced Industrial Democracies.* Princeton: Princeton University Press.

Darcy, R., Susan Welch, and Janet Clark. 1987. *Women, Elections, and Representation.* New York: Longman.

David E. Rosenbaum. 1993. "Beyond the Superlatives: Budget Bill Is Neither Biggest Deficit Cutter Nor the Biggest Tax Rise in Recent Years." *New York Times,* August 5, pp. A1, A1S.

Davis, Charles E., and James P. Lester. 1987. "Decentralizing Federal Environmental Policy: A Research Note." *Western Political Quarterly.*

Deudney, D., and G. J. Ikenberry. 1992. "Who Won the Cold War?" *Foreign Affairs* 62: 123–138.

Devroy, Ann. 1993. "Clinton Faults Hill 'Delay, Gridlock': Stalling on Economy, Flood Aid Cited." *Washington Post,* July 27.

Dewar, Helen. 1993. "EMILY's List Falls Prey to PAC Hunt." *Washington Post,* March 7.

Dewar, Helen, and Kenneth J. Cooper. 1993. "Dust Clears on a Fruitful Legislative Year." *Washington Post,* November 28, pp. A1, A20.

Dionne, E. J. 1991. *Why Americans Hate Politics.* New York: Simon and Schuster.

———. 1994. "The Not-So-Inevitable Republican Landslide." *Daily Camera* (Boulder, Colorado), October 7, p. 3C.

Distribution of Seats Between Men and Women in National Parliaments. 1991. Geneva: Inter-Parliamentary Union.

Dixon, Robert G., Jr. 1968. *Democratic Representation: Reapportionment in Law and Politics.* New York: Oxford University Press.

Dodd, Lawrence C. 1981. "Congress, the Constitution, and the Crisis of Legitimation." In Lawrence C. Dodd and Bruce I. Oppenheimer, eds., *Congress Reconsidered,* 2nd ed. Washington, D.C.: Congressional Quarterly Press.

———. 1993. "Congress and the Politics of Renewal." In Lawrence C. Dodd and Bruce I. Oppenheimer, eds., *Congress Reconsidered,* 5th ed. Washington, D.C.: Congressional Quarterly Press.

———. 1994. "Political Learning and Political Change: Understanding Development Across Time." In Lawrence C. Dodd and Calvin Jillson, eds., *The Dynamics of American Politics.* Boulder: Westview Press.

Dodd, Lawrence C., and Calvin Jillson, eds. 1994. *New Perspectives on American Politics.* Boulder: Westview Press.

Dodd, Lawrence C., and Richard L. Schott. 1979. *Congress and the Administrative State.* New York: John Wiley.

Dodson, Debra L., and Susan J. Carroll. 1991. *Reshaping the Agenda: Women in State Legislatures.* Center for the American Woman and Politics, Rutgers University.

Doherty, Carroll J. 1993. "Aid Bill Moves Smoothly into Law Despite Crisis in Russia." *Congressional Quarterly Weekly* (October 2): 2658–2661.

Donovan, Beth. 1992. "Women's Campaigns Fueled Mostly by Women's Checks." *Congressional Quarterly Weekly Reports* 50: 3269–3273.

———. 1993. "Clinton Reverses Directives; Battle Begins Anew." *CQ Weekly Report* (January 23): 182.

"The Double-Edged Sword of Equal Opportunity." 1988. In Ian Shapiro and Grant Reeher, eds., *Power, Inequality, and Democratic Politics.* Boulder: Westview Press.

Dunlap, Riley. 1989. "Public Opinion and Environmental Policy." In James P. Lester, ed., *Environmental Politics and Policy: Theories and Evidence.* Durham, N.C.: Duke University Press.

Duverger, Maurice. 1955. *The Political Role of Women.* Paris: UNESCO.

Edel, Matthew. 1975. "The Distribution of Real Estate Value Changes: Metropolitan Boston, 1870–1970." *Journal of Urban Economics* 2: 366–387.

Edsall, Thomas Byrne, and Mary D. Edsall. 1991. *Chain Reaction: The Impact of Race, Rights, and Taxes on American Politics.* New York: W. W. Norton.

Edwards, G. C., with A. M. Gallup. 1991. *Presidential Approval.* Baltimore: Johns Hopkins University Press.

Ehrenhalt, Alan. 1991. *The United States of Ambition: Politicians, Power, and the Pursuit of Office.* New York: Random House.

Eisenger, Peter K. 1988. *The Rise of the Entrepreneurial State.* Madison: University of Wisconsin Press.

Eisner, Robert. 1986. *How Real Is the Federal Deficit?* New York: Free Press.

Elazar, Daniel J. 1984. *American Federalism: A View from the States,* 3rd ed. New York: Harper and Row.

Eldersveld, Samuel J. 1949. "The Influence of Metropolitan Party Pluralities in Presidential Elections Since 1920: A Study of Twelve Key Cities." *American Political Science Review* 43 (December): 6.

Elling, Richard C. 1990. "Bureaucracy." In Virginia Gray, Herbert Jacob, and Robert B. Albritton, eds., *Politics in the American States*, 5th ed. Glenview, Ill: Scott, Foresman.

Engelbert, Ernest A. 1961. "Political Parties and Natural Resources Policies: An Historical Evaluation." *Natural Resources Journal* 1 (November).

Epstein, Lee, and Joseph F. Kobylka. 1992. *The Supreme Court and Legal Change: Abortion and the Death Penalty*. Chapel Hill: University of North Carolina Press.

Erikson, Robert S., John P. McIver, and Gerald C. Wright, Jr. 1987. "State Political Culture and Public Opinion." *American Political Science Review* 81: 797–814.

Eskridge, William N., Jr. 1991. "Reneging on History? Playing the Court/Congress/President Civil Rights Game." *California Law Review* 79 (May): 613–684.

Eulau, Heinz, and Paul D. Karps. 1977. "The Puzzle of Representation." *Legislative Studies Quarterly* 2: 233–254.

Eulau, Heinz, John C. Wahlke, William Buchanan, and Leroy C. Ferguson. 1959. "The Role of the Representative: Some Empirical Observations on the Theory of Edmund Burke." *American Political Science Review* 53 (September): 742–756.

Fainstein, Susan S. 1994. *The City Builders: Property, Politics, and Planning in London and New York*. Cambridge, Mass.: Blackwell.

Farney, Dennis. 1994. "Elite Theory: Have Liberals Ignored 'Have-Less' Whites at Their Peril?" *Wall Street Journal*, December 14, pp. A1, A4.

Fenno, Richard F. 1978. *Home Style: Representatives in Their Districts*. Boston: Little, Brown.

———. 1989. *The Making of a Senator: Dan Quayle*. Washington, D.C.: Congressional Quarterly Press.

Fiorina, Morris. 1977. *Congress: Keystone to the Washington Establishment*. New Haven: Yale University Press.

———. 1981. *Retrospective Voting in American National Elections*. New Haven: Yale University Press.

———. 1987. *Divided Government*. New York: Macmillan.

———. 1991. "Divided Government in the States." In Gary W. Cox and Samuel Kernell, eds., *The Politics of Divided Government*. Boulder: Westview Press.

———. 1992. "An Era of Divided Government." *Political Science Quarterly* 107: 387–410.

———. 1994. "Divided Government in the States: A Byproduct of Legislative Professionalism?" *American Political Science Review* 88: 304–316.

Fishkin, James S. 1991. *Democracy and Deliberation: New Directions for Democratic Reform*. New Haven: Yale University Press.

Flammang, Janet A. 1985. "Female Officials in the Feminist Capital: The Case of Santa Clara County." *Western Political Quarterly* 38: 94–118.

Formisano, Ronald P. 1983. *The Transformation of Political Culture: Massachusetts Parties, 1790s–1840s*. New York: Oxford University Press.

Foss, Phillip O. 1960. *The Politics of Grass*. Seattle: University of Washington Press.

Fowler, Linda. 1994. "Political Entrepreneurs, Governing Processes and Political Change." In Lawrence C. Dodd and Calvin Jillson, eds., *New Perspectives on American Politics*. Boulder: Westview Press.

Fraga, Luis, and Bari Anhalt. 1993. "Ethnic Politics, Public Policy and the Public Interest." Paper presented at the annual meeting of the American Political Science Association, Washington, D.C.

Frieden, Bernard J., and Lynn B. Sagalyn. 1989. *Downtown, Inc.: How America Builds Cities*. Cambridge, Mass.: MIT Press.

Friedman, Benjamin. 1988. *Day of Reckoning: The Consequences of American Economic Policy Under Reagan and After.* New York: Random House.

Gais, Thomas L., Mark A. Peterson, and Jack L. Walker. 1984. "Interest Groups, Iron Triangles, and Representative Institutions in American National Government." *British Journal of Political Science* 14: 161–185.

Galderisi, Peter F., Michael S. Lyons, Randy T. Simmons, and John Francis, eds. 1987. *The Politics of Realignment: Party Change in the Mountain West.* Boulder: Westview Press.

Gallup, G., Jr. (multiple years). *The Gallup Poll Public Opinion.* Wilmington, Del.: Scholarly Resources.

Gallup Poll Monthly (multiple years). November 24–27.

Gamm, Gerald, and Kenneth Shepsle. 1989. "Emergence of Legislative Institutions: Standing Committees in the House and Senate." *Legislative Studies Quarterly* 14: 39–66.

Garcia, F. Chris, and Rodolfo de la Garza. 1977. *The Chicano Political Experience: Three Perspectives.* North Scituate, Mass.: Duxbury.

Gates, John B. 1992. *The Supreme Court and Partisan Realignment.* Boulder: Westview Press.

Gehlen, Frieda. 1977. "Women Members of Congress: A Distinctive Role." In Marianne Githens and Jewel Prestage, eds., *A Portrait of Marginality.* New York: McKay.

Gelfand, Mark I. 1975. *A Nation of Cities: The Federal Government and Urban America.* New York: Oxford University Press.

"The Gender Gap." 1993. *The American Enterprise* 4: 98.

"The Gender Gap at the State Level." 1993. *The American Enterprise* 4: 100.

"The Gender Gap in 1992." 1992. *The American Enterprise* 3: 100.

Germond, Jack, and Jules Witcover. 1989. *Whose Broad Stripes and Bright Stars?* New York: Warner Books.

Gilmour, John B. Forthcoming. *Strategies of Disagreement.* Pittsburgh: University of Pittsburgh Press.

Goldsteen, Raymond L., and John K. Schorr. 1991. *Demanding Democracy After Three-Mile Island.* Gainesville: University of Florida Press.

Goodman, Ellen. 1992. "Perot and Women." *Washington Post,* June 13.

———. 1993. "Bean-Counting Through the Ages." *Washington Post,* January 2.

Goodrich, Carter. 1960. *Government Promotion of American Canals and Railroads, 1800–1890.* New York: Columbia University Press.

Gould, Stephen Jay. 1985. *The Flamingo's Smile.* New York: Norton.

Griffith, Ernest S. 1939. *The Impasse of Democracy.* New York: Harrison-Hilton Books.

———. 1974. *A History of American City Government, 1900–1920.* New York: Praeger.

Grove, Lloyd. 1992. "Is Ross Perot a Man's Man?" *Washington Post,* June 8.

Gruhl, John, Cassia Spohn, and Susan Welch. 1981. "Women as Policy Makers." *American Journal of Political Science* 25: 309–322.

Gryski, Gerard S., Eleanor C. Main, and William J. Dixon. 1986. "Models of State High Court Decision-Making in Sex Discrimination Cases." *Journal of Politics* 48: 143–155.

Guerra, Fernando J. 1992. "Conditions Not Met: California Elections and the Latino Community." In Rodolfo O. de la Garza and Louis DeSipio, eds., *From Rhetoric to Reality: Latino Politics in the 1988 Elections.* Boulder: Westview Press.

Hager, George. 1993a. "1985 All Over Again?" *Congressional Quarterly Weekly* (July 24) 1936.

———. 1993b. "1993 Deal: Remembrance of Things Past: With Democratic Congresses and Limited Options, New Package Is Similar to 1990 Version." *Congressional Quarterly Weekly* (August 7): 2130–2131.

———. 1993c. "Latest CBO Figures Support Clinton Deficit Projection: But Forecasters Deflate Reduction Package Total, Warn That Sustained Economic Health Is a Must." *Congressional Quarterly Weekly* (September 11): 2376.

Hagstrom, Jerry, and Robert Guskind. 1988. "In the Gutter." *National Journal* (November 5): 2782–2790.

———. "Airborne Attacks." *National Journal* (October 31): 2742–2747.

Hansen, John Mark. 1985. "The Political Economy of Group Membership." *American Political Science Review* 79: 79–81.

Hansen, John Mark. 1991. *Gaining Access: Congress and the Farm Lobby, 1919–1981.* Chicago: University of Chicago Press.

Harris, Fred R. 1993. *Deadlock or Decision: The U.S. Senate and the Rise of National Politics.* Oxford: Oxford University Press.

Hawley, Willis D. 1973. *Nonpartisan Elections and the Case for Party Politics.* New York: Wiley.

Hays, Samuel P. 1959. *Conservation and the Gospel of Efficiency.* Cambridge: Harvard University Press.

Healey, Jon 1993a. "As Administration Fills Its Slots, Congress Plays Waiting Game." *CQ Weekly Report* (May 1): 1059–1061.

———. 1993b. "Seven Months into Clinton's Term. . . ." *CQ Weekly Report* (September 4): 2310–2311.

Heard, Alexander. 1966. *State Legislatures in American Politics.* Englewood Cliffs, N.J.: Prentice-Hall.

Heclo, Hugh. 1977. *A Government of Strangers: Executive Politics in Washington.* Washington, D.C.: Brookings Institution.

———. 1989. "The Emerging Regime." In Richard A. Harris and Sidney Milkis, eds., *Remaking American Politics.* Boulder: Westview Press.

Heidenheimer, Arnold J., Hugh Heclo, and Carolyn Teich Adams. 1983. *Comparative Public Policy: The Politics of Social Choice in Europe and America.* New York: St. Martin's Press.

Hentoff, Nat. 1990. "The Constitutionalist." *New Yorker* (March 12): 45–70.

Hero, Rodney E. 1992. *Latinos and the U.S. Political System: Two-Tiered Pluralism.* Philadelphia: Temple University Press.

Herzberg, Roberta. 1986. "Blocking Coalitions and Policy Change." In Gerald C. Wright, Jr., Leroy N. Rieselbach, and Lawrence C. Dodd, eds., *Congress and Policy Change.* New York: Agathon Press.

Hibbing, John R. 1993. "Careerism in Congress: For Better or Worse?" In Lawrence C. Dodd and Bruce I. Oppenheimer; eds., *Congress Reconsidered,* 5th ed. Washington, D.C.: Congressional Quarterly Press.

Hicks, Donald A., and Norman J. Glickman, eds., *Transition to the 21st Century: Prospects and Policies for Economics and Urban-Regional Transformation.* Greenwich, Conn.: JAI Press.

Hill, David. 1982. "Women State Legislators and Party Voting on the ERA." *Social Science Quarterly* 64: 318–326.

Hill, Edward W., and Thomas Bier. 1989. "Economic Restructuring: Earnings, Occupations, and Housing Values in Cleveland." *Economic Development Quarterly* 3 (May): 2.

"Hillary Rodham Clinton." 1993. *The American Enterprise* 4: 97.

Hillhouse, A. M. 1936. *Municipal Bonds: A Century of Experience.* Englewood Cliffs, N.J.: Prentice-Hall.

Hochschild, Jennifer. 1984. *The New American Dilemma: Liberal Democracy and Desegregation*. New Haven: Yale University Press.

———. 1988. "The Double-Edged Sword of Equal Opportunity." In Ian Shapiro and Grant Reeher eds., *Power, Inequality, and Democratic Politics*. Boulder: Westview Press.

Holmes, Jack. 1985. *Mood/Interest Theory of American Foreign Policy*. Lexington: University Press of Kentucky.

Hook, Janet, and the Congressional Quarterly Staff. 1993. "Democrats Hail 'Productivity,' But Image Problems Remain." *Congressional Quarterly Weekly* (December 11): 3355–3357.

Hugick, L., and A. M. Gallup. 1991. "'Rally Events' and Presidential Approval." *Gallup Poll Monthly* June: 15–27.

Huntington, Samuel P. 1974. "Postindustrial Politics: How Benign Will It Be?" *Comparative Politics* 6 (January).

———. 1981. *American Politics: The Promise of Disharmony*. Cambridge, Mass.: Belknap/Harvard University Press.

Hyneman, Charles. 1938. "Tenure and Turnover of Legislative Personnel." *Annals of the American Academy of Political and Social Science*. 190: 21–31.

Idelson, Holly. 1993. "Clinton's Unexpected Bequest: Judgeships Bush Did Not Fill." *Congressional Quarterly Weekly Reports* 51: 317–320.

Ifill, Gwen. 1993. "White House Split Over Budget Cuts." *New York Times*. December 16, p. A18.

Inglehart, Ronald. 1989. *Culture Shift in Advanced Industrial Societies*. Princeton: Princeton University Press.

Iowa Supreme Court. 1868. *City of Clinton v. Cedar Rapids and Missouri River Railroad Co.* 24 Iowa, pp. 455–475.

Iyengar, Shanto. 1990. "Shortcuts to Political Knowledge: Selective Attention and the Accessibility Bias." In John Ferejohn and James Kuklinski, eds., *Information and the Democratic Process*. Urbana: University of Illinois Press.

———. 1991. *Is Anyone Responsible? How Television Frames Political Issues*. Chicago: University of Chicago Press.

Iyengar, Shanto, and Donald R. Kinder. 1987. *News That Matters: Television and American Opinion*. Chicago: University of Chicago Press.

Iyengar, Shanto, and Adam Simon. 1993. "News Coverage of the Gulf Crisis and Public Opinion: A Survey of Effects." *Communications Research* 20: 365–383.

Jacobson, Gary. 1990. *The Electoral Origins of Divided Government*. Boulder: Westview Press.

———. 1991. "The Persistence of Democratic House Majorities." In Gary W. Cox and Samuel Kernell, eds., *The Politics of Divided Government*. Boulder: Westview Press.

James, Matt. 1993. "Preliminary Findings, Kaiser/Harvard/NORC Survey on the Problems of Low-Income Americans." Unpublished manuscript.

Jamieson, Kathleen H. 1992. *Dirty Politics*. New York: Oxford University Press.

Jones, Bryan D. 1994. *Reconceiving Decision-Making in Democratic Politics: Attention, Choice, and Public Policy*. Chicago: University of Chicago Press.

Jones, Bryan D., Frank R. Baumgartner, and Jeffery C. Talbert. 1993. "The Destruction of Issue Monopolies in Congress." *American Political Science Review* 87: 673–687.

Judd, Dennis R., and Michael Parkinson, eds., 1990. *Leadership and Urban Regeneration: Cities in North America and Europe*, Vol. 37, Urban Affairs Annual Reviews. Newbury Park, Calif.: Sage.

Judd, Dennis R., and David Brian Robertson. 1988. "Urban Revitalization in the U.S.: Prisoner of the Federal System." In Michael Parkinson, Bernard Foley, and Dennis Judd, eds., *Regenerating the Cities: The U.K. Crisis and the U.S. Experience.* Manchester, U.K.: Manchester University Press.

Judd, Dennis R., and Todd Swanstrom. 1994. *City Politics: Private Power and Public Policy.* New York: HarperCollins.

Kahn, Kim Fridkin, and Edie N. Goldenberg. 1991. "The Media: Obstacle or Ally of Feminists?" *The Annals* 515: 104–114.

Kamber, Victor. 1990. *Trivial Pursuit: Negative Advertising and the Decay of Political Discourse.* Washington, D.C.: Kamber Foundation.

Kantor, Paul. 1993. "The Dual City as Political Choice." *Journal of Urban Affairs* 15, 3: 231–244.

Katcher, Leo. 1967. *Earl Warren: A Political Biography.* New York: McGraw-Hill.

Katz, Jeffrey L. 1992. "Record Rate of Retirements Suggests Major Shakeup." *Congressional Quarterly Weekly Reports* 50: 851–855.

Kelly, Sean. 1994. "Punctuated Change and the Era of Divided Government." In Lawrence C. Dodd and Calvin Jillson, eds., *New Perspectives on American Politics.* Boulder: Westview Press.

Kernell, S. H. 1978. "Explaining Presidential Popularity." *American Political Science Review* 72: 506–522.

Kesselman, Mark. 1961. "Presidential Leadership in Congress on Foreign Policy." *Midwest Journal of Political Science* 5: 284–289.

Kettl, Donald F. 1992. *Deficit Politics: Public Budgeting and Its Institutional and Historical Context.* New York: Macmillan.

Key, V. O., Jr. 1952. "The Future of the Democratic Party." *Virginia Quarterly Review* 28 (Spring): 161–175.

———. 1955. "A Theory of Critical Elections." *Journal of Politics* 17 (February): 3–18.

———. 1959. "Secular Realignment and the Party System." *Journal of Politics* 21 (May): 198–210.

Keynes, Edward, with Randall K. Miller. 1989. *The Court vs. Congress: Prayer, Busing, and Abortion.* Durham, N.C.: Duke University Press.

Kingdon, John W. 1984. *Agendas, Alternatives, and Public Policies.* Boston: Little, Brown.

———. 1994. "Agendas, Ideas and Policy Change." In Lawrence C. Dodd and Calvin Jillson, *New Perspectives on American Politics.* Boulder: Westview Press.

Klebanow, Diana, Franklin L. Jonas, and Ira M. Leonard. 1977. *Urban Legacy: The Story of American Cities.* New York: Mentor.

Klingberg, F. L. 1952. "The Historical Alternation of Moods in American Foreign Policy." *World Politics* 4: 239–273.

———. 1983. *Cyclical Trends in American Foreign Policy Moods: The Unfolding of America's World Role.* Lanham, Md.: University Press of America.

Kluger, Richard. 1976. *Simple Justice: The History of* Brown v. Board of Education *and Black America's Struggle for Equality.* New York: Alfred A. Knopf.

Kolbert, Elizabeth. 1994. "As Political Campaigns Turn Negative, the Press Is Given a Negative Rating." *New York Times,* May 1, p. A18.

Krauss, Clifford. 1993. "Lobbyists of Every Stripe on Health Care Proposal." *New York Times,* September 24.

Krehbiel, Keith. 1993. "A Theory of Divided and Unified Government." Unpublished manuscript.

Kritzer, Herbert M., and Thomas M. Uhlman. 1977. "Sisterhood in the Courtroom: Sex of Judge and Defendant in Criminal Case Disposition." *Social Science Journal* 14: 77–88.

Kurtz, Karl T. 1991. "Understanding the Diversity of State Legislatures: The Red, White and Blue Legislatures." National Conference of State Legislatures, Denver.

Ladd, Everett Carll. 1970. *American Political Parties*. New York: Norton.

———. 1991. "Like Waiting for Godot: The Uselessness of 'Realignment' for Understanding Change in Contemporary American Politics." In Byron E. Shafer, ed., *The End of Realignment*. Madison: University of Wisconsin Press.

———. 1993. "The 1992 Vote for President Clinton: Another Brittle Mandate?" *Political Science Quarterly* 108: 1–28.

Lamb, Charles M., and Stephen C. Halpern, eds. 1991. *The Burger Court: Political and Judicial Profiles*. Urbana: University of Illinois Press.

"Latinos and Representation in the U.S. House." 1991. Unpublished manuscript.

Laumann, Edward O., and David Knoke. 1987. *The Organizational State: Social Choice in National Policy Domains*. Madison: University of Wisconsin Press.

Lawrence, David, and Richard Fleisher. 1987. "Puzzles and Confusion: Political Realignment in the 1980s." *Political Science Quarterly* 102 (Spring): 79–92.

Leader, Sheilah. 1977. "The Policy Impact of Elected Women Officials." In Joseph Cooper and Louis Maisel, eds., *The Impact of the Electoral Process*. Beverly Hills, Calif.: Sage.

Lee, J. R. 1977. "Rallying 'Round the Flag: Foreign Policy Events and Presidential Popularity." *Presidential Studies Quarterly* 7: 252–256.

Lester, James P. 1986. "Federalism and Environmental Policy." *Publius*.

Lester, James P., and Emmett N. Lombard. 1990. "A Comparative Analysis of State Environmental Policy." *Natural Resources Journal* 30 (Spring): 301–319.

Levy, Leonard W., ed. 1972. *The Supreme Court Under Earl Warren*. New York: Quadrangle Books.

Liam, B., and J. R. Oneal. 1993. "Presidents, the Use of Military Force and Public Opinion." *Journal of Conflict Resolution* 37: 277–300.

Light, Paul. 1985. *Artful Work: The Politics of Social Security Reform*. New York: Random House.

Logan, John R., and Harvey L. Molotch. 1987. *Urban Fortunes: The Political Economy of Place*. Berkeley: University of California Press.

Lowi, Theodore J. 1979. *The End of Liberalism: The Second Republic of the United States*, 2nd ed. New York: W. W. Norton.

———. 1985. *The Personal President*. Ithaca: Cornell University Press.

Lubell, Samuel. 1952. *The Future of American Politics*. New York: Harper and Brothers.

MacDonald, Stuart Elaine, and George Rabinowitz. 1987. "The Dynamics of Structural Realignment." *American Political Science Review* 81 (September): 775–796.

Mackie, T. T., and R. Rose. 1991. *The International Almanac of Electoral History*, 3rd ed. London: Macmillan.

MacRae, Duncan, Jr., and James A. Meldrum. 1960. "Critical Elections in Illinois: 1888–1958." *American Political Science Review* 54 (September): 669–683.

Mansbridge, Jane. 1980. *Beyond Adversary Democracy*. New York: Basic Books.

Maranto, Robert. 1993. "Still Clashing After All These Years: Ideological Conflict in the Reagan Executive." *American Journal of Political Science* 37: 681–698.

Massey, Douglas, and Nancy A. Denton. 1988. "Suburbanization and Segregation in U.S. Metropolitan Areas." *American Journal of Sociology* 94, 3 (November): 592–626.

Maxwell, James A. 1952. *Federal Grants and the Business Cycle*. New York: National Bureau of Economic Research.

Mayer, William G. 1992. *The Changing American Mind: How and Why American Public Opinion Changed Between 1960 and 1988*. Ann Arbor: University of Michigan Press.

———. 1993. "The 1992 Elections and the Future of American Politics." *Polity* 25 (Spring): 461–474.

Mayhew, David R. 1991. *Divided We Govern: Party Control, Lawmaking, and Investigations, 1946–1990*. New Haven: Yale University Press, 1991.

———. 1994. "U.S. Policy Waves in Comparative Context." In Lawrence C. Dodd and Calvin Jillson, eds., *New Perspectives on American Politics*. Boulder: Westview Press.

McCubbins, Matthew D. 1985. "The Legislative Design of Regulatory Structure." *American Journal of Political Science* 29: 721–748.

McGuire, William J. 1968. "Personality and Susceptibility to Social Influence." In E. F. Borgatta and W. W. Lambert, eds., *Handbook of Personality Theory and Research*. New York: Rand McNally.

———. 1985. "Attitudes and Attitude Change." In Gardner Lindzey and Elliot Aronson, eds., *Handbook of Social Psychology*, Vol. 2, 3rd ed. New York: Random House.

McMichael, Lawrence G., and Richard J. Trilling. 1980. "The Structure and Meaning of Critical Realignment: The Case of Pennsylvania, 1928–1932." In Bruce A. Campbell and Richard J. Trilling, eds., *Realignment in American Politics*. Austin: University of Texas Press.

Meier, Kenneth J., and Joseph Stewart, Jr. 1991. *The Politics of Hispanic Education*. Albany: State University of New York Press.

Merriam, Charles Edward, and Harold Foote Gosnell. 1949. *The American Party System*, 4th ed. New York: Macmillan.

Milbrath, Lester. 1984. *Environmentalists: Vanguard for a New Society*. Albany: State University of New York Press.

Mitchell, Robert Cameron. 1984. "Public Opinion and Environmental Politics in the 1970s and 1980s." In Norman J. Vig and Michael E. Kraft, eds., *Environmental Policy in the 1980s*. Washington, D.C.: Congressional Quarterly Press.

———. 1990. "Public Opinion and the Green Lobby: Poised for the 1990s?" In Norman J. Vig and Michael E. Kraft, eds., *Environmental Policy in the 1990s*. Washington, D.C.: Congressional Quarterly Press.

Moakley, Maureen. 1992. *Party Realignment and State Politics*. Columbus: Ohio State University Press.

Modelski, G. 1981. "Long Cycles, Kondratieffs, and Alternating Innovations: Implications for U.S. Foreign Policy." In C. W. Kegley, Jr., and P. McGowan, eds., *The Political Economy of Foreign Policy Behavior*. Beverly Hills, Calif.: Sage.

Modelski, G., and W. R. Thompson. 1995. *Growth, War and Innovation: The Coevolution of Global Politics and Economics*. Columbia: University of South Carolina Press.

Moe, Terry M. 1988. "The Politics of Bureaucratic Structure." In John E. Chubb and Paul E. Peterson, eds., *Can the Government Govern?* Washington, D.C.: Brookings Institution.

———. 1990. "The Politics of Structural Choice: Toward a Theory of Public Bureaucracy." In Oliver E. Williamson, ed., *Organization Theory: From Chester Barnard to the Present and Beyond*. New York: Oxford University Press.

Mollenkopf, John H. 1978. "The Post-War Politics of Urban Development." In William

Tabb and Larry Sawers, eds., *Marxism and the Metropolis: New Perspectives in Urban Political Economy*. New York: Oxford University Press.

Moncrief, Gary A., Joel A. Thompson, Michael Haddon, and Robert Hoyer. 1992. "For Whom the Bell Tolls: Term Limits and State Legislatures." *Legislative Studies Quarterly* 17, 1 (February): 37–47.

Moreno, Dario, and Christopher L. Warren. Forthcoming. "The Conservative Enclave Revisited: Cuban-Americans in Florida."

Morgan, T. C. and K. N. Bickers. 1992. "Domestic Discontent and the External Use of Force." *Journal of Conflict Resolution* 36: 25–52.

Mueller, Carol. 1991. "The Gender Gap and Women's Political Influence." *The Annals* 515: 23–37.

Mueller, J. E. 1970. "Presidential Popularity from Truman to Johnson." *American Political Science Review* 64: 18–34.

———. 1973. *War, Presidents and Public Opinion*. New York: John Wiley.

Murphy, Walter R. 1962. *Congress and the Court*. Chicago: University of Chicago Press.

Mutz, Diana. 1991. "Checkbook Public Opinion: The Influence of Horse Race Coverage on Campaign Contributors." Paper presented at the annual meeting of the American Public Opinion Association, Phoenix.

Namenwirth, J. Z., and R. P. Weber. 1987. *Dynamics of Culture*. Boston: Allen and Unwin.

Nash, Roderick. 1990. *American Environmentalism*, 3rd ed. New York: McGraw Hill.

Natchez, Peter B., and Irvin C. Bupp. 1973. "Policy and Priority in the Budgetary Process." *American Political Science Review* 67: 951–963.

Nathan, Richard P. 1983. *The Administrative Presidency*. New York: John Wiley.

National Association of Regional Councils. 1988. *Regional Council Programs and Activities: 1988 Survey*. Washington, D.C.: National Association of Regional Councils.

Neustadt, Richard. 1960. *Presidential Power*. New York: John Wiley.

New York Times Index. 1992 (September–November).

New York Times. 1992. "Conflicting Aims in Health Lobby Stall Legislation." March 18, p. A1.

———. 1993. "A Budget Worthy of Mr. Bush" (editorial), July 26, p. A14.

Newton, Kenneth. 1984. "American Urban Politics: Social Class, Political Structure and Public Goods." In Harlan Hahn and Charles H. Levine, eds., *Readings in Urban Politics: Past, Present and Future*, 2nd ed. New York: Longman.

Norris, Pippa. 1985. "Women's Legislative Participation in Western Europe." *Western European Politics* 8: 90–101.

Novak, Viveca. 1993. "Battered Lives." *National Review* 25: 785.

"Now the Schools." 1994. *Wall Street Journal* Dec. 5, p. A14.

O'Connor, Karen, and Jeffrey A. Segal. 1990. "Justice Sandra Day O'Connor and the Supreme Court's Reaction to Its First Female Member." *Women and Politics* 10: 95–104.

Office of Management and Budget. 1974. *Budget of the United States Government: Fiscal Year 1975*. Washington, D.C.: U.S. Government Printing Office.

Olson, Mancur. 1965. *The Logic of Collective Action: Public Goods and the Theory of Groups*. Cambridge, Mass.: Harvard University Press.

———. 1982. *The Rise and Decline of Nations*. New Haven: Yale University Press.

Osborne, David, and Ted Gaebler. 1992. *Reinventing Government: How the Entrepreneurial Spirit Is Transforming the Public Sector*. New York: Plume.

Ostrom, C. W., and B. Job. 1986. "The President and Public Use of Force." *American Political Science Review* 80: 541–566.

Ostrom, C. W., and D. M. Simon. 1985. "Promise and Performance: A Dynamic Model of Presidential Popularity." *American Political Science Review* 79: 334–358.

O'Sullivan, John. 1992. "A Moral for George Bush." *National Review* (October 5): 6.

Pacelle, Richard L., Jr. 1991. *The Transformation of the Supreme Court's Agenda: From the New Deal to the Reagan Administration.* Boulder: Westview Press.

Page, Edward C. 1991. *Localism and Centralism in Europe: The Political and Legal Bases of Local Self-Government.* New York: Oxford University Press.

Page, Benjamin I., and Robert Y. Shapiro. 1987. "What Moves Public Opinion?" *American Political Science Review* 81: 23–43.

———. 1992. *The Rational Public.* Chicago: University of Chicago Press.

Patterson, James T. 1969. *The New Deal and the States: Federalism in Transition.* Princeton: Princeton University Press.

Patterson, Thomas. 1993. *Out of Order.* New York: Alfred A. Knopf.

Pear, Robert. 1993a. "Drug Industry Gathers a Mix of Voices to Bolster Its Case." *New York Times,* July 7.

———. 1993b. "Doctors Rebel over Health Plan in Major Challenge to President." *New York Times,* September 30.

Peterson, Mark A. 1993. "Political Influence in the 1990s: From Iron Triangles to Policy Networks." *Journal of Health Politics, Policy and Law.* 18: 395–438.

Peterson, Paul. 1981. *City Limits.* Chicago: University of Chicago Press.

Petracca, Mark. 1992. *The Politics of Interests: Interest Groups Transformed.* Boulder: Westview Press.

Petrocik, John R. 1981. *Party Coalitions: Realignment and the Decline of the New Deal Party System.* Chicago: University of Chicago Press.

———. 1987. "Realignment: New Party Coalitions and the Nationalization of the South." *Journal of Politics* 49 (May): 347–375.

———. 1991. "Divided Government: Is It All in the Campaigns?" In Gary W. Cox and Samuel Kernell, eds., *The Politics of Divided Government.* Boulder: Westview Press.

———. 1993. "The Theory of Issue Ownership: Issues, Agendas, and Electoral Coalitions in the 1988 Election." Unpublished paper, Department of Political Science, University of California, Los Angeles.

Petty, Richard, and John Cacioppo. 1981. *Attitudes and Persuasion—Classic and Contemporary Approaches.* Dubuque, Iowa: William C. Brown and Co.

Pfiffner, James P. 1988. *The Strategic Presidency: Hitting the Ground Running.* Chicago: Dorsey Press.

Phillips, Kevin P. 1969. *The Emerging Republican Majority.* New Rochelle, N.Y.: Arlington House.

———. 1982. *Post-Conservative America: People, Politics, and Ideology in a Time of Crisis.* New York: Vintage.

Pierson, Paul D. 1994. *Dismantling the Welfare State? Reagan, Thatcher and the Politics of Retrenchment.* Cambridge, Eng.: Cambridge University Press.

Pierson, Paul D., and R. Kent Weaver. 1993. "Imposing Losses in Pension Policy." In R. Kent Weaver and Bert A. Rockman, eds., *Do Institutions Matter? Government Capabilities in the United States and Abroad.* Washington, D.C.: Brookings Institution.

Pitkin, Hannah. 1972. *The Concept of Representation.* Berkeley: University of California Press.

Piven, Francis Fox, and Richard A. Cloward. 1971. *Regulating the Poor: The Functions of Public Welfare.* New York: Pantheon Books.

Plotkin, Sidney. 1991. "Community and Alienation: Enclave Consciousness and Urban Movements." In Michael Peter Smith, ed., *Breaking Chains: Social Movements and Collective Action,* Vol. 3, *Comparative Urban and Community Research.* New Brunswick, N.J.: Transaction Publishers.

Polsby, Nelson W. 1968. "The Institutionalization of the U.S. House of Representatives." *American Political Science Review* 62: 144–168.

Polsby, Nelson W., Miriam Gallagher, and Barry S. Rundquist. 1969. "The Growth of the Seniority System in the U.S. House of Representatives." *American Political Science Review* 63: 787–807.

Pomper, Gerald. 1967. "Classification of Presidential Elections." *Journal of Politics* 29 (August): 535–566.

———. 1989. "The Presidential Election." In Gerald Pomper, ed., *The Election of 1988.* Chatham, N.J.: Chatham House.

———. 1993. "The Presidential Election." In Gerald Pomper, ed., *The Election of 1992.* Chatham, N.J.: Chatham House.

Popkin, Samuel L. 1991. *The Reasoning Voter.* Chicago: University of Chicago Press.

"Portrait of the Electorate." 1994. *New York Times.* November 13, p. A15.

Posner, Richard A. 1990. "A Tribute to Justice William J. Brennan, Jr." *Harvard Law Review* 104 (November): 13–15.

Preteceille, Edmond. 1991. "From Centralization to Decentralization: Social Restructuring and French Local Government." In Chris Pickvance and Edmond Preteceille, eds., *State Restructuring and Local Power: A Comparative Perspective.* New York: Pinter Publishers.

Price, H. Douglas. 1975. "Congress and the Evolution of Legislatative 'Professionalism.'" In Norman Ornstein, ed., *Congress in Change.* New York. Praeger.

Prinz, Timothy S. 1993. "Perot Voters and Anti-Incumbency in the 1992 Congressional Elections." Paper delivered at the annual meeting of the American Political Science Association, Washington, D.C.

Quirk, Paul J., and Bruce Nesmith. 1994. "Explaining Deadlock: Domestic Policymaking in the Bush Presidency." In Lawrence C. Dodd and Calvin Jillson, *New Perspectives on American Politics.* Boulder: Westview Press.

Raffel, Norma K. 1984. "Health in the United States." In Marshall W. Raffel, ed., *The U.S. Health System.* New York: W. W. Norton.

Ratcliffe, R. G. 1994. "Political Landscape of Texas Receives Makeover." *Houston Chronicle.* Nov. 13, p. 16A.

Rauch, Jonathan. 1994. *Demosclerosis.* New York: Random House.

"Ready or Not, Here Comes Regional Power." 1992. *Governing* 5, 7: 67, 68.

Reichard, Gary W. 1975. *The Reaffirmation of Republicanism: Eisenhower and the Eighty-Third Congress.* Knoxville: University of Tennessee Press.

Renn, Steven C. 1987. "The Structure and Financing of the Health Care Delivery System of the 1980s." In Carl J. Schramm, ed., *Health Care and Its Costs.* New York: W. W. Norton.

Report of the National Performance Review. 1993. *From Red Tape to Results: Creating a Government That Works Better and Costs Less.* Washington, D.C.: U.S. Government Printing Office.

Riker, William J. 1986. *The Art of Political Manipulation.* New Haven: Yale University Press.

Robbins, Carla Anne. 1993. "Squeeze on Foreign Aid Shows Truth of Talk About Shrinking U.S. Influence." *Wall Street Journal,* June 4, p. A16.

Rockman, Bert. 1984. *The Leadership Question.* New York: Praeger.

————. 1990. "Institutionalization, Deinstitutionalization, and Leadership." In Howard E. Shuman and Walter R. Thomas, eds., *The Constitution and National Security.* Washington, D.C.: National Defense University Press.

————. 1993. "Tightening the Reins: The Federal Executive and the Management Philosophy of the Reagan Presidency." *Presidential Studies Quarterly* 23: 103–114.

Rogers, David. 1993. "Brady Bill's Passage Illustrates Growth of Political Concern over Violent Crime." *Wall Street Journal,* November 26, p. A10.

Rogers, Everett M., and James W. Dearing. 1988. "Agenda-Setting Research: Where Has It Been and Where Is It Going?" In James A. Anderson., ed., *Communication Yearbook,* Vol. 11. Beverly Hills, Calif.: Sage.

Rosen, Jay, and Paul Taylor. 1992. *The New News vs. the Old News: The Press and Politics in the 1990s.* Washington, D.C.: Brookings Institution.

Rosenbaum, David E. 1993. "Beyond the Superlatives: Budget Bill Is Neither the Biggest Deficit Cutter Nor the Biggest Tax Rise in Recent Years." *New York Times,* August 5, pp. A1, A18.

Rosenthal, Elisabeth. 1993. "Doctors on the Health Plan: 2 Paths, 2 Kinds of Opinions." *New York Times,* September 28.

Rowland, C. K., and Robert A. Carp. 1983. "The Relative Effects of Maturation, Time Period, and Appointing President on District Judges' Policy Choices: A Cohort Analysis," *Political Behavior* 5: 109–133.

Rubin, Alissa. 1991. "Interest Groups and Abortion Politics in the Post-Webster Era." In Allan J. Cigler and Burdett A. Loomis, eds., *Interest Group Politics,* 3rd ed. Washington, D.C.: Congressional Quarterly Press.

————. 1993. "Reno Supports Protection for Women and Doctors." *Congressional Quarterly Weekly Reports* 51: 1235.

Rule, Wilma. 1987. "Electoral Systems, Contextual Factors, and Women's Opportunity for Election to Parliament in Twenty-Three Democracies." *Western Political Quarterly* 40: 477–498.

Runkel, David, ed., 1990. *Campaign for President: The Managers Look at 1988.* Boston: Auburn House.

Russell, Louise B. 1981. "Inflation and the Federal Role in Health." In John B. McKinlay, ed., *Politics and Health Care.* Cambridge, Mass.: MIT Press.

Russett, B. 1990a. "Economic Decline, Electoral Pressure, and the Initiation of Interstate Conflict." In C. Gochman and A. Sabrosky, eds., *Prisoners of War? Nation-States in the Modern Era.* Lexington, Mass.: D. C. Heath.

————. 1990b. *Controlling the Sword: The Democratic Governance of National Security.* Cambridge, Mass.: Harvard University Press.

Sabatier, Paul A. 1987. "Knowledge, Policy-Oriented Learning and Policy Change: An

Advocacy Coalition Framework." *Knowledge: Creation, Utilization, Diffusion* (June): 649–692.

Sabatier, Paul A., and Hank Jenkins-Smith. 1988. "A Symposium on Public Policy Change." *Policy Sciences.*

Sabato, Larry. 1991. *Feeding Frenzy: How Attack Journalism Has Transformed American Politics.* New York: Free Press.

Saint-Germain, Michelle. 1989. "Does Their Difference Make a Difference? The Impact of Women on Public Policy in the Arizona Legislature." *Social Science Quarterly* 70: 956–968.

Salokar, Rebecca Mae. 1992. *The Solicitor General: The Politics of Law.* Philadelphia: Temple University Press.

Sanders, Elizabeth. 1990. "The Presidency and the Bureaucratic State." In Michael Nelson, ed., *The Presidency and the Political System,* 3rd ed. Washington: Congressional Quarterly Press.

Savage, David G. 1992. *Turning Right: The Making of the Rehnquist Supreme Court.* New York: John Wiley and Sons.

Savitch, H. V., David Collins, Daniel Sanders, and John P. Markham. 1993. "Ties That Bind: Central Cities, Suburbs, and the New Metropolitan Region." *Economic Development Quarterly* 7: 341–357.

Sbragia, Alberta. 1990. "Governance Through Debt: Law and Market in Urban Capital Investment." Unpublished manuscript.

Schlesinger, A. M., Jr. 1949. *Paths to the Present.* New York: Macmillan.

———. 1973. *The Imperial Presidency.* Boston: Houghton Mifflin.

———. 1986. "The Cycles of American Politics." In Arthur M. Schlesinger, Jr., ed., *The Cycles of American History.* Boston: Houghton Mifflin.

———. 1987. "America's Political Cycle Turns Again." *Wall Street Journal,* December 10.

Schlozman, Kay Lehman, and John T. Tierney. 1986. *Organized Interests and American Democracy.* New York: Harper and Row.

Schnaiberg, Alan. 1980. "The Environmental Movement: Roots and Transformations." In Alan Schnaiberg, ed., *Social Responses to Environmental Change.* New York: Oxford University Press.

Schneider, G., T. Widmer, and D. Ruloff. 1993. "Personality, Unilateralism, or Bullying: What Caused the End of the Cold War?" *International Interactions* 18: 323–342.

Schneider, William. 1992. "The Suburban Century Begins." *The Atlantic* 270 (July 1): 33–57.

———. 1994. "Clinton: The Reason Why." *National Journal,* November 12, pp. 2630–2632.

Schubert, Glendon. 1970. *The Constitutional Polity.* Boston: Boston University Press.

Schultz, Stanley K. 1989. *Constructing Urban Culture: American Cities and City Planning, 1800–1920.* Philadelphia: Temple University Press.

Schwartz, Bernard. 1983. *Super Chief: Earl Warren and His Supreme Court—A Judicial Biography.* New York: New York University Press.

———. 1990. *The Ascent of Pragmatism: The Burger Court in Action.* Reading, Mass.: Addison-Wesley.

Schwartz, Herman, ed. 1987. *The Burger Years: Rights and Wrongs in the Supreme Court 1969–1986.* New York: Viking.

Scigliano, Robert. 1971. *The Supreme Court and the Presidency*. New York: Free Press.

Segal, Jeffrey A. 1985. "Measuring Change on the Supreme Court: Examining Alternative Models." *American Journal of Political Science* 29 (August): 461–479.

Segal, Jeffrey A., and Harold J. Spaeth. 1989. "Decisional Trends on the Warren and Burger Courts: Results from the Supreme Court Data Base Project." *Judicature* 73: 103–107.

———. 1993. *The Supreme Court and the Attitudinal Model*. New York: Cambridge University Press.

Seib, Gerald. 1994. "Voters, Having Changed Congress, Now Want Congress to Change Washington." *Wall Street Journal*, November 11, p. A16.

Sellers, Charles. 1965. "The Equilibrium Cycle in Two-Party Politics." *Public Opinion Quarterly* 29 (Spring): 16–38.

Shafer, Byron E. 1991. "The Notion of an Electoral Order: The Structure of Electoral Politics at the Accession of George Bush." In Byron E. Shafer, ed., *The End of Realignment?* Madison: University of Wisconsin Press.

Shanahan, E. 1991. "Going It Jointly." *Governance* 4, 11: 70–76.

Shapiro, Martin. 1965. "Stability and Change in Judicial Decision-Making: Incrementalism or Stare Decisis?" *Law in Transition Quarterly* 2 (Summer): 134–157.

Shaw, David. 1993. "Poll Delivers Bad News to the Media." *Los Angeles Times,* March 31, p. A16.

Shefter, Martin. "International Influences on American Politics." In Lawrence C. Dodd and Calvin Jillson, eds., *New Perspectives on American Politics*. Boulder: Westview Press.

Shepsle, Kenneth A. 1988. "Presentation and Governance: The Great Trade-off." *Political Science Quarterly,* 103 (Fall): 461–484.

Shin, Kwang S., and John S. Jackson III. 1979. "Membership Turnover in U.S. State Legislatures: 1931–1976." *Legislative Studies Quarterly* 4: 95–104.

Shively, W. Phillips. 1971. "A Reinterpretation of the New Deal Realignment." *Public Opinion Quarterly* 35 (Winter): 621–624.

Sigelman, L. 1979. "Presidential Popularity and Presidential Elections." *Public Opinion Quarterly* 43: 532–534.

Sigelman, L., and P. J. Conover. 1981. "The Dynamics of Presidential Support During International Conflict Situations." *Political Behavior* 3: 303–318.

Silbey, Joel H. 1991. "Beyond Realignment and Realignment Theory: American Political Eras, 1789–1989." In Byron E. Shafer, ed., *The End of Realignment?* Madison: University of Wisconsin Press.

Sinclair, Barbara. 1982. *Congressional Realignment 1925–1978*. Austin: University of Texas Press.

Skard, Torild, and Elena Haavio-Mannila. 1985. "Women in Parliament." In Elena Haavio-Mannila, ed., *Unfinished Democracy: Women in Nordic Politics*. Oxford: Pergamon Press.

Smith, Hedrick. 1988. *The Power Game: How Washington Works*. New York: Random House.

Smith, R. B. 1971. "Disaffection, Delegitimation, and Consequences: Aggregate Trends for World War II, Korea and Vietnam." In C. Moskos, Jr., ed., *Public Opinion and the Military Establishment*. Beverly Hills, Calif.: Sage.

Smith, T. W. 1985. "America's Most Important Problems, Part I: National and International." *Public Opinion Quarterly* 49: 264–274.

Solomon, Burt. 1993a. "Clinton's Meritocracy." *National Journal* 25: 1453–1454.

———. 1993b. "Boomers in Charge." *National Journal* 25: 1456–1467.

Stanley, David T. 1965. *Changing Administrations.* Washington, D.C.: Brookings Institution.

Stanley, Harold W. 1988. "Southern Partisan Changes: Dealignment, Realignment, or Both?" *Journal of Politics* 50 (February): 64–88.

Stanley, Harold W., and R. G. Niemi. 1992. *Vital Statistics on American Politics.* Washington, D.C.: Congressional Quarterly Press.

Starr, Paul. 1982. *The Social Transformation of American Medicine.* New York: Basic Books.

Stein, A. 1980. *The Nation at War.* Baltimore: Johns Hopkins University Press.

Stein, A., and B. Russett. 1980. "Evaluating War: Outcomes and Consequences." In T. Gurr, ed., *Handbook of Political Conflict: Theory and Research.* New York: Free Press.

Stein, Herbert. 1993. "Don't Fault D.C. for the Slow Recovery." *New York Times,* September 19, p. F9.

Stewart, Charles, III. 1989. *Budget Reform Politics: The Design of the Appropriations Process in the House of Representatives, 1865–1921.* New York: Cambridge University Press.

Stimson, J. A. 1991. *Public Opinion in America: Moods, Cycles, and Swings.* Boulder: Westview Press.

Stoll, R. J. 1984. "The Guns of November: Presidential Reelections and the Use of Force." *Journal of Conflict Resolution* 28: 231–246.

———. 1987. "The Sound of Guns: Is There a Congressional Rally Effect After U.S. Military Action?" *American Politics Quarterly* 15: 223–237.

Stone, Clarence N. 1990. Personal correspondence.

Stone, Clarence N., Robert K. Whelan, and William J. Murin. 1986. *Urban Politics and Policy in a Bureaucratic Age.* Englewood Cliffs, N.J.: Prentice-Hall.

"Suburbs and the New Metropolitan Region." *Economic Development Quarterly* 7, 4 (November): 341–357.

Sundquist, James L. 1968. *Politics and Policy: The Eisenhower, Kennedy, and Johnson Years.* Washington, D.C.: Brookings Institution.

———. 1973. *Dynamics of the Party System.* Washington, D.C.: Brookings Institution.

———. 1988. "Needed: A Political Theory for the New Era of Coalition Government in the United States." *Political Science Quarterly* 103: 613–635.

———. 1983. *Dynamics of the Party System,* rev. ed. Washington, D.C.: Brookings Institution.

Swanstrom, Todd. 1985. *The Crisis of Growth Politics: Cleveland, Kucinich, and the Challenge of Urban Populism.* Philadelphia: Temple University Press.

Swift, Elaine K. 1988. "The Electoral Connection Meets the Past: Lessons from Congressional History, 1789–1899." *Political Science Quarterly* 102: 625.

Syed, Anwar. 1966. *The Political Theory of American Local Government.* Clinton, Mass.: Random House.

Tatalovich, Raymond, and David Schier. 1993. "The Persistence of Ideological Cleavages in Voting on Abortion Legislation in the House of Representatives, 1973–1988." *American Politics Quarterly* 21:125–139.

Teaford, Jon C. 1979. *City and Suburb: The Political Fragmentation of Metropolitan America, 1850–1970.* Baltimore: Johns Hopkins University Press.

———. 1984. *The Unheralded Triumph: City Government in America, 1870–1900.* Baltimore: Johns Hopkins University Press.

————. 1990. *The Rough Road to Renaissance: Urban Revitalization in America, 1940–1985.* Baltimore: Johns Hopkins University Press.

Television News Index and Abstracts. 1992. Vanderbilt Television News Archive. (September–November).

Thernstrom, Abigail M. 1987. *Whose Votes Count? Affirmative Action and Minority Voting Rights.* Cambridge, Mass.: Harvard University Press.

Thomas, Clive S., and Ronald J. Hrebenar. 1990. "Interest Groups in the States." In Virginia Gray, Herbert Jacob, and Robert B. Albritton, eds., *Politics in the American States,* 5th ed., Glenview, Ill: Scott, Foresman.

Thomas, Sue. 1989. "Voting Patterns in the California Assembly: The Role of Gender." *Women and Politics* 9: 43–53.

————. 1991. "The Impact of Women on State Legislative Policies." *Journal of Politics* 53: 958–976.

Thompson, Frank J. 1981. *Health Policy and the Bureaucracy: Politics and Implementation.* Cambridge, Mass.: The MIT Press.

Thompson, W. R. 1990. "Long Waves, Technological Innovation and Relative Decline." *International Organization* 44: 201–233.

Tiefer, Charles 1994. *The Semi-Sovereign Presidency: The Bush Administration's Strategy for Governing Without Congress.* Boulder: Westview Press.

Toner, Robert. 1993. "Poll on Changes in Health Care Finds Support Amid Skepticism." *New York Times,* September 22.

————. 1994a. "Gold Rush Fever Grips Capital as Health Care Struggle Begins." *New York Times,* March 13.

————. 1994b. "Changing Roles in Health Care Debate: The Man Behind 'Harry and Louise.'" *New York Times,* April 6.

Truman, David B. 1951. *The Governmental Process: Political Interests and Public Opinion.* New York: Alfred A. Knopf.

Uhlaner, Carole, and Kay Schlozman. 1986. "Candidate Gender and Congressional Campaign Receipts." *Journal of Politics* 48: 30–50.

U.S. Bureau of the Census. 1992. *Statistical Abstract of the United States.* Washington, D.C.: U.S. Government Printing Office.

U.S. Department of Commerce (multiple years). *Statistical Abstract of the United States.* Washington, D.C.: U.S. Governmental Office.

Verhovek, Sam Howe. 1993. "Deflate Government? Helium Didn't." *New York Times,* September 21.

Vig, Norman J., and Michael E. Kraft. 1990. *Environmental Policy in the 1990s.* Washington, D.C.: Congressional Quarterly Press.

Walker, Jack. L., Jr. 1969. "The Diffusion of Innovations Among the American States." *American Political Science Review* 63: 880–899.

————. 1983. "The Origins and Maintenance of Interest Groups in America." *American Political Science Review* 77: 390–406.

————. 1991. *Mobilizing Interest Groups in America.* Ann Arbor: University of Michigan Press.

Wallace, Jeremy. 1994. "Analysts: White Men Gave Republicans Control of Congress." *Bryan–College Station Eagle,* November 11, pp. A1, A8.

Waltz, K. 1967. "Electoral Punishment and Foreign Policy Crises." In J. N. Rosenau, ed., *Domestic Sources of Foreign Policy.* New York: Free Press.

Warner, Sam Bass. 1962. *Streetcar Suburbs: The Process of Growth in Boston, 1870–1900.* Cambridge, Mass.: Harvard University Press.

"Washington Wire." 1994. *Wall Street Journal,* December 16, p. A1.

Wattenberg, Martin P. 1991. "The Republican Presidential Advantage in the Age of Party Disunity." In Gary W. Cox and Samuel Kernell, eds., *The Politics of Divided Government.* Boulder: Westview Press.

Weaver, R. Kent. 1986. "The Politics of Blame Avoidance." *Journal of Public Policy* 6 (October–December): 371–398.

Weeks, Lewis E., and Howard J. Berman. 1985. *Shapers of American Health Care Policy.* Ann Arbor, Mich.: Health Administration Press.

Weidenbaum, Murray 1991. "Return of the 'R' Word: The Regulatory Assault on the Economy," *Policy Review* 58 (Fall): 40–43.

Welch, Susan. 1985. "Are Women More Liberal Than Men in the U.S. Congress?" *Legislative Studies Quarterly* 10: 125–134.

Welch, Susan, and John R. Hibbing. 1988. "Hispanic Representation in the U.S. Congress." In F. Chris Garcia, ed., *Latinos and the Political System.* Notre Dame, Ind.: University of Notre Dame Press.

Wessel, David. 1993. "Deficit-Cutting Bill Bears a Resemblance to 1990 Predecessor, But Differences May Be Crucial; Realistic Economic View, Increase in Taxes Are Cited." *Wall Street Journal,* August 3, pp. A3, A9.

Whitby, Kenny J. 1985. "Effects of the Interaction of Race and Urbanization on Votes of Southern Congressmen." *Legislative Studies Quarterly* 10: 505–517.

Wilcox, Clyde. 1993. "Why Was 1992 the 'Year of the Woman'? Explaining Women's Gains in 1992." In Elizabeth Adell Cook, Sue Thomas, and Clyde Wilcox, eds., *The Year of the Woman: Myths and Realities.* Boulder: Westview Press.

Wildavsky, Aaron. 1979. *Speaking Truth to Power.* Boston: Little, Brown.

Williams, Bruce A. 1990. "Regulation and Economic Development." In Virginia Gray, Herbert Jacob, and Robert B. Albritton, eds., *Politics in the American States,* 5th ed. Glenview, Ill: Scott, Foresman.

Wilson, Graham K. 1993. "Next Steps for the British State: The Significance of Reform." Paper presented at the Conference on the Changing Role of the State in Comparative Perspective, Chiang Mai, Thailand.

Wittkopf, E. R., and M. J. Dehaven. 1987. "Soviet Behavior, Presidential Popularity and the Penetration of Open Political Systems." In C. F. Hermann, C. W. Kegley, Jr., and J. N. Rosenau, eds., *New Directions in the Study of Foreign Policy.* Boston: Unwin Hyman.

Wolfinger, Raymond. 1974. *The Politics of Progress.* Englewood Cliffs, N.J.: Prentice-Hall.

"Women State Legislators: Leadership Positions and Committee Chairs 1991." 1991. *CAWP Fact Sheet.* New Brunswick, N.J.: Center for the American Woman and Politics, Rutgers University.

Wood, F. W., ed. 1990. *An American Profile—Opinions and Behavior, 1972–1989.* Detroit: Gale Research.

Wright, Gerald C., Jr. 1986. "Elections and the Potential for Policy Change in Congress: The House of Representatives." In Gerald C. Wright, Jr., Leroy N. Rieselbach, and Lawrence C. Dodd, eds., *Congress and Policy Change.* New York: Agathon Press.

Yang, John E. 1993. "Why Does the Budget Argument Sound So Familiar? Because We've Heard It All Before—Three Years Ago." *Washington Post National Edition* (July 26–August 1): 20.

Young, John. 1990. *Post-Environmentalism*. London: Belhaven Press.
Zaller, John. 1993. *The Nature and Origins of Mass Opinion*. New York: Cambridge University Press.

Supreme Court Decisions Cited

Baker v. Carr, 369 U.S. 189 (1962).
Batson v. Kentucky, 476 U.S. 79 (1986).
Brown v. Board of Education, 347 U.S. 483. (1954).
Dartmouth College v. Woodward, 4 Wheat. 518 (1919).
Furman v. Georgia, 408 U.S. 238 (1972).
Georgia v. McCollum, 120 L. Ed. 2d 33 (1992).
Gideon v. Wainwright, 372 U.S. 335 (1963).
Harris v. New York, 401 U.S. 222 (1971).
Hudgens v. National Labor Relations Board, 424 U.S. 507 (1976).
Mapp v. Ohio, 367 U.S. 643 (1961).
Memoirs v. Massachusetts, 383 U.S. 413 (1966).
Miller v. California, 413 U.S. 15 (1973).
New York Times v. Sullivan, 376 U.S. 254 (1964).
Planned Parenthood v. Casey, 120 L. Ed. 2d 674 (1992).
Reynolds v. Sims, 377 U.S. 533 (1964).
Roe v. Wade, 410 U.S. 113 (1973).
St. Mary's Honor Center v. Hicks, 125 L. Ed. 2d 407 (1993).
Texas v. Johnson, 491 U.S. 397 (1989).
United States v. Eichman, 110 L. Ed. 2d 287 (1990).
United States v. Leon, 468 U.S. 897 (1984).
Wards Cove Packing Co. v. Atonio, 490 U.S. 642 (1989).
Warth v. Seldin, 442 U.S. 490 (1975).

About the Book
and Editor

Since the 1992 election, we've heard a lot about "the new American politics." Bill Clinton. Hillary. The environmental V.P. A Cabinet that "looks like America." New Democrats. Unified government. NAFTA. Health Care. The end of welfare as we know it, not to mention the end of the Cold War. Town meetings, talk radio, the information super-highway. And now, the backlash of 1994.

Does any of this—or all of it—constitute a significant new direction in American politics? Was 1992 a realigning election? Did the midterm elections of 1994 realign the re-alignment? Will 1996 carry the United States forward on yet another changed trajectory? In this volume of original essays, leading political scientists examine key components of the American agenda and assess the current administration's position in light of histori-cal precedents and future trends. Each conclusion is unique, born of a combination of the empirical record and its interpretation, but essays by Bryan Jones and Larry Dodd help to put the wide ranging views represented here in long-term perspective.

The New American Politics is must reading for all interested in an informed assessment of the first two years of the Clinton administration and is designed to accompany courses in American government from the introductory level on up.

Bryan D. Jones is Paul Puryear Professor of Liberal Arts and professor of political science at Texas A&M University.

About the Contributors

William G. Mayer is assistant professor of Political Science at Northeastern University.

Shanto Iyengar is professor of Political Science at UCLA.

Sharmaine Vidanage is a Ph.D. candidate in Political Science at UCLA.

Rodney Hero is associate professor of Political Science at the University of Colorado–Boulder.

Barbara Norrander is associate professor of Political Science at the University of Arizona.

Frank R. Baumgartner is associate professor of Political Science at Texas A&M University.

Jeffery C. Talbert is a Ph.D. candidate in Political Science at Texas A&M University.

David R. Mayhew is Alfred Cowles Professor of Government at Yale University.

Morris P. Fiorina is professor of Government at Harvard University.

Lawrence Baum is professor of Political Science at Ohio State University.

Bert A. Rockman is University Professor of Political Science at the University of Pittsburgh.

William R. Thompson is professor of Political Science at Indiana University.

Billy Hall is a Ph.D. candidate in Political Science at Texas A&M University.

Dennis Judd is professor of Political Science at the University of Missouri–St. Louis.

James P. Lester is professor of Political Science at Colorado State University.

W. Douglas Costain is lecturer in Political Science at the University of Colorado–Boulder.

Lawrence C. Dodd is professor of Political Science at the University of Florida.

Index